AT PERIL

AT PERIL

Stories of Injustice

Thomas J. Cottle

University of Massachusetts Press

AMHERST

Copyright © 2001 by University of Massachusetts Press
All rights reserved

Printed in the United States of America
LC 00-056832
ISBN 1–55849-278-X
Designed by Dennis Anderson
Set in Janson Text by Graphic Composition
Printed and bound by Sheridan Books, Inc.

Library of Congress Cataloging-in-Publication Data

Cottle, Thomas J.
At peril : stories of injustice / Thomas J. Cottle.
p. cm.
Includes bibliographical references.
ISBN 1–55849-278-X (alk. paper)
1. Social problems—United States. 2. Social psychology—United States. I. Title.
HN59.2.C676 2001
361.1′0973—dc21
00–056832

British Library Cataloguing in Publication data are available.

To the memory of Eloise Mikkelsen

CONTENTS

CONTENTS

III. SCHOOL PERIL 147

IV. SOCIETAL PERIL 191

FOREWORD

AT THE heart of Thomas Cottle's illuminating and disturbing book are stories; stories of trauma, passion, pain, resilience, and hope. The stories bear Cottle's signature. They are told with compassion and discipline, power and restraint. He is a discerning and generous listener, a probing and respectful questioner, and a lucid and lyrical writer. Long after we read them, the stories linger; the images haunt us.

How can we forget "Mind Shadows," the poignant and aching story of little Annie, whose best—and only—friend Sarah leaves town, leaving Annie with a broken heart and a loneliness from which she will never recover. Or "Hocking a Life," the gritty tale of Ina Merman, a mother and wife who believes in hard work and clean living, who keeps an impeccable home where you "can eat off of the floor." But even though she has labored hard her whole life, she watches everyone around her get ahead while she and her husband feel as if they are "drowning." They can't even put together the cash to pay for their meager meals or the medicines they need for their frequent illnesses. Ina struggles against the currents of grief and bitterness that rise up in her and threaten to overwhelm her optimism, the single source of her survival. Annie and Ina's stories seem particularly painful in their ordinariness. But they are made extraordinary by Cottle's telling.

This volume, however, is also filled with more exotic tales of lives that may, at first, seem more remote to us. How can we forget "Women Who Kill," the searing narrative of Lenore Kingsley, the mother of four, who is serving a fifteen-to-twenty-year sentence for murdering her husband Henry. The murder followed years of cruel infidelity and violent abuse, when Lenore's sadness and shame finally turned to rage and retaliation. Now she waits in jail and the shame has returned. And how can we forget "Man with No Answers," the painful saga of Bob Grober, an atomic war veteran who suffers from a rare skin cancer, the result of nuclear fallout contracted during his tour of duty in the navy. First, his illness is misdiagnosed by physicians, who offer misguided remedies. Then, he is lied to by government officials, who refuse to take responsibility or action in the case. Now he fights the ravages of the cancer; tortured, waiting, hoping for a medical miracle. Lenore and Bob's stories may at first strike us as unusual, somewhat removed from our everyday realities. But soon these two people are no longer strangers to us. We identify with their struggles; we cheer their fortitude and courage. The exotic is made universal by Cottle's telling.

But Cottle has done much more than tell memorable stories. He has also ordered the narratives into a framework, with chapters designating domains that represent the broad ecology of human development. His framework helps to remind us that the sources of peril are found in a variety of places— in families, schools, health institutions, and the wider society—and that the policies and remedies we develop to respond to the endangered among us must appreciate these complex origins. There is no simple answer to society's injustices, no magic bullet. Rather, we must be attentive to the multiple forces and spheres of influence. We must chart the interactions among these arenas of human vulnerability, and understand how they are perceived and negotiated by the people who inhabit them. Cottle's heart-wrenching stories are given a scaffold by his analytic perspective, which allows us to see the stories in a new light and hear the tonality and texture of the voices with greater acuity.

But as a social scientist—who knows the challenges and casualties of collecting, recording, and interpreting people's lives—I am most intrigued by the way Cottle enters and exits from this volume; by the insights and lessons that are found in his introduction and afterword. It is in these chapters that we hear his voice most clearly, that we experience his thinking and have access to his methods. It is in these chapters that he reveals himself as the instrument of inquiry, as the co-creator of these narratives.

The introduction offers a compelling perspective for considering the issue of "peril" in human experience. Cottle's conception is probing and thoughtful. It does not fall into—in fact, it resists—the typical social science preoccupation with pathology, with crisis, with deprivation and focuses instead on the broader cultural, economic, developmental, social, and psychological threats that may imperil the healthy growth of *all* human beings in our society. Cottle is clearly most interested in examining the lives of those who are most severely oppressed and excluded in our society, but his analysis not only offers us new ways of considering the phenomenological *experience* of "injustice," it also offers us a broader gauged interpretation that includes those of us who are not typically considered to be "at risk" in our society.

I found his interpretive analysis intriguing and refreshing in the sense that it is both deeply compassionate and intellectually rigorous, both moving and informative. He reveals his deepest concerns; the urgency in his voice is not masked. But he also presents a discerning interdisciplinary discourse that helps us see and understand the broader and deeper meanings of "peril." I was particularly interested, for example, in the ways he joins Bronfenbrenner's notion of human ecology with Dewey's perspective on the marriage between individuals and their social and cultural worlds. This is just one example of Cottle's movement across disciplinary and theoretical boundaries, as he works to elucidate and refine our view of "peril." He also considers philosophical inquiries into fairness, psychological themes of identity formation, spiritual concerns about self-actualization, and sociopolitical issues focusing on welfare. Throughout, he borrows from the works of an eclectic range of writers and thinkers, both classical and contemporary—Fromm, Friere, Nathanson, Durkheim, May, Maslow, and Grant among others. But these references to the literature never feel like name dropping; they never seem confusing or too far-reaching. Rather, Cottle embeds these references into an emerging conceptual structure that becomes both convincing and coherent by the chapter's conclusion, and, most important, he offers the reader a lens for engaging the narratives that follow.

In the afterword, Cottle makes his methodology vivid and transparent. He tells us about his approach as witness, listener, griot, and narrator—a form of "story sociology" he has practiced for more than thirty years. He talks about the complex and subtle issue of voice and the mix of voices—the storyteller's and the narrator's—that combine to inform the life stories. He talks about the thorny and controversial methodological issues of "objectivity," "reliability," "validity," and what I would call "authenticity," offering interesting angles on each, challenging traditional definitions in the research literature. He also talks about the purpose of this work—why he does it, what he hopes will be its impact, his stance, his preoccupations . . . and he admits that these "subjective," interpretive lenses thread their way through all of the stages and phases of his work from conception, through data collection, through narrative development. And finally, he refers to some of the difficult ethical dilemmas faced by those of us who do face-to-face work. What I found useful and fascinating about this chapter—and this is from one who is fairly sophisticated about the methodological conundrums of qualitative inquiry—is not only that Cottle is self-revelatory and manages to demystify his craft but also that he does this without defensiveness or combativeness. The afterword maintains a tone of clarity, confidence, and generosity, and it—retrospectively—deepens the reader's understanding, and appreciation, of the narratives.

We reach the end of this wonderful book moved by Cottle's powerful blend of art and science.

SARA LAWRENCE-LIGHTFOOT
Emily Hargroves Fisher Professor of Education
Harvard University

PREFACE

As a child, I often heard my father, a physician, say that for a lifelong endeavor to be worthwhile, it somehow had to deal with life and death. Clearly, my father felt that life was too short to work on frivolous matters when so many people were hurting and needing care and attention. I joined this lesson with some primitive sense that many things in life were unfair. I doubt that my early perceptions were especially altruistic. That in my eyes my sister might have received a better present or my cousin a larger allowance assuredly led me to my earliest encounters with injustice.

What I didn't know as a child was that almost all people struggle with these matters of unfairness, injustice, and inequity and, if given the opportunity, speak about them eloquently. Nor was I sufficiently aware of the precarious state of so many lives, lives typically called imperiled. For me, risk was something you took when your pals dared you to do something dangerous. I was simply not aware that so many people in this country were living in genuinely perilous circumstances.

One cannot claim that only the hurting peoples of the world know injustice, intolerance, and inequity, but they do experience it and feel it. Peril is part of their existence. This is a book about people living their lives at peril. More specifically, it is a collection of accounts of peril told by children and adults, which means it is also a collection of personal descriptions of perceived injustice and inequity. Not surprisingly, the people in this book describe illness and health, family and school experiences, and conditions whose origins they locate in the institutions and conventions constituting our society and culture.

It is often said that because surviving in the face of injustice or peril is a monumental feat, stories of people at risk offer magnificent testimonies of the human spirit. Frankly, I am not always certain what this means. I suppose it has something to do with the fortitude, perseverance, and even forgiveness of perfectly innocent human beings when so many things stand in their way and the odds are stacked against them. But to listen to the people in this book is to hear that even the most private recesses of the human spirit can be put at peril and that the youngest of children can sense this and perhaps in some elemental fashion describe it.

In an individualistic, even narcissistic culture like ours, where psychological theories tend to dominate our thinking, perceptions, actions, and even destinies, the people whose stories are presented here offer a significant corrective: almost all of them are able to recognize the social and cultural, the very public, features that serve to put their lives at peril. They see social institutions, rules, laws, political and economic systems and policies, rituals, and conventions in the most palpable terms. Perhaps as evidence of that proverbial indomitable spirit, they refuse to perceive themselves as victims, although all recognize the degree of personal responsibility they bring to their own story of human peril.

The book is divided into six sections. In the introduction, I explore what will be called the "ecology of peril," a term meant to capture the richness and complexity of the environment in which human needs and lives develop and evolve, as well as theories of justice and how they affect these needs and our thinking about people whose lives are led at peril. The next four sections, respectively, present personal accounts of health peril, family peril, school peril, and social and cultural peril.

Finally, in an afterword, I discuss the theory and process of collecting the sort of stories found in this book. Bearing witness to accounts of peril allows us to view our own roles in the lives of others, our own place in society, and recognize the degree to which we identify ourselves as just, moral, compassionate, or even beneficent persons or perhaps persons living a perilous existence. In a sense, the act of bearing witness symbolizes a connection with another human being, who for us may be nothing more than the stories he or she tells. It symbolizes, as well, the connections we have to one another as fellow residents of not only a world community but an environment of peril.

A HOST OF people must be thanked for their contributions to the writing and publishing of this book. There is, first, a group of scholars at Boston University, notably my colleagues in the Special Education Department: Arthur Beane, Leroy Clinton, Donna Lehr, Rose Ray, Kathleen Vaughan, the late Frank Garfunkel, and, above all, Gerald Fain. In addition, Edwin J. Delattre, Allan Gaynor, Roselmina Indrisano, Victor Kestenbaum,

Mary Shann, and David Steiner have all been terribly helpful and generous. Special thanks as well to Lisa L. Paine, chair of the Department of Maternal and Child Health at the Boston University School of Public Health. Finally, there are my many students, who are devoting their lives to the well-being of children and are willing to undertake the study that this work requires.

Sara Lawrence-Lightfoot, Robert Melson, Gerald Platt, and Barry O'Connell not only are wonderful friends but also happen to be wonderful readers offering superb counsel. In this same regard, I want to thank Daniel Frank, Salvador and Patricia Minuchin, Richard, Ruth, and Roo Rogers, and Richard Rosenfeld, brilliant scholar, dear friend.

At the Press, Clark Dougan has been especially helpful and encouraging, making our collaboration perfectly joyous. Special thanks go to Carol Betsch and in particular to Deborah Klenotic, a kind but disciplined editor of the finest quality.

My family continues to grow, which means that the center of my life, Kay, Claudia, and Tony, Jason, Sonya, Luke, Nicole, and Anna, is as rich as ever it has been. And it continues to be filled with parents no longer here. Writing projects are solitary enterprises, but I am never alone.

Finally, I owe profound gratitude to the people whose words are heard in this volume. With full and complicated lives, they were nonetheless willing to work with me, speak with me, and allow bits of themselves to be made known to others. I hope they approve.

THOMAS J. COTTLE
Boston, Massachusetts

AT PERIL

INTRODUCTION
The Ecology of Peril

We become just by doing just acts, temperate by doing temperate acts, brave by doing brave acts.

ARISTOTLE, *The Nicomachean Ethics*

Virtues travel faster than the edicts carried by the royal couriers.

MENCIUS, *Works of Mencius*

THE PAST few decades in America may be called the period of self-consciousness. The term, of course, is a complicated, almost cavalier one. *Self-conscious* may connote self-interest to the point of wasteful vanity. On the other hand, it may connote a cautiously discerning approach to matters private as well as public. Self-consciousness, after all, can emerge in the form that Ellen Langer calls "mindfulness."[1]

In recent years some Americans have reveled in narcissistic behavior that may have surprised even the late Christopher Lasch, who wrote brilliantly on the subject.[2] The concept of self-interest and particularly self-esteem has been glorified—or is it the self that has been glorified?—and whether or not we admit to it, there is little incentive in society for generous, much less altruistic, morally motivated, or what Gerald Fain calls "beneficent" behavior.[3] In short, there is little incentive to contribute to the goodness of another person's life.[4]

Consonant with this philosophy, such as it is, and the lifestyle it breeds, the people who are most at risk in our culture claim they have seen little improvement in the state of their well-being. The commonweal, they argue, has not been properly attended to, particularly during eras in which government scandal and celebrity activity loom more exciting than the improvement of someone's immediate circumstances. State and federal policies have

I

come and gone, they note, but whatever the effects of these programs, a sizable group of people remains at peril.

The point is well taken. Never in our country have we witnessed more children growing up in poverty. Between 1979 and 1990, the actual number of poor people increased 41 percent, and half of the increase was accounted for by children age eighteen or younger.[5] It is estimated that without the earned income tax credit, the poverty rate might have climbed as much as 25 percent.[6] And although the rate of poverty appears to have declined over the last few years, there has been a rise in the number of children living at or below the poverty level who have one or both parents working. Significantly, almost two-thirds of children living in poverty report at least one parent working. More white children than any other group live in poverty, although disproportionately large numbers of African American and Hispanic children live in poverty. It goes without saying that education becomes the critical variable: the lower the educational level, the greater the likelihood that people do not find jobs and end up in poverty.

Given the manner in which contemporary programs are often administered, a sizable population of imperiled people will continue to exist. Keep in mind that America celebrates rates of unemployment as "low" as 4 or 5 percent, when in truth these numbers denote hundreds of thousands of people out of work, many for long periods of time, with some destined never to return to work.[7] And then there is the condition of the family members of these unemployed workers.

An intriguing aspect of America's at-risk populations now presents itself. If one scans the social and economic boundaries of the culture, and sometimes they appear almost palpable, one finds an extraordinary panoply of people, all of them having one thing in common: the belief or hard-earned knowledge that their group, if not they themselves as individuals, is at peril. They are struggling, suffering even. Along with legions of experts, these people would allege that their group's imperiled status is due directly to acts, well intentioned or not, of social and personal injustice, which often means for them acts performed by people with legitimate power to shape their circumstances. "The United States," Cynthia Crosson-Tower reminds us, "is the only industrial nation that has no national policies or standards for the welfare of young children and their families."[8]

Surely the poor of the land—the parents of the one in five children who grow up in poverty, the homeless and jobless, the children obliged to attend poor schools or enrolled in schools slated to be closed, the people without health care, and those unable to find the slightest morsel of nurturance and security in their families—feel this way.[9] One would predict this. What can be said about a culture that permits children to live without adequate shelter or go malnourished for years and produces children who have been described as having lost their ability to feel, react, or respond to any facet of the human conscience or social morality?[10] Surely there has to be some standard, some "minimum level of decency," as Stephen Nathanson calls it, beneath which we cannot allow people to fall.[11]

Remarkably, one hears the same refrains of peril and injustice among families of all socioeconomic classes in schools, child care centers, and health care facilities in all sectors of society. People either sense they have been excluded from something significant offered by the culture or know it with assuredness. They have been deprived, they claim, of basic living requirements, access to power and institutions, or other forms of valuable resources.[12] They are out of touch with some agency or some information, or they feel isolated from powers (and people) that appear sometimes mystical or magical and other times as tangible as the injustices they continue to experience and internalize as part of their identity.

These sentiments coalesce in an intriguing feature of injustice, namely, that people of all social classes and circumstances believe that they have been deprived of, have permanently lost out on, or are lost in the pursuit of real and imagined life goals, purposes, and dreams. As Rollo May suggested, these individuals sense that their own potentials have never been nurtured or seen the light of day.[13] Although they possess the same competitive sense as anyone else living in a society with certain standards of accomplishment and worth as well as limited resources, they have determined that the playing field isn't fair and because of this they have lost the game. The loss is felt, moreover, to be irrevocable and places them in the difficult position of being forever sequestered from successful, seemingly invulnerable people, who appear never to find themselves in harm's way.

Driving this sense of loss and separation is the belief that a person is legitimately entitled to, well, something—at least more than the little he or she has presently. Television, after all, advertises what everyone possesses, so no longer can anyone honestly report, "We grew up poor but we thought everyone lived like us." We may not know our own history, we may not know the statistics of injustice, but we know well the lifestyles of the rich and famous. And we all know something about dignity.

Politics, social history, one's unique set of experiences, the intensity of one's loyalty to one's country, years of hard work—anything at all may evoke a deep-seated resentment or, for that matter, invoke justifications for one's

3

sense of entitlement, a sense not so incidentally born from the public virtue of individualism or individual-based achievement. "One person, one vote" becomes transliterated; "I am; therefore I am entitled." As a result of people's clamoring for what they believe should be their own, the entire structure of political action has been transformed. Mass movements of a voluntary nature are more complicated and treacherous to establish and maintain than they were even a decade ago. As Theodore Roszak pointed out, America exhibits a chain of voluntary associations, each championing its own special political concerns and focus, each feeling that its rights have been jeopardized or compromised, and each alleging its own political claim to be legitimate, whether or not that claim touches on the political legitimacy or claims of the next group in line.[14] How is it that so many people feel they have been victimized by injustice? How is it that so many people feel themselves to be at peril?

To be sure, many political associations transact their business to call attention to themselves or, more precisely, to their causes. In a culture, generated by television, of visual confirmation (and creation) of social action, recognition is an inevitable step in the evolution of political reform. Indeed, some people act as if personal recognition constitutes the entirety of their politics. It is hard to avoid this when a so-called recognition factor becomes an indispensable element of political campaigns and social movements. Still, whatever anyone's claims and strategies, it cannot be denied that disenfranchised groups everywhere assert that they have experienced injustice of one sort or another through systematic courses of social or, more likely, political action. Accounts of their circumstances reveal a truth, and we hear them, especially the dramatic ones. Stories of children found unattended in homes stinking of filth and garbage become national headlines, along with domestic violence cases and murders of children by children. However accurate or distorted the media's coverage, we can no longer claim ignorance of these storied accounts, and we must make our way through the interpretations of them. On the one hand we are people who proclaim that one case here or there hardly constitutes a social ill or injustice, and on the other are those who transform an individual case into the poster child for some issue or cause. In the interpretations of the event lie the interpreters' philosophical and ideological positions. The murder, the battering or the lengthy duration of unemployment merely confirms the preconception.

Then again, in some cases, it seems as though the story of injustice is presented merely because of its appeal to sensation. What is more powerful than an image of a man being dragged to death along a country road by his murderers, a picture of children huddling together, barely alive, in a filthy apartment, or the bruised and bloody face of a woman battered by her assailant?

Usually the stories of social injustice include descriptions of someone lacking something necessary and tangible: attention, care, food, shelter, security, medical assistance—some basic human requirement or fundamental right. When one observes situations such as the lack of adequate health care among the poor, the condition of men and women experiencing long-term unemployment, or the plight of men who, as soldiers, were exposed to dangerous levels of radiation by their own government, one tends to become increasingly sympathetic not only to the person living in the particular circumstances but to the political cause advertising commitment to others living in these circumstances. In one's mind, it often comes down not to asking, How did this particular person get in to this position?—as if one were seeking to blame the victim—but to wondering how it is possible that so many people live in such circumstances and that governments, by dint of policies that are enacted or fail to be enacted, actually permit these circumstances to exist.

In many cases, furthermore, the observer cannot fail to be impressed by organizations, most of them operating on the proverbial shoestring budget, dedicated to assisting those still called "the needy." Soup kitchens, shelters, and respite houses are filled with people who the rest of society apparently feels are not its responsibility. Interestingly, surrounding many of these sanctuaries are voluntary associations committed to what they consider just causes. Their number and variety would have surprised even Alexis de Tocqueville, who saw in these associations the genuine strength of America's political will.[15] Indeed, the string of voluntary associations founded to combat injustice remains extraordinarily impressive, despite accusations from some quarters that they are essentially self-interested or individually driven organizations.

No one can set forth with perfect objectivity a hierarchy of America's political needs or even its imperiled populations. No one, moreover, can offer the accounts of populations at peril with disinterest. In the most personal of terms, I cannot visit the people whose stories are presented in this book and not be influenced—changed, really—by the circumstances of their lives and the amalgam of political, social, and economic conditions that creates them. Compassion, described by Edwin Delattre as the ability to take into account people's perspectives of their lives and hold these perspectives as vital facts of the whole story, demands interest and involvement, or at least some form of engagement.[16]

In the face of imperiled individuals, I find it virtually impossible to remain aloof and objective. It would be easier, I imagine, to attain a scientific level of objectivity and disinterest if all I had to do were to calculate the numbers—which themselves tell a remarkable story. Consider, for example, that more than 44 million Americans, 11 million of whom are children younger than eighteen, have no medical insurance. Data from the U.S. Census Bureau indicate that in 1998, about 25 percent of poor children had no insurance.[17] Among the country's children, Hispanics were the most likely to be uninsured, followed in order by African Americans, Asians, Pacific Islanders, and whites.[18]

Consider also these figures: with all of America's exquisite medical technologies and facilities, African American babies are twice as likely as white babies to die during their first year of life, and African American men with early-stage lung cancer are less likely than white men at the same point in their illness to be operated on and hence possibly cured, a factor that accounts for a significant disparity in the death rates of these two populations.[19]

Finally, consider that African American women are four times more likely than white women to die in childbirth.[20] Not so incidentally, although the actual deaths of these mothers are due to medical matters related to hemorrhage, pregnancy-induced hypertension, and the occurrence of an embolism, most research indicates that lack of access to care and poor quality of care are the reasons behind these maternal deaths, which number 20 per 100,000. As I say, numbers of this sort make the confrontation with injustice easier; faces and stories make the confrontation painful, if not outright unbearable.

We are in many respects a culture reeling out of control partly because of the irreconcilable nature of the excesses at one end of the social spectrum and the deprivations at the other. We react to the bureaucratic neutrality foisted on us by institutions that cannot rise above an almost childlike obedience to mindless rules to the level of simple human care or, in the eyes of imperiled people most affected by these institutions, sometimes actually appear to revel in dehumanizing processes and policies. Too many people are stymied and demeaned by bureaucratic mazes, red tape, regulations, and at times the most uncompassionate legislation and demeanor.

Our mental representations of ourselves and of the world are profoundly affected by still unresolved matters of racism, sexism, poverty, even colonialism—matters no longer inexplicable. Consider, in this regard, one simple research finding from the literature on special education. We know that medications such as Ritalin have been beneficial for people of all ages who exhibit attention deficit hyperactivity disorder, and we should not be surprised to learn that these medications are administered three times more often to boys than to girls. Clearly, boys' heightened activity or aggressiveness can become a serious problem for teachers and administrators, who only naturally recommend that the boys be medicated. But how are we to explain the finding that these same beneficial medications are given twice as often to white students as to African American students?[21]

In a sense, stories of injustice suggest that America has not yet determined at just what developmental age it wishes to be viewed at this point in its history. The country offers up all sorts of claims, but one still wonders what America is going to be when it grows up and whether the goal of genuine liberty, the blueprint of which appeared first in the Bill of Rights, will ever be reached. Although some would find the country's ideals, as set down by the Founding Fathers, to be as glorious as those established by any country in the history of humankind, historians remind us that the Constitution in fact did not attend fully to the fundamental needs, dignities, and rights of all the country's citizens. Glorious though it might have been in concept, vast populations of people remained imperiled, and despite invaluable amendments, some still do.

America seems to have passed through an era—as short-lived as most American eras—in which it appeared that certain imperiled groups received not only the attention they required to perpetuate their social movements but the benefits they coveted as well. I say "seems" because, after all, we do live in an age of public relations, a mentality that often masks enduring political and social realities, such as the continuing rate of poverty and the constant existence of those 20 percent of America's children growing up at or below the poverty line. Against a backdrop of omnipresent racism and generalized antipathy toward reforming poverty, many Americans nonetheless found they could tolerate popular political movements aimed at redressing the inequities of those who had been victimized by acts of injustice. This sentiment went only so deep, however. In time, while different groups within the country responded to the antipoverty and civil rights movements, perhaps even to the feminist movement, other groups took the existence of these social movements to mean that they, too, could begin to orchestrate their political demands and launch campaigns against what *they* saw to be the grand injustices of America. So while one group argues that poorer communities are destined to send their children to inferior public schools, another fights for the right to pray in those same schools, or at least at the schools' football games.

If some groups appeared to be receiving special attention and, as a result, valuable resources, why couldn't other groups enjoy commensurate attention and tangible benefits? What was just about someone else's group getting something while ours goes without? Even more, how can anyone justify *our* money being used for *their* well-being? If the families of children with disabilities were demanding that their children be allowed to attend regular classes with all the other children, even if this meant that teachers had to provide them extra time and resources, then why wouldn't the parents of children without disabilities demand additional teacher time and resources for *their* children? Why, in other words, should the movement for inclusion of children with disabilities result in some parents' feeling their children were being excluded? And couldn't one make a case that intellectually superior students were also exceptional people requiring additional time and resources? If certain Americans resented the national attention paid to poor, minority, or special education populations, then they resented as well the fact that these populations seemed to have their demands for tangible rewards met.

Compounding the problem was that belief, sometimes valid and sometimes not, that benefits were accruing to certain populations at the expense of other populations. Nothing has given rise to this perception more than the civil rights movement and the more recent inclusion movement in special education. In many cases, however, the resentment of one person's receiving even minimal attention only exacerbated other people's contention that they were the genuinely dispossessed and hence the most imperiled. Affirmative action, like the inclusion movement in special education, has aroused the deepest of human sentiments and ignited the most complex discussions of justice. Both of these social movements, presumably, are intended to compensate for or rectify fundamental social inequities that occur in an unlevel playing field. As wrongs are righted, injustices addressed, and the playing field leveled, someone inevitably feels shortchanged and aggrieved, and so the battles continue to be waged. He got into the school, it is argued, merely because he is black or Hispanic or, sadly, was born with some disability. But what about my child, who earned her place in school through hard work and demonstrated performance? Is she to be punished, made the fodder in some social revolution, merely because she is white and lives without a disability? Yes, comes the response, but what about the years of abuse and exclusion predicated on that very same color or that very same disability?[22]

These are the sorts of discussions, many of them rancorous indeed, heard daily in this country as institutions attempt to shift their ideologies, legislation, and practices. At one level, these discussions invoke complex and compelling philosophical and sociological arguments about justice and the nature of what is good, virtuous, and right. On another level, they evoke deeply personal and autobiographical responses and narratives.

In this book, I recount some of these narratives. Although I review several major theories of justice later in this introduction, my focus in this volume remains the single life and hence the single account of human experience, told not by philosophers and social scientists but by individual men, women, girls, and boys, wishing to express their own accounts of an experience: a reaction to a diagnosis of a learning disability, an observation of a neighbor unemployed for months, an idea that city living might be associated with physical discomfort and illness, the lack of proper medical care, the desperation in a family that leads a child to take her own life.

The stories reveal the sorts of conversations we all have with ourselves and the world. They reveal the ways in which we explain ourselves to ourselves and those who will listen to us. They reveal, in other words, the mental representations we hold of ourselves as well as our worldviews as we hunt for the meanings of events such as an illness, a school closing, long-term unemployment, or perhaps just teaching or learning in a school. Stories reveal our ideologies and beliefs, which means that individual stories offer accounts of human action and perspectives on it that are shaped by ideologies and social and cultural forces of all stripes. Inevitably, the voices of societies and cultures are heard in our narratives, for they shape and direct our most personal reflections and visions.

Equally intriguing, as Stephen Kemmis reminds us, is the possibility that social institutions, cultural forms, and ideologies are themselves shaped in part by individual reflection and action and hence by the very stories we tell and witness. Culture, after all, is predicated largely on transmission of the meaning of matters such as justice through stories. Culture is kept alive through stories that emerge in allegory, metaphor, ritual, and mythology. So although it may be true that our stories naturally change over time or, as John Kotre has observed, as a function of those to whom we tell them, they are at least attempts to make sense of or account for experience. This means they also reflect attempts to make sense of how a personal or intimate environment touches or, in some cases, collides with complex social and cultural environments to define the single human being and eventually give rise to his or her stories, which in this book involve an experience or felt sense of injustice.[23]

9

In the following section, I offer a discussion of these environmental factors and influences, if only to elucidate one point: no human story is ever purely idiosyncratic. Inevitably, no matter what the detail or nuance, whatever the poignancy, inherent in the story are systematic social and cultural features, abstract or very real, which define our lives as well as bind us together with the storyteller. It is the *ecology* of the story, in other words, that provides much of its meaning and allows us, the witnesses, to make our connections with the story and its teller. Of course, we understand more fully the story of injustice because we ourselves have felt forms of slight or outright injustice. Yet in our connection with the storyteller, we recognize that abstract, philosophical, and most assuredly ecological elements of injustice drive these stories, just as they are formed by them. In the final analysis, the story allows us to learn not only about the teller but also about the teller's society and culture. We learn about an instance of hurt and, beyond this, about ongoing, complicated matters of lifelong peril and social injustice.

AN ECOLOGICAL APPROACH TO JUSTICE

Ecology is the study of the relationships between and among living organisms and their environment. That the word derives from the Greek *oikos*, meaning "house," suggests the symbolic state of the house as a structure protecting its residents from external circumstances, the membrane between the self and the external world of societies and cultures.[24]

Urie Bronfenbrenner's ecological scheme provides a useful model for exploring the ecological nature of a single life, which in a sense is what this book is about.[25] In Bronfenbrenner's scheme, the child is surrounded by a series of concentric circles, each representing a sphere of environmental influences on him or her. At the center of the scheme, in the innermost circle, stands the child. For Bronfenbrenner, this innermost realm represents the child's mental and physical health, a significance borne out in the fact that most studies of people at peril commence with examinations of health, illness, and access to care.

The first circle surrounding the child, the *microsystem*, represents the somewhat expansive setting in which the child lives. Residing here are the child's parents, teachers, doctors, religious leaders, and anyone else having a direct effect on his or her welfare or, in cases of peril, lack of welfare. Outside this circle is the *mesosystem*, the realm of relations between the various microsystem features. It is from this slightly removed perspective, Bronfenbrenner theorizes, that we observe the child operating in her child care center or watch what happens if a parent abandons or abuses her.

The next circle represents the *exosystem*, the world of extended family, friends, and neighbors. These are people, seen or unseen, who may in fact have little or no direct personal role in the child's life but whose influence nonetheless may be significant. Residing here is the woman upstairs who brings the child cookies when he is ill or runs an errand for the child's parents. Importantly, the exosystem also contains members of the school board or city government, whose legislation enhances or fails to enhance the child's life. The cookies for the ill child are akin to the resurrection of the local park or the failure to install a stoplight at the corner where many accidents have occurred. The Headstart program, the condition of schools, the mechanics of health care delivery, employment regulations, and unemployment benefits are features of the exosystem, whether the child is aware of them or not.

Outside the exosystem lies the *macrosystem*, the ecological realm of belief systems, ideologies, and values—the literal and symbolic material of culture that, as Clifford Geertz reminds us, is passed on from one generation to the next.[26] In the macrosystem are the sources of definitions and of the meanings of our lives and ourselves. Macrosystem elements, such as ageism, racism, and sexism, are powerful forces in the shaping of one's life and worldview, as we have already seen, even though the child in question may have not the slightest understanding of the dynamics of culture, if he or she even recognizes the word.

Macrosystem elements might also be said to contain the realities of social class. Although this is not the place to discuss these matters in detail, it seems illustrative to point out that when adolescents were asked to rate their health, it was discovered that self-reported depression and obesity were linearly associated with families in which parents engaged in manual occupations.[27] Social class, in other words, plays a role in both the existence of certain disorders and the self-assessments of young people.

Finally, we encounter what Bronfenbrenner calls the *chronosystem*, and now the spatial model of concentric circles may seem slightly inappropriate. The chronosystem contains the patterning of environmental events and transitions that take place over the course of a lifetime. Obvious examples present themselves. A divorce of the child's parents will have an effect on the child throughout her life, as will the relationships between her grandparents and parents, relationships constituting the essence of the transmission of healthy or pathological patterns of family interaction.[28] The chronosystem reminds us that events do not happen in a finite instant, but create ripples of affects on the child well after the creators of these affects have disappeared. Men who experience long-term unemployment know this phenomenon only too well, as we shall see in a later chapter.

Whether or not anyone at the center of the concentric circles can identify any aspect of such a theoretical model is irrelevant. What is essential is that children, as their cognitive abilities mature, become better able to speak about their lives from the perspectives of these various realms. Whether children know it or not, their definitions of the world and themselves become profoundly affected by these ecological realms. We have only to note the developing ideologies of an adolescent to confirm this point.[29] It should come as no surprise, therefore, that a person would recognize how, for example, a law, an esthetic feature of a city, or the behavioral rituals in a hospital would directly affect his or her sense of well-being or lack thereof. We should not be surprised to hear a man say that he dies from the existence of unrepaired potholes or a woman state that her stomach cancer is caused by living in the crowded, hostile, noisy environment of a housing project. Patients' narratives of their illness, what Anne Hunsaker Hawkins calls "pathographies," reveal not only specific medical issues but the ecological issues defining their experience or felt sense of illness.[30]

An ecological model reveals how people develop their various schemes of justice and injustice as their thinking matures from a belief in something merely because their parents taught them it was true to the ability to debate others, and themselves, on the meanings of justice and injustice. In time, they come to recognize how these meanings shape their definitions of wellness and illness, living and dying. An ecological model, moreover, enriches our understanding of the evolution of a child's cognitive skills from concrete to abstract reasoning, as well as the child's emerging recognition of the complexity of human action, and of the degree of thoughtfulness required to recognize the social and cultural forces that influence our innermost thoughts and feelings and, for that matter, our reasoning. Ecological factors delineate the most personal of narratives, many of which may never be told.

At a very young age children begin to recognize that they are being put at peril for no reason other than that their skin is dark or that they are poor. An event occurring years ago, for example, the death of a sibling or a parent's abandoning the family, may imperil a child. The child is also imperiled by unseen people—legislators, perhaps, who are unfamiliar with the circumstances of the child's life or merely insensitive to them. Peril is also the result of societal and cultural processes, rituals, and long-standing belief systems.

That a man suffers from long-term unemployment is the result not merely of psychological reactions to stress. Nor is his life wholly defined by his capacity to cope with the daily peril of being out of work, peril that surely constitutes chronic trauma.[31] A life is also put at peril by a belief system held by society enunciating a necessity for certain groups of people to be out of work, or poor, or homeless, or without adequate medical care, in order for the greater system to survive. In the case of long-term unemployment, as Seymour Bellin and S. M. Miller suggest, the ideology actually becomes morally acceptable to a culture, thereby yielding what André Gorz calls the "non-class of non-workers." The influence of social structural forces on our most personal narratives and self-definitions is what Abraham Maslow had in mind when he wrote that "inner problems and outer problems tend to be deeply similar and to be *related to each other.*"[32]

In a similar vein, to understand John Dewey's philosophy is to understand the relationship between the individual and the democracy in which, ideally, he or she lives. That Dewey believed in the uncommon story of the common man and woman was underscored by his belief in the need for people to participate in the workings of democracy. Readers of Dewey are familiar with his assertion that a child is not born with wisdom but learns it from those willing to enlist the child's innate interest in solving real and practical problems along with intellectual and artistic ones.[33] Intriguing to think that those without wisdom could also be called imperiled.

Again and again, Bronfenbrenner's so-called ecological orientation elucidated an intimate marriage between individuals and the social and cultural worlds in which they survived; we will detect this strain in the voices presented in this book. For the person to thrive, there had to be a marriage of individual integrity and social solidarity.[34] Authentic individual growth, Dewey, too, argued, meant the deepening of social engagements. Conversely, an unjust society could destroy any possibility of human growth. Dewey's pragmatism, in other words, was almost an ecological model itself and demonstrates the perilous state experienced by the isolated individual or the victim of injustice.

If Dewey disdained the dualism of the mind and the body, he also deplored the concept of nature versus culture, for he knew that human growth requires a social and cultural scaffolding. If the child at the center of Bronfenbrenner's innermost circle is to thrive, the forces and influences generated in the other circles must be properly arranged and operating at full capacity. Aristotle was right: no one is independent and wholly self-sufficient. No one does it alone; without societal supports, too many people are put at risk. The human being triumphs only when the ecological environment is itself essentially just.

THE REALMS OF PERIL

We review now the realms of potential peril and the membranes of protection against peril that derive from the writings of Bronfenbrenner and Dewey. These realms form the sections of this book.

The child's physical and mental welfare, one would think, represents the commencement of protection against peril, and hence we may establish the category of risks to individual health. Next, as Bronfenbrenner suggests, is the immediate and extended family, which offers a second layer of protection against peril, although, of course, it is also a potential source of peril. We are reminded in this regard of the research indicating that people who report having been abused or neglected as children are four times more likely to exhibit some form of personality disorder. These include borderline, narcissistic, antisocial, and avoidant personality disorders, as well as symptoms of anxiety and depression.[35] On a brighter note, we are also reminded by Herbert Anderson and Kenneth R. Mitchell that the family "is the context in which we discover our gifts in such a way that we can give them away. We are held in order to be sent."[36]

Third, as Dewey reminds us, education is a source of peril or a protection against it—though schooling is rarely conceived in these terms—and a force for liberating the human mind. In Dewey's words, "Education has accordingly not only to safeguard an individual against the besetting erroneous tendencies of his own mind—its rashness, presumption, and preference of what chimes with self interest to objective evidence—but also to undermine and destroy the accumulated and self-perpetuating prejudices of long ages."[37]

In the most humanistic of terms, the educator William Ayers writes not only of school but of the teacher's role in safeguarding the child from various external factors: "There are still young people who need a thoughtful, caring adult in their lives; someone who can nurture and challenge them, who can coach and guide, understand and care about them. There are still injustices and deficiencies in society, in even more desperate need of repair."[38]

Fourth, and ideally, society and culture must offer a final barrier to peril—Bronfenbrenner's macrosystem—through what Dewey calls democratic institutions, especially those regarding work and education.

There is one more dynamic that is sometimes omitted in discussions of people at peril. I call it the imperiled spirit, referring to the person who is unable to experience genuine self-realization, or what Maslow called "self actualization." Likewise imperiled is a culture that prevents entire classes of people from engaging in these quintessential human acts: self-realization and the exploration of identity.

Students of Dewey know that he was concerned with the matter of self-realization, a concept we typically associate with psychologists such as Maslow and May. At bottom, Dewey observed that the result of individual life lived in a just society should be genuine self-realization, something that ought to be possible for all people and not merely the culture's economic or educational elite. Indeed, this uniquely human capacity for self-realization not only is made possible by democratic orderings of work and education but is the very ideal of the democratic ethos. It may in fact be what the Founding Fathers called "the pursuit of happiness." So we are faced with another form of peril: the human spirit denied the appropriate societal and cultural machinery and resources to attain its full potential. For freedom, too, is a promise to the child in the innermost circle, or it ought to be.[39]

The very nature of self-consciousness, the fundamental experiencing of oneself, is an essential ingredient of humanness, argue many philosophers, May among them. Humanness is represented by a capacity to construct images of the self, May asserted, as well as a continuing sense of oneself as responsible, so that one may experience one's own humanity. If you don't let children pursue their curiosity or inborn intelligences, potentials, and individualism, May argued, as did Fromm before him, you cause them to feel insecure and ultimately anxious. Dewey would have argued that in addition, the children are enslaved.

A relationship is founded, therefore, between the self and its potentials. More generally, in the mode of being that May called the *Eigenwelt*, in which the self is thrown against itself, we come to know ourselves, feel ourselves, and react to or experience ourselves and, in the process, come to recognize our potentials and how and why they are being actualized or repressed. May defined the *Eigenwelt* as the realm in which identity and consciousness evolve. Ultimately, he argued, the self is responsible for itself, for others live within us; indeed, whole relationships live within us. This means that cultures and societies, too, live within us, precisely as the sociologist Émile Durkheim and the psychoanalyst Fromm argued.[40] This also means that justice and injustice live within us and in part come to define the *Eigenwelt*.

In this manner, a just society also makes possible the sojourns of the self. If the world seems fair, I can extend myself into it, explore it, live in it, experience it, and eventually be nourished by it. As Arthur Beane writes, summarizing May, "The Eigenwelt was more than a subjective experience. It's the 'basis on which we see the real world in its true perspective, the basis on which we relate.'"[41] When I experience injustice, I am thrown against myself, unable to successfully develop my potentials or discover my genuine identity, which some would label my "calling." I am by definition inhibited, forced to live a solitary, isolated life filled with anxiety, shame, and the feeling that I am unacceptable. I live, moreover, with a sense of ostracism rather than a sense of inclusion, and hence my existence is dominated by thoughts of death—what Freud called "Thanatos," or the death instinct—rather than of life. I am closed off, repressed (though not necessarily in Freud's meaning of the word), uncreative, self-absorbed, and perhaps unable even to love. In not being able to find meaning in the world or in myself, I feel alienated from the exterior world and myself. Experiencing this alienation, as Paulo Friere reminds us, I become alienated from the very decisions I must make about my own life and well-being.[42]

Finally, in my search for personal welfare, a welfare ultimately denied by social injustices, I am unable to provide another person selfless love or the welfare he or she may require. I am unable to do good even for my own family. Most probably, too, I shall never know the feeling of pursuing joy, much less attaining it.

Do we reflect often enough on the role of injustice in what May called the "shaking of the self world," or the assault of the spirit? As we study Bronfenbrenner's ecological scheme, does it strike us that cultural, economic, and political forces ultimately shape the substance of one's consciousness, identity, and spirit?[43] Do we in fact reflect often enough on the tentativeness or outright fright we observe in people at peril and ask ourselves whether tentativeness, surely a symptom of their identity, is caused by societal features? Or do we prefer to perceive peril as the product of psychological factors somehow inherent in the individual, who, if he just had the wherewithal to pull himself up by his own bootstraps, could make it in the culture like all the rest of us who did? At the very least, these questions demand that we consider various theories of injustice.

THEORIES OF INJUSTICE

One place to begin a discussion of injustice is the concept of equalitarianism. If we hold that all people are equal, then all people are entitled, somehow, to equal protection and due process. As argued by Stephen Nathanson, whose work I draw on in this section, the notion is well meaning, but the fact that no two of us are equal means that equalitarianism fails to supply the solution to injustice.[44] Different people require different goods and services. The education of the child with cerebral palsy, for example, presumably requires more money than does that of the child who doesn't need special services. It is also clear, Nathanson argues, that in a society that derives part of its income from property taxes, children in poorer communities have access to fewer dollars for their schools than do children in richer areas.

In the end, Nathanson observes, we are inevitably confronted with different forms of equality and inequality. The mere fact that I may need more calories to be healthy than you do suggests that an equal distribution of food may not solve my own particular nutritional needs. Thus we enter the realm of theories of distributive justice and must now formulate the telling question, How do we distribute society's goods and services so that no one is imperiled? Or fewer people become imperiled? Or everyone faces the same chances for peril? The just society, after all, is the one in which, all things being equal, the differences in human destiny are accounted for purely by genetic chance or luck.

The theory of entitlement holds that in the context of a free market economy, if all parties engaged in any negotiation deem every step of the negotiation process to be just, the ultimate negotiation must also be deemed just. As Nathanson observes, to each according to his or her own market value. To be sure, the government promises public education, the one institution that continues to symbolize, if not always enact, the central dynamic of democracy. "The answers to the problems of a tragic world," wrote the editors of the first volume of the *Journal of Education*, "can come only through more effective education of people." Similarly, Gerald Grant wrote that "schools were the major channel of the nation to bring about a more equal society." Nevertheless, no person is naturally entitled to more than another, and not because some theory says this isn't just, but because not all parties involved in the negotiation of such an entitlement consider it just.[45]

Utilitarian theory, as Nathanson reviews it, emphasizes the belief that the "right" thing to do is that which will bring the "best" results to the greatest number of people. As the expression goes, we have to weigh the upside against the downside and hope that our decision falls on the upside for most of the people involved in the decision. In this process, there is no guarantee that all people will be treated equally or even fairly. Alas, utilitarianism promises only to offer the greatest *sum* of beneficial effects; the reader recognizes the familiar cost-benefit feature of utilitarianism. As Nathanson muses, if you want a theory of distributive justice that tends to the needs of all people, utilitarianism is not for you.

Still another theory of distributive justice is the difference principle. On the surface, this theory is often acceptable to those expressing concern with a culture's imperiled populations. As Nathanson explains, the theory recognizes that an unequal distribution of goods and services may well be permissible and hence just if in the end it is found to benefit the people who are the least well off.

Essentially a social contract to which all people must agree, the difference principle, as put forth eloquently by John Rawls,[46] argues, first, that liberty must be granted to all people equally and, second, that society can justly aid the people who are better off if it can be shown that as a result the less well off people also benefit. As Nathanson observes, the theory represents a "trickle-up" economic flow, inasmuch as all people presumably benefit to some degree in the negotiation. But here's the catch: even if the lower reaches of the society benefit somewhat from trickle-up economic dynamics, nothing is said about the standard of living in which they ultimately find themselves as a result of the trickle. While in principle the trickle-up theory appears philosophically just, there is no guarantee that people will end up in what the society would define as "decent shape."

Examples of this predicament are numerous, with special education again providing a perfect illustration.[47] A school wishes to grant money to special education students, just as it wishes to be fair and grant money to its gifted and talented students not involved in special education programs. Ostensibly, the just solution is to allocate money to both groups. But what if the money afforded the special education students does not allow them to reach some fundamentally decent level of functioning, a level already attained by the gifted and talented students, who now desire to reach an even higher level? As Nathanson suggests (although he does not use this wording), the trickle-up economic dynamic of the difference principle, while better than nothing, fails to directly address people at peril. The societal objective of justice, after all, is to remove all people from peril or at least those forms of peril over which we maintain some degree of control.

For Nathanson, the solution to the vexing concerns of distributive justice is found in what he calls the "decent-level" theory. Using the notion of safety nets or minimum standards, Nathanson claims that it is just to offer the culture's goods and services to all people only when it can be demonstrated that with these goods and services, all people will live at a so-called decent level, that is, without peril. In order to make certain that all people live free of peril, however, we may have to reduce the overall well-being of everyone in the society.

Responding to traditional criticisms of the entitlement, utilitarian, and difference principle theories, the decent-level theory states that many people in the culture may have to wait to travel until everyone is on the train. Because this is so, decent levels of existence, by definition free of peril, represent an argument against the unequal distribution of goods and services and the inevitable charge of inequality. To reiterate, the decent level theory states that in a free market economy, all people can get what they can get, just as long as no one lives at peril. As John Gardner put it, "all men are equally worthy of our care and concern."[48] In a sense, Nathanson offers a corrective to what sociologists call ascriptive wealth, or wealth into which one is born. Given that people do not start off on the proverbial level playing field, the decent-level theory assures that at least all children have a reasonable position on the field.

It appears that Nathanson has cast his lot with Dewey and, for that matter, the Founding Fathers, for it is evident that the fundamental ingredient of the decent-level theory is the maximization of educational opportunities. The school, as Dewey's disciple Francis W. Parker claimed, must be "a model home, a complete community, and an embryonic democracy."[49] At the same time, we recognize that the institution of the school must guarantee a democratic playing field where success is earned through individual achievement and not by fortuitous genetic accident.

The decent-level theory implies that a culture cannot call itself democratic if, from the time of birth, certain citizens are placed at peril by forces other than idiosyncratic misfortune. No one would dare to publicly deny anyone access to the finest doctors and most advanced medical technologies in the land, but the fact is that certain populations of people *are* denied the best doctors and the most advanced medical services in the land. How else can one explain the statistic that four times as many African American women as white women die giving birth? How else can one explain the absence of health insurance among so many children living at or below the poverty level? It is precisely these sorts of sociological facts that led Nathanson to ask how we reconcile a desire to seek the best medical care with the knowledge that some people go without even the most elemental care, which places them permanently at risk.

Nathanson may also have cast his lot with Aristotle, who associated justice with equality but added that justice demands that goods and services be distributed to each according to what he or she deserves.[50] The decent-level theory suggests that in the context of a culture's resources, we *deserve* a fundamentally peril-free life. Yet having said this, it is obvious, as Fain points out, that laws of distributive justice, morality, and acceptance of differences cannot fully describe the dynamics that ultimately extricate people from peril. "A civil and human society needs more than law, more than justice, and more than toleration," writes Fain. "It depends also on other civic virtues including respect for and commitment to beneficence."[51]

Fain is thinking here of simple human acts of kindness, or what is commonly called charity. He writes, "When we know that life is not fair, that being born with a life limiting disability is not fair, that disease is not fair, that poverty is not fair, that child abuse is not fair, then we know that justice is not enough. Justice applies to the many, but it cannot always fulfill our voluntary duty to the exception."[52]

In the next section, I turn to the inherent human needs. The satisfaction of these needs is not only prerequisite to personal fulfillment and the capacity to remove oneself from peril but also essential if people are to act charitably, with beneficence, so that they may free others from perilous states. For if Fain is correct, the fulfilled person is also a beneficent one.

THEORIES OF INDIVIDUAL PROTECTION AND FULFILLMENT

Although we recognize that even the most ideal form of justice cannot remove everyone from peril, it is nonetheless essential that we examine the metaphoric playing field. What are the fundamental needs of people that, if met, would reduce the chances of their living at peril? We begin with children and the work of Mia Pringle, who identifies four needs (reminiscent of Maslow's hierarchy of five needs) that, if unmet, cause a child to be "doubly vulnerable" to risk.[53]

The first need is for love and security. Children's formation of an identity, Pringle asserts, rests on these two powers. They are necessary, furthermore, if children are to establish relationships and to believe they can affect action or, more simply, elicit help, as Robert Kegan suggests, and thereby successfully navigate in the world.[54] Love and security make it possible for children to believe that they are creators of their environment as well as products of it.[55]

Second is the need for stimulation, novelty, or what Pringle calls "new experiences." Clearly, this need refers directly to the development of the mind, learning, and education. Perhaps nurturing of the spirit is involved as well.

Third, children must receive attention, recognition, praise, and, let us add, moments of sublime success, for ultimately, says Pringle, these are what allow the formation of confidence and healthy esteem.

Finally, Pringle offers the concept of responsibility, which first introduces children to their culture's rules and regulations, what we would call morality, and then asks them to act in responsible and hence competent and constructive ways. In all meanings of the term, children learn that they are *responsible* for their actions.

As noted, Pringle's need inventory is closely aligned with Maslow's hierarchy of needs, which includes physiological needs, safety needs, love and belonging needs, esteem needs, and finally the need for self-actualization.[56] But the need inventory advanced by Fromm more than half a century ago does even more to elucidate our appreciation of populations at risk. Readers of Fromm are familiar with his assertion that human beings possess a drive to attain security and escape loneliness and at the same time a conflicting need for freedom and the ability to create the individual self.[57] All of these human cravings, as Fromm called them, are essentially determined by the opposition to these drives, as manifested in six distinct needs.

First is relatedness, or what Fromm called sibling love, parental love, and erotic love. Ecologically, relatedness represents Bronfenbrenner's microsystem, the realm in which we recognize our essential need to care for others; know them; respect them; and, importantly, commit ourselves to their well-being.

Second is transcendence, or the need to rise above our animal instincts (Fromm, we recall, was still somewhat bound to Freudian theory) so that we might undertake purposive and creative action. When creativity is blocked, producing what May called anxiety, Fromm claimed we become destructive.

Third is the need for rootedness. This notion is akin to Bronfenbrenner's macrosystem, the realm of kinship, community, and attachment to one's nation.[58] Rootedness also compensates for our evolving separation (even alienation) from nature.

Fourth is the familiar identity need, a need that Erikson later thoroughly articulated, as did Salvador Minuchin, who posited that identity combines the seemingly paradoxical dimensions of community and belonging, on the one hand, and autonomy and the sense of being separate, on the other.[59] For Fromm, each of us lives with the need to establish our unique identity, derived not from our identifications with groups—for this would be tantamount to what he called a "borrowed identity"—but from our own personal searching, the mode of being May described as the *Eigenwelt*.

Fifth, Fromm argued that humans have a need, stemming from our natural powers of imagination and reason, for a frame of orientation and object of devotion. What Fromm meant was our need to formulate a rational and coherent view of our environment, a so-called objective perspective of reality, as well as some object or icon to which we are devoted and through which we find meaning.

Finally, Fromm asserted that human beings require stimulation and excitation (Pringle's new experiences). We need what Maslow labeled as "peak experiences" and the psychologist Mihaly Csikszentmihalyi called the "experience of flow."[60]

In addition, as Pringle, Fromm, and Erikson point out, each of us must formulate compromises between our fundamental needs, indeed our biological inheritance, and the environment. These compromises or resolutions of psychosocial dilemmas, as Erikson called them, essentially determine our personalities.[61] This in turn means that satisfaction of all six needs identified by Fromm ultimately depends on social and cultural opportunities, precisely as ecological theory asserts. By definition, furthermore, if any of these needs goes unmet, we are imperiled. We are also at peril, Fromm's theory indicates, when individuals or the culture acts to harm or deny us and in reaction we withdraw. Similarly, when individuals and cultures withdraw from us, we are again imperiled and in reaction become destructive.[62] Both scenarios are illustrated in the narratives presented in this book.

The balance between security and responsibility—a good place to begin a discussion of people imperiled by social institutions—finds its origin in the parent's love and respect for the child. Fromm urged that the same love and respect be shown each person by his or her culture, as each of us ultimately reflects the values of the culture, its richness as well as its shortcomings. That a child's personality is profoundly affected by his or her parents must not conceal the fact that it is parents who carry the seeds of security *and* peril from the culture to the child. This becomes a critical feature in what social scientists call the "transmission of culture." The child ultimately learns that a powerful cultural apparatus supports or does not support his or her development. Fromm noted that from this involvement with the culture, the child develops a "social character," which for many populations in contemporary society is an imperiled one.

Two last points regarding Fromm. First, still holding somewhat to Freud's notions of instinctual life and death forces (Fromm spoke in terms of a life character, biophilous, and a death character, necrophilous), Fromm theorized that people are born neither good nor evil but can become evil when they are unable to achieve their potential. Through love, brotherhood and sisterhood, solidarity, and humanistic and communal orientations, an ideal society yields productive citizens. These notions were set in a more modern context by Roberta Wollons: "Unlike times past, the language of risk today is an indictment not of children's moral failure, but rather of the social institutions that fail children: the family, the schools, and the government . . . Deepening the complexity of the problems, institutions to which we look for solutions are too often faced with conflicts that arise when the needs of the child are at variance with the needs of the institutions themselves."[63]

Second, Fromm believed that human beings are not determined by unseen, uncontrollable instincts, a point that reveals the optimism of his philosophy in contrast to Freud's. Indeed, we have an innate instinct, Fromm averred, for justice and truth.[64] Somehow we know that something is not right, good, or just and, whatever our efforts, we probably will not win. Granted, we may act as if we were unaware of an injustice or an untruth, but we know. So the task of living is not merely to fulfill our innate potentials— become self-actualized in Maslow's terms—but to create a society in which all people can know genuine gratification and fulfillment. In the absence of this fulfillment, an absence created in part by a society unable or unwilling to generate justice and truth, we live at peril.[65]

IDEAL VISIONS AND REAL DANGERS

It was just another night of university teaching. I stood on a stage in a large, windowless lecture hall, teaching theories of adolescent development. The education majors faced me from their seats in the amphitheater, the last rows seemingly a hundred feet high and a thousand miles away. I launched the discussion with a question on the advisability of maintaining elementary, middle, and high schools as separate entities. Alleging the foolishness of allowing little children to run around in the same building with older ones, most of the students saw the wisdom of maintaining separate schools. It would make no sense, they argued, to have children who are barely able to reason logically cavorting with youth working on the budding formation of their adult identities. Then they poked fun at me. The next thing you'll want, they said, is to blend students of all ages in one classroom.

I began my response to the animated discussion with a brief review of various social scientific studies and then gave an account of my own educational history, which involved attending one school for fourteen consecutive years, prekindergarten right through high school, with practically the same thirty-six boys and girls. Designed by the philosopher John Dewey and the educator Francis W. Parker, the school advocated Dewey's notion that in all children there live grand ideas and beautiful innate gifts and it is the teacher's job to discover them.

Because of those fourteen years, I explained, my conception of an ideal educational institution remains a tiny school with tiny classes, plenty of teachers (generously compensated, of course), and the opportunity for everyone to engage in all sorts of activities, with all classes mainstreamed—a buzzword meaning that no matter how you learn and how much time it takes, you're entitled to the best seat in the house.[66] And if, for some reason, your learning strategies are different from those of your classmates or you require more time than normally is prescribed for performing certain tasks, you ought not be set back or shamed. In fact, your fellow classmates should be part of the cadre of people assisting and encouraging you.

And one thing more, I told my students, as long as I was spinning dreams of an ideal education: if a school cannot house all of its students, staff, and faculty in one auditorium, the school is too big. Never enlarge auditoriums, I counseled; reduce school populations. It is in the auditorium, not the gymnasium, where the school presents itself in an ecological light and as a miniature democracy. More than a classroom, the auditorium or meeting room becomes a communal (and communing) space, a place for human connections, the authentic center of the school's culture. It is a place in which people of all ages convene as a genuine body politic in as pure a democratic atmosphere as is humanly possible. On display in the auditorium is a rich panoply of human beings and human endeavor, which takes on added meaning because of the presence of the entire school's citizenry.

Then came the inevitable and perfectly reasonable question: How can you advocate all of this—small schools, auditoriums to seat a miniature body politic, tiny classrooms, loads of well-paid teachers, students tutoring students, equal opportunities, just institutions caring for their citizens? It's not cost-effective!

As the young man spoke, I felt emotions rushing back in me that I knew were born in the 1960s. Not cost-effective? Perhaps not. In the public realm of America, I was thinking, the federal government underwrites the construction of a building whose function no one seems to know, and a governmental agency receives from the President $7 billion it didn't even request. In the private sector of America, an actor earns $20 million to perform in one film, and a baseball player in salary talks with his team's owner compromises—his word—and settles for almost $20 million for three years of play.

Still, I did my best to answer. I referred to a study undertaken in Boston in which it was found that one out of ten children treated in a particular hospital had witnessed firsthand a crime of violence: a stabbing, rape, or murder. I reminded them of a statistic indicating that the most dangerous person in America is a sixteen-year-old boy with a gun after school in the late afternoon. I cited Children's Defense Fund data on the number of children born and raised in poverty, as well as the number of children killed every year by other children.[67]

I told the students of the Fordham Institute's annual reports on the social health of children. The institute examines statistics on teen suicide, runaways and latchkey children, physical and sexual abuse, and teen pregnancy. I thought it might interest them to know that in the years 1950–1954 almost 30 percent of first births were out of wedlock, but by the years 1980–1981 this percentage had risen to 72 percent. Every year the institute reports that the circumstances for children appear to grow worse. Every year the numbers of runaway and latchkey children go up, along with abuse of various sorts. The *1999 Kids Count Data Book*, a government report, confirms the rise of teenage sexual activity, pregnancy, childbirth, and abortion.[68]

I also reminded the students what the *1999 Kids Count Data Book* suggests are the primary reasons for more than 9 million children's being considered at risk. First, the children live in single-parent homes. Second, the parents of the children report low formal educational attainment. Third, the children reside in areas of high unemployment. Finally, the children lack medical insurance. In short, what these more than 9 million at-risk children confront is poverty.

Then I raised with the students the notion of people at peril. I spoke of large-scale institutions' failing children and reminded them that nothing about the school I attended put children at risk, psychologically, physically, intellectually, or spiritually. I spoke of just institutions' taking people out of harm's way, giving them opportunities to build wonderful character and citizenship, and making them aware of their culture and the hundreds of cultures that comprise it. I told the students that just and moral institutions are perhaps best defined by their capacity to enable people to discover their intelligences and use them to make valuable products of all forms for their culture.[69]

I spoke of the metaphor that is often used in discussions of peril, that people fall between the cracks. Facetiously arguing that even newborn babies are too big to fall between cracks, I suggested that, instead, some institutions simply lose track of people or perhaps push them aside, ignore them, avoid them, or simply don't know how to deal with them and so don't. Merely inquiring about people, visiting them, and listening to their stories are ways in which people at peril are protected, possibly even rescued. A simple communication may bring a chronically truant child back to the classroom, a patient back to a hospital, or a homeless person back to a shelter. Each of these communications represents an act of beneficence.

Invariably in discussions of this sort, I think of the high infant mortality rates in some American communities, many of them located in sight of our greatest hospitals. With arguably the best birthing technologies in the world, the United States nevertheless continues to have babies and mothers dying in childbirth at frighteningly high rates. The problem, clearly, is that despite our good intentions, we don't allocate state-of-the-art medical technologies universally. And, truthfully, sometimes we do not exhibit the best intentions. Only a bleeding-heart liberal left over from the 1960s, I thought, could assert that the culture might be better off building new schools, hospitals, and child care centers instead of constructing new football stadiums and basketball arenas where old ones are perfectly fine and oblige the elite crowd to sit among the common folk with their uncommon folklore. I was also put in mind of Delattre's statement that "just persons do not play favorites and avoid exceeding their own authority or treating people in ways they do not deserve. They feel as indignant at the unfair treatment of others as of themselves."[70]

Finally, my student's important reminder that social programs be cost-effective caused me to reflect on several children I know, and one in particular, a child whose story does not appear in this book.

Jamal Hinnion is a sweet-faced boy of twelve whose eyes always look misty, as if he's about to cry, which in truth I've never seen him do. He lives with his mother and two sisters in one of Boston's poorer housing projects. Jamal is always well dressed and remains one of the most well-mannered young people I've ever encountered. I've known his mother for many years, and partly because of this relationship, her son and I have developed a little friendship of our own.

About a year ago, Jamal telephoned to say he wanted to meet. He said he had something for me. This seemed unusual, so I drove to his home as soon as I could. I was barely out of the car when Jamal handed me an audiotape that I assumed was a mix of songs and rap music that he likes, which I work diligently to like as well, though not always successfully.

"I want you to have this," he said, looking grave. It was clear the tape was neither an attempt to convert me to rap nor a gift. "Keep this in a safe," he ordered. "And if I get killed, make sure they play it at my funeral. It only runs like ten minutes."

We have to take stock, I reminded my class that evening, of everything that happens to all of America's children and adults, be it in schools, in homes, in hospitals, on ball fields, in law courts, in employment offices, in places of business, or simply on the streets. Having successfully achieved that, we might then sit down and assess the cost-effectiveness of all these imperiled lives.

In this book, I present a collection of stories from men, women, boys, and girls. I hope to show that their stories are indeed of interest to us, just as their lives are essential in ultimately defining and enlightening our own. If nothing else, these stories, these people, dissolve some of our self-fabricated isolation, which too frequently is our response to not knowing how to handle human differences and possibly, too, the reality of imperiled destinies. The stories may also reduce some of the shame in which we tend to wrap ourselves, believing ourselves to be imperfect, or even defective. For shame and an anger stemming from hurt come upon us when we imagine our lives to have fallen short of some standard that either we have imposed on ourselves or others have imposed on us. Likewise, shame grows in us when we do not have those aforementioned requisite needs met or are directly wounded by people close to us, our caretakers even, or when people in society whom we will never confront act or do not act in a certain manner.

When a person tells a story and another listens to it, a covenant is created between teller and witness, which allows both participants to transcend the fear that they are perhaps troubling someone with their story of injustice or merely with their own being. It allows people, moreover, to relate to another through the narrative, which ideally yields a capacity to care for another, as well as for ourselves. In other words, a genuine covenant has the power to diminish the shame we all carry. Interesting, isn't it, that we often describe storytelling or memoir writing as a form of unburdening?

Somehow we find our way through the facets and tendrils of human differences and accounts of peril. Then, bound together through the words and evocations, and the echoes, we together rise above them, meeting the promise of—the responsibility, really—of the covenant, simply to honor another life, and then another, and then another. And then, just simply, life.

I

HEALTH
PERIL

I N MANY respects, what goes on in the field of medical care is merely an extension of the most elemental care offered people by one another. The parent cares for the child, a friend cares for a friend, neighbors look out for one another; even strangers may offer assistance in time of need. In a culture like America, it is expected that women will give birth with minimal peril, that their children will be born also with minimal risk, and that most people will live productively well into their seventies, eighties, or even longer.

It surprises me to learn, therefore, that in a span of forty years, when life expectancy rose more than it had in the previous four thousand years in an economically prosperous era and in a prosperous state like my own, Massachusetts, infant mortality rates actually rose in the middle to late 1990s after declines in this rate had been reported over the prior ten years.[1] It also comes as a surprise that at this same time, as many as twenty African American women per one hundred thousand die during childbirth. But if these numbers seem small to some, then surely "imperiled" is the proper term for the almost 35 million people in the world presently diagnosed with AIDS and the 1.5 billion people without access to safe water.[2]

If mysterious bacteria and viruses cause illness and death, so, too, do the behaviors of individual citizens and the structures of human societies. We know that Americans kill more children with automobiles than will die from the five most lethal childhood illnesses. Some of these deaths surely are accidents, but some are completely avoidable. Some children and adults are imperiled because they are ignored, avoided, or neglected or because medical technology simply does not reach them, or they cannot reach it. Sometimes people simply do not have access to the transportation that would allow them to reach local or neighborhood medical services. More often, reaching the services is not so much a problem as paying for it. And some people stay away from health care facilities for fear that confidentiality policies will not safeguard them.[3]

Sometimes, the very nature of our cities, the machinations of our complex economic system, or the structure of our social lives eats away at people and causes them to feel ill or outright kills them. We recall those areas of cities known as "death zones." Some people, after all, cannot recover from the fact that as crowded as cities have become, there is still no one around to care for them. Cancer kills, but so do loneliness, worry, isolation, population density, and poverty.

Counteracting the peril is the most obvious resource of all: a person who is there to care, frequently in ways that go completely unknown to the caring one. It may be the physician or the pharmacist. It may the nurse, the ambulance driver, or just the upstairs neighbor. Always, however, the notion of the ecology of peril seems appropriate. Cultures, laws, and social conventions contribute to the nature of the health, or lack of it, of every single human being. Of course, part of being healthy is mere luck. Some people are born to live in what might be called "life zones," areas where resources of all varieties are greatest. Even these people understand that at any moment a single human cell may embark on a disastrous course of malignant development.

Another part of health, however, is not attributable to misfortune. In some cases, decisions that may involve millions of people are made or not made which allow a society to move on without caring for those people properly called imperiled. It has been decided, apparently, that a portion of the population simply has to go without, with the result that some of these people choose to engage in action they know is dangerous and immoral in order to gain access to required resources or coveted luxuries. It is extraordinary, really, that so many could turn a blind eye on all of these people.

More extraordinary, the child in me keeps saying, is that the structure of the culture has turned so forcefully away from human care. Administrators at a Boston-area hospital of great repute, where researchers appear to be on the threshold of understanding the cause and ultimately the cure of no less an illness than schizophrenia, rightly take pride in the fact that in one year its staff was awarded almost $27 million in research grants. Next year, of course, this number may go down, thereby inhibiting investigative progress. Across town, a football player is given a $50 million guaranteed contract over seven years. He is one of fifty-three athletes on the team. And in still another part of this same city, a child sells drugs and makes a fair amount of money, some of which he spends in capricious ways and some of which he uses to pay his mother's hospital bills. Are these not good illustrations of what I call the ecology of peril?

CHILDREN AT RISK
The Case for Youthful Offenders

SEVERAL YEARS ago in speaking with young people in jail, a boy of seventeen recounted a chilling tale of murder. Late on a hot, still Friday afternoon in the middle of summer, he told his listeners, a large group of kids gathered at a basketball court not far from the local middle school. Most of the youths knew one another, but some there were not part of the crowd. Suddenly this seventeen-year-old boy pulled a gun and fired two bullets into the head of a twelve-year-old whose name he did not know.

"I was just standing there, talking to my friends, figuring out what we were going do that night, right, when I see this kid, kind of over my shoulder, you know, and I notice he's standing on my shadow. There's this long black shadow, you know, you couldn't miss it, everybody could see it, and he's standing on it. So I tell him, 'Would you mind getting off my shadow.' The kid doesn't move. I don't know if he doesn't hear or he hears me and he doesn't care. So I tell him again, loud, 'Would you get off my shadow.' This time he's just looking at me, but he still doesn't move. Third time. 'Hey, man, would you get the fuck off my shadow.' The kid just looks at me. So, I did it. I warned him three times, right, and I shot him."

IN AMERICA we are once again in one of those periods when our outrage toward youthful offenders causes us to rethink the juvenile justice system, the methods of adjudication, and the punishments that ought to be meted out in cases of serious juvenile crime. This debate has been reopened by the grizzly murders of children by children that we have witnessed recently in Colorado, Massachusetts, Kentucky, Arkansas, and Pennsylvania, not to mention the false accusation of murder of two boys in Chicago, both younger than twelve.

The debate typically pits those who say, "If you do the crime, you do the time," arguing that crime is crime, be it committed by a thirteen-year-old or by a forty-year-old, against those who claim that something horrendous must have gone wrong for a child of eleven or thirteen to commit a murder or rape. This child may be immature, abused, or neglected, they say, but he is not evil and, quite possibly, because of his youth, he can be rehabilitated. Besides, the critics ask rhetorically, what could prison possibly do for the child other than permanently galvanize his furious impulses and turn the still malleable youngster into a hardened lifelong criminal? Then there is the matter of placing children in jail with adults, an act that many believe will eventually bring great harm to these children.[1]

It is sobering indeed to learn that possibly the most dangerous person in America is the sixteen-year-old boy drifting about after school with no place to go and having access to a gun. "Juvenile crime triples starting at four P.M.," Jonathan Alter wrote in *Newsweek*. Not yet old enough to drink (legally, that is) or join the army, he is, however, old enough to drive; in some states drop out of school; and most definitely kill if he has the opportunity, the inclination, the desire, or just a momentary urge that quite often even he can't explain.[2]

What our society elects to do with a young offender depends on how we choose to perceive him, which means the decision has something to do with how we conceive of the child or what we believe him to be, although we would normally say "know him to be." More generally, the decision has something to do with how we define and view the child at risk.[3] For in looking at children's risky behavior, we in fact are examining children at risk, children who for various reasons, social and personal alike, are unable to make it safely through to adulthood in a manner that society judges proper, mature, healthy, and moral. In this essay, I focus on the most extreme form of children at risk, those who find their way into crime and ultimately the juvenile court system, and discuss their expressed attitudes, and their explanations for their behavior as well as others' explanations for it.

It may help to begin with some facts on the general state of American children. According to government statistics, one in five children grow up in poverty, and one in four girls and one in seven boys report some form of abuse.[4] A 1989 Fordham Institute index on children's social health, which comprised rates of infant mortality, child abuse, child poverty, teenage drug abuse, suicide, and high school dropouts, revealed that American children were faring far worse than they had in the seventies.[5] Only teenage drug abuse has abated somewhat in the last few years, and this trend, too, may be in the process of reversing itself. As shocking as these findings seem, they pale next to the following data gathered by the Children's Defense Fund in 1990.[6] Consider that in one day in America, 67 infants will perish before their first month of life; 2,800 teenagers will get pregnant; 135,000 youths will bring a gun to school; 30 youths will be wounded by and 10 will die from guns; 1,850 will be abused or neglected; 6 will commit suicide; and 3,300 will run away from home.

In the last half of the 1980s, juvenile arrests for murder doubled nationally from about one thousand to two thousand. Experts who predict a 7 percent increase in the juvenile population foresee that by the end of 2000 the number will have climbed to six thousand. Federal statistics also reveal that about 10 percent of all homicide arrests are youths younger than 18, more than 90 percent of whom are male.[7] Statistics from the Federal Bureau of Investigation indicate that juvenile arrests for weapons offenses have doubled in the 1990s, while aggravated assaults committed by teenagers have increased by 70 percent. The number of juveniles arrested for murder has increased by one-half. The only optimistic note in all of this is that murder continues to be a relatively small, although obviously unacceptable, percentage of youth crime.

Finally, more than a decade ago, it was demonstrated that cities contain communities notable for their high degree of poverty, where physical injury and death emerge in disproportionate frequency given the number of people living there. Not surprisingly, these areas, appropriately called "death zones," are found to be the very neighborhoods in which, over the years, most murdered children have been killed.

In attempting to discover who these child murderers are, social scientists invariably report similar sorts of findings. To begin, there is no question that certain juvenile murderers are conscienceless people, clear-cut psychopaths, who either were born this way, which I believe is doubtful, or somehow learned to separate a violent act from its consequences, something, quite frankly, America inadvertently teaches through the epistemological structure of its popular culture. Everyday, children receive all sorts of messages that seemingly have nothing to do with one another, which I think in effect teaches them not to hunt for cause-and-effect associations between and among stimuli and events. The result of this subliminal learning may be the inability to construct or perceive temporal and behavioral interconnections, which in turn may explain some of the alleged psychopathy.

More to the point, what psychologists continually find in their studies of juvenile murderers is the degree to which these children have experienced abuse of some sort. The data in this regard are overwhelming. Abusive parents and other child batterers as well as molesters leave their physical, cognitive, neurological, and psychological marks, and no one, especially not children, escapes unscarred. The association, moreover, between abuse and juvenile murder is strong. Some research, for example, suggests that early childhood abuse tends to increase the likelihood of a child's developing chronic aggressive behavior.[8] In addition, researchers have observed in these children what they call "biased and deficient" patterns of dealing with people generally. Said simply, the abused child lives with anger all too close to the surface, and one false move, or perhaps merely a thirst for entertainment, will bring forth that anger, and then some.

Similarly discouraging are the results of a study of young men arrested in Michigan. According to this work, the majority of juvenile murder arrests were youths with divorced parents—and likely fathers who were absent—who either had been expelled from school or had dropped out. Most of the young men, furthermore, revealed histories of alcohol and drug abuse. These patterns, of course, are familiar to all of us. What we perhaps don't think about often enough is their link to more general patterns of poverty, a link that is painfully complex, but not so complex that we should avoid examining it.

A publication from the Children's Defense Fund (CDF) confirms this emerging picture. According to CDF, "a black baby born in Boston in 1988 had less chance of surviving its first year than a baby born in Panama, North or South Korea, or Uruguay."[9] In addition, American children in general rank fifteenth in childhood immunization against polio; America's black children age one year or younger rank forty-ninth. To the dismay of those valuing teacher-student closeness and the benefit of having teachers know their students and be able to watch out for possible trouble signs, America ranks nineteenth in teacher/student ratios, behind countries such as Libya, Lebanon, and Cuba.

Given these statistics, it's ironic that, according to the Nickelodeon/Yankelovich *Youth Monitor*, 61 percent of America's children believe their family is like most other families and want it to remain this way. (Not surprisingly, the percentage is lower for children of divorced parents.) Eighty percent of America's children think it is better to have a sibling than to be an only child, and 76 percent report that they wish they could spend more time with their parents.

If that's not sufficiently bittersweet, a study of middle and high school students published several years ago indicated that of all the concerns facing American children and adolescents, and with all the talk about jobs, money, music, sex, esteem, school, homework, sneakers, girls, boys, brothers and sisters, the matter most important to these young people was the physical well-being of their parents. For those who may be interested, the number one concern for children of the Soviet Union that same year was achieving world peace.

Having considered some of the more general statistics and findings, let's now look more closely at the profile of the typical boy, if there is such a person, brought to the attention of the Massachusetts Department of Youth Services.[10] From such an examination we learn these facts:

According to statistics compiled in 1995, the average young Massachusetts offender is a sixteen-year-old male with roughly a 50 percent chance of being white, 28 percent chance of being African American, and 24 percent chance of being Hispanic. There is a 50 percent chance that he is coming from a residential placement situation, which means that he has not been living with a parent or guardian. Importantly, he is a school dropout (44 percent of youthful offenders have left school by ninth grade), reads at only a fifth-grade level, and has a one in two chance of requiring special education attention.[11]

In addition, there is an 86 percent chance that the boy uses alcohol (the average age at which American children generally begin to drink is eleven), a 75 percent chance that he smokes marijuana, and a 50 percent chance that he smokes it at least once a week. (The average age at which American children begin using hard drugs is twelve.) Finally, there is a better than 50 percent chance that he has been arrested for personal assault and battery. Needless to say, the crime that finally got him an assignment with the Department of Youth Service was by no means his first; most likely he is a repeat offender.

Equally interesting are the facts pertaining to his parents. On average, their annual income is roughly $11,000. There is only a one-in-seven chance that they are married to each other and a one-in-eight chance that both are the guardians of the young man. Half of the mothers and 60 percent of the fathers are unemployed, and fewer than half of the parents have completed high school. Obviously, none of these figures comes close to resembling the American average for adults.

There is something else in the profile, something that comes to us from personal accounts and interviews. The typical young offender is the product of abuse. He has been physically, sexually, emotionally, verbally, or spiritually abused, or any combination of the above.[12] Most likely, and this fact is often forgotten, he also has witnessed the abuse, if not actual deaths, of family members and friends. In fact, he probably has attended numerous funerals.

Indeed, attending the funerals of friends is for some young people at once an extraordinary and commonplace occurrence. In a study of one thousand middle and high school students in Chicago, 35 percent reported having witnessed a stabbing, 39 percent had witnessed a shooting, and 25 percent had witnessed an actual murder. Half of all of these victims were friends, family members, classmates, or neighbors.[13]

In fact, the typical youthful offender, not to excuse his crime, reveals practically every symptom psychiatrists outline as constituting posttraumatic stress disorder (PTSD). He reports heightened anxiety; intense distress and agitation; sleeplessness or night terrors; the experience of flashbacks; outbursts of rage stimulated, seemingly, by nothing at all; an inability to concentrate; intensive levels of masturbation; a characteristic hypervigilance, as if he were constantly on guard against some inevitable attack; recurrent and intrusive memories and thoughts; and, most characteristically, a feeling of detachment, isolation, and alienation.[14] Needless to say, he is predisposed not to trust anyone, something that may change, though, if he becomes a member of a gang.

Interesting, too, are the studies involving schoolwork and the lack of academic advancement. A 1990 study indicated, for example, that not only were children who had experienced abuse found in disproportionate numbers in special education classes, but they were far more likely than their nonabused peers to be forced to repeat a grade or grades in school. Not surprisingly, the national test scores of abused children were significantly lower than those of their nonabused classmates.[15]

Finally, in the fourth edition of the *Diagnostic and Statistical Manual of Mental Disorders*, we read, "the worse or more enduring the trauma, the greater the likelihood of developing PTSD... About half the patients recover within a few months; others can experience years of incapacity."[16] While this may be true, child psychiatrists suggest that PTSD in children normally is chronic and debilitating.

FROM A fifteen-year-old boy who has been in jail five months: "What do you want me to tell you, man, that I stay up all night waiting for people to come and get me? That I think I hear my father coming down that corridor out there, like I'm ever going to see him again? Like maybe my mother is going to come in and tuck me in bed? Or maybe she's going to come and knock the shit out of me for something maybe I did, or maybe one of my brothers did, or maybe no one nowhere ever did? This is a good place for me, here, believe me. You don't trust no one, not the man, not the guy to the left, not the guy to the right. Turn your head away just one time, man, and they'll take your food, or grab a part of your body, you know what I'm saying? You learn a good thing here: Don't rely on no one but yourself. You're the only person looking out for you. You don't learn that here, you ain't never going to learn it. Then at night sometimes, I tell myself, who am I kidding? I don't even trust me. You know what I'm saying?"

THIS IS a boy who lives with a sense of a foreshortened future. He would scoff at Jesse Jackson's familiar mantra, "Keep Hope Alive," for he cannot imagine living too much longer, much less achieving a successful career, marriage, or family. Further, he reveals a restricted range of emotion, almost a numbness, which most people discern at once but often fail to consider when he is unable to exhibit the slightest sense of regret, remorse, or guilt.[17] Only naturally, we see the emotionless kid standing before the judge with that characteristic posture that veritably screams, "I couldn't care less about anything" as a prime example of a psychopath, a macho thug, a heartless animal, or the embodiment of evil. Only rarely do we think of him as a traumatized patient. Only rarely might we think of the child's emotionless bearing as a self-protective means of preserving boundaries between himself and the entire world. If we do, we are quickly labeled bleeding-heart liberal, and few take our diagnosis seriously. In fact, there are many who would oppose even the label "child at risk," inasmuch as it emphasizes the child as victim rather than perpetrator or instigator.

Who, for example, would be sympathetic to any sort of explanation for the murder of an innocent child merely because he stood on someone's shadow? For years, this scene of a boy first warning the child and then killing him in cold blood for where he stood perplexed me. Of course I could never excuse the crime, but somewhere in this ostensibly meager rationale, there had to be a rational psychological premise. All I could associate to this reckless act was, first, the familiar notion of construing an action as being one of presumption and disrespect—young people speak all the time of "dissing" people—and, second, the peculiar and mysteriously hostile expression about walking on cracks in the sidewalk: "Step on a crack, break your mother's back."

The explanation ultimately was found among the more subtle symptoms of posttraumatic stress. Many people who have been traumatized develop something psychologists have termed "omen formation." Innocent, mean-ingless acts and expressions assume extraordinary import because it is be-lieved they bespeak one's fate. Hardly bizarre, familiar superstitions are something we all experience, although usually without extreme reactions: "Never walk under ladders," "Beware of black cats," "Step on a crack," "I told him three times, 'Get off my shadow!'"

Granted, society must do something about the criminal, be he young or old. After all, laws must be observed if there is to be civil order. The offender represents a risk to us personally, as well as to that desired civil order. Yet the sheer epidemic proportions of youthful offenses indicate that a host of factors has placed these very same children, now standing before a judge or sitting in jail, at risk. The epidemic alerts us to a slew of young people, wounded not by intrapsychic processes and conflicts, but by actual experi-ences that others witnessed as well. How do these children control such hor-rific thoughts, such intense emotions? How do they come to feel any satis-factions, any sense of reward, when their interior worlds remain in utter disarray and the exterior world provides nothing that resembles genuine sat-isfaction, gratification, or reward?

Tragically, crime is one of the ways that injured or traumatized boys react to earlier wounds. It will take a great deal of work to get them in touch with the pain, humiliation, and sense of shame in them that stems not from a perception of themselves as having done bad, as we would hope, but rather from their knowing themselves to be bad. And although many traumatized children believe they can do something to stop the trauma or believe, some-how, that they will be rescued from it, other children—and these may be the young men we meet in jail—imagine that they can punish the "cause" of the trauma.[18]

The crimes, ironically, only confirm the boys' fundamental image of themselves as bad, worthless, and pathetic. How counterintuitive to think, for example, that cutting another person or, better yet, oneself actually might serve to soothe a child.[19] If crime, in some perverse manner, is not a coping strategy, then at least it proves that one is alive. How strange to think that intense action like committing a crime could allow a boy to feel that he is alive or that the broken bits of himself for a few precious moments fit together in some sort of wholeness and bring joy, no matter how twisted. But let us hold in mind the notion, from psychiatry, that in cases of PTSD the unconscious is always at work, attempting to recapture or, even better, replicate some early experience.[20] Psychiatrists call this phenomenon "action memory." Essentially, when some external event or stimulus evokes an earlier hurt, the original event comes forth in memory along with internal emotional reactions attendant to that event. Examples of the outward manifestations of action memories are adolescents' familiar thrill-seeking experiences along with their need to take total command of certain social situations.

FROM A sixteen-year-old boy in jail less than one month: "I'm going to tell you the same thing I told everyone else who's been here. There is no feeling in the world like putting a knife at someone's skin. You haven't seen no blood yet, you hear me, you haven't seen nothing. All you got in front of you is that steel blade about to go right into the person's skin. Doesn't make no difference to me if it's my skin or your skin or her skin or his skin, no matter who you are you got to feel the rush, or you are one dead person. Then whip, in it goes, and the blood starts, first slow, then big. Another rush. You want to touch it, you want to taste it, you want to put your whole face in it. Then, seconds later, and I don't know for sure why this happens, comes the sting. Whoa, the pain, like a burn, like somebody put a torch to you and for some reason I can never explain to no one, it feels like nothing you have ever felt before, no matter how many times you done it. It's like you are coming alive all over again, all over again, all over again. It's like you been dead to that point, like you hadn't eaten in centuries and here comes your feast. Not the blood; I ain't no vampire. It's the sensation in your body, like you've been jolted into another planet. It's like you been electrocuted only this electrocution doesn't put an end to you, it makes you comes alive, which it does every time you pull that knife. Your whole body's breathing, my man, every last bit of it."

IF THE arguments presented here seem far-fetched, let us recall that the logic or "psychologic" of the injured mind is hardly the logic of the healthy one. In fact, it is the nature of this logic that prompts our definitions of psychological health or illness in the first place. Still, psychology has answers for why it is that people in pain but unable to feel that pain, constantly undertake actions that somehow make the pain with which they cannot connect go away.

Felonious actions are symptoms as well as crimes. They are representations of the way the inner world comes to be expressed or, as the clinician might say, "presents." One presents what one is feeling, no matter how well the feeling may be disguised in the act. Typically, boys are said to "act out" their symptoms, aggressiveness being an example, while girls "act in," for example, with eating disorders. In commenting about his book *Real Boys:*

Rescuing Our Sons from the Myths of Boyhood, psychologist William Pollack noted, "A boy in pain will initially retreat. He wants to be silent and alone. It's what I call the timed silent syndrome."[21]

Essentially it is the hurt of early experiences—the word *trauma* means "wound"—that the child is attempting to forget or keep away from. Acting out symptoms is a way the boy can keep memory out of sight and hence, he imagines, out of (conscious) mind. Actual amnesia will come to his rescue. Without amnesia—and people are able to recall a great deal of the horrors of their childhood—the child must play all sorts of mind tricks in order to keep away not only from these events, but from the feelings generated by them. Let us not forget, in this context, that Freud proclaimed well-known defense mechanisms such as denial, repression, and displacement to be conceits or mind tricks.[22]

More generally, there is now evidence to suggest that the brain stores traumatic events and experiences in places apart from where it stores normal, unthreatening experiences. Indeed, recent evidence points to the notion that trauma alters the very neurology of a child, thereby affecting processes such as the ability to reason and regulate emotion. Psychologists Janae Weinhold and Barry Weinhold cite the work of Bruce Perry, who takes these notions one step further. According to the Weinholds, Perry argues that "early experiences in the family of origin produce a 'socio-cultural DNA' that if left unchanged will be transmitted from generation to generation. His research indicates that if the child's home environment 'is characterized by structure, predictability, nurturing and enriching, emotional, social and cognitive experiences, a vulnerable and powerless infant can grow to become a happy, productive, insightful and caring member of society—contributing to us all.'" Unfortunately, the Weinholds comment, "the family is the most violent place in the U.S."[23]

It is in the mind tricks and the recognition that the mind operates in this mode of self-trickery that we begin to make some sense of the offender's behavior and expressed psychologic. Feeling weak, distrusting, vulnerable, alone, and at risk causes him to take risks, appear tough and invulnerable, compete, eschew closeness and intimacy, and at all costs pride himself in needing no one. The child has moved from a healthy position of dying to please to killing to displease. He cannot face reality, which means his own actions and the repercussions of them, for to face this reality would mean having to confront the realities of the interior world, as well as the original trauma, which means the return of the pain.

One is reminded here of the notion put forth by the Canadian psychiatrist

Allan Young that anger is pain remembered.[24] Not ironically, anger is also one of the early responses to death.[25] In mere instants, horror turns to pain and fury. When one cannot get beyond the pain of death, there is a good chance one will remain preoccupied with death and hence wish to recreate it, as if in some mysterious manner one is able to expiate the pain associated with it. The trick of the mind, therefore, is returning to the scene of the crime or, more precisely, to the emotions or internal framework that existed or more likely erupted at the original crime scene. The novelist Bernhard Schlink wrote of this matter, "The tectonic layers of our lives rest so tightly one on top of the other that we always come up against earlier events in later ones, not as matter that has been fully formed and pushed aside, but absolutely present and alive."[26]

The ultimate mind trick to holding back the pain and humiliation caused by childhood trauma is simply to stay away from the remnants of the trauma, or any reminders of the trauma, which means staying away from oneself. Keep the lines of communication with oneself tied up at all times. One does this by trying to forget, never speaking intimately about past experiences or present feelings, and, for that matter, working hard not to have any feelings whatsoever. The game is to pretend that one is totally armored when in fact one is totally vulnerable. So the child, most likely incapable of intimacy, becomes a superb actor. In this context, we might remember that in the wake of extreme trauma, the normal (and normative) uses of play and imagination generally are impeded, if not lost altogether.[27]

Ironically, it probably helps the boy that our culture teaches him not to reveal his inner feelings, be strong, "suck it up," so that no one, not even he himself, knows what is going on inside his mind. Adding to this psychic noise and confusion is the child's internalization of the family's disorganization, what popular culture calls dysfunction. It may be argued that within all of our minds live the sound and pictures of our families, their individual personalities, their unique styles of communication, their messages, and the needs that each of the members in one way or another has imposed on us. Some psychologists even theorize that our very personalities are little more than the accumulation of the roles that as children we played in our families and the psychological residue of the attachments we make to family members.[28]

More intriguing, some theorists allege that without proper attachment to parents, or at least one parental figure, the child can only rarely control impulses and hence achieve compliance to any authority.[29] Said differently, the very process of socialization, which ensures compliance, the sense of responsibility, duty, and ultimately civility, is predicated on power. Yet it depends as well on internalizing the psychological attachments we make to (and with) authority figures. From this internalization we develop a capacity to speak to ourselves and ultimately to reason with ourselves about such matters as morality. In this context, Felton Earls and Mary Carlson suggest that children emerging from so-called democratic families emphasizing nurturance, security, and the achievement of intimacy reveal such personality characteristics as warmth, friendliness, responsibility, loyalty, honesty, and moral courage.[30]

Indeed, proper attachment, it has been theorized, affects not only the child's sense of contentment, something each of us can observe in babies, but the actual brain chemistry of the baby, which ultimately affects the maturing child's capacity to control impulses. Let us recall that brain chemistry plays a significant role in a child's ability to learn and assume another person's perspective and outlook, as well as contemplate the consequences of actual or imagined action. So while we often focus on the injuries of the soul or spirit of the child at risk, we must think as well of very palpable wounds to the brain that ensue as a result of breakdowns in parenting. Neuropsychologists refer to the wounds of this sort in their models of "dysregulation" and the biochemistry of stressors.[31]

Attachment, therefore, is essential for the proper development of interior dialogues and discourses regarding issues as disparate as solving conflicts and self-soothing. Attachment makes possible such musings as, What would dad do in a situation like this? and How did mom comfort me? In the end, our personalities may be merely the products of all these internal musings and conversations, features of what some psychologists call "self-speak."

The magnitude of our internalization of attachment figures has lead some psychologists, moreover, to speak of people as being relationships rather than as having relationships.[32] It is for this reason that worshipful attraction to popular cultural figures, the notorious role models from sports and entertainment worlds, rarely, if ever, provides the psychological stuff required to calm impulsive drives. Amorous attraction, after all, is not to be confused with the rewards and ramifications of genuine attachment and intimacy.

Only naturally would the mind want everything to go away. It does this magnificently with amnesia, leaving a person feeling practically bereft, empty. The traumatized person may feel precisely this. In fact, some victims of trauma cannot get in touch with their own bodies; for them the physical has vanished as well. All of life is perceived as being foolishly superficial, without substance, skin deep.[33] At last, as someone once remarked about Oakland, California, there is no there there.

From a fourteen-year-old boy in the custody of the Department of Youth Services: "I don't think I'm any different from nobody else. If you give me some wishes, like a genie, you know, I'd make a whole lot of things go away. Maybe I'd make half my life go away; maybe more. Come to think of it, I can't come up with much from my childhood I'd keep. The genie can have it all. Like I say, most of this stuff isn't worth the saving. We're not talking about money here. But like, some of the stuff, you sort of want to get a hold of, have back, you know, like, you don't have to deal with it, but it would be nice to know if someday you wanted to deal with it, you could. But I can't. I'm, like, the guy whose room's so messy he can't find nothing, and his mother keeps telling him, 'Straighten it up, straighten up so's you can find things you need.' But I don't know what I need so I don't ever bother to straighten it up. So what you do is you sort of walk all over the stuff, step right on it, like you was walking on mud or something. I have no idea what's underneath all that mud. Maybe I don't even want to know. Maybe if the genie said, 'Go ahead, man, you can look under the mud, take whatever you want,' I'd be like afraid to do it, you know. So I, like, play it safe, keeping all that mud up there in my room, but I'll never know if old genie gave me the chance I could even find something that I, like, wanted to find. I feel, like, even if it was there, I couldn't, like, touch it. Couldn't touch it."

How then to fill the emptiness and regain the power and sense of control? How then to be comfortable living with the emptiness? How then to regain the capacity that almost defines the healthy person, that of asking people to assist you, teach you, and care for you? How then to soothe yourself, for, clearly, part of feeling healthy is the capacity to self-soothe.[34]

Criminal action, no matter how seemingly illogical or perverse, answers a lot of these questions. Crime empowers; it makes one highly visible and filled with feeling. It surely draws attention, even a form of care, and for an instant makes one feel impenetrable and invincible; the actor finally has gained his audience. Crime may not pay, but for a certain cadre of injured boys, it, like drugs and alcohol, provides an uncanny experience simultaneously of numbing and soothing; almost magically, the self is mastered. It does this by responding, as it were, to the symptoms of trauma, but of course not to the actual root trauma itself. It represents a momentary resolution of the conflicts, nay, crises of the interior world, as well as of the physiological stresses caused by the exterior world. When the frightened child finally admits he would give anything to go back minutes before the crime took place and refashion his life from that point on, not only is he telling us he feels remorse, he is attempting to get in touch with the defining moments of childhood trauma he might wish to have reenacted; redone; or, even better, undone.

By this same psychologic, crime has one more appeal. It has an almost perverse spiritual element. It allows one to rise to the level of some higher power, even if that power normally is associated with the demonic. Whatever the substance of this spirituality, it serves to take a person out of himself and his present circumstances, rid himself of his ego, and feel as though there is nothing inside him. It is not surprising, therefore, that in describing their crimes, young offenders often appear transported, as if recounting a meditation in which their emptiness is experienced as comforting.

Surely these meditations are aided by the enormous amount of entertainment violence that enters into the lives, really, of all of us. Merely watching movie and television violence for fun, violence for action, violence for relief of tension in some manner must teach young people the exhilarating connections to be made between psychological feeling states of all kinds and the felt sense of real and imagined criminal activity. In this regard, I recall sitting in a movie theater one night and hearing a man behind me tell his friend as the lights dimmed, "There better be a lot of killings in this flick, 'cause I have had one miserable day!"

Still in the context of the felt sense of crime, it is interesting to think of the historical antecedents of anorexia nervosa.[35] We recall the figures known as Anorexia Mirabilis, female saints in whom fasting denoted purity, holiness, and humility. As for the miraculous maids of the Reformation, the destruction of the body revealed divine intervention. Is it possible that in the psychologic of the young male criminal, the destruction of the body, in this case, someone else's, bespeaks an appeal to divine intervention? Is it possible that boys' criminal offense has been all these years the symptomatic counterpart of characteristically female anorexia?

Again, our society must do something about this youthful offender, the child at risk, for he represents a risk to us personally and to the social order, not to mention himself. Something must be done in response to his immoral or amoral conduct. But in light of the line of youthful offenders who continue to file through the Department of Youth Services offices in every state, one might also argue that something must be done about all these children at risk. If the child is immoral, then so, too, are the conditions that spawn his immorality. Indeed, the whole notion of the child at risk rests in great measure on the notion of immorality in the society. A child in trouble here or there, every so often, and we take another philosophical position. But generation after generation of offenders tells us that social pathology and immorality must breed this condition. And these young people, hurt and hurtful, raging inwardly and outwardly, will keep on coming; of this we can be certain. As they say, the parade of the princes of our disorders seemingly is endless.[36]

We are again in one of those periods when our outrage toward youthful offenders causes us to rethink the juvenile justice system. Productive or not, changes will come. But we might do well at this time to rethink the morality of a culture that continues to perpetuate a population of children seriously at risk. These aren't children falling between the cracks; children are too big to fall between any cracks. These are children shoved away, out of sight, out of mind, or just plain shoved. Clearly, it is far easier to think about political and legal change than it is to consider the development of moral character, moral courage, motive, and turpitude. It is far easier to label children with the name of some disorder than take a detailed history, a genuine accounting of their lives. It is also easier to think about so-called good kids and the victims of crimes than so-called bad kids and the perpetrators of these crimes.

In the absence of thoughtful moral reasoning about these children and, more precisely, the conditions that create their personal trauma as well as their internal deliberations and outward conduct, be they witnessed or not, we will forever be left with debates about legal changes in the juvenile justice system and an ever growing population of youthful offenders for this system to adjudicate. And so the children will continue to live at risk.

In the end, the entire argument of this essay may be summarized in the most personal, almost cinematic of terms. We watch on television as the reporter provides a gruesome account of a man who has just killed his wife and then turned the gun on himself, while his four-year-old son watches. My God, we wonder, what must that child be thinking? How can a child live through something like this? What ever will become of that child?

Now fast-forward, say, twelve years. The scene is that proverbial one of the judge admonishing the youthful offender for his history of criminal activity, his remorseless manner, his practically uncivilized demeanor. Sixteen years old, and what has he got to show for it other than a list of offenses as long as his arm! What, furthermore, does he envision his future to be, and what possibly is his role in life?

The answer to this last question is simple: his role in life is witness to crime and keeper of trauma. He does in fact have something to show for all these years: the experience of the murder of his mother and the suicide of his father. Then again, the judge may be right, for trauma rarely shows, only the symptoms and repercussions of it do. Whereas some of these symptoms are sufficiently poignant and touching that we feel compelled to aid the child, others are so ugly and repellent that we apparently forget the very questions we ourselves asked twelve years before: What ever will become of that child?

THE WAITING TIME OF
WILSON DIVER

WILSON DIVER is the smallest, thinnest, and most frail looking of the nine Diver children. At twelve, he appears considerably younger than his eleven-year-old sister Theresa and ten-year-old brother Curtiss. On meeting Wilson for the first time, everyone imagines he either is on his way to a hospital or has just come out of one. His mother, Mrs. Claudia Diver, claims the boy eats as much as his brothers and sisters and has the same energy as they do; he just looks sickly most of the time. It doesn't help Wilson's condition that he and his family are among the poorest in the state.

From the moment of his birth, it was clear to Claudia Diver that her eighth baby was not as strong as the others. Wilson had a lovely disposition and seemed to walk and talk when it is normal to begin these activities, but he was, somehow, an unwell child. The first real sign of illness came when he was two, when for weeks at a time he would lie in his crib whimpering, struggling to breathe, and running extremely high temperatures. Trips to the local hospital emergency room were common, although difficult since the Divers did not own a car.

As Wilson grew, the periodic bouts of asthmatic bronchitis, as they were later diagnosed, came more frequently, perhaps seven or eight times a year. Like all children, Wilson would exhibit the beginning signs of a cold or flu. He coughed and sneezed and his nose ran profusely. Then, usually at night when he was lying down, the coughing became unbearable. He coughed without respite until his chest ached and ominous rings circled his eyes. He could barely talk, and even by flaring his nostrils and opening his mouth, he barely drew sufficient air into his lungs. Cold weather added to his misery, particularly at night when there was no heat available in the Diver apartment. The Divers' landlord saved money by turning off the furnace from ten in the evening until six in the morning, so there was no way to keep Wilson warm or provide him much relief. His mother would prop him up in bed and hold him while she and his sleepy brothers and sisters would stare at him, expecting him, surely, to expire at any moment. One day he was fine, the next morning he would reveal symptoms of a cold, and by that same evening he would look to be on the brink of death.

Wilson was examined once by a medical student in the large hospital six miles from the Diver home. At the time, the young doctor, who Wilson's sister Cherise thought looked like a movie star, said that he heard nothing in Wilson's chest to indicate a chronic problem. "Some kids," the doctor advised Mrs. Diver, "are just susceptible to pulmonary and bronchial infections and complications when they get sick. It's not anything to worry about." He prescribed medicine to use the next time Wilson came down with these same symptoms. The medicines seemed to help greatly; at least they provided Wilson relief in breathing. Strangely, though, they also seemed to stimulate him so that he was unable to sleep. Mrs. Diver had to decide what was more important, relief in breathing or Wilson's and, for that matter, the entire family's getting some rest.

By his twelfth year, Wilson was accustomed to his periodic illnesses. He did his best to avoid catching colds, but he simply was more susceptible to them than anyone he knew. No matter how warmly he dressed or how wisely he ate, the infections got to him. Mrs. Diver kept promising she would move the family to a warmer climate, for she did have relatives near Birmingham, Alabama, but the constant shortage of money never allowed for this. There was no way she could find a job as good as the one she held in the small wool factory near her home. Nor, she imagined, could she ever replicate the child care system she had in place—she called it her "little person's industry"— what with her friends and a few relatives taking care of her various children throughout the week. "Wilson has survived this long," she would say, "and everyday he's only getting bigger and stronger. He'll survive the rest of the way, too. He has to."

In mid-February, two months before Wilson's thirteenth birthday, he once again grew ill. All the usual signs appeared: the unrelenting cough at night, the running nose and eyes, the pains in the sinuses behind his cheeks and forehead, and the chest aching from strain and fatigue. This time the infection seemed to hang on longer than ever before; the medicines were not making their old magic. Moreover, a new symptom emerged. Early one morning, Wilson suddenly became nauseated and began to vomit violently.

Even when he had rid his stomach of its contents, a muscular reflex continued to grip him and he gagged until he felt he would actually expel his lungs. When blood appeared in the vomit, he became terrified and began to cry.

Awakened by the sounds of Wilson's retching and crying, McCay, his older brother, found him in the bathroom and promptly woke their mother. At 6:00 in the morning the family decided that as difficult as it would be, they had to take Wilson to the hospital at once. A portion of that trip was described by Wilson himself several months later:

"First we called the police, you know, and they said they couldn't send nobody 'round our house, 'less we could prove it was an emergency. McCay and Danielle said I should get on the phone and cough big for 'em. They wasn't joking, neither. But they wouldn't come out, so we went down to the corner and waited for the bus. It was so cold out there we might as well froze together, even though my mom brought Cherise's favorite blanket for me. Everybody was standing 'round me trying to keep me warm, you know. Must have had ten coats and jackets and blankets on me. And I kept up this gagging and choking. So after a long time, the bus comes and we get on. All of us. The whole family 'cause they were really scared.

"Then we had to transfer to another bus, and finally we got there. We were real early, too, but this waiting room they got there was crowded like all the whole city got sick that morning. It was like we were sitting in a bus station or something. Nurse told me everyone gets sick when it gets so cold. Every chair was filled up. Everyone had to stand. Some old man, you know, he gave his seat to my mother but my brothers and sisters and me, we sat on the floor. Place was cold, too, man, and there wasn't nothing to eat 'cept coffee which I hate, man. They had a real nice water fountain, I remember.

"Now here's the truth. We must have got there by eight o'clock, you know, and we didn't talk to no one, no one, man, 'till like ten-thirty, or maybe later. And that was this woman who took our names and stuff like that, you know. She wasn't even a nurse. She was just taking down people's names and their addresses. And the place was getting more crowded every minute. Like every minute another bus came and dumped all those folks in there on top of us. You should have seen the people coming in there too, man. Broken legs and arms and bleeding and stuff, and coughing. They brought this one guy in on a table and they said he died. Man died there right after the doctors saw him. Doesn't make you feel too good.

"So then, like at twelve, maybe, the woman calls our name and we go up to this desk, and she tells my mother—oh, I forgot, she kept thinking Wilson was my last name—we don't have the right kind of insurance for her.

She needed to prove where she worked or something like that. But anyway, McCay has to go all the way home and get this card, like, that proves she can come to the hospital, and we live in the neighborhood, something like that. And we can't telephone anybody in our building 'cause they can't get into our house or bring us what we want. And anyway, all the kids are at school, or supposed to be.

"So McCay, he goes and he comes back, and he is mad like I never seen him. But he comes back with the police. He just went there and told 'em his problem, like, and this cop gave him a ride all the way, back and forth. Now it's like one-thirty and I still ain't seen no doctor yet. So finally they get all the stuff straightened out on the papers, you know. Oh, I forgot, here's what it was. The woman thought it would be better for my mother to say she was on welfare than to tell 'em she had a job, which she does, you know. It worked out better for me and them too if they did it like that. So they did. My mother didn't care none, she just wanted me to see the doctor 'cause I sure wasn't getting no better sitting in the bus station there. So finally after all this they call my name, and don't you just know they call me Mr. Wilson again, and I go see this doctor.

"Man tells me to take off my shirt and lie down on a table, one of these tables like that other guy I told you died on, only this one had a clean sheet on it. So I get on the table and I'm really coughing now 'cause it's always worse when I lie down, and I'm thinking to myself, this doctor looks way too young to be a real doctor. And it's real cold in this hall they got me in, too, 'cause it's not like a room, you know, it's just a hall with a sheet hanging down from the ceiling to kind of hide me, you know what I mean. Then the doctor goes out and he don't come back. I'm lying there all by myself 'cause they don't let anyone come back in there with me, and my shirt's off and I'm freezing, man.

"So finally I just get up and walk out and ask this other man there, can I put my shirt back on? 'Cause it's right there next to me on the table, and this man there, he say, 'You can put your hat on for all I care. If you can walk around and ask all these questions you ain't sick enough to be in no emergency room.' So I get really disgusted now, you know, and go back to my little sheet room in the hall, you know, and get completely dressed.

"While all this is going on, McCay, he goes back home again 'cause he's so hungry he can't stand it no more. Mind you now, he should have been in school that day like all the rest of 'em but my mother wanted them there with me. But McCay, he asked someone before he left, how come no one's helping me? And the woman at the counter tells him it's her job to choose what people coming into the room look the sickest. I guess that since I didn't look that sick to her she kept me waiting to see the doctor. But she heard me coughing. So then I go out again and tell someone, but not that other man I told you about, 'I'm really hungry, man.' This time it's a doctor and he looks at this little piece of paper they had me carrying with me, you know, and he say, 'You been vomiting, so you better not eat anything right now.' So now, when I went back to my little sheet room I saw the clock said three thirty. Still nobody come to see me.

"You ain't going to believe that nobody came until four thirty, man. Then finally this doctor comes, not the first one, but a different one. And this dude is tall, man, like he's a basketball player, 'cept he's looking so tired like I must have looked too, and he's talking to so many people at the same time in the hall there, he's starting to look sort of sick himself, you know what I mean. So he say, 'Take your shirt off, young Mr. Wilson.' Man's trying to be nice. I say, 'My *first* name's Wilson.' He don't hear me. He's got that thing in his ears, you know, and he's starting to listen to my chest, and then he puts it on my back too. That's how they hear your lungs breathing. Then he lays me down and the man pushes his hands so hard on my stomach I thought the man was going to kill me 'stead of cure me. Then he asks if I'm hungry. I say, 'I ought to be, haven't eaten nothing since last night.' So do you believe this, the man reaches into his pocket and gives me this candy bar he's got in his pocket, and tells me where he buys it and how it will give me energy, or something like that. Then, do you believe, he pats my face. Nice guy.

"'How do you feel?' he say. I tell him I want to go home. 'You're going to be fine, Wilson, my boy,' he say. 'You're going to be good as new. You just got to eat my special candy bars.' Man, did I feel good after that. I ask him, 'Can I go now, Doc?' 'Hold still a bit longer,' he say. All this time he's writing on this pink piece of paper, and now he's eating another candy bar like the one he gave me. And I can see he's got lots of 'em in his pocket. 'You got a phone number?' he say. I tell him. "What's your address?' I tell him that too. "Now can I go?' 'Just hold still,' he say. Man was getting sort of tough and I wanted another candy bar but I didn't have the guts to ask for another one.

"So now I have to wait some more. But when he leaves he promises me he'll come right back. 'Don't worry,' he say. Then he leaves and I hear him tell this nurse there's a boy in there who's very sick. We got to find a bed right away for him. I didn't know what he meant at first. Then I figured maybe they want me to go to the hospital 'cause I wasn't fine even though he say I'm going to be fine. So I started to cry. Real soft 'cause I didn't want no one to find me. When nobody came back I put my shirt on for like the tenth time, you know, and went out to get my mother, but she was gone. They was all gone. The room wasn't crowded no more neither. Then I really got scared. But there was this new woman there and she had this note for me saying my mother would come back and I shouldn't worry. I figured she had to take all of 'em home and fix 'em dinner, you know. Shouldn't worry, why not? They wanted to put me in the hospital which meant I was real sick, sicker than I thought. I'd been there all day, and only one person saw me, the candy doctor, you know, and he was only there a couple minutes. 'Course he did give me that candy bar which was my breakfast, lunch and dinner. He did give me that! So then I waited some more.

"Then like about ten o'clock in the night, a nurse comes in the room, they had me in a room with other people there where they got a television on. She say a policeman's outside, in the bus station area, you know, waiting to take me home. She say I should be in the hospital and they've been waiting for like a bed to open up for me, but since they couldn't find anything they were sending me home. Before I left she had to take some blood from my arm which hurt, man, like out of sight pain! 'You going to drink it?' I say. 'I been here all day, lady,' I told her. 'Me too,' she say. Angry old bitch. Anyway, the cop took me home. Had a new car, too. I fell asleep and the cop had to carry me into the house. Everybody was asleep 'cept my mom and McCay. They tried to get back to the hospital but the buses wasn't running any more that night.

"That was the longest day of my life, man. Started out with me vomiting up my lungs, end up with a policeman carrying me home. I knew I was going to have to go back to that hospital pretty soon. I told my mother, couldn't she find a better hospital? She say they were all the same, and anyway, this one had all the records on me. I told her, 'Yeah, they got all the records for Mr. Wilson. They still don't know my name.' I was doomed there, man. I told McCay later, 'If I go back there I'm going to die there, man. Hospital's going to kill me off just by all that waiting.' My mother told me not to talk that way. She say I have to show the doctors respect. But McCay, he say, 'Wilson's right. What about that man we saw died on the table like the one they put Wilson on?' My mother told him to shut his mouth for good, but he was right, McCay was. Only I didn't want nobody to talk about it like he did. He didn't have to go back to that hospital like I did."

Ten days after Wilson Diver's examination, the hospital sent a letter to his mother saying that the results of the blood tests indicated that Wilson should be admitted to the hospital for further tests. The hospital would notify the Divers when a bed was free, but it would be helpful if they could return to the hospital before that time for a chest X ray. It was three weeks before the X ray was taken.

"This time," Wilson said, "I only waited two hours, only I was by myself. But it was all right 'cause I didn't have to go to school that day. People were nice to me, too. The one woman remembered me from before. I didn't see the candy doctor that time. 'Bout a week later they wrote to my mother saying they had a record of me coming in for X rays but no record of the X rays. So I had to go back all over again, and like I told you, each time you go you got to take two buses each way, you remember that? Each trip takes about two hours, too, maybe, if you don't have to wait too long for the buses. My mother couldn't go. She say if she keeps going to the hospital she's going to lose her job. Each time you got to wait outside in the cold too, man, and you're getting so cold you don't know whether to go on or go back. One time I went back and told my mother later that I went. You should have seen how mad she got that time. Then I had to cut school another day so I could go for real. So they did the same X ray all over, which is okay 'cause that doesn't hurt none. I was feeling how my chest seemed to be getting smaller. For a while I was thinking so much about going to the hospital and worrying about if I was sick, I didn't even think about *being* sick. But I never vomited again like I did that one night. I just couldn't ever shake my cold, you know. It was like stuck to me, like I was going to have it forever. I don't know. Maybe I will."

Four months after his initial examination and the decision to hospitalize him, Wilson Diver was finally admitted to the hospital. He was placed in a room with three other boys. On this occasion he was examined by new doctors. He claims he rarely saw the same doctor twice. A third chest X ray was taken and a variety of medical tests performed. On the third afternoon of his hospitalization, Mrs. Diver was called into the second-floor office of one of the doctors for a consultation. The physician told her that Wilson was suffering with pulmonary problems, which of course she already knew. But there was more. The X rays had revealed a spot on his right lung that indicated tuberculosis. Furthermore, although the doctors remained uncertain about this, some of the tests suggested the possibility of his also having a form of leukemia, although hopefully it was a treatable form of the disease. He was also malnourished.

As Claudia Diver reports it, the doctor was stern but helpful. She notes that he was about to reprove her for failing to provide her son with proper medical attention, but then he looked at her and stopped himself. She did not have to explain Wilson's circumstances, or her own, for that matter.

MOTHER ON A TRAIN

ESTHER CRIGHTON looks considerably older than her forty-eight years. She says she has been through lifetimes in her lifetime. Two husbands walked out on her after she gave birth to their children. She had a child by a man she never identifies. Her first child was born when she was sixteen, and her second, when she was eighteen. She hasn't seen the inside of a schoolroom since the first time she learned she was pregnant. She was on welfare, worked, and then returned to welfare when the doctors told her she had breast and uterine cancer. She knows precisely why she gets the best medical care that money can buy while her friends wait out the long hours in hospital emergency rooms, hoping that some resident will finally call their names. Long ago, she claims, she dispensed with any moral conflicts about her son's activities, lifestyle, and occupation. They had their talks, she harangued him, but the time of words has come and gone. She takes without shame, apparently, a sizable portion of his profits. The exact amount of his earnings is something she will not disclose. I know that he is a thirteen-year-old drug dealer earning, on average, more than $200 a day.

I seldom visit Esther Crighton's house without noticing some change. Blinds on the windows, a new couch with dazzling yellow throw pillows. A desk in front of the porch door, brass flowerpots, fresh plants. Then, within months, another couch; the old one has been removed. There is a television set in every room, including the bathroom. In one closet three VCRs sit piled on top of one another; they have never been unwrapped. From our visits, I recall six different tea sets. I have been graciously served by her from them all.

"I know what you want to hear from me," she tells me, with a trace of bitterness in her normally gentle voice. "You're looking for some word from me that I disapprove. I should just take the boy by the collar and jam him up against that wall and say, 'That's it with the drug act. You just bring down the curtain or *I'm* the one going to call the police.' That's what you wait for, right? Well, I did that routine for months. Threw him up against the wall, told him there will be no more of this. I have a son in prison. Boy stole cars from the time he was ten, court said. Used to make that trip up there to see him. No more. I don't want any of that no more. Where the hell were all the men when they were supposed to be here with me? I carry their babies, I born their babies, they take one look and run off. Anybody leave me any money? They hide it from me before they went away? There a mess of presents waiting for me and the babies somewhere? Anybody leave me anything when I had my abortions by myself because these bozos left the second they found out I was carrying? Where are all the people when you need someone to provide for you? So yeah, I threw the boy against the wall more than a couple of times, only now that wall has been painted three different times with money Dr. Paulie provided me. Men came in here and painted this whole place for me, three different times. Finished my floors too. Made 'em shine like the sun. We're not talking mop 'n glow here, we're talking hardwood floors like people who like those sorts of things are supposed to have. Lamps and curtains, blinds, levoler or something like that. Thin ones that change their look with the twist of a rod. And when I change my color scheme and want to make a change like rich ladies do everyday of their lives, I have a man who says to me, do what you want. I'll pay for it.

"I got TVs in every room here. Have more than that if there was any way a person could watch more than one at a time. Why the hell not? What did I ever have that folks aren't meant to have? Paulie didn't even know his father. I knew my father. Beat the hell out of my mother and sister. Didn't care enough about me to even hit me. Used to think, if the man would only beat me like he does my sister, maybe I'd know he cared 'bout me. Least it would prove he *saw* me. So what did I have? I had babies, more than one by the time I was eighteen years old, and three miscarriages, then more children, then two abortions 'cause the doctors thought I'd be sick if I had more children. Now I got one breast left, no uterus, and we're waiting aroun' to see where cancer's going to grow in me next. You want to bet on my liver, or my spine, or my brain, you tell Paulie, he'll take your money.

"You don't call all those years a life. You call 'em a waste. No one's foolish enough to believe that material things ever going to make up for lost mothers and fathers who wouldn't even hit you to let you know they loved you, and husbands and children, and a son in prison. But it's funny how those material comforts can make a person feel *real* good. Maybe they take your mind off the fact that people are laying bets on where your cancer's showing up next. Maybe they take your mind off something *you* don't want to think about. Or maybe you pretend you're somebody, lying in your bed, clicking all those TV sets like they were going out of style. Maybe I just like serving tea in one of my settings. Maybe I just like to sit in soft chairs and put my magazines and things on new tables with perfect wax finishes on 'em. That sound so wrong? All that supposed to be reserved only for certain people? Do I have to spell this out any more for you?

"This is America in this house right now for the first time ever. If you can pay for something, then you go out and pay for it. Everything you see in this house is paid for. I don't owe a dime to anyone! No one asks; it's nobody's business. Not a dollar was stolen. No one was threatened. No one asks anybody how they got their money. Do I enjoy it? You better believe I enjoy everyday to the last second watching Mr. Letterman on a twenty-seven-inch TV. Man makes me laugh. You know his stupid people tricks? Well, he could come into this place and I'd show him people spending their money on killing themselves. That's stupid people tricks.

"All this comes from grown men and women getting high on a drug I will not let come into my house? People paying all that money to kill themselves. Stupid people tricks! You want to call me a hypocrite, be my guest. I don't use the stuff. If *they* want to, that's their business. You ever notice how when people look at other people and see they have all these things in their home they stay away from 'em and let 'em live their own lives? When you have all these things, and your house looks so beautiful a person would think you took it from out a magazine, they leave you alone. They respect you. And you know why? Because you have arrived. You have earned what you are supposed to earn. You tell folks you lost men, hated your father, never had a family, lost babies, maybe even killed babies, live with cancer, they feel sorry for you, maybe. They may even want to help. But they don't *respect* you for none of that. They don't think you're somebody special 'cause of that. Pretty soon they'll get tired of you 'cause you have nothing good to bring 'em, just complaining. But you tell 'em, like I told my friends at the hospital where I used to work, why don't you come over, watch the Super Bowl with me? You know what they said? They said, how big's your TV set? That's what they want to know. They know the Super Bowl comes but once a year and they want to watch it on a *big* screen. I told 'em, it's as big as it gets, and damn if I didn't have thirteen people sitting in this room watching the Super Bowl. They were proud to be in this house. They told me to my face. They were proud. And I was proud to have 'em. Everyone of 'em invited me out after that. Respect. It came right out of that TV set over there. That's the way it works. You don't have to love it; it just works just that way.

"Super Bowl Sunday, Dr. Paulie sits with me, lets me hold his hand. We don't say a word, just watching San Francisco do its thing. But he knows when I worry about my cancer. He knows when I veg out with my soaps. He knows what I'm getting away from. So, if the stuff he sells makes it possible, then I have made my peace with it. Cocaine, I hate that word. But everyday I take what it brings me. It's the way me and my son get on the train. You understand what I'm saying? Big train. Never been on it, but when you live in this country you see it all around you everyday. I'm riding on it now. First class. I want to change those blinds over there? I just make a telephone call. Make it on any one of my phones. We'll do it 'til they catch us, or the damn train goes and slides off the track.

"I have talked enough with my boy. We have our agreements, but he's not stopping. I cannot get him to go to school. So, I quit trying. I'll never believe this life is better than his going to school, but I can't control what I can't control. Maybe someday his show, like he calls it, will make it possible for him to lead a whole different life, but right now, the train is a long way from the home station and a long way from the next one.

"It's a non-stop trip, and like I say, I ride first class. Call it dirty if you want. I have all the things I want. Most things he can't buy me, though I got the best medical treatment around. Words like 'moral' and 'legal' used to bother me. But when that train pulled out I opened the window and threw them out. I don't forget them. But for the while I had to throw them out the train."

Without warning, Esther Crighton has begun to cry. It feels to me as though the walls of a castle have crumbled and a modest building, but a castle nonetheless, stands pristine and undefended. She refuses to look at me. She wants no part of my eyes, my looks. She knows I will not offer rejoinders. She has shown this face many times before. But she is crying and turning away from me, glancing in the direction of the kitchen, where an unopened box labeled MICROWAVE sits on the floor.

"This play will come to no good end," she continues. "I know like a mother always knows. I feel in my heart I'll outlive my thirteen-year-old boy. He'll never survive out there doing what he does. I can't stop the train now. Maybe once I could, but no more. It wouldn't do no good even if I gave it all back. The train pulls him and he's in such terrible danger. Maybe if you have time next week you could speak to him, although it's not going to do any good. Speak to him about his work. It's going to get him killed. And when that happens, I won't care where the cancer hits me. I'll pray in front of all the TVs that it will come and destroy me. Be a good friend, please. Speak to him. My confusion must never get in the way. He's all I have. The only provider I ever had. He must survive. On this side of the law or the other, makes no difference to me. He must stay alive. I'll make more tea. I can see you want it."

A CHILD WATCHES TELEVISION

CHILDREN'S TELEVISION viewing habits are regularly studied by social scientists. For that matter, so are the children who watch the programs and, just as important, the commercials. Indeed, we are coming to know a great deal about children's "television behavior," that is, what they watch, what they do as they watch, and what they become and how they think as a function of what they watch on TV. Purchasing patterns, brain patterns, attitudinal patterns, speech patterns, and social patterns have all been examined by researchers in the hope of better understanding not only the effects of television on children, but the rather mysterious and often scary marriage made between children and television.

As a psychologist who speaks regularly with children about a host of matters as part of my research, I have had more than a few opportunities to discuss television shows with children. Although I would never call these discussions basic research, still, a friendship with a child, which implies hours of conversation, often turns up some intriguing information about television; the child; and, more specifically, the relationship between television programming and the child's sense of self.

The invisible connection between a child and a television program or, just as likely, a commercial, has been studied, but as yet it remains somewhat enigmatic. What we do know is that the not-at-all-simple act of watching television has the most profound effect on a child's thought processes and personality. We know, too, that the world in which the child lives will have an equally profound effect on his or her attachments to television images and information. We know this partly from observing children, but mainly from speaking with them or, I should say, listening to them speak about television and themselves.

What follows are pieces of conversations with three children. None of the conversations, undertaken quite a few years ago, as the reader will soon recognize, began or concluded with the topic of television. Yet somewhere in these conversations the subject of various programs and commercials arose, and I encouraged the children to tell me as much as they could about their likes and dislikes and, more generally, their feelings about television programs—I am, after all, a psychologist—and just watching television on a day-to-day basis.

I

To listen to twelve-year-old Michael Ruber speak about television was to hear a young man's anger, sense of betrayal, and rather intense expressions of human needs. Michael had just come home from school when we began chatting.

"I've watched television, man, when I was so low, you know, and all I wanted was some guy to get up there on that screen, a hero, you know, and *move*. Guy didn't have to talk, you know what I'm saying. I just wanted someone up there, anyone. Talk, walk, move around, he could stand on his head for all I care, long as he didn't go away. Didn't make no difference if it was a commercial or the best show, like *Chuck's Chicks*. Then other times, like, I'll get in this mood where I want to see folks get knocked around. Folks beating up on some guy, kicking the shit out of him. I know while they're doing it they're only messing around, pretending. They got those stunt men can practically fall out of an airplane without getting hurt, but that don't make no difference. I want action, I want 'em fighting, hitting one another with sound and noise. I'll be sitting there, still as a brick, you know what I'm saying, but inside my head I'm getting off on it. Let 'em club each other. Someone has to die. I know who's going to win, you understand. Kojak, for one, ain't going to lose to no one. My man Baretta ain't going to lose to no one, neither. Old Rockford, poor guy, he's always getting beat up in the beginning, but in the end you, like, know he's going to win too. I like that guy Columbo, too. Peter Falk. That's his real name. Man's out of his mind. Funny guy. He could be your friend. Like Rockford could be too.

"See, I don't mind that it's all made up. Stuff has got to fit my mood. I know it's fake. If I didn't know it's what my brother calls the 'fake and bake,' I wouldn't watch the tube. You follow my meaning? I'd get in the world one way or 'nother. When I get into the TV I want the fake and bake. I don't want no kid show. I want my mood satisfied. Folks on TV get to be, like, friends with you. So you wait everyday to see your friends, and then hope

63

they club hell out of some dummy, if that's the way you're feeling that day. Now that don't mean I don't watch educational stuff. Mainly I do 'cause my mother makes us. But after a while, man, you seen all the ships and the fish and the lions you ever want to see for the rest of your life. All this nature stuff, I don't see how that's going to help me. I ain't going to spend my life in some forest somewhere. I don't get off on that stuff.

"Like I say, I don't watch the kids shows no more. You outgrow all that noise. I used to watch 'em. I still peek at 'em once in a while, shake my head, you know, and move on with the channel. Too silly now, no fake and bake. You sort of can't believe you used to watch some of those shows. Hey, what the hell, all of TV is for kids. I don't know a show that's on TV that's just for adults. Like you can go to the library and pick up a book and read the first two sentences and you know that that's a book for adults only. You don't even get to the bottom of the page 'fore you quit reading. But TV? Every show they got's for kids like me. Smart kids, dumb kids, all kids. Hell, if I could get to stand the weather forecast I might just watch all day. Well, *that* is one thing they got for adults only: the weather man. You know one kid gives a damn what the temperature is outside, or what's it going to be tomorrow? 'What's the weather forecast, Reggie?' That's my mother asking my brother every twenty minutes. 'You been watching the damn box, what's the weather going to be?' 'Going to be weather, Ma. It's going to start tonight when it's really dark and it's going to continue all day tomorrow when it's really light. Weather everywhere, for the little kids, too.' Like, I got a grandmother, she lives with us. It gets cold outside and we don't always have enough heat at home, you better believe I'd like to know, just for her, when the cold's going away.

"You want to do a good thing for TV? Tell 'em to send some heat through the box. Tell 'em everybody in America will watch their show, no matter *what* they put on, if they blow out a little heat from where the sound comes out. Then in the summer, man, a little fresh air. Little air swirling around the tube. Man, you'd *really* have something then. You do that, and I'll buy any product you tell me to buy in your bullshit commercials!"

II

Brenda Griffith, thirteen years old, watched what she called "a whole lot of the box." According to her parents, she sat in front of the television set utterly dumbstruck, as though her mind had gone dead. She barely moved for minutes at a time, as if she weren't even breathing. Yet the conversations I had with Brenda revealed that her mind was far from dead. In fact, television evoked a whole series of questions about her capacity for recall, her need to escape, and even her assessment of her own sanity.

"People watch television, they always talk about what's on, right. Like, they'll go over in school the whole night of shows. You see this one? You see that one? He did that, she did that. Lots of times I know I'm only watching 'cause I'm so afraid I'm going to miss something. Not on the show, I mean, at school. I can't believe how I remember some things. Like once it's there, once I've seen a show, I'll know it for the rest of my life if I see it again. I can see a show two seconds and I'll say, I saw this one. She gets murdered, he's the stealer, I mean, you know, the robber guy. I can't figure out why my brain works all right in front of the TV and goes to sleep in school.

"I can read fifty pages of a book and suddenly I'll be saying to myself, hey, I know this book. How come I already know this book? Did they make a TV show out of it? Did I read it before? I *must* have read it before. Not with TV. I know. Maybe it's the pictures. Maybe it's like I read with my eyes, but other than that I'm blind, if that makes any sense. Like, if I meet someone I'll know their face again. And if I talk to them, I'll know their voice, too. But reading doesn't make any impression on me. It's like, they're just words and they don't sink in and stay there. Couple days after I read something, I forget it, and it just won't come back no matter how I try to make it to. I can't get it anymore. I want it, 'cause if I can't find it I got to read the same book all over again, but it's not there. I'll always be wondering where it goes.

"I must *have* a brain 'cause I remember TV, but it's not working when I look at books. Well, it's working all right, but not in the same way. It's like it's working against me. And you want to know something amazing? If you ask me how many hours a day I watch TV I'd say maybe, five. And if you ask me what I watch I could tell you every show and probably most of the commercials, too. And if you ask me what my favorite shows are, I could tell you that, too. And then if you ask me, do you like TV? I mean, you must like TV if you watch it all the time and you remember so much of what you watch, I'd say, *wrong!* I hate most of it. I don't like much on it at all. But I watch. I don't know why I do, I just watch. It's like I need to have it on. I pick shows and I watch 'em, and I sort of feel myself disappearing, like. Like a part of me is fading up to the ceiling. I watch and I eat, or I watch and I don't eat, or I watch and I pay lots of attention, or I watch and I don't pay any attention. Half of me is sitting in the chair, and half of me is floating on the ceiling somewhere. That's just the way I am. That's the way I think I've always been with the TV. Come back in ten years, you'll probably still see me like that. I'll still be watching. I won't like it anymore, but I'll be watching, and still remembering everything I see, even with half of me floating up there near the ceiling out of sight.

"You're a shrink, right? So what's the verdict? Sick? Healthy? How 'bout temporarily insane when she watches TV? Right? Temporarily insane. But when am I sane, when I'm watching TV, or when I'm *not* watching TV. You got an answer for that one?"

III

Finally, there is fourteen-year-old Kathy Cheevers. On the afternoon we had the conversation that I am about to recount, a light snow lay on the ground. In two hours we talked about a great many things, generally jumping from one matter to the next somewhat rapidly. Television, television shows, and the latest heroes were only a few of our concerns, but they occupied a rather generous amount of time. What follows are excerpts from that one conversation with Kathy.

"I think my favorite television show is *60 Minutes*. No matter what they show I learn something, or I think about something new for the first time. I learn a lot from the news, too, although it's best when it's Walter Cronkite. He's by far my favorite television teacher. You can tell he knows a real lot. And he cares what he tells you, too. He doesn't just read it. He cares. Let's see. Sometimes I watch *Face the Nation*, but I have a hard time concentrating. I know I should but it just goes down too hard, you know what I mean? It's like this one thing my mother makes. You got to chew it forever before you swallow, and even then you know it's going to get caught somewhere. Besides, there's not too much to see. *Little House on the Prairie*, that's always good but it always makes me cry, which I can use; helps me to know what I'm feeling. The children are wonderful, and the parents are always kind. Michael Landon is dreamy. Cop shows. *Baretta*. If I could pick a friend, I think it'd be Baretta. Him and his bird. Great! Cop shows are always the same, though. But I guess that's the way I want it. But it's only all right if the good guys win if you really like the good guys. I think the man on *Vegas* is too slick, if you ask me. *Love Boat*'s sometimes a little too hard to follow; too many stories going on at the same time. I think I understand what they want to do there, but I sometimes don't get with it all quickly enough. No soaps for me. They hook you by getting you all depressed. I only watch 'em when I'm home from school and all my homework's done. They're sort of soggy and predictable, like they always leave this big problem hanging over you for the weekend. It makes me think they're for adults whose lives must be sad and very boring.

"I like weird shows. There's something real strange in me that likes weird and unnatural people. Different kinds of people help you to understand who you are, and what you are. It's too hard to explain. Your mind has its own weirdness to deal with. Sometimes television confuses the weirdness in your mind; sometimes it helps straighten things out. You know there *are* cartoonlike parts of all of us, not that I like the cartoons on TV. I don't. Not to watch them, anyway. Can't get my teeth into them. They sort of melt away before I can eat them. Know what I mean? Poor food. *Laverne and Shirley*, *Happy Days*, shows like that, kind of hard to talk about. Once, like, they were friends of mine. Now I think I may be tired of them but I hate to admit it. I even feel guilty telling you that, as though what I think would get them off the air. The Fonz is all right though, isn't he? He's kind, he pretends he's tough but not so much that you ever believe him. Archie Bunker, he's a lot more complicated than you might think. Sometimes I really don't like him, then a couple minutes later I do. So I have to tell myself, he's one complicated guy. I've got to keep giving him a chance. A guy like that you can't quit on. You shouldn't quit on anybody.

"*Chips* is too noisy sometimes, like *The Dukes of Hazzard*. I can't always follow those plots. They're simple and all that, but I lose it. *Charlie's Angels*, too. They lose me. I suppose they're all beautiful, though, huh? Don't tell me; you think they're gorgeous. *The White Shadow*. That's great because the coach there really does things real people do. He's honest, and he uses his brain. You can admire him. A man like him has to be handsome. Even if he isn't, he is to the people who know him. He's like a wonderful father.

"Let's see. Sometimes I watch plays on PBS; good plays with all kinds of interesting people in them. Very serious. That's when I can convince myself I'm finally doing something educational. Most of the time I watch TV I tell myself I really should be reading. Maybe I like PBS 'cause I don't have to feel guilty about something when I watch it. *Eight is Enough*. Maybe eight is too much! They do okay things there, but it always works out too easily, like sweets. One candy bar's enough, you know what I mean? Too many make you sick. Besides, the world doesn't run that way, and I think I'm glad of that. It may not be wise to have kids believe family problems just work out so nice and easy *all* the time. There is pain in the world. Some people's problems, you know, don't always go away. *The White Shadow* is better. Children shouldn't ever be afraid of true things. You can't always close your eyes and pretend things aren't there. Some things you have to face. That's why I like *The White Shadow* and *Baretta*. Baretta makes me feel courageous. He makes me feel, keep going, keep going. You'll make out one way or another.

"You know who I like? Barbara Walters. She's how I get to know people. She asks, and all those famous people answer her. I can't see what she's doing to them, but she must be getting the information out of them one way or another. She's like Walter Cronkite. I think they see things and hear things not a lot of people even know are happening. And that's very important. Sometimes I think Barbara Walters knows things that are happening to people that they don't even know themselves.

"Who else did I forget? Oh, oh my God, *The Gong Show*. I forgot all about *The Gong Show*. They should really gong *The Gong Show*. They make fun of people on that show and that's bad. Nobody likes to be made fun of. Everybody knows that. I sure don't, anyway. People always laugh, but they shouldn't be allowed to laugh at other people like that. Oh, children's television programs. I used to like Mr. Rogers. I still see him in his neighborhood once in a while. He still has that power over me to sort of calm me down when I'm too excited or upset. He's like good warm milk or cocoa. I don't need to drink him a lot anymore, but once in a while, when it's cold, like today, I might want some Mr. Rogers. It's cold today, isn't it?"

"Kind of, Kathy," I said.

"Is it snowing? I didn't hear the weather report."

"Light snow. Half hearted, like it's not sure it really wants to give it all it's got."

"White snow."

"White snow."

"White, white snow with crystals."

"White, white snow with millions and millions of crystals."

A few excerpts from a long and rich conversation I had years ago with Kathy Cheevers, who, from the age of three, had been totally blind.

JUST A PHARMACIST

EILEEN O'GRADY would never attempt to fool anyone about her age. "I'm eighty-three," she says neither proudly nor self-consciously, "and I'm still going weak!"

She has said these same words for decades. She hasn't felt strong since her own mother died twenty-five years ago. Doctors have found nothing but the normal evolution of an aging body. If Eileen's reports are accurate, doctors aren't all that happy examining her, because it means listening to her complain. They tell her everything is just as it's supposed to be. "Just keep taking your pills." That was the phrase she so detested: "Just keep taking your pills." She heard it from the doctors, nurses, even some of the hospital managers. For her it always meant, Go away, lady, you're becoming a nuisance. But the pills turned out to be the best thing that ever happened to Eileen O'Grady, because they were the reason she met Jack Simon.

Tall, thin, and more handsome than Clark Gable and Basil Rathbone, Eileen proclaims with a hint of rapture in her voice, Jack Simon works as a pharmacist like his father before him. He is what Eileen calls a "people's pharmacist," meaning he's more involved in the person than in the colored capsules he dispenses. To say the least, Mr. Simon has endeared himself to the white-haired widow whose pale hand he can describe from all the times it has reached over the high counter. Mr. Simon, whose white coat never shows a wrinkle, has a coterie of women and men who consider him their family physician. But for Eileen, there is only one Jackson Henry Simon, and it remains the man, not the pills, who has kept her alive. Jack has never taken a day's vacation in fifteen years without making certain her prescriptions are up-to-date. Word of his departure inevitably makes her feel ill:

"I'm just not as safe when he goes away, no matter how good my stock is. And I've got a stock almost as big as Jack's. I could open a branch office over here in the [housing] projects. But when he leaves, my safety feeling goes away. Hard to explain. Makes me think about when I was a girl and my mother took care of me when I got ill. All she had to do was go out the house and I'd feel worse. Second I'd hear her key in the lock, I knew she'd be coming to my room, and I'd feel better. Jack goes 'way, I lose my safety; he comes back and I can do it again. I might dump out some of my pills just to have an excuse to go see him. Used to, anyway. Now that excuse's gotten too expensive. But he knows what this old girl's up to. Best damn doctor a person could have."

A string of clichés holds these two people together. The man in his late forties attends to the woman nearly twice his age. He neither interrupts nor contradicts her. Both know that the words uttered today are the same as those uttered years ago. Eileen O'Grady is no pill popper, addict, or complainer. She's not even a senior citizen in his eyes. She's his client and friend. Someone, he claims, from whom he learns. He may even admit to depending a bit on her, as she does on him:

"Eileen reminds you of your job, what you're supposed to be doing with your training and experience. These are people with lives, not inflamed gallbladders, uneven heartbeats, arthritic joints. They're people. You like my clichés? Blame my dad. He's the one who taught them to me."

Eileen O'Grady watches America grow and laments its new forms. She laments the raw power of technology. "People," she says, "are so concerned with their machines, they forget the real people; what we're feeling, and what we need." Then, almost reflexively, her thoughts jump to Jack Simon, as though this neighborhood pharmacist might join her in trying to ward off the arrival of the twenty-first century. They both know that it is not in the filling of her prescriptions that their communing is accomplished, but rather in the dialogue they contrive, however awkward, to fill the minutes of their encounters.

In truth, Eileen cannot even see over the lofty counter to catch a glimpse of what her personal Basil Rathbone does. But she trusts the man, his intentions and his competence, because his interaction with her convinces her he's trustworthy:

"You don't go to school to learn what that man has. All he has to do for me is count to twenty-four. I never buy more than twenty-four of anything. Dr. Simon's learned from the old ladies like me who talk our damn fool heads off to him. We made him patient. We locked him in there with all our talking and complaining. But damn if that man isn't happy to see me coming. Never rushes me. Treats me with respect like not one doctor I ever knew. Knew a judge once who acted that way. No one else. My own father didn't take the time that man does. Can you beat that? My own father. So I figure, maybe Dr. Simon likes me a bit. Tell you this: he's a lifesaver. Not the pills; the visits. Bet you'd find his pills don't keep my blood pressure down as much as the sound of that man's voice. I'd like to tell you my arthritis goes away when he shakes my hand, which he does every visit. With both his hands, too. The man reaches over that fool counter with both his hands. Like I say, doesn't help with my arthritis, but it helps an old woman's heart."

Jack Simon observes the effect he has on the eighty-three-year-old widow from County Waterford, Ireland. And what he neither senses nor observes, he learns from their chats. He knows he's part priest, part psychiatrist, part physician, part father. More clichés perhaps. He knows that to treat this dear woman in mechanical fashion would break her spirit. She would never say anything, but he would sense it. She'd make certain to have him sense it.

Still more clichés. And one more. He knows he is a lifeline. He knows the weekly pharmacy encounters have become life-sustaining rituals. He knows that Mrs. O'Grady attends church when her joints permit her to walk to Saint Anthony's. He himself prays for her, although he would never admit this to her. He prays for the pills to continue carrying their mystical chemistry, and he prays that when the interval seems right, the white-haired woman wearing the gray cloth coat and purple knit tam will push open the heavy glass doors of the pharmacy and beckon toward him as if to say, We can both breathe easier; I'm still walking the earth.

He often bemoans the training received by pharmacy students. He bemoans the fact that it is the rare individual who chooses to perceive people as they are, and not to inspect them through the lenses of training, theory, ideology, even chemistry. Chemistry matters, pharmacy matters, science matters. But so, too, for Jack Simon, do manners, civility, care, and respect.

Probably just more clichés. But what Eileen O'Grady herself would find surprising is that Jack Simon has told friends that he has learned from her what professors omitted in pharmacy school. What he discovers in Eileen O'Grady and his other regular clients—"his flock," as Eileen refers to the older ones who return again and again on their appointed days—is the energy to battle "all the evil and ugliness that come," he says, "from people not caring about one another. It's no more complicated than that. If I'm just a pill dispenser, then a computer and a vending machine would do a far better job."

Eileen O'Grady refuses medical attention now. She's too frightened, too worn out from being seen as little more than a complaining machine, an old, arthritic Irish lady who can barely make out the writing on the bottles, much less appreciate the pills they safeguard. And "safeguard" is the proper word to describe a younger man's role in an elderly lady's final years.

"He's just a pharmacist, I s'pose," says the teenager dawdling in the aisle, hunting for chocolates, one afternoon. "He looks real pale too, don't he? Who'd ever want *that* job!"

Jack Simon hears the remark. He glances at the glass cabinet behind him as if assessing his skin tone. Then he smiles and continues color-coding the little plastic canisters for eighty-nine-year-old Owen Whitmore, the gentleman who occasionally arrives soon after Eileen O'Grady. He has seen neither of his elderly friends in several days now, and neither of them owns a telephone. So this afternoon he will pay them a visit, just to make certain. It is part of the bargain he has made with his father and his profession. He considers the effort standard operating procedure. No one has ever "studied" his role in the community. He would never even think in these terms. He's just a pharmacist, as the lanky young man said.

Buck the culture and compensate people for some of the indignities endured in an often nasty and thoughtless society—Jack Simon's mind never operated that way. People came to him with life-and-death concerns. He offered assistance and worked with every person to nurture the life, no matter the form that work took. No rewards were required, and no recognition coveted. He saw all he needed to in Eileen O'Grady's soft blue eyes that always moistened by the time she reached the imposing counter. Strange sort of barrier, Jack Simon mused on many occasions, although it never seemed to intrude on his friendships or his business. Something else he successfully bucked, one might say.

Cliché or not, he has always thought of the Eileen O'Gradys, whose belief in him silenced any doubts he might have harbored about not going to medical school. Eileen's presence and bearing, but mostly her abiding faith in him, confirms the rightness of what lately he has felt is his calling. And so he is profoundly saddened this unusually warm January afternoon, when he, his father, and one of the police officers for whom he also filled scripts find Eileen O'Grady lying dead in her small, spare apartment in the Grace Street Projects.

He might well have foreseen her death. He was, after all, a student of medicine, and of people. But he could not have been prepared for what he finds on the shelf above the tiny sink in Eileen O'Grady's darkened kitchen. There, neatly arranged, are the bottles and canisters of pills he himself had filled. And next to them, a photograph of himself, a photograph he simply could not remember giving her.

FEELING ILL WITH THE CITY DISEASE

IT IS BECOMING increasingly clear that environmental factors may be as powerful a source of illness as pathological factors within the human body. A growing body of data, for example, confirms relationships between long-term unemployment,[1] and ailments of the heart, lungs, arteries, and kidneys. Indeed, one study has indicated that self-reported happiness is not as good a predictor of longevity as job satisfaction.[2]

Even without the research of biomedical and social scientists, each of us is familiar with phrases such as "My job is killing me," "This city's beating me down," and "It's a dog-eat-dog world." Granted, these are merely figures of speech, which, while surely describing certain attitudes and feelings, rarely have been taken seriously as indicators or causes of illness. Now, however, it is becoming evident that stress inherent in the physical and social patterns of daily living may actually cause severe illness, perhaps even death. In other words, the phrase "This city is killing me" may turn out to be far more than mere metaphor. We already know that in various areas of cities, typically areas of extreme poverty—which, in turn, suggests the presence of high unemployment rates, inadequate housing and medical care, and malnutrition—there are disproportionately high rates of physical and mental illness and death. These areas have been called "death zones."

How something vague called "city life" could actually destroy someone has not yet been thoroughly investigated. Still, we are hearing more and more people attributing their physical and psychological problems to the city, and not necessarily to any specific aspect of the city, such as poverty. When we listen to these people outside of work and hospital settings and in places where they seem freer to speak about how they lead their lives, we become increasingly impressed by that sentiment, that metaphor connecting physical pain to the throbbing stresses of city life.

Herein a brief account of a conversation I had with a woman who was certain that the pain she carried in her body had as one of its sources the very real experiences accumulating in someone living in a city. By speaking about her illnesses in this, well, city metaphor, she gave voice to a host of connections among the social world, the most personal world, and human tissue.

SARAH MORRISON sits at the front window in her living room, her eyes moving back and forth as if studying every detail of the dusty sill. She is thirty-four years old, a mother of two children, and a grandmother of one child. She looks no older than her seventeen-year-old daughter Paula, who visits her regularly. She has not seen the father of her children in more than ten years. Some people tell her that he died; others claim he just ran off. Sarah says simply, "He's not here. There's not much more a person has to say when their man isn't home. You don't need to ask when he's coming back. That's the business of only two people in the world."

A short, attractive woman with deeply set eyes, pronounced high cheekbones, soft skin free of even a single wrinkle, Sarah repeatedly has warned me never to be deceived by her appearance. I am not to be taken in by what she calls her "grand cosmetic job" or her handsome clothes. "Don't pretend along with me. Let those other folks out there in the streets do that. You just listen to what I tell you and go forget what you see, even though I spend hours every day trying to make for the best appearance. You'd do best closing your eyes when I talk to you."

Sarah Morrison has worked more jobs than she can recall. She has known weeks of making so much money she found herself giving it away to friends. She has known weeks where "there wasn't a dollar in sight, and don't you think for a moment I didn't go looking for it, too. Couldn't even get a loan from folks I gave it to during the rich weeks." She has been a prostitute, she once drove a getaway car for two men who she believes robbed a filling station, she has worked in a child care center, she has worked with heroin addicts in a local clinic, and she has had her days when heroin was all that she imagined kept her alive. Now thirty-four, she remains a youthful-looking, handsome, and gentle woman whose energy level seems to be dropping more each time I visit her. She has advised me of this fact as well:

"You come to see me often, and I think that's all right, 'cause you can be sure I wouldn't tell nobody about nothing if they showed up once and never came back. But if you want to hear the whole story, and let me tell you I got a story even in the short time I've been walking and talking on these streets, then you better get your sweet self over here as often as you can, 'cause I don't honestly think the pretty woman you think you see's going to stay around all that much longer just to talk with you, as much as I do love hearing the sound of my own words. You know what I'm saying?"

"Are you ill, Sarah?" I ask. The question is rhetorical. Of course she is ill. It is shorthand for a thousand questions I wish to ask: Do you want to talk? Do you want to see a doctor? How do I help? Are you really dying? Why is it me here, and not your family? And who do you speak to when no one is around?

"Am I ill? You are asking me that again, aren't you, Thomas, when I told you the answer so many times? Yes sir, for the one hundredth time, I am an ill woman, though I tell you I feel like a little girl. Been ill a long time, 'cept no one's meant to know it. No one's meant to even hear about it. I sit at this window, can't get my eyes to look outside, just staring at the ledge here, feeling the paint bubbles with my fingertips. How can it be, I tell myself, that I could see a healthy person looking at me from the mirror over there, when inside I know everything's caving in, or caving out, or whatever which way the insides cave? It ain't the children. I've asked myself about that, all right. Is it the children going on having children as fast as I did? Is that what eats me up inside? Is that the voice I hear talking back to me? No, ain't that. When they come into the world don't make all that much difference to people now. Well, it makes a difference all right, but that ain't what it is.

"You know who fathers all those children born out there faster than most of us has the time to think about? The city, the politicians, the people with all that power, that's who. The city fathers 'em. Child still grows up like we all did, living the kind of life we all did, you know what I'm saying? First part of our life is spent dreaming 'bout all the things we're gonna be and all the things we're gonna have when we get older, even if we never tell nobody about these dreams. That's true for all of us. Then, when we ain't even halfway grown up yet, we find out about all the luck it takes to make it out of here into someplace where we can be happy. So then we think, why make a plan? Why work your way toward anyplace? Don't make no difference to no one, does it? Plan only gonna work out if someone else picks it up for you. You ain't going nowhere 'less somebody picks you up, and no one's about to pick you up 'less they hear you talking to them. And when do you have the chance to talk to anyone? When do you have the chance to let another person know you have something in your heart to say? So then, like, you begin to see who's bossing you around, who's holding all the power. City's bossing you around. Welfare office, politicians, state workers, office of children, they're the ones making all my plans for me. Ain't no one giving me no rides anywhere, not even if I say I can pay for 'em. Ain't no one coming to this door and saying, 'Let's hear your plan, Sarah. You tell us your plan and we'll make it possible for you. Let's just hear what you got to say for yourself. Just don't make no trouble for us, Sarah.' See what I'm saying?

"Children grow up living like this, city begins to surround 'em, push 'em together. Everything 'round here makes 'em think ain't nothing out there waiting for them, so why should they wait? Why should they wait 'round in a school, wait 'round after school, wait 'round in jobs, wait 'round just looking at the bed? Might just as well do it. Do it right now, and tomorrow or the day after go find out what it all comes to. No one stops long enough to listen to no one. So no one says a word to no one and that makes everyone think, woman has nothing to say, that's why she don't speak to no one. But then you speak up about these matters and people say, like all those self-important folks in those government offices, 'Lady, you got a pretty face, all right, but you got a big mouth, too.' This here's a woman talking to me like this. 'You got one big troublemaking mouth on you, you know that! And let me tell you, if you want help from this office, you would do us all a huge favor by putting a clamp on that mouth of yours 'cause no one wants to listen to you. You come back here with success written all over that face of yours, and a helluva lot less makeup, and then we'll let you say a few words. But 'til that time, take my word for it, put a sock in it, honey!'

"City's crowding my insides these days. Folks pushing at me, silencing me, jumping at me. Can't breathe good like I want to. Things inside hurting all the time. Sometimes it's my private aches, aches about my life, you know what I'm saying. Sometimes it's my inside getting frightened, again and again, by what's happening all 'round here. It's the folks coming in and going out and nobody saying nothing 'bout what they all know is happen' right in front of their eyes. What is that word about them I need?"

"Silent?" I ask.

"No."

"Gagged?"

"NO!"

"Mute?"

"Yessir. There it is. Mute. It's all those mute folks coming in and going out. Coming and going in the building, in the employment offices, in the welfare building, in my grandson's day care center. Hell, in my bed too! I don't care if you know about all this. Got a man there one day; don't see him the next. Ain't said a single word to one another. You picture that? Nothing's steady. Start out the morning with my best plan, hell, by lunch time I got to give it up already. City takes it away from me, you know what I'm saying. It's got us all figured out before anyone even sees how that plan might work out. And that plan could be the one to make it for you, too. You don't know. You don't know. And if no one ever tells you what they're thinking about way inside, ain't no one ever gonna know whether your plan's the one that just might work out.

"City's squeezing me, choking me, making me stay in here and be silent." Sarah looks at me and smiles broadly. "Mute. Makes me mute. Am I making sense now, Thomas? Don't have to worry about no cold apartment, or nothing about no food prices over at the Stop and Save. Don't even get to worry about that stuff 'cause the city's got its squeezing dirty hands all over me worse than any man I ever knew. Gets up inside me, chokes up my throat muscles, climbs inside my private parts, creeps around with its dirty fingers in my brain. When it ain't squeezing it's picking me apart from the inside, feeling all around my insides, makin' 'em ill no matter how hard I'm trying to make 'em healthy. I cannot tell you how I am wanting to scream. Scream out to someone out this window and I don't even know who I want to have listen to me. Hell, they'd only say, that woman up there screaming has to be mad. Put her away somewhere and shut her up. Who the hell's up there making all that racket anyway? Woman that age ought to know better, ought to be ashamed of herself, making all that racket, screaming out her lungs like that, like she's getting some kick out of hearing her own ugly voice. Didn't her mother teach her nothing about manners? Somebody get a sock for that woman!

"City does the same thing to my children, and my grandson too. I see those buildings out there, all those goddam cars going every which way, right through the stop sign most of the time, folks getting stuck in the snow, brand new batteries dying on them, probably, all them flat tires and the trucks trying to pull those suckers out. I tell myself, Sarah, look at them. Listen to them. They had plans, too, those folks, and they ain't even able to up and go nowhere. They ain't got no money, they surely ain't got what you would call security; knowing that it's coming and where it's coming from. Holy Jesus, they got folks out there so squeezed up in those housing projects with all their broken up basketball courts and those smelly hallways and all those apartments looking just like the next one to it and the one on top of it and the one underneath it.

"You ever ask yourself how come those buildings are so full of noise, like a prison is always filled with noise? How come with nothing to do and nowhere to go all these people make so much noise twenty-four hours a day? You ever ask yourself that? You know why that is? 'Cause the noise they want to make they know they can't make. It's the quiet noise, simple talking noise, sharing what's in them noise. But they can't make that noise. That noise is against the law. So they go out everyday and make all the noise they can 'cept for the noise they really want to make, 'cause those folks in those housing projects like all those folks in the fancy prisons they keep building, they're mute just like me. Now how you going to make a plan to be different when all you see is folks living exactly like one another and never saying a word about nothing? How you even going to sit down and write a letter to someone feeling that way, or take the time to make a nice meal for someone, even for yourself, if you can eat anymore, 'cause that's who you got to feed first?

"I don't talk to myself much no more; I don't feed myself no more, neither. I don't want to feed myself no more. Don't even make no plans to go out and buy myself something to eat. I don't want to believe in food no more, like I don't want to believe if you got a friend he's going to let you talk to him. All's I do is eat and the city squeezes it out of me, or squeezes so tight I can't get it down. It can squeeze me up so tight I can't get rid of what I'm supposed to get rid of, you know what I'm saying. Ain't going to leave none of us alone, neither. You get born in this city, my Lord, the city puts a squeeze on you the minute you take your first breath. It's like someone has to remind you just who's got the power 'round here, so don't get uppity on us, little baby. City puts a squeeze on the magic cord. They got you in a hospital, don't they? They're starting to close in on you right then. Right then those buildings and all those problems folks are having are putting the squeeze on you. And what's that little baby doing? Baby's crying his little lungs out, like he wants to talk already and tell you what he's been thinking about. He's just dying to confess everything!

"I see a pregnant woman in the hospital with me one time, belly sticking out like she was fixing to pop it out while we were talking. 'Feel tight to you?' I ask her. 'Tight like a drum,' she says to me. 'Well, it ain't only that baby of yours pushing out,' I tell her. 'City and all those insurance folks already squeezing you back into shape. They like to give you the pleasure of a big fat belly, but you got the squeeze on you, sister,' I tell her. And she nods at me; she knows what I am telling her, you know what I'm saying. She knows how the city lays its dirty hands all over your insides and makes you just be quiet about it. Men 'round here feel the same way 'bout it, too. Warm weather fools folks every once in a while, but not too long. Warm weather don't make no difference. City squeezes you twelve months a year, rain or shine. Most reliable thing we got 'round here. You want to depend on something? You just depend on having your insides squeezed by that mean thing and realizing you got nothing to say about nothing.

"They're going to take me soon, Thomas. Some doctor's going to cut into my insides. Feel now like the man's going to cut out half my insides 'cause he ain't going to figure out no way to take the squeeze off of 'em. This year they'll take one part of me, 'nother year they'll take another part. That's what they build the damn city up with, isn't it, the squeezed-out parts of folks like me? Hell, the city will put the squeeze on that doctor even as he's taking the squeeze out of me. If he's working in a city hospital it'll put the squeeze on him, too. Can't even take a breath no more without feeling a pinching inside me. 'Spect to see blood coming out from somewhere every time I turn 'round. Feeling like I'm bleeding all the time. Somewhere inside that helluva mess my body's in, I feel like I could have a leak. One part leaking, one part squeezed, one part dead already, for all I know. Blame it all on that death-life out there going on everyday and every night, whether I'm out in it or just sitting inside looking down at this window ledge. Got to blame someone. Sure can't blame folks who've been squeezed all their lives same way I been, you know what I'm saying. Blame 'em and the city thanks you for putting it on that much tighter.

"Like to face it dead on one night. Like to say to it, please, please back off me. Get your hands off me. Listen to me talking now: let me breathe easy for one lousy week. Take those steel bars out from inside me, bars you go building your buildings with. Get 'em out of there and let me feel free inside again, all alone, talking just to myself, no screaming, I promise, with just what's supposed to be in there. I am feeling ill, Thomas, ill with the city disease. Did the best I could to describe it to you. Can't say it no better than that. I'm a mute little girl who's got the city disease, that's all there is to it."

TWO MONTHS after this conversation took place, Sarah Morrison underwent major stomach surgery. Her gallbladder was removed along with several feet of intestine. A biopsy performed at the time of the surgery revealed the intestinal tissue to be cancerous.

II

FAMILY
PERIL

A PSYCHOLOGIST friend of mine suggests that people don't have relationships as much as they are relationships. The statement is more than a provocative reminder that people are not to be likened to possessions. It is meant to suggest that we incorporate people, psychically connecting to them so that in our minds we carry people not only through memory, but as living parts of our personalities.

How people live in us is, of course, profoundly complex. What really is meant by the process of identification? Do we at some level imagine that we are identical to another person? What happens when we lose someone, and why does it seem as if a part of ourselves disappears when someone close to us, someone with whom we feel we have been intimate, leaves, abandons us, or dies? Or, for that matter, chooses to harm us? Given that most people say either that their birth family—what anthropologists call the family of orientation—or those who provide them the same sorts of powerful connections are rightly called family, what really are these people claiming family to be?

It is always fascinating for me to engage in classroom discussions on the nature of family. Inevitably, conversations turn to definitions in which anybody a student strongly cares for at any particular point in time is called family. Anthropologists have a term for this as well, for the "family of affinity" is just that, people whom one chooses to label family, whether one is technically related to them or not. And that's the point: if there is any positive sentiment associated with the people being described, the students normally consider them family. This means, first, that the term "family member" is reserved for those with whom we have intensely significant relationships and, second, that, if my psychologist friend is correct, I am constituted of entire families or at least one big family, which in its best sense, as D. W. Winnicott reminds us, is a holding environment.[1]

Rollo May spoke of this complex mode of human attachment when he postulated the concept of the *Mitwelt*, the "with world," the world with others, as distinguished from one's biological inheritance, on one hand, and the self engaged with itself in the form of self-consciousness, for example, on the other.[2] At the heart of this "with world" is one's family; it remains the model of attachment and intensity of bonding, as well as the template of intimacy.

Anyone seeking to arrive at a rock-solid definition of family is in for some difficulty. Definitions suddenly become slippery and tend to vary from one person to another. Still, when one hears the word "family," it is hard not to think of grandparents, parents, siblings, and children. It is difficult, moreover, to think of family and not recall Salvador Minuchin's three worlds of family interactions: the parental world, the sibling world, and the parent-child world.[3] Each of us can identify with these concepts. My own students typically reject the traditional notion that family is partly defined by those with whom one resides. They almost always omit the incest taboo feature of family, forgetting somehow that one of the functions of the family is that it must provide sexual boundaries among its members. Yet they universally choose to use the term for those people with whom they feel an attachment predicated on trust, care, love, concern, respect, warmth, acceptance, responsibility, morality, and decency. I take from this their abiding desire to perpetuate the concept and reality of family, no matter who precisely occupies the particular family constellation they have in mind.

Not surprisingly, students seem to appreciate Erich Fromm's writings in *The Art of Loving* and find helpful his categories of parental love, sibling love, and erotic love, although hardly a class on this subject goes by without grand discussions of Platonic love.[4] Regardless of what ignites our discussions, there is always the feeling that families support and protect us, keeping us somehow from harm's way or outright peril. In this regard, the definition of family offered by Felton Earls and Mary Carlson at first strikes the students as highly unusual and then ultimately as helpful.

For Earls and Carlson, the family is the sum of the strategies that parents and children together use to resolve matters of nurturance, security, and intimacy.[5] Importantly, these authors appear not at all self-conscious about focusing their definition on parents and children; for them, successful families make it possible for people to engage in fruitful and enduring relationships, which of course is required for the next generation to perpetuate nurturance, security, and a comfort with intimacy. Earls and Carlson would agree with my students about the need for parents to keep children from peril, although they would quickly recognize the need of cultures to protect the families, however defined, who protect the children. When students point out that Earls and Carlson fail to mention love, I propose that the triumvirate of nurturance, security, and intimacy constitutes a rather lovely definition of that most elusive term.

There can be no doubt about the power of family or family-like interactions. It seems that no people can make us feel as strong, courageous, confident, and bold as our family members. What Erik Erikson called the "basic strengths" that ideally emerge as a function of successful development—notably, hope, will, purpose, competence, fidelity, and eventually the capacity to love—all have some of their roots in the connections one makes with family members. Theoretically, these strengths are the results of successful adaptations to the various needs and demands of psychosocial development. Erikson also observed, however, that when maladaptations dominate the early stages of development, people emerge withdrawn, ashamed, compulsive, willful to the degree of ruthlessness, inhibited, promiscuous, rejecting, and disdaining.[6]

The following accounts of family peril should bring to mind Urie Bronfenbrenner's ecological orientation, discussed in the introduction. For surrounding these intimate family relationships, whether they produce the strengths and virtues of personality or what Erikson called "maldevelopmental tendencies," lie the cords of society and culture. In fact, the very term "psychosocial" implies a collision of the psyche with the society and culture. For Erikson, they were practically inseparable. At every stage, the human being faces a dilemma caused by the psyche's encountering of society and culture. The resolution of the dilemma determines either the strength, theoretically yielding psychological health, or the maldevelopment, potentially yielding peril. And lest we forget, justice, or the lack of it, in part defines the dilemma.

MIND SHADOWS
A Suicide in the Family

AFTER ACCIDENTS and homicides, suicide is the third leading cause of death for people fifteen to twenty-four years of age, the suicide rate being 11.3 deaths per 100,000 people. Suicide rates in this age group have more than doubled over the last two decades, and suicide rates among children ages five to fourteen tripled from 1980 to 1995.[1]

Almost 10 percent of the American adolescent population has attempted suicide, with white adolescents attempting far more often than African American adolescents.[2] Generally, suicidal ideation is noted in girls more often than in boys, and hence it is not surprising to discover that girls attempt suicide almost four times more frequently than boys. Because boys use more lethal methods, however, they complete suicide about four times as often as girls.[3] Girls contemplating suicide are not unique in expressing intense hopelessness along with their depression, even though many of them give the impression that they are able to handle loneliness and lowered self-esteem.[4] Finally, about one-third of all adolescent inpatients have been hospitalized because of suicide attempts. Predictably, suicide rates increase among mental patients hospitalized for various psychiatric disorders.

Among young people who attempt and complete suicide, one discovers a familiar array of psychological traits and symptoms, for example, relatively high rates of substance abuse; the presence of narcissistic traits; impulsive dramatic traits or low levels of impulse control; and, most especially, mood disorders, particularly depression.[5] Approximately 40 percent of adolescent suicide cases involve major depression.

Significantly, adolescent suicide also involves factors related to family dynamics, many of them even considered to be predictors of adolescent suicide.[6] They include interpersonal loss or conflict (approximately 70 percent of adolescent suicides occur within one month of intense conflict with or separation from significant people), lack of family supports or cohesion, parental strictness, parent-child discord, family histories of mood disorders, parental psychopathology (60 percent of adolescent suicide cases reveal parents with emotional disorders), families revealing intense competition in areas of academics and careers, and violence of any sort in the family.[7] It is known that adolescents who have been physically abused are four times more likely to commit suicide than adolescents without a history of abuse. What is not yet known is whether merely witnessing abuse increases suicidal ideation. In sum, adolescent suicides often occur in families experiencing stress on an almost daily basis.[8]

SERVING AS a background for the present study of an adolescent suicide, the literature on family systems theory advances several relevant principles.[9] First and foremost, irrespective of its individual constituents, the family constitutes a system, which means that what happens to one family member has ramifications for the lives of all the others and that the system itself executes functions and contains properties and characteristics that represent more than the sum of the individual functions, properties, and characteristics of family members.[10]

Second, as Minuchin postulates, the nature of boundaries among family members contributes not only to the definition of the system and quality of interactions between members, but also to members' individual representations of themselves and their family.[11] More explicitly, in cases of relationships in which boundaries appear to be unclear and permeable, and it is difficult to discern where the emotional life of one person ends and that of another begins—what Minuchin calls "enmeshment"—individuals experience a chaotic feeling that they often attribute to personal or psychological distress rather than to the form of family system in which they are operating. Improper boundaries also lead to what is called the "parentified child," the child obliged to assume inappropriate responsibility in families unable to successfully manage authority issues.[12]

Third, families may be assessed in terms of health and pathology in part by dint of the way they are able to handle the problems, however severe, of individual members.[13] Pathological families often designate a particular person the "family problem" or "family patient," thereby avoiding a host of potential problems existing in the relationships of other family members. The labeled patient, in other words, assumes the heat and attention of the family. Labeling a child a "patient" derives from what Minuchin calls "family coalitions," a term meant to suggest inflexible alignments of family sub-systems, as in, for example, cases of children playing too significant a role in the parental subsystem.[14] It is not uncommon in families in which coalitions emerge to observe parents teaching their children to act publicly as if the family were free of problems, if not altogether perfect, in order to lessen the tensions witnessed in other family members as well as in their relationships. In contrast, the healthy family, the one presumably exhibiting appropriate boundaries and an absence of coalitions, appears better able to assimilate individual struggles and development into the ongoing workings of the greater system.

Finally, a fundamental axiom of family systems theory states that healthy family members are able to deal on intellectual and emotional levels with each of the other members of the family.[15] This notion assumes that individuals recognize what others in the family are able and not able to provide and hence what they themselves are able to provide members of the family. A healthy family is not only a good place to be; it is a place where every individual is allowed his or her own emptiness.[16] Presumably, the opposite holds true for the unhealthy family.

Conversely, family systems theory proposes that psychiatric symptomatology typically develops when families unsuccessfully attempt to handle problems of everyday life. In altering the system, presumably for the purpose of dealing with an individual family member, all members of the family run the risk of experiencing excessive tension or disturbance.[17]

I COLLECTED the data for the life study of Annie Mansard, who killed herself at age eighteen, over a period of several years as part of a larger study of teachers whom students in various schools designated as being significant in their lives. After getting to know these teachers, I drew up a second list of the students these teachers felt were significant in their own lives. I then obtained permission to speak with the students and their families.

I learned Annie's story from a series of visits in the Mansard home with family members together and meetings with individual family members that might take place anywhere; all visits focused on Annie. Over time, in work of this type where researchers become implicated in the lives of families, various family members become friends.[18] Conversations therefore frequently contain personal information one normally reserves for one's intimates or even psychotherapists. Importantly, the Mansard family perceived me as just a researcher, someone interested in their child and their family, someone attempting to describe Annie's and the family's circumstances. The meetings with the family were not intended as therapy sessions.

Clearly, the researcher's relationship to family members, and particularly the quality of trust established, affects the stories that are told and the events that are recounted.[19] Presumably, the closer the friendship, the more detailed and richer the story. In addition to directly observing and conversing with the Mansards together and individually, I examined materials such as letters, personal notes, and diaries for relevant information.

A significant turning point in the account occurred when I witnessed scenes of the Mansards fighting. Witnessing events normally kept secret by families further implicates the researcher in the family's ongoing interactions and history. In this case, my presence during family conflicts allowed some family members to speak openly of personal matters, while others chose not to speak of these matters at all.

In life study research, family members may use the researcher as a sounding board if not unconsciously as a quasi psychotherapist. Quite possibly, the researcher becomes the only person to whom the family members can speak about certain issues. It should be pointed out that on more than one occasion the Mansards refused referral to family and individual counselors.

In the account, any reference to a person's insight into his or her own thinking comes directly from the person. The people I spoke with either volunteered an insight or interpretation or attempted one in response to a request from me. My interpretations are clearly indicated. The interpretation of an experience is as significant in life study research as the original description of the experience. In this account of Annie Mansard, as in the rest of the accounts in this book, I have attempted to accurately describe events as they occurred and reproduce language as close to the original as possible.

Each of us is constantly attempting to make sense of the effect on us of external events and internal sensations, as well as the effect we have on the external world.[20] When we ask people to tell us how they feel about or perceive some experience, we are collecting information through their spoken accounts, or stories. People's recollections of the past, perceptions of the here and now, and expectations of the future are contained in their stories. Significantly, too, in their accounts we discern their interpretations of these distinct experiences. The interpretation, in other words, is part and parcel of the telling.[21] Donald Polkinghorne notes, "Narratives exhibit an explanation instead of demonstrating it."[22]

In many respects, the following narrative of Annie Mansard tests the limits of life study research. The child and the family or, more precisely, the psychological state of the child and the social structure of the family, are revealed. There is also the matter of my role. In many respects, the complexity of this account is captured by Daniel Frank: "The most value laden areas to study are mental states and social institutions; to study them together forces the researcher into the abyss of the subjective world."[23] It is precisely this subjective world that the life study, and autoethnographic research generally, seeks to approach.

AT THE TIME, no one had a good explanation for the way Annie Mansard reacted to the departure of her best friend. Sarah Halkins moved away from Bristol Town when her father's employer transferred him to Houston. This sort of thing happened frequently in Bristol Town, an affluent suburban community of handsome homes near Boston. Many families moved there, only to learn six months or two years later that the insurance, brokerage, or computer firm where one or the other parent was employed had decided the person would be more valuable to the company in another city.

So Sarah moved and Annie felt sad. She was only eleven at the time, but in her parents' eyes, the sadness never lifted. An aunt of hers, Maggie Carlisle, said it was like something had been lifted out of the child, and one had the distinct feeling that nothing would ever again fill that emptiness. Maggie's husband, Arthur, never forgot his niece's peculiar and somewhat exaggerated reaction to Sarah's departure, not that Annie ever talked about it with him. Arthur said, "You get used to hearing a piece of machinery which, let's say, has several engines working in it. Then suddenly, for no good reason, one of the engines shuts down. You say, what was that? Something's different now. Damn thing doesn't make as much noise as it used to." He added, "When it comes to kids, you hate all the noise. But you worry yourself to death with them when it gets too quiet."

One girl left, the other stayed, and it was said she was never the same. "Utter foolishness," Annie's father would remark when the subject came up. "Annie grew sad, depressed," he would say. "Why make so much of it? Why make anything of it? You have two kinds of children in the world. You have the ones who love all kinds of kids. They go to school, they go into a new neighborhood, and all of a sudden there they are with ten thousand new friends. Bees to flowers and they're the flowers. The other sort of child prefers one or two friends. They trust these friends, lean on them. Annie's a leaner, a truster in one or two friends. At the time little Sarah went away, the children were close. Each was the other's only friend. You don't make a case about that. Believe me, you look for all sorts of clues. There is no evidence for anything! If a child has a million friends and one goes away, they barely know the child has gone. If a child has one friend and she goes away, then of course it's like the world has caved in on you. I'm just as happy making the case that the troubled child is the one who needs a lot of friends to protect himself from the one going away. Why not? Why not make the case that way, too?"

Annie's older brother Timothy said he didn't remember Annie going through any changes when Sarah Halkins left Bristol Town. He didn't think Annie was a person who "leaned"—he recognized this word to be his father's—"all that heavily on one friend. You don't *have* a friend with Dad," Tim said, his lips looking as though they dared not break into a smile, or was it perhaps pain he wished to express? "You lean on people. You get the image? The old house of cards routine? One card falls, they all fall. And if it's nothing more than a two-card house, then you've got yourself a little problem, don't you?"

Two years younger than his brother, Jonathan Mansard remembered Sarah Halkins well. "She had a dumb, cute face, you know the kind? She sort of looked at you, and it was kind of nice, but you couldn't remember what she looked like five minutes after she walked out of the kitchen, and you could have been staring at her the whole time. But she was cute. And those two, her and Annie were very close. She was always in the house. Or Annie was at her house. She was here as much as anybody else in this family. I'll go you one farther." Jonathan had an intriguing way of pulling a listener into his stories. He appeared as if he were reading words he barely could discern off his shoe tops. It was as if he were urging you to crouch down and peer at the words with him. If Timothy pushed people away, Jonathan drew them to him.

"If Annie had her way, she probably would have gone to Texas with the Halkins. Maybe she loved them, I don't know. She loved Sarah, I'm sure. But she wouldn't have had to love the parents. She would have gone anyway. I'm sort of sure of that."

Asked to describe the old days, Melinda Rafters, the oldest sister of Annie's mother, Jeanne, had more thoughts about her sister than her niece. One felt Melinda's anger when she described her sister's ways as a mother. "There she was, Dr. Freud, offering the reason for some matter or other. A child make a mistake? You didn't accidentally make a mistake from the time you were six months old. God gave you and my sister six months of grace, but after that, it was Dr. Freud all the way. If a three-month-old baby fell out of her crib it was accidental. Things like that could happen. But a six-month-old baby falls out of her crib, and we're into the realm of the deeply psychological.

"What a pathetic thing when psychology takes over for religion. Both are necessary, I'm sure; otherwise neither one of them would have become such thriving businesses. But they substitute for one another about as easily as, what shall we say, a man standing in for a woman. Children make mistakes. They serve up more faults than all the tennis players in the world, if you'll pardon a horrible pun. But you know, puns say something, too; they express some of my anger. Jeanne analyzes and analyzes. It's not that she should have left that job to the people who can do it, or at least get paid for doing it. She should have let her children grow up without all the psychological razzmatazz.

"You want analysis? Here's one. The kid that falls out of the crib? It's the will of the mother or the father. You want to try that one on for size, Jeannie dearest? Whose unconscious are we talking about? You can break a kid with too much psychology. I'm convinced of that. You beat kids into a pulp with that stuff. The name of the game is to open the flower; you don't have to worry about it dying and going under, the world will take care of that for you. It's cruel out there in the garden. But the parents' job is to bring up that flower. It's supposed to be a perennial, says so on the package, each year to flower again and again. But from my standpoint the job is done, forever, completed after you've done it the first time. Once around for each child. No puns this time."

Melinda Rafters always indicated she had come to the end of an outburst by peering about at an imaginary audience and holding out her hands, palms up, to them. The gesture made one believe she would have happily accepted a bouquet if one were offered.

"But look at me," she concluded. "I'm analyzing exactly like my older sister would have me do. Although one best not indulge in this in front of the master. Didn't Freud say that sometimes a cigar can just be a cigar? Besides, murder comes in many packages, but I shall say no more."

Annie Mansard grew up listening to classical music. The first thing her father and mother reached for when they got out of bed each day was a radio or the stereo. Every other day, it seemed, someone was building shelves to house the growing record collection. She tolerated most of the music, loved some of it, but never felt the courage or desire to tell her parents that she liked a piece of a symphony or sonata. She found the romantic composers to be the most pleasant and the modern forms utterly disgusting.

Various pieces of music were always playing in what she called the entrance porch to her mind, just as records lined the walls of the family home. It was constant background noise in the house, although her parents hardly would have condoned use of the word "noise" to describe passages from Brahms, Lalo, Honegger, and Bartók. Occasionally Annie offered a rejoinder: it was noise—noise that hid the world behind it. If you could pretend anything when the music was loud enough, then you could pretend that things simply were not real. You could conceal the fighting between Timothy, Jonathan, and your father with a big hunk of a Beethoven symphony.

Sitting atop his younger brother, Timothy would have him pinned down on the kitchen floor. He would drive his knees hard into Jonathan's upper arms and then pound him on the chest and stomach with his fists. Timothy would be yelling, crying, and swearing. Periodically he would blow out his breath, exhausted from the fight and clearly in some pain. Annie would watch from her accustomed station in the doorway, half amused, half terrified. She told me how in these moments she thought about being a boy and having the freedom to pound her fists into someone and be pounded by them. She rooted for Jonathan, though never outwardly. When she was younger and watching the boys fight, she said, she would climb on top of Timothy, which made it impossible for the boys to carry on their battle. So they would cease and her parents would embrace her, calling her the family's pacifier. She recalled these moments of praise as being support not so much for her as a person as for what she was able to do for the family that her parents could not.

At some point, however, she decided never again to referee and to let the boys fight. During the fight she would put music on loudly, which succeeded in bringing her mother's fury to a fever pitch. Jeanne Mansard knew the music was meant to taunt her. If she were truly a good mother, Jeanne always questioned, then why did the boys fight incessantly? Why did her husband join the fights? And why was the only person capable of stopping the violence a young girl?

Annie described hearing her mother scream at the boys in the kitchen. She heard her calling them horrible names. They were ugly, ferocious, bestial, idiots, morons, bastards. One minute she was screaming to her husband to stop them, and the next minute she was urging them all to kill each other. If it meant that at last the house would know peace, then let them go all out! At this point Annie would rush into the livingroom, pick out a record,

Wagner, Beethoven, or Shostakovich, and put it on the stereo. In a bizarre frenzy, everyone in the family was crying and screaming, while the music exploded from the livingroom speakers like giant airplanes revving their engines. Annie would rush back to the kitchen and witness the effects of her action. Holding her hands over her ears and jumping up and down, she watched her mother screaming at her to shut the music off.

It seemed as though Mrs. Mansard never stopped shouting during these horrendous sporting events. "All right, kill each other, but do it already! Annie, stop that damnable music! I don't understand you. I simply do not understand what's wrong with you. And them, and all of us! Kill the house, burn it for all I care! I don't want anything to do with any of you anymore! Just once, I beg of you sick and rotten animals to stop it! All right, all right, that's it. I'm calling the police. That's it." And on one occasion she did reach for the phone and dial some numbers. Then she looked at her daughter and tried not to listen to the swearing and yelling of her husband and sons as they threw themselves over the hard stone floor, desperately trying to free their arms and legs. By now, the boys were drenched with perspiration, and Timothy was bleeding from the nose and mouth. Everyone was crying.

Annie reported that at times Bill Mansard would hit one of his sons, for now he had lost interest in separating them and bringing peace. It appeared to her that in these moments he wanted to destroy them. The boys would groan with pain and Annie would see this sick and dazed look come over their faces and watch their bodies grow weak. They could not afford to lose consciousness. All the while the boys were shrieking at the top of their lungs, "You animal bastard! You sick animal bastard!" And Annie would sense the music growing louder, which only fueled the fury.

In the doorway, Annie could be seen grimacing one moment, screaming the next. She would describe feeling a "sickly, empty sort of pain" inside, as if she weren't there at all. With the battle raging on the floor in front of her, she watched her mother dial the phone and waited for it to be slammed down. Annie knew there was no way her mother would have policemen arrive at her home on a Saturday morning to quell a family fight, as if this were some inner city housing project. Her mother never followed through with her threats to call anyone. Annie would grin derisively at her mother's helplessness, which only infuriated Jeanne, who now would run past Annie and turn off the music. This one sound, at least, she could control.

It was an emptiness that Annie always felt, as strange as this seemed even to her. As much as she was overcome with the fury and excitement, she was particularly affected by her mother, normally so controlled and rational, being reduced to a raging, helpless child. Also strange was that there was a mysterious sexual side to these scenes, not that she would dare tell anyone about these sensations. These belonged only in her diary. Then, in reaction perhaps to all that happened in that "wrong house," as she would later recount it, she would "go dead inside." "Empty," "hollow," what other words could she find to describe this state of feelinglessness? Fright was part of it, but this, too, would disappear as soon as she tried to put a word to it. Dislike was another part. "All alone," she could be heard to say, standing in the doorway, trying to determine who in the world she liked and why it was that she could completely tune out the very music that transformed her mother into a raging, broken human being. "All alone."

Sarah, with whom she kept contact over the years, heard about all of it—about Annie putting on the music and watching her father fight and her mother storm off in that slumping way of hers, when it was evident she considered herself the ultimate loser in the kitchen battles. When the boys fought in their bedrooms, the family took it as a sign that they were not to be separated. Whatever was destroyed would remain that way as long as the fight was restricted to private turf. Annie grew to believe that the kitchen fights were staged to provoke her mother. Perhaps her mother even instigated the "royal battles," as the family had come to call them. Annie called them "the battle of the kings for the queen." These words, too, lived behind the smiles she would show her mother as she propped herself against the wall in the narrow passageway leading from the kitchen.

Yet with all this, she reported, there were still no feelings she could hold onto long enough to define or control them. Why, exactly, did she wish to dissect her emotions? Because that was what her mother did? Might she have been content merely to have a feeling last long enough to allow her to define it, before it leapt back into the shadows as if playing some trick on her? There was no mistaking those special feelings, the ones evoked by the fighting and the predictable final scene of her mother's spirit slowly breaking and her body folding forward as she trudged, the actress in anguish, across the kitchen floor toward the dining room. Annie wrote often of this in her diary.

Each of these visions had a life of its own. They all leapt about in her mind like shadows. They did tease and taunt her and often, too, hurt her. Still, no matter what feelings arose and appeared to dance about in the visual field into which she could at will transform her mind, which she did in speaking as well as in writing, the final result was always the same: her mind grew larger and then emptier, eventually causing her to feel even more alone. It was worse at night in bed, she admitted, in the darkness and silence.

One thing could be said about the tempestuous fights on the kitchen floor: they brought forth noise that Annie came to associate with living. Annie's aloneness was aroused by the fights, but at least all five Mansards, as intelligent or as primitive as they were, as human or bestial—her mother's word—were all there. Alone and together. Then, as always, Annie's emotions produced even more mind shadows, which quickly disappeared behind the obstructions her own mind created to contain and conceal them. At least this is how she described these emotions.

Sarah Halkins knew all about this. Whatever details she didn't know before, Annie made certain to tell her during the last days they spent together, and then again in letters and phone calls. Sarah listened to all of it. Annie remembered that Sarah never smiled or laughed, even when Annie did. Sarah always felt the seriousness of the accounts and especially the manner in which they were told. But she did cry when Annie cried, which was often. They cried too often, Sarah recalled years later, although, being only eleven at the time, she didn't even fully understand how dangerous the situation at the Mansard's house had become. How could she know, when Annie herself struggled to describe the scenes and the feelings associated with them? How could she possibly foresee the consequences of the stories she was hearing on the eve of her own rather scary voyage to a new home hundreds of miles away?

Still, Sarah never forgot those last meetings with her best friend. Annie's words and moods were far too strong ever to forget, even though Annie herself had seemed strangely weak, or at least resigned. Still, Sarah remembered a veil of sadness. Even at nine and ten, Annie had just seemed sad. Sarah's going away only made matters worse, not that anyone could ever blame her for whatever might happen in the future.

"OH, DEAR GOD," Jeanne Mansard wailed one evening as outside a snow fell that looked heavy enough to bring down even the strongest roof. "Where was the beginning of this horrible, horrible story? Where did it start, start, start? How could it have been going on without us seeing it? We did, you know. We did. Oh, Christ, yes, we did. And we went blind like soldiers terrified by war. Damn the war! Damn all of them! We went blind. Oh, Jesus, yes, I have been blind from the beginning, and it was my job not to be. That's the excruciating pain: it was my job not ever, ever, *ever* to be blind. I killed her! He killed her! Her brothers killed her! This house killed her! The music killed her. We were blind, and the whole rotten world was blind, too.

"We weren't the only ones. They were blind in the schools. Where were they all those years? And her friends, and their parents? All blind, all blind. If you knew her and you didn't *see* anything, or you didn't *say* anything, which is so much more terrible, then *you* were blind! That's the whole story, oh, Jesus, Jesus Christ. And there is no comforting or communing with anyone about it now. There's nothing now, because that kid is gone. Damnable, damnable. It's all such a waste. All my life I heard about it, but darken *our* door? Oh, no! Not here. Not here where the rich live. Not here where *I* live, in the home *I* created. Jesus, what a waste. What a colossal crime against *all* of us. I mean it. I want to blame and blame more and more people. All of them. I want to drag innocent people into this house from I don't care where. I don't even want to know them and I want to blame the hell out of them, and the hell out of me! Jesus, Jesus, it is so wretchedly miserable. You want so much back. You want to take so much of your life back and kill it. I swear to God: I want to kill so much of my life, the future too. If I could see it, I'd probably want to kill it, too. I have no words for this. I'm broken apart. Jesus God, I am broken. This whole house, and family, this whole world is broken. Broken and unfixable. Just broken."

THERE IS a story to be told of a happy day. Later, Annie remembered it well. She had gone shopping at the sprawling complex of stores two towns west of her home. She, Gloria Brenning, and Cynthia Ducksworth; there were others, too, but it was difficult to remember all the details of what you did at age twelve when almost four years had passed. The trip, Annie recalled, required the girls to go on a bus, which was always an adventure, and not just because one saw—well, stared at—people and usually laughed at them (although one hated to admit this). Trips on the bus or trolley rides into Boston were always more exciting than car trips with her family because she felt she was "getting out," being in the open world, doing what others did. It was the glory of action and activity, the glory of movement.

To digress a bit, Annie thought often that she would travel when she got older. Perhaps she would spend five to ten years doing nothing but going around the world. She imagined traveling by boat and train, learning several languages, and working her way through peasant villages and industrial cities where not one person could understand her. She would make out by relying on her intelligence and ingenuity. If she needed money—although she imagined she could devise a lifestyle that required no money—she would find a way. She certainly would never write home requesting funds from her parents. The whole point was to survive on her own, free of anyone's assistance and influence.

She knew, however, she would never undertake such a voyage. Ultimately, she imagined, it would prove to be too much of an ordeal. It would only exhaust her. One grows exhausted traveling, probably bored as well. It is not that the different countries start looking alike. Rather, the experience of picking up and starting out all over again in a new city or village becomes repetitive; once again one must struggle with the problem of finding places to stay and figuring out how to earn even small amounts of money. Then there's that painful process of meeting new people, over and over again the new people. Making friends is difficult enough when you don't speak their language, although sometimes she felt it was easier to meet friends when you don't speak their language. Sometimes words just get in the way. But, no, that wasn't it. The problem was leaving people after establishing a friendship with them.

On second thought, it wouldn't be a defeat to ask your parents to send money. The whole point of traveling was to make new friends. Earning money in foreign countries was more a test of one's ingenuity and courage. But after passing the test once or twice, why keep doing it? At that point it's better to work on friendships and have Mommy and Daddy pay the way. Leaving new friends would be difficult. It would be better to become a hotel manager and have people visit you. This way you know at the time of their arrival the time of their departure. So you could hardly blame yourself for their leaving. In the end, it was better perhaps not to travel but to learn of other countries through books and movies. No need to pester Mommy and Daddy for money. In all of Annie ruminations about world travel, the word "lonely" never came up.

Returning to the happy day, the bus ride to the shopping mall took thirty minutes, the girls giggling all the way. Annie was one of the crowd. Her descriptions of the experience revealed her enjoyment of being with the other girls, being lost among them. As she listened to their animated conversations, she wondered whether they had been having experiences about which she had no understanding. It was a peculiar concern, related, she said, to the feeling that all kids have knowing that a friend has something you wish you had or did something you wish you'd done. But there was more. Her concern was not to miss out on the understanding or appreciation of a single human experience. No emotion, mood, or fantasy must ever convince her that she might be missing out on something. If the others had something that was kept from her, it meant that she was herself lacking. It meant, too, that something was wrong with her mind.

The girls never stopped talking. More noise, Annie noticed, came from their little nest on the bus than from all the other people combined. She watched the girls watching themselves, just as she watched herself watch herself. It was an exhausting exercise. Why did she think so much about these matters and write of them so often in her diary? Why did she watch anyone or anything so closely? Why all this vigilance? Why did her mind have to work so hard all the time? Why at age twelve wasn't she able to ride a bus to a mall, shop, browse, eat, talk endlessly as the others did, and for once not go through these tedious and fatiguing acts of self-reflection? Why couldn't the motors of her mind just once shut off or, as she would say, just break down completely?

That was the one psychological experience others must have known she lacked: the capacity to go for hours, months, a whole lifetime, without having a single psychological experience at all, to be totally unaware of one's mind. The others, she believed, had quiet inside them, comforting, enduring quiet. Comforting quiet like lying in your mother's arms. Lying there, the two of you, breathing together, no one speaking. Feeling your mother's chest expand and contract and the fabric of her blouse on your skin. Feeling the muscles as well as the fleshy parts in her shoulders and arms. And her hands, not quite as smooth as years before.

What would be nice in such moments would be to put your face against your mother's breast and fall asleep. For these moments, surely, it is permissible to envy a baby, or even wish to be one. Merely observing a mother and her baby reveals how much the mother enjoys holding the baby and has no desire to place her back in the crib. It is always quiet when a mother holds her baby. Everything else seems so far away.

The girls must have peered into a hundred store windows that one afternoon, although the jewelry stores were always the most tantalizing. Tiny rings and bracelets, and the earrings—always the earrings provoked the same conversations about finally getting one's ears pierced. The girls were standing in front of the window of Hemion's jewelry store, where earrings hung like stars on fine wires, when Annie abruptly made her decision. Inside the store she found a tall, blond woman who pierced ears. Best of all, if you had your ears pierced you received a set of earrings as a gift. Some of the girls acted disgusted by the piercing, but Annie could sense their excitement.

Some were already examining the display cases, hunting for the appropriate gift set. Cynthia chose a simple gold ring design. They were perfect.

After using a liquid to clean the lobes, the woman performed the procedure with a small gadget that looked sort of like a paper hole punch. The girls crowded around Annie, who grimaced as though experiencing intense pain. There was a stinging sensation, but it was less frightening than she had imagined. The new earrings were inserted at once. Annie remembered that a doctor had once advised her that if she ever had the procedure done, it would be best to have a small string placed in the holes while the puncture healed. The discussion with the doctor, Jeanne Mansard had said at the time, was merely an exercise of the tongue. She would never allow Annie to have her ears pierced. If it was to be done, Annie knew, she would have to make the decision on her own, and it would have to be spontaneous.

That afternoon, she had looked at the earrings floating behind the window on the silver wire and announced that she was going to have her ears pierced. The girls loved her for doing it; she was going to make this the best shopping day of their lives. One thing was certain, Annie thought as the tall woman finished locking the earrings in her ears: this was no exercise of the tongue!

The woman did not speak during the procedure. The girls, however, never stopped talking. Annie loved that they so enthusiastically acknowledged her courage. Finally, when they were outside in the colorful aisles of the mall, the girls admired how she looked. For an instant the psychological nonsense, as she called it, was put aside. She loved what she saw reflected in every store window of the mall. She did look beautiful, with her thin straight nose and light brown hair with reddish glow barely falling over the new earrings. The girls had grown silent in admiration. All they could do was stare at her, their silence a tribute to her beauty.

Annie stood stock-still, turning her head dramatically from side to side, and holding back her hair in such a manner that a great wave of it would flow back almost over the ear, but not so much that the earring was concealed. Each time she modeled her earrings for them, she imagined the whole world growing perfectly still. It was the loveliest of all days. There was no future to be concerned about, no past to upset her. Her friends did find her beautiful, and they loved her. No one could call this day an exercise of the tongue.

Two hours later when she returned home, she was slapped across the face by her mother. Sentenced to her room, she was told that for one month she would not receive an allowance and could go nowhere except to school and piano lessons. She was not to speak to any friends on the telephone unless the conversations involved schoolwork. All calls would be monitored. And she was never to wear the earrings again.

As she went to her room, tears cascading down her cheeks, she heard her mother telephoning the family physician and asking his nurse if the holes in recently pierced ears would automatically seal shut if earrings were never inserted. She was advised that infection was less likely to occur if something, even a small string, were placed in the lobes. But Mrs. Mansard did not abide by the nurse's instructions. Nor did she ever receive the little bracelet with the tiny bauble hanging from it that Annie had purchased for her. The bauble revealed a mother holding her baby's head on her shoulder. The gift, still wrapped in its yellow-and-white striped box, was buried that same evening in one of the garbage cans alongside the garage. That night in bed, when she reflected on the events of the day, Annie comforted herself with the thought that at least she hadn't wasted money on a card.

Annie's reflections on the trip to the shopping mall revealed to me the way she experienced thinking. There was so much commotion inside her mind, noisy, crushing-sounding motors that seemed to me to be her wishes and their built-in inhibitions. One moment she imagined traveling, and the next moment she resigned herself to staying home or near enough that she could safeguard her parents' support. It was one of many puzzles that seemed to have no reasonable solution: how could it be that one moment she lived with intense hatred for them and the next moment she felt as if she required them merely to stay alive? She looked to the other girls for clues on managing this vacillation in feelings. She yearned to hurt her parents, but as this thought crossed her mind, it boomeranged, returning in the form of self-punishment. What she hoped to resolve in listening to the other girls—she never expressed an interest in hearing how boys managed these delicate affairs of the mind—was the balance not so much between hating and loving her parents as between wanting to hurt them and needing them to be close to her.

This may have been the most terrifying conclusion that Annie reached early in her teenage years, a conclusion that unfolded as if it constituted a significant scientific discovery. Her reflections appeared like the tedious activity of psychological research. Daily, it seemed, she was absorbed in her attempts to understand a particular mood, sensation, or psychological event that previously had been misunderstood or ignored. Somewhere around her thirteenth year she reached the conclusion that what her mind had done—

"long ago" she had determined that her body worked independently from her mind although this conclusion, too, would eventually be altered—was chew up and digest her parents. She determined that something had gone wrong in her development. Describing herself as defective, she conjured up the image of ingesting parts of her parents, the very parts, she quickly recognized, she most despised.

The process was similar to mimicking the qualities one dislikes in another person. But not *any* person, only special persons. One way to rid the person of the qualities one finds distasteful is to eat them away. One does this, after all, with food. First, the food is presented beautifully on the plate. It seems a tragedy to touch it, much less devour it. By all rights, Annie would say, when something beautiful is laid out in front of you, you should either leave it alone or destroy it. The handsome painting or sculpture can always be destroyed. It hardly takes sophistication to understand why a child would destroy her parents' most prized possession, she thought. Clearly one is breaking a piece of one's mother or father.

Destruction of a beautiful painting, Annie also described, had political ramifications. One makes a bold public statement, indeed, when one destroys not merely a personally prized object, but a public treasure. The point was to leave the beautiful object, or person, exactly as it was or destroy it for personal and public gratification. Destruction, therefore, was not simply an impulsive action, as, for example, deciding suddenly to have one's ears pierced. Destruction had reason behind it. It was neither thoughtless nor a simple rebellion. For Annie, rebellion, like revenge, represented retrogressive action. One never gets even with anybody, of this she was convinced. She said this often. One hurt people simply to hurt them. And no one could dispassionately judge whether hurting someone was equal to that person's hurting you.

The point stood: no rebellion, no revenge. The history of the action that had upset her in the first place could never equal the action of retaliation. You either leave the beautiful painting on the wall, she would remind herself, or you rip it to shreds. As for eating beautifully prepared food, that she found absurd. This is why people photograph food on the plate. Of all the bizarre reactions to beauty, she said, nothing could compare with stuffing food into your mouth, transforming it, and, most important, making it disappear for good. Then again, if food came from her mother and was meant to be nourishing but wasn't, then it might not be absurd to eat it after all.

Annie often used the word "absurd." What the others called "yucky" or "gross" was for her absurd. Absurdity was like a disease. Starting slowly somewhere in the body, it came to light spreading its tendrils into every-thing, a metastasis of the absurd, with the effect that anything and every-thing could become absurd for her and then suddenly lose its meaning alto-gether. How satisfying this metaphor was for Annie. It grew to be another of those silencing mechanisms. When something became difficult or pain-ful, she could obliterate it merely by labeling it "absurd." Someone's question was absurd, changing underwear was absurd, combing one's hair and brush-ing one's teeth were absurd, and so were the conversations with her mother. The only things not absurd were her brothers' fights, especially when her father joined them. It was the sexual nature of the fighting, she decided, that kept them all alive. Neither her father nor Timothy had much on the feeling side of the ledger, but when they fought they were alive and vibrant. In those ugly moments, nothing about them could have been called absurd.

Even at thirteen, the lovely girl with the long straight hair and elegant, thin nose, appeared to be neutralizing the power of objects, ideas, feelings, and entire experiences. It was not an all-consuming task; there were periods of grace, excitement, and delight. Still, a great deal of effort was devoted to siphoning off the psychological life from objects by designating them absurd and then sucking their energy into herself. This is what brought her early on to the notion of eating bits of people and objects she disliked. It gave her the private gratification of destroying those transformed yet still disliked portions. In her own language, consuming someone else's ugliness cleansed that person for others. Disgust was deleted. So there was a self-destructive aspect to it, this she acknowledged, but there was a generous, gift-giving aspect to it as well. Stimulated by what she called the "algebra of staying alive," she devised psychological formulae for herself. Here was one:

She shared a mother with her brothers. For that matter, she shared one woman with three men. All of them appeared to suffer from being alive at the same time as their mother. No one in the family would ever admit this to anyone, and especially not to themselves; it was taken as a given. Ac-cording to her daughter, Jeanne Mansard was breathing death in to her fam-ily. She was polluting them, making them ill. Annie would laugh to herself: Mother pollutes us to the tune of three packs a day. And *she* doesn't even have to inhale her own debris. She leaves it around for us to breathe, and eventually drown in, though that's not her conscious plan. It may well have been unconscious, Annie debated on more than one occasion. Perhaps her mother really did wish for the family's destruction. There are many ways to murder people, but the perfect crime is the psychological destruction of the soul.

"You did it to them, Mother," Annie wrote. "You did it because you always hoped all three of them would fight each other to the death, and then you'd be free and able to tell the world, I did exactly what I was meant to do: get married and have children. I was a wife and mother, right? So I was complete. Isn't that what was wanted of me? Nobody can blame me if I'm free of all that because I *did* do it, and they were the ones who killed themselves. I never touched them. You saw me. I stood there and begged them to quit. You saw me, Annie. You saw how I urged them to quit, how I demanded that he break them up. You're my witness."

In her mind, Annie assumed the role of star witness at a trial in which the entire family became judges, attorneys, and, in the end, jailers and prisoners.

The psychological solution was to save her family by destroying the sort of disequilibrium she had learned about in algebra class. She could remove pieces of the equation, no matter on what side they fell, by ingesting them. That's what her algebra teacher preached. "If you take it away, Annie old girl," Mr. Daltman would say, leaning his face next to hers—"a little too close, don't you think, Mr. Daltman, for a crummy old ninth grade class"— "if you take it away from one side of the equation, it's got to appear somewhere on the other side. Numbers don't just disappear. I mean, you didn't *eat* the quantity, you merely subtracted it. Nothing just disappears. You took it away so the other quantities on that side would feel a little lighter. But now, Annie old girl, you got to put it back. That's only fair, isn't it? You didn't eat it, did you, Annie?"

"Move away from me," Annie described wanting to tell him, "with your smelly face. It's bothering my thinking, and everybody in this room knows what you're doing, or would like to do when your face gets that close, 'cause we're the sophisticated generation, Mr. Daltman. We know which end is up. But I do like the idea of making one side of an equation a little bit lighter by eating it. If it's all right with you, I don't want to put it back on the other side. I'm just going to take little bits away, away from her, Mr. Daltman, and that way all of us in the Mansard equation will be a little bit lighter. It's absolutely ingenious, this idea of eating bits that nobody likes. And you know why it's going to work, Mr. Daltman? Because it's perfectly absurd. You'll see, everyone's going to end up happier. And that's all that counts in the big equation, isn't it, Mr. Daltman? Making everyone in the equation happier? So if you're worrying about what happened to that one quantity in little old Annie's equation, I'll tell you, as absurd as it sounds: I ate it, Mr. Daltman. Honest to God, I ate it, although I almost said I hate it. Now, Mr. Daltman, what do you think *that* means? Hate and ate? Would you say that's like mixing apples and oranges? Well, it is. It is just as absurd, thank you very much!"

It was amazing how many days felt pleasant to her. One of Annie's favorite expressions was "It isn't always bad." Truth be told, her attitude toward being alive was impossible to fathom, even though she tried her best. She told herself that even as she went to understand the patterns of her moods they would shift, and she lost any chance to analyze or photograph them. Part of the time she believed herself to be on a roller coaster, one moment feelings running high and fast, and the next moment, everything slow, nearly immobilized. At other times she felt herself to be ambling through life in what she called "submerged tones." Her style, she determined, was slower, more deliberate than other people's. But no, she corrected herself, it wasn't style; it was the constant feeling that things felt heavy, that life weighed down on her.

For Annie, it wasn't proper to go through a day without having some serious purpose. Clearly that was her parents talking. Every instant for them had to be a learning experience, or so she reported. They despised small talk, the meager descriptions of what happened at school or the amusing thing that happened to a classmate in the cafeteria. The Mansards wanted talk of grades and college, intellectual inquiry, and proper grammar. That was the worst for Annie. Couldn't they understand that sometimes, when you get excited about something, you don't speak correctly, as especially her mother invariably demanded. It became a curse, the constant need to watch what she said—watch herself—in the presence of her parents. They appeared to be listening, but it wasn't the content of her communications to which they attended; it was her language.

"So anyway, me and Cynthia went out after—"

"Cynthia and I."

"Cynthia and I. We went to the caf and who's there but this kid—"

"What kid?"

"I'm about to tell you." Her anger already was building. "There's like, this kid, Neil, you know—"

"A kid, and no I don't know. . ."

It went on like this until finally Annie, utterly frustrated, felt her energy reduced to nothing. But when she made a move to walk away, it was her parents who grew angry. The pattern repeated endlessly, and always she told herself these words, as if hoping they would conclude the exchange: "You'll see, someday I'm going to do one thing right." Later she would think, Wouldn't it be wonderful to have something written on my gravestone that was grammatically incorrect? Those two would be so busy correcting it, they'd forget I died!

"Here me lies. Like, there ain't no 'nother one down here but I. Resting in pieces, sincerely yours. . ."

FRANCINE CAVANAUGH remembered teaching her first class of junior English at Bristol Town High School. She could see at once that her students were interested in books and curious about a variety of matters. Affluent looking, despite the overalls, work shirts, and sloppy jeans, most of Ms. Cavanaugh's advanced-study junior English students had completed most of the summer reading assignments. She remembered clearly the first discussion about the nature of the hero in literature. She remembered, too, the girl seated at the desk near the window beneath the poster of Windsor Castle. There was a special look about this studious young woman. She took notes, consulted her books, and communicated a host of gestures that signaled her attentiveness. Annie Mansard, she recalled, was one of only a few students whose full names she had memorized by the end of class.

Francine Cavanaugh had to smile when she thought about her first Bristol Town classes: so many bright students. But what burdens they lived under. Every one of them was getting pressured by parents. Many students had older siblings who had performed successfully, which meant that teachers approached them with still higher expectations. "You must be Timothy Mansard's sister. . ." More pressure. Then there was the school itself, with its lofty standards and ideals, competitive test scores, and need to maintain an outstanding reputation in the state. It didn't look good if graduates shunned college or the number of seniors admitted to prestigious colleges declined. More pressure.

Francine was the first to admit she was haunted by Annie's presence in the school. There was the student's fierce dedication to learning and gaining admission to one of the so-called better colleges; Annie was reading five times more than anyone else in the class, five times more than anyone she had ever taught. There was the fact that she could be so outstanding and still attract people to her. There was always the good looks, and always the sadness. It seeped through the personality, Francine would say, as a slow but significant leakage. Still, it wasn't her role, Francine believed, to intervene in students' personal lives. After all, she wasn't a psychiatrist. If a student volunteered something, it was legitimate to talk it out. But teachers had to know their place as educators, not psychotherapists. Still, anyone could see that Annie needed help. With the whole world, seemingly, hovering about her, she displayed a deep sense of aloneness.

As best as she could recall, Francine Cavanaugh met with Annie no more than six times during the student's final year in high school. No real friendship ever evolved. No matter; senior year for Annie was filled with tribulations, and Francine, now in her second year on the faculty, felt more a part of the institution and its rituals. Annie had her chums; Francine had a new class of eager students. No one in her classes was as compelling as Annie Mansard had been that first day of school a year before, but who was to say that the attraction to Annie hadn't derived from the fact that Annie was the first person she'd noticed in her first class on her first day teaching in a new school.

It is always sad, Francine thought, when friends separate or a friendship fails to materialize. Teachers, of course, are used to this, but Annie was different. Annie was someone who would have felt the grief of a woman whose only child died at age three from a rare illness and whose marriage dissolved partly because of this. Annie would have understood this feeling of perpetual mourning, Francine thought, because that was the feeling she herself evinced. This was a young woman one could speak to about loss, even if she were twenty years younger.

That Annie never knew of little Keith Cavanaugh was one thing; that Francine might have failed to notice the clues in Annie was something else again. Wasn't that what they always said about cases like this? There are always clues; it's just that the witnesses choose to look away. Yet Francine hadn't chosen to look away; she swore to God that she hadn't once looked away. Anyone could see she was not responsible. If she hadn't indulged in wishes and desires, it was clearly in the child's best interest. Anyone could see that. Anyone could see she was not responsible, in the same way that she was not responsible for her son's death years before or for the ensuing divorce. But to be so close to the deaths of two such beautiful children became an overwhelming burden for the teacher.

Francine Cavanaugh took a leave of absence from school the year after Annie's graduation and left the state forever the following spring. On her final day in Bristol Town she paid a visit to the cemetery to have her last talk with the attractive young woman whom she first saw, face so alive and bright, though not without sadness, on a brilliantly clear morning, sitting so poised at the desk near the window, beneath the poster of Windsor Castle.

Six weeks after graduating from high school, while her family believed she was making plans to attend the prestigious university to which she had been accepted, Annie Katherine Mansard committed suicide by overdosing on medication. At the time of her death, she was eighteen years, one month, and three days old. While she left a note at the time of her death, the family has not revealed its contents to anyone.

THERE IS perhaps nothing as frustrating for social scientists than determining patterns of human behavior while knowing full well that these patterns can rarely do more than suggest or indicate behavior. Only on occasion do the patterns we draw actually construct how someone conceives of and perceives behavior. Family members work in this same manner. A host of variables and courses of action make sense to the researcher, but evidently only a small portion of behavior can be accounted for by any series of studies.

Studies of suicide bear this out.[24] Patterns emerge, familiar elements hover about families that experience a suicide of one of their members, but when one goes to assemble even the most well-researched data, the patterns frequently appear thin. "Broken homes" was the politically incorrect term that once dominated the thinking of suicide researchers. It is, of course, a misleading catchall, since any form of deviation from normal routines and circumstances may appear to constitute a so-called broken home. To the actual family members, a separation, a divorce, or even abandonment of the family by one member may not be construed as *breaking* the home.

Truth be told, the "broken home" notion of social pathology was applied more often to families of lower economic status than to those of higher economic status. More affluent families typically were labeled "problematic" or "under stress." As it became evident that divorce rates among affluent families could not be underestimated and that domestic violence also was no stranger to these families, the term "broken home" fell by the wayside. Suddenly, critics of the term began wondering if *any* American families were not broken or "dysfunctional," as the term from family systems theory suggests. Still other critics contended that perhaps "broken homes" were the result less of individual psychopathology than of erosion of social institutions, values, and economic circumstances. Given the lack of opportunities experienced by many families, it seems almost impossible for the family system not to break up in one manner or another.

Although the term "broken family" fails to delineate the precise nature of a particular family's stress, it nonetheless carries a peculiar power. Danger and violence, abuse perhaps, and an almost warlike assault are suggested by that term, "broken home." If by now it isn't overworked, the term should imply that something momentous has occurred. The family system has broken into pieces, or at least it seems so in the minds of some of the members.

Some have suggested that "broken homes" serve as foundations for teenage suicide. I take this to mean that for the child in question, something of a precious and portentous nature has been destroyed. A father or mother has violently or permanently quit the family, or fighting frequently marks the family's history. A series of powerful events has taken place that has profoundly altered the child's destiny and internal makeup.

Using the language and concepts of family systems theory, I identified several characteristics in the Mansard home that are often found in so-called problematic families.

First there was the boundaryless behavior, the confusion of roles, the infusion of one person's emotional world into the emotional world of another, with the result being an internal chaos whose origins a young child could neither fathom nor explain. Second was the "parentification" of a child,[25] the transforming of young Annie Mansard into the family peacekeeper, a role she felt to be essential for the well-being of her family yet essentially impossible to enact.

Third, Annie had to play the role of perfect child—successful, calm, and happy—in part to preserve the image of the family as successful, happy, perfect. The act was a sham, and the child, already feeling defective from the shaming rituals that were often part of the family's interactions, experienced the same degree of psychological isolation that her family, too, had created. Isolation was her only armor. At some level, they all felt ashamed and defective.

That at a very young age Annie knew there was something wrong with both her and her family speaks to the notion of how precisely the internal world, the world of self-consciousness and identity, the mode of being that Rollo May called the inner world "thrown against itself" (*Eigenwelt*), derives in great measure from the mode of social interactions, the family world, the mode of being May called the "with world" (*Mitwelt*).[26] It is essentially from family interactions that children derive their sense of the inner world as well as their ongoing definitions of the substance of this world. Children's profound calculations of their own sense of independence, confidence, intelligence, competence, and worth derive in great measure from the sorts of interactions born in families. It is possible that even styles of cognitive operations derive from these same intimate interactions. To listen to Annie was to learn that she believed this to be so.

Fourth, there was the almost prosaic matter of family communication, which in the Mansard family was complex, indeed. They communicated through words, fighting, gestures, music, yelling, and interpretations of behavior. They communicated directly and indirectly, new coalitions forming, old ones dissolving. They hated as they loved and expressed independence even as they sought nurturance and attachment. Just as they knew things had gone seriously wrong, so did they communicate to each other how they themselves felt wronged. They blamed, they accepted blame, and in the end they found that even the most elemental family decisions were transacted with unneeded complication and tension. And always the inside worlds were confused with the outside worlds, the lack of boundaries serving to weaken friendships and individual psyches. The violence that raged on the kitchen and dining room floors raged in their minds as well. To hurt another, one hurt oneself; to hurt oneself was to hurt all the others.

Several additional points should be made about youth suicide. Like most significant social psychological phenomena, it typically does not come as a bolt out of the blue. To some it may seem this way, but in most cases (though not all), the signs and symptoms of suicide have been evident for a while. Suicide, furthermore, is not the result of one distinct event or experience. It is the result, usually, of long-standing, day-in, day-out personal and social experiences that drive people's anger and despair to the point of self-destruction. Somehow the children direct their anger at themselves; their pain is more than they can endure.

Of course, anger is not the only emotion involved in suicide. There is never just one emotion connected to any human action, destructive or not, just as there is, normally, no single event that explains an entire piece of human behavior, although studies reveal depression to be a common companion of suicide.[27] People and families undergo profound changes, particularly during their childhood and adolescent years, or, conversely, they resist the inevitability and naturalness of change and evolution.

A child has acted up at school for several years. He is the classroom terror, uncontrollable, notorious to all his teachers. Suddenly, and for want of a better explanation, maturity seems to take hold and the child improves. His grades go up, and his demeanor is different; he has taken a wondrous turn. The reverse is also possible. The excellent student falters, the well-behaved child becomes brittle, recalcitrant, bitter. The once happy and carefree child becomes withdrawn, unyielding, and demanding. Teachers and parents perceive new qualities in the child, new facets of an emerging personality. Sometimes these facets are welcomed; sometimes they seem frightening. It is clear that the child is heading for trouble.

Something intriguing does indeed take place during the middle school years. It has to do with subtle transformations not only in the child but in those who describe the child and thereby construct his or her world. In

American culture, anyway, as children enter their teens, the words used to describe them take on greater psychological import. Simultaneously, less technical and more human terms seem to fall out of usage. "Modesty" and "shyness" vanish, and "disturbed," "hostile," "rebellious," "aggressive," and, most dangerously perhaps, "depressed" assume new importance. Evidently, what the "child describers" are doing is declaring that the period of "kid stuff" is over. In turn, children come to be described by hard-core psychological, if not pathological, labels, which only naturally affect their conceptions of themselves and one another. Labels construct, the Mansards learned, even as they describe.

There is no denying the cognitive maturity and psychological sophistication of many young people. But even in saying this, I wonder whether we are not about to stumble over one of the most complicated obstacles to understanding the suicide of an adolescent. Why is it, for example, that so many children, even as they move into adolescence, are such vigilant surveyors of the psychological scene, their own and everybody else's? Does this derive from their natural drive to understand their own being or from the work they perform in family interactions? Will we ever know why some children become consumed with psychological pressures and their own interior worlds? Why some children spend so much time ruminating on their interior worlds is answered in part by this simple explanation: because for the first time in their lives, cognitively, they can.

Why is it that once some adolescents engage in personal ruminations, they reach the conclusion that little of value exists inside them? Is this, too, linked to family interactions and to rituals of shame? Does the sense of worthlessness perhaps grow from these interactions and the experience of pain? Is it true, moreover, that this pain, this extra parcel of authentic human sensitivity, is the result of constantly having one's self-esteem, not merely one's self-concept, challenged by the world as well as oneself? Is it the case that all too many young people battle the poison of shame?[28] And does this same pain, derived from family worlds, create a sensitivity or numbness that so many teachers detect and worry about?

The term "broken home" seemingly describes so much that it barely describes anything at all and hence in the end may not be useful for making sense of adolescent suicide. But if the term "broken" connotes broken spirit, broken will, and broken esteem, then it may prove useful after all. Many suicidal youngsters feel that after years of taking a pounding of one sort or another, a pounding others may know little about—some of it, actually, self-induced—they finally feel something break. It may seem to an outsider as though one particular event brought down the house of cards, but, having sustained a heavy bombardment for a long period of time, the house was ready to go.

From the outside, the Mansards were hardly what anyone would call a "broken family." Neither Jeanne nor Bill Mansard ever spoke of divorce or even thought of abandoning the family. They never engaged in physical fights between themselves. Bill drank every so often, but he never exhibited unusual behavior when he was intoxicated. From the outside, the Mansards appeared to be a successful family: prosperous, respected, attractive, liked, and well educated. But are we now combing through, not superficial material exactly, but the stuff of which "broken homes" presumably are constructed? It is difficult indeed to follow a family, especially one that had its share of crises, and not reflect on the signs that may have been missed and the warnings overlooked when later a child decides to take her life.

Feeling the child's hurt, one examines the evidence, as it were, with some self-blame, self-doubt, and self-hate. In the long run, it is not a missed clue; it is a missed life, a series of missed lives, and anyone even slightly implicated in the interpretation process finds himself or herself caught up in the sadness, guilt, rage, and pity that lie heavily in the rooms and passageways where a short time before a child lived. One's words come out so naturally in the past tense, as though the whole family has died, instead of just one of its members. And in a sense a family *has* died. In a similar context, David Luterman suggested that when deaf children are born into families, to some extent all family members become deaf.[29] A lingering danger is that one can write about a family that has experienced a suicide in such a manner that the whole experience quickly disappears into the past. Or is it that a researcher suddenly discovers that he or she has become, in some small measure, a member of someone else's family?

In the end, the Mansards were a broken family. They were broken by Annie's death at age eighteen and, as they would later tell, they were broken long before that.

RETIREMENT ACCOUNT

Eugene Lancaster wasn't interested in reflecting back on his life, not even now, in the hospital weeks before his fifty-seventh birthday. He never was the sort of person to figure out why things transpired as they did. What's done is done, he said, and what is yet to be must be accepted in its own time. It was a philosophy that had always lived within him. He had never read it or had it preached to him. Very little, in fact, had been formally taught to him. He'd left school at the end of his second year of high school, gone to work, and then entered the military; he said he can count on one hand the number of books he read in their entirety. His philosophies derive from living life. They're simple, even simplistic, particularly now.

One of five children from a home he remembered as being stressful and unfriendly, Eugene Lancaster spent much of his childhood steering clear of his father's wrath. All the children learned early on to note the warning signs: the bulging veins in the neck, the reddening cheeks and forehead, the rash erupting below the Adams apple. If one of them didn't receive the anger, then their mother surely did, for the fights raged almost every night.

Tacitly acknowledging that they didn't have much of a family life, the Lancasters rarely sat down together at the dinner table. Mrs. Lancaster prepared the food, but people were on their own to serve themselves. She might sit with one of the children, while others might eat standing nearby. Still others might not show up for meals at all. Later the dishes would be cleared, people would spread out around the small house, and then, ineluctably, the arguments would begin.

Hushed voices at first, then shouting and the slamming of doors, and finally a crash, like a dresser drawer pulled from a bureau and slammed to the floor. Eugene would lie on his bed, his small body turned toward the wall, and talk to himself: "Pretend that none of this is happening. It just isn't happening. Nothing you can do about it, anyway." Occasionally, his sister Marsha would huddle at the foot of his bed. He would hear her weeping and would want to touch her or comfort her, but he never did. He just performed his nightly ritual, staring at the rough plaster wall, whispering to himself, "It's not really happening. Nothing you can do about it, anyway."

When Eugene was very young, his mother would visit the children at night—the five of them slept in two bedrooms—to check on them. It seemed as if she wanted them to know she had survived another night. Her arrival meant that Mr. Lancaster was drunk and asleep. The mother's night vigils stopped, however, when Eugene was eight. He would learn that his mother, too, had taken to drinking as a way, she explained years later, to cushion the verbal attacks of her husband. She always assured her children that she had never been physically assaulted, as if this fact exonerated their father.

Eugene missed his mother's nightly visits. He always pretended to be asleep when she arrived, but he never fell asleep until after she had left the room. His mother spoke soothing words to him, making him suspect she knew he was awake. But the visits ended, his mother's drinking became increasingly apparent, Marsha's sadness more disturbing, and then somehow, childhood disappeared in a dry mist. Slipped away. Gone.

Where the past fifty years disappeared remained a puzzle for Eugene Lancaster as he lay in the hospital bed. Significant events now were blurry images with few feelings attached to them: getting discharged from the army; being offered his first real job; marrying Michelle, which his mother had warned was a mistake, because she reminded everybody of his father; and the birth of their four children, particularly the second one, Mickey Edward, who everyone could see from the moment he took his first breath had something wrong with him. Mickey Edward, who was born with Down's syndrome, turned out to be the most loving of his children. His death at twenty-four was his father's saddest moment. It was far sadder for Eugene than the afternoon he learned of his father's sudden death from a stroke, and it was certainly up there with that July morning when they buried his mother. Marsha's death, too, had been difficult; she had suffered so long with cancer. One minute the surgeons were saying they had gotten it all out of her, and the next minute they announced it had grown back. He lost faith in medicine during Marsha's illness and disliked the priest's sermon at her funeral. Every day he had visited her at the hospital, just as he had done when Mickey and his mother were gravely ill.

The guilt of not being with his sister, mother, and son at the moments of their death never completely left him, though he didn't let himself reflect on it. Nor did he blame himself. He had been a good son, brother, and father. A particularly good father. Fortunately, he had not inherited his father's wrath or his disinterest in children and family life. He and Michelle ate dinner with the children every night when they were growing up, and breakfasts and lunches on the weekends as well. The family took vacations when he could afford them. They were never lavish, but for a week or two in the summer he would rent a cabin where the children could play and swim and he could fish. There was something else he made certain to accomplish that his own father had not: all the children completed high school, even Mickey in a special education program. Two of the four graduated from college, and a third, at age twenty-six, had recently announced that he was taking university extension courses as a sort of trial run. So Eugene Lancaster assured himself that he had been a good father. Maybe not the most loving or demonstrative one, but he had never failed his children. He had spanked them, and hollered plenty in his day, even during the vacations, but he always provided for them. And he had stayed. He had stayed when anyone could see that living with a vengeful and angry wife, who did turn out to be like his own father, was hardly an easy task. His own mother had told him he could be excused for walking out on his wife. God would excuse him if he just up and left. He needn't get a divorce. After all, he was entitled to some happiness in his life, and she and his father hadn't given him much when he was a boy.

Although he threatened to on numerous occasions, he never did leave. Likewise, he never quit a job until he had a better one in hand, and he never was fired. He didn't even quit work two years ago, when the pains in his stomach brought him to his knees and the doctors at the hospital where Marsha had died removed several feet of his intestine. They told him they thought they had got all the cancer. He never said a word to them but just stared straight ahead, remembering how he had believed Marsha's surgeons when they uttered almost these same phrases after her first operation. He requested that the children, now fully grown, not be told much about his illness. It would only upset them. What could they do about it, anyway? His siblings could be notified, but not the guys at work. Not yet, anyway.

Since Eugene's first hospitalization, Andy Kelly, his boss for twenty-three years, had made certain that his employee was retained on the payroll. He could understand that Eugene would not want to inform him of the cancer. It made a man feel weak, helpless, ashamed. But a man like Eugene had more than paid his dues; the company would continue to cut his checks as if he were putting in his forty hours a week. They would help as well with the costs not covered by medical insurance. Sad, though, that he wasn't accepting visitors, especially if the stories were true that he had only a few months to live.

It was becoming clear to Eugene Lancaster that he wouldn't make it. The trips back and forth to the hospital for chemotherapy and other treatments were becoming foolish, and extremely painful. He had grown thin and weak, and the dosage of morphine constantly was being increased. He slept most of the time, and awoke bathed in sweat and feeling frightened. He asked the nurses to move his bed closer to the wall. It gave him comfort, he explained, facing the bare white plaster. They wanted to oblige him, but the wires attached to the bed made moving it even a short distance impossible. So he came to hate the four-foot chasm between his pillow and the wall. It was hard for him to pretend at that length.

He dreamed a great deal during the hospital stays, mostly of his mother, sister, and Mickey. He told himself he would be meeting them soon. Perhaps the religious notions he had so despised were actually true; they merely were meant for the dying. He spoke little with his wife, who visited him daily, and enjoyed the one time his fishing buddies dropped by unannounced. They assured him they would hold his place in the boat and he managed to laugh. His lifelong dream had been to own a lakeside cabin with a small motorboat at the end of a dock. Why hadn't he bought them when he had the chance? And why hadn't he taken more vacations? He always complained he had no money, which was true, but he could have borrowed it. He could have borrowed all he needed. It was his inability to live with the itchy feeling when he owed money. He should have bought the cabin with the dock and the boat and just scratched a lot. "I should have bought that pretty little girl we saw that time at the boat show," he whispered to his friends. "She'd have looked all right on a trailer in the yard, wouldn't she?"

"Still can," they answered.

"Still will, Geno," they said.

He looked at them and smiled, and then turned toward the wall. "It's not really happening, is it, guys?"

Nobody spoke.

THE FINAL hospitalization lasted two-and-a-half weeks. He woke every morning hoping to feel strong enough to go home, for he didn't want to die in the hospital. There were promising afternoons, but the strength he imagined was returning disappeared in minutes. In previous stays, he had felt weepy, but during this hospitalization the tears were due to pneumonia and fever. He barely had the energy to talk, but his mind was clear, and, miraculously, visions of his childhood returned more clearly than ever before. He saw the faces of his family, heard the discussions and fights, and, surprisingly, remembered happy times, scenes in the kitchen of his brothers and sisters teasing one another or torturing the neighbor's golden retriever. He could smell his mother's baking, especially her honey cake, the pies she made with graham cracker crusts, and the wheat bread with raisins she made on special occasions. He remembered his father laughing when the clothesline fell down in a mud puddle. His mother had been furious at first, but then they laughed uncontrollably, and there was his father stomping about in the muddied clothes, making his mother laugh even more, while Eugene and his brother Willy watched in confusion and delight. He remembered his father once kissing his mother on the mouth. Then there was the time Marsha swept the magazines off the coffee table, stood on it, and sang for everyone. For the first time in fifty years, he could hear her sweet voice, and even recall words from the song. Then he saw his family applauding and Marsha turning beet red with embarrassment. Everyone was smiling. Thousands of scenes were returning, and being played out as if projected onto the white hospital wall. Now, too weak even to turn in bed, he searched the whiteness for more scenes, and endlessly they rushed at him.

Amid the memories came flashes of unfinished business: bills that had been left unpaid, concern over some house insurance, an income tax rebate check. What occupied the top right-hand drawer of the small desk in the basement floated about in his head. But there were more serious matters. He had never visited the graves. Surely he could have found time to stand near his mother's headstone and to make certain the family plots were neatly maintained. They had looked so shabby on his last visit, years before. He also should have made private peace with his father. The man wasn't evil; he merely had been a failure as a father. But the family had never gone without a roof over their heads or a meal on the table. How could anger and sadness last so long? Why had he waited? And where were his own children now? Why hadn't they even inquired about him?

Eugene Lancaster often fell asleep asking the nurses whether Mickey was coming to see him. Able to recall these requests the following day, he admitted it was his other children he longed to have near him. Of course he knew Mickey had been dead for years. But where were the other children? Was someone keeping them away? What was Michelle up to? Was everything settled with the will? Could someone please bring him the will?

For a while his murmuring sounded like the familiar terror and worry of any dying man. Michelle assured him that everything was in order. But then a friend of the children happened by the hospital. Learning of Eugene's illness, he paid a call. The visit lasted two hours. Eugene told the friend of his concerns, frights, disappointments, and of course the memories playing out on the wall. After leaving Eugene, the man telephoned the Lancasters' oldest son, Paul, who obviously had no idea of his father's critical condition. Michelle successfully had kept them away. She had kept away everyone, except for the fishing buddies, and had even told some nurses that she and her husband were childless. It was her final attack on her husband.

A rainy snow fell the night the children visited with their father. They held his hand and spoke softly to him. They agreed to stay with him on round-the-clock shifts. He would not again be left alone. Desperate to make up for the lost weeks, they inquired about sleeping in the hospital, but the request was denied. It wasn't necessary, a doctor told them. "He's barely conscious now; he doesn't know who's here with him."

The children's fury with their mother continued to grow, but they revealed none of it to their father. All of their conversations were punctuated by expressions of love for him. He loved them, too, he whispered, one by one, over and over. They did their best to hide their tears from him. He could not hold his back.

Then, miraculously, three days after Paul had been advised of his father's condition, Eugene Lancaster began to show signs of growing stronger. He could turn slowly in his bed, his voice seemed less frail, and his talks with the children lasted longer before he fell back asleep. On the fifth day, he ate some of the food his daughter Emmy had prepared at home. And he enjoyed listening to Jerry read the sports pages to him. Michelle was no longer paying visits. She hovered about aimlessly in the visitors room. Eugene never inquired about her. Soon there was talk of his going home. He begged the children to arrange it so that he wouldn't die in the hospital. They discouraged him from all talk of dying. Couldn't he see he was improving? Couldn't he feel it? He had to admit he could.

Late one afternoon, Paul brought him the contents of the infamous desk drawer. He examined the pile of papers and familiar objects dumped on the bed and grinned. "You can work on it someday," he instructed his son. Then he told the children of the time Aunt Marsha had stood on the living room table and sang to everyone. The children laughed. Jerry showed his father a baseball box score from spring training. They were laughing just as his family had laughed when Marsha sang. Eugene Lancaster was rebounding. The doctors had no explanation other than the boost he received from the children's presence.

The improvement was so extraordinary that when the family friend who had learned of his hospitalization looked in on him a second time, he found Eugene sitting up in bed. Again the two talked for a long while, the patient newly energized and the visitor incredulous.

"It is all in the children," Eugene told the astonished friend. "Work and money mean nothing. It's children. I know that. I knew it years ago, too, but never did anything about it. But I know now. It should be the family, but I picked wrong. She just couldn't be what she should have been. My mother told me, but I was too important to listen, even though I knew she was right. It's supposed to be a partnership. You're not supposed to end up alone in a place like this. The grave's for people to be alone, not here. Not when you're breathing. My kids saved my life. Not religion, not doctors. I don't have any faith in anything. I saw their faces and made myself live. How can I tell you? I pushed myself to keep going. Like I gave myself a pep talk or something. Like a runner, you know. You tell yourself, keep going. Keep going. You don't have to die. You can live. Just keep going. Keep going.

"It's all in the kids. Isn't it something how a thing like this could work! Weeks I stared at that wall, trying to get my past to come back, just like when I was a kid listening to my parents fight all the time. I had my own movie theater going in here. Then in come the kids and the past goes away and in marches right now. Everything's right now. I'm not telling you I'm suddenly planning out the next ten years, though I'd love to. But I'm telling you, I'm stronger. I'm not watching the movies on the wall no more. And if I get out of here, if a real miracle happens—'cause I know the cancer is all over the place in there—I'm going to buy a boat. I swear on my mother's grave. If those kids of mine pull this off and the pep talks works, and I get out of here, I'm going to buy it. It may be three feet long, and I may not even get to ride in it, or go fishing, but it'll sit in the yard on a trailer like it should have all these years.

"How do you like this. You get your kids right up next to you and I swear to God, they breathe life back into you. You breathe it into them when they need it, and they breathe it right back to you when you need it. Talk about a helluva retirement account. If that don't take the cake. See what I mean? I wasn't a half-bad father. I was there for them. I could have left. I had someone to go to, too. I'm not going any farther with that one, but I had a place to go if I wanted to, but I never did. You do it for the kids, and you get it back, with interest. I'll tell you, that is one amazing retirement account. You talk about an I.R.A. And I'm taking it all out premature without penalty, and getting all the interest and all the principal and the government isn't getting a cent! They aren't getting a lick of this one. And I ain't even . . . how old you have to be to get that money out? Did I blow that thing, too? What is it, fifty-nine? Fifty-seven-and-a-half? What's the difference, I'm not even close to that. I just got the dividend of my life. Would you believe it? You saw me the other night—when was that?—would you believe it?

"Kids. Who ever told anybody about this? You see what I mean? Mothers don't own it. A father can get his share. Mickey's here with me in spirit. He's right here. I got all four of 'em with me. First thing I should have done when I got in here the first time was put their pictures up, like I got 'em on the desk. You can take and flush all the medicine down the toilet. Those pictures would have done just as good. Believe me. You want a miracle drug? Get your children to show up when you need 'em. God bless 'em. God bless 'em. Listen to me, will you. God blessing my children all over the place here. All right, we'll throw Him in there, too. God bless 'em. I won't mention her name in the same breath. I won't say out loud how I think maybe she put that stuff in my gut in the first place. We'll just see who's standing around the bed when her time comes up. Would I love to see that sight, even if it sounds mean. Just the kids. That's all we're talking about tonight. That's what we're celebrating. Tomorrow I get pictures in here. I'm telling you, I'm getting out of here. Few more days and I'm gone. I'll make it. With the kids now, I'll make it. You see, I was alright. I was a good father. They love me. You heard 'em. They love me. They told me. And I told 'em right back, didn't I? Each one I told: I love you. I love you. I love you. I love Mickey, too. I tell you, I'm going to wake up tomorrow and find the Easter bunny in this bed.

"Thank you very much for coming by. I haven't thanked anyone until you. You're the first. Thank you. I haven't even thanked the kids. Tomorrow. You take it for granted. You don't ask; you don't tell. Thank you very much. Really. Thank you."

Eugene Lancaster's miracle lasted only three hours more. Death came to him moments past midnight, four days before his fifty-seventh birthday. The children rushed back to the hospital that evening after the nurse telephoned and told them of the massive heart attack and stroke, but he died before they arrived. For hours, all anyone could talk about was the short-lived miracle. None of the nurses had ever witnessed such a remark-able turnaround.

The family friend was called early the next morning and asked to report everything Eugene had said the previous evening. After learning of her fa-ther's expression of his intensely loving feelings for his children and of his gratitude, Emmy needed to know his last words. When told of the numerous "thank you's," she sobbed. Then, after a long silence, she said, "Paul wanted to tell you that when dad died, he was on his back, but kind of facing the door. He wasn't facing the wall. He said to be sure to tell you that. He wasn't facing the wall. Is that supposed to mean something?"

WOMEN WHO KILL

THE FREQUENCY and severity of violence against women are widely known, albeit difficult to comprehend. They are captured in two dramatic statistics: somewhere in America a woman is battered every fifteen seconds, and every five years the number of women killed in this country is equal to the number of Americans who died in the Vietnam War.

Add to these numbers the facts that each year 50 percent of American families report some form of domestic violence, 20 percent of all police fatalities occur during intervention in incidents of domestic violence, and for every case of child abuse—a well-known phenomenon—is a case of grandparent abuse—a barely recognized phenomenon—and you have the background for the rising number of cases in which, in apparent self-defense, women murder their husbands.[1]

As shocking as these numbers seem, historical precedent laid the groundwork for them. A little more than 150 years ago, various forms of domestic chastisement, as it was called, were perfectly acceptable. Indeed, the law entrusted the man of the family with the responsibility for domestic chastisement. In the very concept of *familia*, which referred to the number of slaves owned by a man, battering was sanctioned, although the law often revised the rules governing chastisement. In 1824, for example, the infamous Rule of Thumb Law required that the stick with which a man hit his wife not exceed the circumference his own thumb. Though a statute fifty years later rescinded the Rule of Thumb, it did not replace it with harsh restrictions against domestic violence, although one judge did write that it is better to forgive and forget.

Not that long ago, social scientists, unaware of the frequency and extent of domestic violence, assumed it to be an isolated, infrequent, and hence private and deviant phenomenon. Indeed, the thinking of the time went that in those "certain" families, wife battering actually helped to establish equilibrium: the man needing to be violent, the woman needing to be the recipient of his violence. Society and psychiatry thus believed female masochism to be normative and in those families an almost necessary part of "normal" functioning.

Granted, hundreds of thousands of women do remain in abusive relationships. Some of them even physically retaliate against their husbands. But masochism no longer is seen as the main reason for their staying in seemingly unlivable conditions. More likely, these women have no alternative housing options and remain economically dependent on their husbands. Even more significant is their fear of punishment should they make the slightest attempt to escape.

Simply said, the terrorized woman in the typical domestic violent scene lives much like the prisoner of war every day facing the same sadistic enemy. Terrorized, traumatized, even brainwashed by the captor to whom she is bonded, she lives with self-hatred and frozen fright, as it is called in the language of posttraumatic stress disorder, a hostage in her own home. Vacillating between rage toward her captor and the feeling of being reprieved, she threatens to leave or even kill in one moment, only to thank him for allowing her to survive in the next moment.

In some instances, her imprisonment is reminiscent of the world in which she grew up. Often, though not always, her history, in yet another captive scenario, was one of abuse by a parent. Denied, deprived, endangered, humiliated by those she trusted, she lived as a victim of and witness to all varieties of family pathology and dysfunction: alcoholism, drug addiction, incest, infidelity, battering, suicide, or homicide. As a worshipfully dependent victim, she now only naturally clings to the persons who have hurt her. Interestingly, studies reveal, the longer she stuck by her original family, the greater the chances she will remain in her abusive marriage.[2]

Underwriting her decision to perpetuate her marriage are rationalizations, derived in part from social myths, that have roots in childhood and hence are elaborated in childlike reasoning. Violence, she tells herself, is normal. Like her father or mother, her husband merely is experiencing excessive stress, but it will pass. For that matter, violence at times is justified. Besides, if she is good, she will be safe.

The phases of family violence only strengthen her rationalizations. She becomes keenly sensitive to the tension buildup that precedes the violence and believes, moreover, that she may have participated in inciting the eventual assault. Then, after the tension release, in the familiar phase of post-violence reconciliation, she believes fervently that he will at last change. Meanwhile, her husband's short-lived, childlike, and remorseful pleas for forgiveness—the only moments, perhaps, in which his own plaintive cries for nurturance are heard—convince her that she is loved and needed. They support her reasoning, furthermore, which she holds to be perfectly logical. Although initiating an assault may be mistakenly interpreted as masochism, in fact there is little about her thinking that depicts a perverse pleasure in experiencing pain.

Nor, for that matter, experts report, is a woman's decision—be it premeditated or impulsive—to take her husband's life an act of sadism. Rather, it is an act of self-defense, one that may have its origins in childhood but now stands as the ultimate response to years of outright abuse and imprisonment, if not physical and psychological torture. Supporting these contentions are the legal cases in which women have been acquitted of the charge of murdering their husband precisely because of the self-defense argument.

But self-defense is hardly a surefire protection for all women indicted for murder. What follows are accounts of two women who argued self-defense and were convicted of murder and sentenced to prison. Neither woman denies her crime, and neither denies her shame and despair. They spoke with me on various occasions in their respective prisons, where they continue to serve time.

I should note that I received permission from the women to publish their words with the understanding that I take all precautions to preserve confidentiality and anonymity. Both women, moreover, independently requested that I share these accounts with certain members of their families from whom they long to receive a morsel of compassion, if not renewal of the love they once felt.

I

Late morning light streams through the windows of the prison chapel. Lenore Kingsley, a woman in her late forties and the mother of four children, sits across from me, tears flowing down her cheeks, her hands holding tightly to wads of tissue. A prison guard, a man in his late twenties, sits behind her in the corner, occasionally dozing off during our conversation. We are allowed twenty minutes. This is the eighth time I have visited Lenore in prison, though it's the first time we have been allowed in the chapel. She is in the fourth year of a fifteen- to twenty-year sentence for the murder of her husband, Henry Kingsley.

"Can you understand if I tell you it was a different sort of day? It was like a film covered everything, like the clouds were low or something. I just saw things different that day, not fuzzy, but like through steam. I don't even know how many years I had been going through this thing with him, coming home whenever he wanted and yelling at me for something absolutely stupid. It took me a while, but I came to understand that when he came home yelling he had been with someone. He put it on to his drinking, but I knew it was because he had been with someone. He'd yell at the kids, too. I remember telling him early on, 'Take it out on me; don't take it out on them.' He'd always say, 'You poison me with them.' I'd tell him, 'I don't have to poison you for nothing, you do it all yourself. Your whole life's poison.'

"That would be the sort of thing that would set him off, and he'd hit me. In the beginning it might be a slap. Oh, he'd deck me, all right, but I'd be more in shock than in pain, you know what I'm saying. Then, later on, he'd really give it to me good. When I was pregnant with my second, he kicked me in the stomach. Like a football player. I remember him standing there, stock-still, I didn't know what was coming. We were fighting. Then all of a sudden he just punted me, you know what I'm saying, caught me in the side of my belly. I went down that time like a ton of bricks had landed on me. I lost consciousness. When I was coming to, all I could think of was the baby, and why'd he do that? Why did he possibly do that?

"It's absolutely amazing the baby was all right. I cannot figure out to this day how that child is healthy and normal, 'cause he kicked the living hell out of that child two months before he was born. I couldn't stand up to him anymore, not after that. No more. It was too much. Always the same. He'd come home, drunk most likely, and pick a fight. Then I'd say, 'Who you been with this time?' and I'd get it. Man, would I get it. Up towards the end I could feel myself baiting him, not wanting to get hit, but wanting to get him in some way. My sister told me I had to get out of there, but I wasn't going to no shelter. No way in the world I'd take myself to the shelter. And he'd say anytime I want to go that's fine with him, but if I move the children one inch he'd kill me. I believed him, too. Three times I went to the emergency room with injuries from that man. Each time the doctors said they had to report him and I begged them not to. 'Please Doc, don't make trouble for me,' I'd tell them, and they'd let it go. Maybe they put it on the records somewhere, but no one ever took action, that I knew about, anyway.

"Toward the end I just felt mean all the time. It wasn't like me. I don't remember feeling mean. I used to cry a lot, and feel ashamed, but I never felt mean. It was something more than anger; it's hard to describe. You see it in children once in a while; they get real mean and there's no stopping them. You see a child get angry and you get angry or frustrated in return. When you see a child get mean, you get frightened, 'cause you figure that child is capable of doing something that even he doesn't know he can do. I had become mean, mean as my husband. And then I had that terrible need to know what the hell he was doing and who he was doing it with when he wasn't home which was more and more with each child. By the time we had our fourth, I was actually shadowing the man. Not that I had much free time, but I followed him whenever I thought he was going up to see some woman. It killed me that he had women. I could take his kicking and the hitting, I could watch him scream at the children, even slap them around once in a while—'cause he didn't spend that much time with them. But I couldn't take the other women. Something in me said I had to see them, I had to get a glimpse of them. And then I plotted catching him in the act, not that I had the slightest idea what I would do if I did. But I felt I had to catch him.

"So this one day I followed him, through the steam, like I tried to describe. I watched him leave the pub where I knew he always went and I followed him. It was just like I was in a television show. Out he comes, and I followed him. And I know where he's going. I know who he's seeing. All my girlfriends were telling me every time he set foot in that woman's house, which was something like two, three times a week. I knew where he was all the time, but I had to see it for myself. I had to see that man come out of her house this one time. Through the steam, you know.

"Like clockwork out he comes and I'm standing there across the street, just waiting. Cold day, I have my black coat on and my dark blue knitted hat, but I don't feel the weather. I don't feel a thing. Out he comes and now, what I'm about to tell you is going to sound strange. On the one hand, I can tell you I haven't the slightest idea what I'm doing. It's almost as though I'm some sort of a puppet and somebody else is pulling the strings. I guess they call that a marionette. I'm perfectly numb. Yet, at the same time, I feel like every motion I make, my hand moving into my purse, my taking out his gun, which I brought with me, watching him walk across the street toward me, it was like everything was perfectly rehearsed. I can't say I did much thinking about this, or if in fact I ever did any thinking about it. But it all seemed rehearsed, almost as if I were doing it for the second or third time.

"So now he's walking across the street and damn if a car goes by so close it almost hits him and I feel scared that he might get hurt. I feel myself taking in my breath, like I was frightened. Then he's maybe fifteen feet away and I pull out the gun, his gun, like I say. And now, in an instant this thought crosses my mind. I don't know if there are bullets in it. He's always threatened to kill me with it, brags how he keeps it loaded at all times, which I've been telling him is bad because what if one of the kids pulls it out and plays with it. But he says they won't find it. But like I say, I don't know if he's really loaded it. Man had told so many lies in his life, this could be a toy gun for all I know. But I remember in the street how heavy it was. It was cold and heavy. Heavier, it seems to me, than it was when I took it from the closet and stuck it in my purse.

"Man's fifteen feet away. This is my husband coming toward me and he is angry. The man is dreadful angry. I remember, when he was coming down the stairs from her house he was starting to button up this tan overcoat of his. I always liked that coat. But then I called out his name and he is stunned. He can't believe I'd be there. So now he's coming at me and his coat's still unbuttoned. I have the gun out, and I still can't believe I do this, 'cause you remember me saying it's like steam and like someone's pulling the strings. I think I was already in shock, or something like that. He looks absolutely stunned, and for the slightest second I think I see what his face looked like when I met him some, well, what is it, seventeen years ago. Then I think, I can't believe how our youngest looks exactly like him and he seems so ugly and she is adorable, well, you know her, and they look alike.

"He's frightened. I wish I could have kept him that way longer, 'cause the man deserved to feel how I felt. Frightened all the time. I tell you this now as if I knew what was happening, but I don't know for certain whether I really remember it or not. It just seems as if this is what happened. I lower the gun and pull the trigger. I aim the gun right at his groin. I swear to God I did, and I pull the trigger. Two shots. I hit him. Both times. Now the man looks more shocked than before and he's feeling pain, but goddamn if he isn't still coming toward me. He isn't slowed down by nothing. I raise the gun, only a little bit. It's all part of the same motion, like an exercise or something. Two more shots. This time I aim at his chest. I hit him dead on. He looks up like there was something on the roof of the building behind me. I almost want to turn around. Now I see all the blood. It's the first time I see all this blood, his blood, pouring all over his nice coat and into the street, and I think I hear something like a puff of air go out of him. Maybe I just made that up.

"The man died right there, not ten feet from me. I can't move. I cannot move my legs, I cannot let go of the gun, and I'm wondering if there are more bullets in there. There's supposed to be six, I think. People there told me my face was frozen. Couldn't speak, couldn't cry, nothing. I'm standing there like one of the buildings. Before he dies he whispers, 'Fuckin' whore. Fuckin' whore.' I heard him say that. I heard other people talking and yelling and shouting. I think I remember some kid talking real soft to me and telling me he was going to take the gun. Boy must have been petrified that I'd shoot him, too. How'd he know I wasn't some mass murderer. I couldn't possibly have told him there was only one person in the world I wanted to kill, and I just did.

"I couldn't take it anymore. I just couldn't control myself. He had beaten me down, down to the point where I wasn't a person anymore. I wasn't a good mother, I wasn't a good daughter. He made me into a crying animal. I was hurting from him all the time. From his hitting and yelling at me and criticizing me and screaming at the children. And all the women. He killed my spirit and my womanhood with all those women. I never once cheated on the man. I never looked, I never spoke wrong to another man and he knew it. I made his meals, I cleaned his house, I let him have at me whenever he wanted. There was no way, no time I could say no to the man. He wanted his sex and he knew he'd get it from me. He couldn't have cared how I felt, or what I needed. But why'd he have to go with those other women? Just to feel his masculinity? Just cause of his little appetites?

"So now my life is completely ruined. I won't be out of here for another ten years at least; it could be longer. My children are ashamed. I see it in their faces when they come to visit me, which isn't all that much. My oldest won't come at all. He's going to change his last name, if he hasn't gone and done it already. He can't understand any of this, and I can barely speak to the others about it. I don't understand all of it myself. I've ruined everything. My husband is dead, and I'm as good as dead. I'm forty-six years old and my life is over. When I come out, where do I go? What do I do? I'm a convicted murderer. A person can cry self-defense all they want, but no one will accept my story. They will see me as crazy, a maniac, a murderer, like I say. Hate the man, hit the man. But why'd you go and kill the man? Because he had it coming! He had it coming. A man would have done the same thing; they do it all the time. You hear them talk revenge, but a woman can't do it. A wife can't do it. And sure as hell a mother can't do it!

"I feel so ashamed, more ashamed than anything else. I don't know that I wouldn't do it again. He shamed me and I killed him, and now I feel ashamed. And now, the only person I have in my life who'll talk to me, who'll come and see me and send me cards is my mother. My mother. Folks say, well, that's what mothers are, that's what mothers do. They stick with their children no matter what, like I'd like to stick to mine if they can find it in their hearts to let me. But my own mother looking out for me, trying to love me. You know what my mother did when I was a little girl? I haven't told this to my own children. She beat the shit out of me day in, day out. She put cigarettes out on my arms and my back. I have scars today from burns that woman gave me. Woman tried to get me to smoke dope with her when I was eight years old. Woman wanted me to have sex with her boyfriends when I was eleven. You believe that? She'd get drunk and want me to perform for her men. And there were more men running through our home than you could count. Never once did that woman ever touch my brothers, but she busted me every time she could.

"She burned me. My own mother. She broke me down again and again. I guess she must have wanted me to lead the same life as her. Screwing around, getting pregnant, having abortions, miscarriages, doing dope, making me feel ashamed of myself and her everyday of my life as far back as I can remember. And now the only person I have in the world is the one who's maybe responsible for all this. My own mother. The woman who introduced me to shame."

II

Elaine Haloran sits across the table from me in the prison cafeteria. At the far end of the room, several women wash the steel serving tables in preparation for lunch, an hour away. I have spoken with Elaine on numerous occasions, and never once has she appeared without her sunglasses, even on the darkest days. Today is no different. I am not certain that I have ever seen her eyes. Elaine Haloran was convicted for the stabbing death of her husband, who was twenty-one at the time, the same age as Elaine. This is the second year of her incarceration.

"There isn't much to tell about that night. Both of us had been drinking, and when he drank he would do anything. He didn't mind pushing me, or grabbing me, or poking me. He thought if people were married there couldn't be rape. But he raped me all the time. He saw nothing wrong with coming into the room, I might even be asleep, and waking me up and making me take my clothes off or pushing my head down on him. He said wives had to do these things. Those were the rules of marriage. Or he'd come up from behind me and start touching and putting his fingers in me, and God help me if I protested. I mean, you just didn't say anything.

"I fought him all the time and he hated it. I kicked him out of the house five times. More maybe. But then he'd promise never to do it again. And like a fool I'd believe him. Of course I never really believed him. I didn't want to be alone and I thought I'd never have another chance with a man if I messed this one up. I should have divorced him right away, but I didn't have the guts to go to my parents and admit I made a mistake. My father hated him. He told me a thousand times I shouldn't marry him. An hour before the wedding he said I was a stupid fool. The more he talked, the more I promised myself I would marry Billy. I didn't want my father to be right. My mother didn't have a say in our house. She never did. She was always silenced by my father. It would really have been nice to have a mother I could speak to, but I wasn't born that lucky.

"I don't want to talk much about it. I don't like to think about it. It was hot, I remember that well enough. I was walking around that night in not a lot of clothes, which I knew I shouldn't do because it would only turn him on. I swear to God I wasn't asking for anything or trying to get him up. We're in the kitchen and he says, 'Well, well, well,' like he wants me to do something sexual. I tell him I don't want to. 'You deaf?' he yells at me, 'Do it!' 'I won't.' We go back and forth, and then he's pulling my hair, real hard, harder than I ever felt before, like he was lifting up my scalp underneath. Then he hit the side of my neck, just under the chin, and I feel myself falling on the floor. I don't know, maybe he kicked my feet out from under me. He ripped off my clothes and he's unbuttoning his pants. I remember I hit my head falling to the floor and he yanks me away from the cabinet and pulls me over to the middle of the floor, still trying to get his pants down at the same time.

"I don't remember everything, but there's a moment when he hits me in the chest, like thud, right into the middle of the chest. I remember him mumbling something like, 'You deserve this. You really deserve this.' I don't even know if I ever said anything. I know I was crying, which he always hated. 'Why do you always have to be a crybaby?' he says. 'Jesus Christ, you're such a fuckin' crybaby. You know you were fucked when you were a little girl, so why the hell you act like this is all so new to you? What'd you expect marriage to be?' Then he's yelling, 'Put your fuckin' head here, put your fuckin' head here,' and I just lost it. I became crazed. They say things snap in people and that's what happened. I snapped. The next thing I know I'm reaching for the knife and he's still taking off his pants. He's thinking I'm getting up to get on top of him 'cause I sort of stretched myself out over him to reach for the knife on the counter and he sort of moans and says, 'Well, shit, I can live with that.' He was more vulgar but, like, you know.

"I just struck at him in the dark. I didn't plan anything. I never thought I'd do anything like this in a million years. You don't think about it. Oh, you say, I wish he'd die. I said that a million times, but you don't think, some night when it's hot and he comes at me I'll lure him into the kitchen and put a knife in him. But I remember the knife going in. I watched it disappear in his stomach. Way in. Way in. He was sort of watching, too. He was standing on one leg when it happened, pulling on his cuff, I think, and for a second he just sort of hung in space. Then he fell over. I couldn't believe how much blood there was. It seemed like gallons were all over the kitchen floor, along with half our clothes. I remember thinking, do I have to wash them out or are they going to be used as evidence? Maybe I really went crazy that night, I don't know. I know I didn't know myself that night. I certainly didn't know my own mind. He was in the hospital two days before he died. I wasn't allowed to visit him. Then I heard he died."

There is a long pause. Elaine reaches up beneath her glasses to wipe her eyes. She looks down, as she has throughout her account. The women continue to scrub the tile walls and metal serving tables. When I feel she is ready to continue, I ask, "What did your husband mean when he said—"

She cuts me off. "I knew you'd ask me that. It just came out. You mean because I was screwed all the time when I was little. I don't like talking about this. I promised myself I never would. Let me just say that my father was two different people. He was wonderful during the day and horrible at night, at least when I was five up until about when I was ten or eleven. I don't remember all of it, but I know he molested me. Lots of times. Always in my room, always at night when everyone was sleeping. He'd wake me and do his thing. I didn't have to do anything but stay quiet. He grew angry only if I cried. He would let me weep, sort of, but I couldn't cry. I couldn't make a sound. He told me if my mother wakes up or I say anything, something horrible is going to happen to her. 'Do I really have to tell what that is?' he would say. His voice would get very low. Those were his exact words. I knew he kept a gun in the house, although I never saw it, so I always assumed that's what he meant.

"I sort of do and sort of don't remember those years. I know there are lots of things I've made myself forget. I've never forgotten it all, but once in a while something will come back, like a flashback. I think it was worse than I imagined. There was something I felt one night when my husband had my head in his hands and was pushing me down. It's like a chill went across me. I remember lying in my bed those nights, when I was little, trying to memorize the patterns of the wallpaper. I can see all the furniture on that one side of the room, and a picture of a lamb and toadstool I had over my bed. I would turn toward the wall and lie still, but he always pulled my shoulder and turned me around to face him.

"God, it never has seemed to go well for me. There are so many things I still don't want to face. So many things I don't want to know about because I'll only have to cry over them. I think I hated my husband most when he made me cry, when he'd say things that he knew would make me cry. I never wanted to show kids in school that I was sad or upset or just about to cry. I hated having to cry. I've always been that way. First it was my father demanding that I wasn't supposed to cry. Then it was my husband. He knew he had something on me with my crying. I fought him as hard as I could not to cry, not to break down, not to show him that he had beaten me, or controlled me. I never want to give in. I hate sitting here and talking with you when I feel that right behind my eyes there may be tears coming up. I hate that anybody can make me feel that. My husband knew I'd rather be hit than forced into a position where I'd cry.

"It's strange. I just remembered something the other day, or sort of remembered. I think maybe I was forced to do something by my father in front of my mother. I know I was in their bedroom. It doesn't seem possible, but I'm sure it happened. I was very young. Maybe I made this whole thing up. But just once, I think, I was in their bed and she was forced to watch something I was doing. I think it was on my birthday. For some reason I remember him saying, 'We're going to celebrate your birthday tonight.' That's all I can remember. I don't know if it was with him or just me alone. But I remember her crying. She couldn't stop, and he kept saying things like, 'Go ahead and cry, it'll do you good. It'll clean you out. Go ahead, cry!' I wonder whether this happened or if I'm making it up. I do remember her crying that time. It seemed to go on forever, even after I was allowed to go back to my bedroom. Walking down the hall I could hear her crying. And she was screaming at him, 'I want you to die. I want you to have a heart attack and die.' Good things for a little girl to hear, huh?

"God, how she cried that night. Maybe that's why I can't bear to cry. It's almost like I'm crying her tears, or her tears are coming through me and her for what he did to us. Funny, I always thought I hated her as much as him, because on the days after those things happened they acted as if everything in the world was perfectly wonderful. I don't remember her ever wearing sunglasses. That's my invention. Don't let anybody see your eyes; they'll find truth in them. I guess I was never supposed to let anyone know the truth. I never told it all to my husband, only small amounts. He thought he knew it all. I knew he'd use it against me.

"And you know, my father would have killed him for how he treated me.

133

My father could have saved me from this whole conviction. All I had to do was tell him what my husband did and my father would have had him killed. I know he would. Despite everything that happened, my father would have done it, because like he tells everybody still, he would do anything for me because he loves me. He says that still, and like a little girl, a little girl the age I was probably when he started doing his little night acts, I want so much to believe him I sometimes think I do. I sometimes actually believe he loved me, like I tried to convince myself my husband loved me. The police told me I actually said that when they came that night with the ambulance. I don't remember it, but I was told I was saying, 'He does love me. Whatever else you may think, my husband loves me.'

"I think my mother could have saved me, like I tried to save my younger sister from my father. Sometimes I think my husband's father could have saved him, too, if he hadn't been such a flaming alcoholic who walked out on his wife and children when my husband was something like five months old. Sometimes I think my grandfather could have saved us all, because I always believed he sensed something horrible was going on. That's the sort of things a person thinks about in prison.

"Actually, nobody could have saved us. We were all hit by the same virus. It got to all of us and killed us one way or another. My husband with a knife, me in prison, my parents and my husband's parents with all the secrets and the actions nobody ever took. And all those tears. All those poisonous tears. Or at least I thought they were poisonous. Maybe if I had cried it would have been an alarm for someone. Maybe I could have cleansed away the memories by crying. But not that one night. Not that one night."

Again and again Elaine reaches behind the glasses to wipe her eyes. Her head stays down. I imagine her eyes are staring at the floor.

"This is all bullshit. Everything I'm saying is bullshit. I've fucked everything up. I did when I was small, I did my entire life, and now I wait for fifteen fucking years before I can start again, or try to, as if anyone will ever want to be with me again. I've fucked everything up. Believe me. God doesn't hear you in here. He doesn't care a rat's ass if you're crying or not, or wearing sunglasses or not. When you pay your penalty he takes you back. Maybe. At least I hope so. I pray for that."

Three weeks later, Elaine Haloran made what would be the second of three attempts to commit suicide. Given prison regulations and budget shortfalls, she has been unable to receive psychotherapy.

A SON DIES OF AIDS

DANNY MANGIONE has been dead nearly three years now. His family finds it difficult to believe that so much time has passed; the hurts and sadness have not diminished. The ceremonies at the church and the cemetery were especially painful. Danny Mangione, the priest had reminded the congregants, was only twenty-six years old when he died. Need anyone really comment on this tragedy? We cannot only always look to what is fair and what is not.

Father Ted's words had been strong. He spoke openly and directly about AIDS, the disease that had wrenched the life out of Danny Mangione, the fourth child of John and Theresa Mangione. He spoke of Danny's illness, which had lingered for so many months, the sores on his face and chest, his loss of weight, the terrifying way his voice changed in its growing weakness, and the shocking disappearance of his handsome looks. It seemed as though each day his brown eyes had grown smaller and fallen further back into his skull.

Angela Mangione found some relief in her brother's death. He had fought so hard and cried so often, especially in the last weeks, that in her hatred of the illness and pain of watching him suffer, she found herself praying for God to take him. His brothers Stefano and Marco, Steve and Marc to everyone outside the family, seemed bewildered by the whole matter, as if they would never allow themselves to understand the illness or its consequences. Even in the hospital visiting with their brother, they acted as though they had never heard of AIDS, but of course it was the force of the illness that mystified and angered them. Marco said that if he could smash someone and cry a lot he might feel somewhat appeased. Crying by itself only frustrated him more. Neither brother found solace in the church until after Danny died.

Theresa Mangione kept her pain inside. Whatever feelings and sentiments she may have expressed during her son's long illness and after his
death were heard only by her older sister Carlotta, and Carlotta revealed
nothing of their conversations. With Mamma Fiorella gone almost ten
years, the two daughters came to rely on one another as never before. They
had the church, Father Ted, and each other; no one else. Not their four
brothers, not their husbands, not even their own children.

John Mangione, sixty-four years old, was a man seemingly alone in the
world. He was not brought up to express feelings or tell people of his problems. Instead, he was raised by a father who emigrated to America from
Calabria in southern Italy as a young man looking for nothing more than a
steady job. It didn't have to be creative work or even high paying; it needed
only to be regular and certain. A man's whole purpose for living, John was
told as a boy, was to provide for a family. You make money, pay taxes, write
checks, keep the books. Having joy and being happy were not part of one's
bargain with life. A father provided for his family and taught his children
how to make their own lives better than his had been. But feelings were
meant to be kept to oneself.

Giovanni Mangione had become a first-rate stone mason. His son Johnny
chose the wholesale food business. At thirty-two, he bought his own two-
family home, something that clearly pleased his father. It was the ultimate
sign of making it in America, Giovanni announced, the night final sales papers were signed. Theresa, the four children, the steady clean work, not like
pushing stones around in sand and concrete, and now the house were the
benchmarks of success. Papa Mangione could die in peace when he saw the
complete success his son had made in his beloved adopted country.

The elder Mangione died five years before his son would learn that his
own youngest son, Daniello, was gay. John Mangione thanked God that his
father never learned the truth of Danny's life, and he himself could never
accept it, never deal with it, and certainly never talk about it.

Daniello Mangione knew that his father would not take kindly to the
news of something he had suspected when he was eleven or twelve and knew
for certain by fifteen. According to Angela, Danny never spoke of his homosexuality to members of the family until well after he learned of the disease
that had taken hold of his body. Theresa said that Danny was her son, no
matter what "his problem" might be, but everyone else saw that John was
devastated by Danny's unacceptable lifestyle. A religious man, he had no
place in his world or his heart for homosexuality.

Upon completing high school at eighteen, Daniello was asked to leave the house. He was old enough now to earn his own way in the world, his father told him. Besides, he was no longer welcome in the family home. He could come for the traditional Sunday dinner once a month, but he was never to bring one of his friends. He never did. Danny went to work for a picture framing company, first as a delivery boy and later as a framer.

Upon hearing from his son's internist that Danny had contracted AIDS, John Mangione reaffirmed his policy of no discussion of feelings. He announced to his wife, not his son, that he would assist with the medical bills as much as possible, but he would not become personally involved with "the matter." He would prevent no one from visiting Danny when he was hospitalized or otherwise dealing with him. But if their relationship had had a ray of hope left in it before the diagnosis, it now vanished.

John Mangione did visit Danny in the hospital during the young man's many periods of intense illness, but he never visited him at his home during the periods of remission. Two years after his son's death, he would admit that he purposely had arranged to take a business trip during the weekend the doctors thought would at last bring death to Danny. He took the phone call from Marco and arranged to take the first plane home. He arrived later that evening and proceeded to stay in the house for the next week. He never visited the funeral home and was conspicuously absent from the final church service and graveside ceremony. His behavior shocked his friends and infuriated his wife. His children tried to understand his actions, but their private conversations were unsatisfying. There was no talking with their father.

"It all died between Daddy and my brother," Marco would say later, "when he recognized Danny was gay. Some men can deal with it; some can't. Honestly, I don't know how I'd react if it was my son. My father could never handle it. He's like his father, a perfect specimen of the nineteenth century!"

To his family and friends, John Mangione became an enigmatic figure, if not an outright monster. How could a person act this way toward his own son? It was a cruel, inhuman treatment. "You can only pity him," Angela would mutter bitterly every time the subject of her father's absence from the church and graveside ceremonies came up. "It's totally pitiful. His father, his great hero, would never have gone so far. He only thinks he would."

So John Mangione lived his life very much alone. He maintained his business, where, apparently, few of his colleagues knew of the family's lasting anger and resentment in the wake of Danny Mangione's life and death.

On the second anniversary of the death, the entire family, with the exception of John, visited Danny's grave near the grove of cypress trees. One by one, they laid flowers near the headstone, and each spoke a few words to him. When they finished, they knelt and crossed themselves. Some waved when they left the grave, and others never looked again at the soft, damp ground where Daniello was buried. Theresa and the children remained nearby to welcome some of Danny's friends, who had come to pay their respects. From time to time they glanced in the direction of the narrow winding driveway leading from the cemetery gates, hoping that John might this day break his silence and visit his son's grave. He never came.

With all the children living in their own homes, the Mangione family house had grown colder and darker. Theresa and John's relationship had deteriorated. They dined together, speaking almost not at all, and barely spent time doing household chores or watching television. The taboo on speaking about Danny had spread to all subjects. The house, too, was dead.

At last acknowledging that their marriage was a sham, John Mangione proposed that the couple separate. They need never divorce. Neither wished to violate the tenets of their church; neither would ever remarry. Theresa offered only minimal protest. Within weeks of proposing the dissolution of their marriage of almost forty years, John Mangione moved to a small, dim, one-bedroom apartment. He took with him only the barest belongings: some clothes; important papers for work; and a few small objects that meant something to him, such as a paperweight his father had given him for Christmas years before.

For a while he telephoned Theresa on a regular basis, checking in with her and inquiring whether she needed money. He also called his children now and then, something he had stopped doing altogether when Danny became ill and he felt himself alienated from the family. Then the phone calling ceased. Theresa took to phoning him at work, since he either was never home or chose not to answer the phone. People at the office notified Mark and Steve that their father looked tired and ill. It seemed as if he had aged ten years in a few months. No one at the company knew of John and Theresa's separation, and whatever friends knew, they never revealed. But everyone who saw John Mangione remarked on his sickly pallor and loss of energy and appetite.

One night at Angela's, after a rare and tense family dinner, Marco, no longer able to take his father's bitter silence, finally erupted:

"Have you got one topic in the world we can talk about? How about college swimming championships, is that safe enough? I mean, how far away do we have to go? You have worked very hard to destroy Daniello's memory, but it isn't taking hold so don't get excited about it. People either laugh at you or pity you. I don't feel either. I think you should be punished for what you did. I don't care what the guy was or what he did or with who. He was my brother, your son. He even happened to be your father's grandson. You want to pretend he was never on this earth, that he was never born, go ahead, have a good time. There was never any Daniello Mangione. I don't know why people keep coming up with that name. I know I only had one brother and Stefano only had one brother. So who's this Daniello guy people are always talking about, and crying about? Nuts, huh? All these people going to church, going to a cemetery, putting flowers on a grave of a person who isn't there. Can you imagine all these people paying respects to a man who never even existed? Talk about weird.

"God will punish me for this. But I wish you were in that grave for the way you acted, not him. You deserve to be there, not him. He never did a bad thing to anyone. He never said a bad thing about anyone, and he could have, the way you treated him. He could have said plenty, and don't talk to me about what the Bible calls a sin. You want to talk about sinning? How many times did Angela have to make an excuse for you when he asked are you going to visit? You don't think that tore her up? You don't think that maybe that made death come a little bit quicker? You played it the way you wanted to, but you played it wrong. Real wrong, and God can punish me for saying it, but you belong in that grave, not your son. Your son. You hear that? Your son! And my brother."

With the members of his family watching, John Mangione never said a word. His face remained free of expression. He just stood there a few feet from his son, looking old. Marco could only shake his head. Angela wept. Theresa's shoulders were shaking, and Stefano went to put his arm around her. Angela's son Tony bounced a large blue-and-yellow beach ball.

Marco began walking out of the room, muttering to himself, "It's like talking to a rock. The man's got the feelings of a rock." Suddenly he stopped and turned back for a last look. "I got news for you. I don't have no father anymore. You want to talk disowning, I'm disowning." He studied his watch. "As of right this minute, I don't have a father. They might," he went on, glancing at his sister and brother, "but not me. You want me back, you show it by taking Daniello back. When he's your son, I'm your son. That's the deal!" Then he was gone, and the family heard his angry footsteps thudding down the stairs toward the front hall.

For the Mangiones, time had come to be measured around the events of Daniello's life and death. It was so many years since he'd moved out, so many years since he'd learned he had AIDS, so many years since that one hopeful autumn remission. It was now almost three years since his death.

Marco had taken charge of planning a small Sunday graveside ceremony to mark the third anniversary. Afterward, friends were invited to Angela's for refreshments. More than forty people accepted the invitation.

On the Thursday before the ceremony, someone telephoned Theresa to say that John had been absent from work for five days without notice. This launched a series of phone calls, with no one able to offer information about his whereabouts, although some people commented on how sickly he'd seemed the last time they had met. It was suggested that the police be notified, but Marco and Stefano said the first job was to go to John's apartment. Marco hadn't visited the shabby dwelling in months; Stefano had never been there and was shocked by the condition of the neighborhood and building.

The front door to the building was unlocked, and the halls gave forth a rancid odor and mustiness. The apartment door was also unlocked, and the apartment itself was completely empty except for a few pieces of functional furniture. The closets, bureaus, and few kitchen cupboards held only a few objects and a small amount of clothing. The room looked as if only transients lived there.

The sons found only two objects of note in their father's home. The paperweight his own father had given him rested on a large notebook with a black grainy cover that looked to be old leather. Inside were unused bank checks as well as the carefully recorded stubs of all their father's expenses of the last years.

In the light of late morning they read through the only written history of their father they would ever know. All the usual expenses were represented: rent, utilities, telephone, taxes. But there was something else. John Mangione had been donating money regularly to AIDS and cancer research programs. It was evident that he had deprived himself in order to meet Theresa's expenses, give money to the children, and still have money for these charities. More surprising, the first contributions were dated before Daniello's death.

A few more phone calls, and John Mangione was located. He had been admitted to a city hospital several days before, suffering from severe chest pains. A few days after his family found him, he died of congestive heart failure, with his wife and children at his bedside. After a requiem mass, he was buried next to his youngest son, Daniello. It had been one of his last requests.

KIDNAPPER

NO ONE who knew Norman and Bernice Kehlman would ever have believed that someday they would be divorced. For fifteen years most people called theirs a good marriage, but in private the Kehlmans were pulling away from each other. Only their three children witnessed it.

From the beginning, Bernice spoke to her husband about needing to lead her own life and not being tied down to housework and child care. Besides, as the children were growing older, they did not need her as much. Norman supported her. He cooked more, and they ate out, even though his salary as a book designer hardly afforded the family luxuries. Gradually he assumed responsibility for the laundry and for cleaning the house as well. Bernice began to speak of taking a job. She scanned the newspapers, but few positions seemed promising. She went for interviews, but these only convinced her that the right thing had not yet come along. During this time she began gaining weight and the children teased her about it.

Eventually she decided to return to school as a special student. She signed up for a full course load but could not handle the pressure of the work. Unable to admit this to Norman, she withdrew. For weeks no one said anything about school, but Norman watched for signs of shame or sadness. There were none. In fact, Bernice seemed void of any feelings.

Then one morning, with the children at school and Norman finishing some work in the living room before going to the office, Bernice walked up to him and slammed her fist on the desk. A vicious argument ensued, and within weeks the Kehlmans had arranged for a legal separation.

In time, Norman rented a small apartment near his office. He was unhappy there, although his friends helped him to make it pleasant. He also began seeing a psychiatrist. Whereas once he had been sympathetic to his wife's needs and behavior, he now realized he was filled with fury. Bernice, on the other hand, seemed happier than she had ever been. Norman suggested that they try living together again, but she refused, insisting it would do them good to meet other people. Anyway, she already had met another man. Eventually Norman found a woman who treated him kindly and even talked about wanting to marry him. He told her he could never again consider marriage. All he thought about was custody of his children.

A year after the separation, Bernice's lawyer notified Norman that divorce proceedings had commenced. At that point, Norman Kehlman's smoking and drinking increased. His fingers became stained yellow and brown, and his hands shook slightly. Although his weight had not changed since his college graduation eighteen years before, his face appeared drawn. In his own words, he was a "desperately angry, desperately sad man, getting old faster than anyone in the world."

In light of Bernice's frequently irrational behavior in front of the children, it seemed doubtful to Norman that any judge would grant her custody. "Push for the divorce," he was advised by a neighbor who frequently heard the couple arguing. "You can't miss. Everybody will testify you're a great father and that she's mad, out of her mind nuts!"

"Don't say that," Norman admonished him. "You've only heard my side. She's still my wife. It's not about her. All I want is the kids."

The acrimonious divorce negotiations stormed on for months. At last, a court date was set. Visiting the children as often as possible, Norman had made certain that his wife would not bring them to the first hearing, but she arrived with eleven-year-old Gerard, the oldest son. After consulting with her own attorney, she decided to send the boy home with a family friend.

Although everyone could observe the anger between the litigants, the legal process began politely enough. The lawyers calmly presented their arguments. Because of the complexities of the case, it was continued one month, but the second session turned out to be even more heated than the first. Repeatedly reprimanding the lawyers and the Kehlmans, the judge concluded the proceedings with these words:

"Sometimes I can make an argument that a husband doesn't care about his children. In this case I cannot. And in some cases it can be demonstrated that a mother is unfit to care for her children. In this case, again, I cannot. It's a new time, and men like you, Mr. Kehlman, are challenging the custody laws and traditions. In the old days, it was a foregone conclusion that mothers got the children. Let me say, too, Mr. Kehlman, that I am impressed by your willingness to consult a psychiatrist. Some people avoid this because it can be seen as jeopardizing their case. In fact I want to recommend to Mrs. Kehlman that she follow your example."

One could see the judge looking about the courtroom as if searching for the right words. "Well, then," he resumed, "having indicated that I lean to the ways of the past, I have decided to award custody of the three children to Mrs. Bernice Kehlman. I have considered your challenge, Mr. Kehlman. Times are changing, but I continue to believe that half any mother is better than a whole father. You will be able to visit them . . ."

Norman Kehlman barely heard the details of visitation rights (one day a week, three weeks in the summer, an alternate holiday schedule). Bernice's expression never changed. She appeared tired, bored. Norman begged his attorney to appeal the decision. Charlie Donovan tried to silence him, assuring him that appeal was a normal step, though not one about which he should feel too confident. Within minutes, the proceedings had concluded.

Outside in the corridor Norman walked up to his ex-wife. "Congratulations," he said bitterly.

"For what?" she muttered. "What did you expect him to say? Men are all alike. They put kids with their mother; that's all they know. Didn't you get what he was doing? He gave you freedom. Go on, you've got what you wanted. You got your freedom."

"You mean you didn't even want the kids?"

"What's the difference what I wanted. I got them. Men plant them, and men make sure you never get rid of them!" With that, she walked away.

Weekly visitation proved insufficient for Norman. That his day to have the kids was Sunday made it even worse, for Bernice had enrolled the children in Sunday school. A day together meant the afternoon and dinner. Gerard, furthermore, wanted to go to sporting events, Annette preferred museums and movies, and Billy didn't like any of these options. Still, they wanted to be with their father and did what they could to be close to him.

An additional problem was Norman's living arrangement. As alimony and child support cut deeply into his income, he barely could afford even his small one-bedroom apartment. Having the children there was difficult for him, as was hearing their constant references to their mother's house as "home."

As he took a walk one evening a peculiar thought came to Norman Kehlman. Something about being a father had prevented him from openly feeling love for his children. No matter what he said publicly, he had accepted the traditional notion that fathers come last. He actually had been unaware of the intensity of the love he held for the children. It had never been Bernice he wanted. Whether or not he had been part of the children's lives when they were little now seemed irrelevant. What mattered now was that he needed to be with them.

The following afternoon he left work early and drove to the front gate of Annette and Billy's school. As always, the two children came out together. When they heard their father's call, they raced toward the car and embraced him. Then they went for ice cream and a drive. Upon bringing them home, he cautioned them not to say anything to their mother and to tell Gerard "to be prepared to be kidnapped some afternoon."

"When will you do it again?" the children wanted to know.

"You never know. Might be tomorrow," he teased. He hugged them and watched them disappear into the house.

The kidnapping routines continued for months. There was no one at home to care for the children, and as Bernice was away when the children returned from school, there was no way she could know how late they had been, or why. Their disinterest in dinner easily was explained by their regular habit of cheating with afternoon sweets. Indeed, the children did not regularly dine with their mother, who now often went out in the evening.

When, finally, Bernice did learn of the kidnappings, she forbade the children to see their father except for the appointed Sunday afternoon visits, but they chose to disobey her. She telephoned Norman and warned him. Charlie Donovan, too, made him promise to cease the kidnappings. The three August weeks with his children only reaffirmed his need to see them, though, and fueled his anger at his ex-wife and the judge.

With the arrival of winter, Norman appeared at the school gates less often. The children grew upset with him. They interpreted his absences as meaning he had lost interest in them and decided that their mother, finally, was winning what they always called "the battle." Nothing Norman said could dissuade them. He spent all his money on the children, treating them to lavish Sunday night dinners and constantly buying them expensive gifts that he could not afford.

"I thought this divorce thing was going to break you, Dad," Gerard said to him one night. "But you're really rich! You're richer than this guy mom's been seeing."

"What's he like?' Norman asked.

"He's terrible. She'll marry him, though."

"Why do you say that?"

"She doesn't want a good man. She wants someone she can push around."

"He's a hamburger," Annette said. The children laughed.

"I don't like to hear you talking about your mother that way," Norman reprimanded them gently.

"Come on, Dad," said Gerard. "You don't love her anymore."

Norman was surprised by his own response: "I do love her."

"Dad," Gerard groaned. "If you loved her you'd still be married to her, and we'd all be living together."

"Well, that's not exactly . . ." Norman began hesitatingly.

Christmas that year was a shabby, unsettling affair. Norman arrived at Bernice's home carrying presents, but she refused him entrance. When he protested, she motioned for help. "My former husband in one of his scenes," is the way she introduced Frank Tennenberg to her ex-husband. "I guess we'll just have to call the police." As Norman turned to leave, he heard her add, "You get them on Easter."

That spring, walking with a friend not far, actually, from Gerard's school, he said, "They do so much talking about women's liberation. But men are going to have to start to fight. We've all been brainwashed by this mother-child business. The whole world thinks men don't want to be fathers; all they want to do is work. You know who makes it hard for me, is the guy who lets his wife do everything for the kids. He's the one who makes that tradition impossible to bust. I can't break it. My wife is afraid to be without them.

"So what do I do? I go to court, I keep hoping something will make her change her mind, but it's got to be more than that. America has to change its mind. The first breakthrough was the acceptance of divorce. Now it's child custody, and so far, everybody's just gone along with history. Children come from the mother, so you give them back to the mother. The traditional family still exists: Pop works, Mom tends the kiddies. That's not changing. What we have to do is start thinking about the way people are, not about *marriage* all the time. One family, the kids go with their mother; another family, with the father, even though the father's working and the mother has no career. *That's* what liberation's all about.

"I'm the goddamn guinea pig in this thing. I know damn well that it's on my case that the next case gets tried. All those scenes in court where she wasn't even happy she won, that's part of it. But the big part is what happens to me? Do I go back to court? Do I ever get my kids legally? Do I kidnap my kids?"

Norman Kehlman wiped the perspiration from his forehead. Then he looked about and ran his hand along a row of shrubs, just beginning to blossom. He squinted at the blond oak door of a house across the street as if he were listening for some sound or other signal.

"Does he ever get his kids legally?" he whispered. "When they answer yes to that one, the gates will open. Women will feel better about it, too. They'll stop pretending they have to be mothers every minute of their lives. That's the biggest hurt of all: That she feels she *has* to love them. Strange, isn't it, how your parents teach you that if you don't do well in school and come out with a good job and a fat income you're unsuccessful? The only way to be unsuccessful is to fail with your children. There's not a thing I can do to put my life back where it belongs unless I have my children. She knows that. That's what she's breaking me with, and the courts go along with it. I'm fifty years too soon. I'm a goddamn male suffragette for the family. How can it be that men always come first, and fathers always come last?"

He looked up, suddenly focusing on the houses and small front lawns that lined the street.

"Where are we?" asked Norman. "We near my kid's school? Gerard goes to school around here. Two blocks, that's all. You see how it is with me? I take a walk with nothing on my mind and end up heading for them. That's the way it'll be the rest of my life. Twenty-five years from now I'll be walking around near their homes, peeking over bushes like these to get a glimpse of my grandchildren. Walking and peeking. And kidnapping. You add them up and you get a father who, if he behaves himself, gets to see his kids on Sundays for a few hours, three weeks in the summer, and alternate Easters!"

III

SCHOOL
PERIL

As I mention in the preface, I've never forgotten my father's admonition to always undertake research with life-and-death matters at the heart of it. Although his work as a physician clearly dictated this sort of philosophy, I know that research on education also meets my father's standard: there is no doubt that school can destroy people, adults and children alike, just as it can redeem people and breathe life into them as no other institution can. While national attention often is paid to the murders committed on school grounds, the fact is that life and death are played out every day in the schools of this country. The writings of Jonathan Kozol, William Ayers, Robert Coles, Sara Lawrence-Lightfoot, Neil Postman, Herbert Kohl, Alfie Kohn, and George Dennison document this fact over and over again.

The delicate balance confronted by schools is that between development of the mind and development of the personality and character. This combination of cognitive, affective, psychosocial, and intellectual skill development would seem to be more than any one school could ever accomplish, and yet these are the skills that children require in order to become good citizens and complete human beings.

Craig Ramsey and Sharon Landsman Ramsey have listed six psychosocial "priming mechanisms" that they believe reveal not only the intellectual requirements of school, but the nature of the arena in which these skills must be born: encouragement to explore the environment; mentoring in basic cognitive and social skills; celebration of new skills; rehearsal and expansion of new skills; protection from inappropriate punishment and ridicule for developmental advances; and, finally, stimulation in language and symbolic communication.[1] As one studies the Ramseys' list, one recognizes how schools indeed have the power to destroy or redeem the child.

On an individual level, schools are commonly expected to pick up the pieces of irresponsible or inadequate parenting or, more generally, protect the lives of imperiled children. In fact, this has become automatic for many schools. Newspapers are filled with accounts of their offering programs (that many contend should be taught at home) on subjects such as sexual behavior, substance abuse, the effect of divorce on families, violence prevention, sexual harassment, hate crimes, gender issues, racism, sexism, health issues of boys, health issues of girls, and pregnancy prevention. There is now even a movement afoot for schools to offer courses on parenting. All this, and driver education, too!

While many people advance reasonable arguments for abolishing schools of education because they fail to produce people of sufficiently high academic quality and focus too much attention on the tools of the teaching trade, rather than on the intellectual substance of classrooms, the list of requirements for teachers grows almost exponentially by the year. In addition to possessing competence in an academic discipline, a teacher now has to be an expert on psychological, social, medical, and legal matters of all varieties. In some schools, a teacher's commitment to mathematics, history, or languages seems almost incidental, given the amount of hours he or she spends on the aforementioned (life or death) extracurricular activities.

If individual lives are damaged or resurrected in schools, so, too, are ideologies, policies, and entire social movements. Almost every major social revolution is played out, or fought out, in classrooms. The busing movement for racial integration put schools on center stage in America. Affirmative action surely is played out in the labor market, but its focus has always been schools. The battle for Title IX entitlements, ensuring scholarship money for female college athletes, centered around schools. Although national laws have been instituted to protect the rights of people with disabilities, once again the focus of the social movement for inclusion has been the school.

A new movement for standardized testing and a resultant ranking of students, teachers, and entire school systems is underway, for an argument has been made that children also are imperiled when they do not receive the very best education. Only naturally, there has been an attack against this position by those who suggest that no tests accurately measure what the proponents of standardized testing seek to know. Teachers want accountability but complain that teaching to tests makes their jobs nearly impossible or, if possible, limited and uncreative.

But consider the personal aspect of standardized testing, for example, the child who *knows* he is stupid because the tests say so, even as the educational community debates the validity and value of intelligence tests, along with fundamental definitions of intelligence. Whereas some people cling to the notion that intelligence can be defined by literacy and mathematical skills coupled perhaps with some commonsense wisdom, others rejoiced at Howard Gardner's assertion that there are seven inherent intelligences existing to some degree in all people.[2] (Recently he added an eighth.) Suddenly the athlete, dancer, and painter could be as honorable as the scientist and literary critic. And when the special education community introduced the concept of learning disabilities, a whole other population of students and their families was somehow ennobled. The child wasn't lazy or purposely inattentive, after all. Rather, he had a lazy cortex caused in part by the shortage of a natural substance called dopamine.[3]

For years in this country, governmental records listed the fundamental purpose of schools to be socialization. The single most important goal of the school was to turn children into civilized, productive citizens. At one level, this meant that getting children to stop chewing gum and running in the halls was seen as important as their becoming competent in mathematics. Surely this was the case for girls, for whom manners were deemed more valuable than arithmetic. At another level, socialization can be viewed as character development, which is essential if a country is to remain a civil democracy.[4] In other words, there appears to be a tension, as Amy Gutmann has written, between "living a good life according to one's own best lights and being educated as a democratic citizen with civic responsibilities such that everyone is able to live a good life."[5]

The only problem in these early days of educational reform was that too many people were left out of the mix. Or if they attended school, as, of course, the law required, they were too easily neglected, ignored, or outright dismissed. It was a group of young people called, interestingly enough, young Arabs, who ran about the streets of developing urban areas, committing what we now call minor property offenses, that encouraged authorities in Chicago to launch a juvenile justice system a little more than a century ago.

Now, in an era of inclusion, student rights, and standardized testing, another problem emerges that only a few people, such as David Steiner, attempt to address.[6] If all people are required to attend schools, if all people are truly considered part of the commonweal, and in strict moral terms it is proclaimed imperative that all receive the finest education, who will perform society's menial jobs? How is it that following this inclusive ideology, we continue to have, as Katherine Newman documents, vast populations of people, some of them young, continuing to constitute the working poor of America?[7]

The school will continue to be the playing field, level or unlevel, of the democracy. Teachers and administrators know this fact well, and students learn it at surprisingly young ages. For all we know, the school is properly designated the centerpiece of the commonweal, which makes one wonder about the country's priorities. Apart from the literal and symbolic meanings of starting teachers' or long-term career teachers' salaries, consider that one professional basketball player will this year be paid almost $14 million. In the same city in which this man will perform, a summer program designed to tutor thousands of children so that they can be promoted to the next grade is in jeopardy, because the state government could not come up with the program budget of $7 million.

Few scenarios better illustrate the notion of the ecology of peril, or the fact that what goes on in the greater society and culture directly affects the sacred acts of teaching and learning. Perhaps this is what my father had in mind, what determines whether students and teachers will flourish or perish. As William Ayers wrote, "Education, then, is linked to freedom, to the ability to see and also to alter, to understand and also to reinvent, to know and also to change the world as we find it."[8]

SCHOOL CLOSING

AN EDUCATIONAL battle has been waging in the home of Donal and Regina Stafford. The family was hit hard this summer by the closing of their son's high school. Budget cuts, they learned, were causing several of the city's schools to be closed, and seemingly overnight, Delmont's school was shut down. Regina Stafford likened hearing the news to a woman's going for her annual physical examination and learning she had three weeks to live.

Delmont Stafford, just turned eighteen, described himself as a good and earnest student. He'd never thought too much about college until Mrs. Treadway, his English teacher in his junior year, planted a seed in him. Or perhaps her belief in him encouraged a hope he secretly had held. Then, with the school closing and the Staffords dashing around to find any place where Delmont might feel happy, all the residents of the three-family house on Cornwall Street felt themselves to be unraveling.

"I'm not sure that a divorce wouldn't have been easier for this family," Regina said, shaking her head and wiping perspiration from her neck. "Everything we worked to achieve, there it goes, knocked out in one punch. There have to be sure things in life. You have to be able to take some things for granted. You can't live wondering whether the roof's going to fall in on you, or the road underneath's going to give way.

"The moment you give birth to a child you think schools. Where can we live where the schools are good? Families like ours make all sorts of compromises. You live where you can. You live with your own kind, or where you come from. Whoever dreamed that a school this size in a city big as this would suddenly just up and go 'way. We're stranded now. It's one thing if we move them and they feel dislocated. But this is like we all got abandoned. All this tax money paid and we're going out hunting for new schools. And the boy has to find a whole 'nother job and apply to college. I went to bed one night and put on the television and heard the man say, 'City school closings, details coming right up.' They mentioned all these different schools, but I never imagined even once it would be us. You got to learn it from television. Nobody warned us. Nobody mumbled a word. I'm lying there in my bed, watching the television, and I see the words come up on that screen, and they say our school. In a year, maybe it'll shut down, I say. No sir. It's this minute, and I've got a boy going there, a good boy, and he's about to start his senior year!

"I know this would insult folks, but some folks could understand. I heard those words on television and for one moment I felt like the government had just come into my home and told me my son had been killed in a war. That's the way it hurts. Like we had been robbed, or our house burned down to the ground where you couldn't see nothing of it anymore. I feel invaded. My body's hurting from it. Why live here? Why we have to put up with this? Why even go through the trouble of making a good home for a child, work like a dog on your marriage, push your values on your children? Doesn't the government have to support you, stand with you? Is it always us against the world? That's how I feel this thing. The big against the little. We can't do nothing about it. The meeting at the school was a farce. Parents protested, of course they protested, and all those folks listened to us. But the decision was made. No one's going to change their minds. Someone has to go, and we're it.

"So many parents have so many worse things to contend with. I'm embarrassed saying this. But this is a deep wound, and it's unnecessary. Those folks have mismanaged the whole educational system. You don't see private schools closing like this without warning. You don't see suburban schools closing up. We pay the same percentage of taxes as those folks—more, probably. Why do we deserve this? At least they could have closed it out over a period of time. Two years, three years. You don't take a group of seniors and throw them out on the street. How they all going to fit in anywhere in a year! All their grades going to drop. All their chances and opportunities going to drop.

"This isn't a challenge; it's an unjust act. I'm sure they care. I can't see them being happy making these plans. But they don't ever pay the price of their faults. We do. We always do. Same people always do. You just begin to find yourself, get yourself settled, and they take it away from you, like they just don't want you to make it too good. Our first son, our first child. You put so much into him. It's like he's carrying the family to the next place.

Now they go and cut off his legs and tell him, 'Oh, you'll find a place to stand somewhere else.'

"I don't want to feel I don't have legs, or that my children don't have legs. I know I'm insulting some families when I say it, but it feels this way. They let some children run, but when we start running they close us off and demand that we crawl. That school was hardly outstanding, but it was ours. There were good families, and good teachers. We were together. Now we're all by ourselves again. No central issue, no school, no community. It's like a big plane crash. I'm going to say it: it's like we've been hit in the face with a plane crash. Once again the little people are told they got to crawl, and the big people spend their money getting their children tutored for the college boards. Who helps us now? Who's ever helped us?"

Delmont Stafford heard all of his mother's outcries. He attended the meeting with representatives of the city's school committee during his junior year. Sitting in the poorly lit auditorium with his friends, he found himself, surprisingly, free of anger. It was sadness that he felt, as if someone had died. He looked around for Mrs. Treadway, his English teacher, and as the acrimonious debates continued, he remembered his friends poking fun at her. They mocked her for her flamboyant clothes, the handmade jewelry, and her peculiar outbursts when she felt excited by some piece of literature. "Weirdo" and "goob" were the words his friends used to describe her. Delmont laughed with them; he was careful never to reveal his true feelings about the one person in the school who had given him what he called a "belief in his brains."

He had always been somewhat shy, a fair athlete, and a mediocre student, but then came Mrs. Treadway's required English course. It began with George Orwell's *Animal Farm* and Mark Twain's *Huckleberry Finn*. The students protested the choices. Offering superficial arguments, they charged the books were irrelevant, racially offensive, and just plain too hard. Mrs. Treadway approached Delmont after the first written assignment, on which he had received a D, and asked what he thought of the readings. Were they understandable? Were they in any way relevant and useful? He lied. He told her he enjoyed them. Mrs. Treadway just looked at him and grinned. "You lie terribly, D," she said, using his nickname to provoke him. "Read them again and write the paper again. We'll forget the grade."

"Yes, ma'am," he had whispered, heading quickly for the door. He dreaded the thought of not only repeating the work, but trying to convince his mother that Mrs. Treadway actually was giving him a second chance. No way my mother's going to believe me, he thought. She's going to call the school, or worse yet, she's going to pay a visit to that woman. She's always meddling in my life. She says she knows she does, but she still don't stop it. Promises me every day to stop, but she never does. Woman meddles too much in my life.

Mrs. Stafford did call the school to make an appointment with Mrs. Treadway. Delmont was ordered to attend the meeting. When the English teacher confirmed Delmont's report, Mrs. Stafford remained silent. She simply tucked away the teacher's words about her son as a woman might hide her mother's favorite broach for safekeeping. Never to be worn, it was meant only to be kept safe, like a promise. The promise offered by Mrs. Treadway was the assurance that Delmont was able and intelligent and if he used his mind, a new sense of life would be his. The promise was college, a respectable career, and personal gratification of a sort he might not now recognize.

His mother and he sat quietly in the English room. Mrs. Treadway did all the talking after Mrs. Stafford discovered her son had told the truth. Delmont alternated between feeling bored and somehow sensing his life was being changed. For once, nobody was arguing, and nobody was complaining or finding fault with an unseen system or directing their fury at unknown officials and administrators. Mrs. Treadway was drawing a plan, a simple human blueprint, and all three people sitting in a classroom in a large high school—that nine months later would be shut down—knew that one woman had succeeded another in directing the intellectual life of a quiet young man. One form of energy had given way to another, and a high school junior felt lighter, unburdened, hopeful.

Mrs. Treadway never did enter the school's auditorium that evening. Delmont would not see her again. If he continued with his work successfully at a new school, it would be without her, although he maintained a vision of her showing up in his new school. The politicians took it away, he thought as the raucous debates went on into the night, but Mrs. Treadway with her amazing clothes and jewelry gave it all back. She gave it to several of his friends as well, he had discovered as his junior year progressed. Each of them reacted to her as he had. All the families, all the students, like his mother, silently indebted. "Bless that woman," Mrs. Stafford had said on more than one occasion. "She's the one going to get him through."

Delmont Stafford spoke little about his school closing and his anger, disappointment, and fright. "I'll get it together," was about all he said to those inquiring about his feelings. "Got it together once. I'll be prepared."

Late in August, when it was still not decided where he would attend school, and his mother was venting her anger at the city's school committee so vehemently that Delmont couldn't speak with her, a postcard arrived from Yugoslavia. An aerial view revealed a charming seaport town with glistening blue water and handsome sailboats. The message on the back read;

Dear Delmont. Schools can close or be closed in your face, but they cannot close your mind. It is too good and too strong. The mind can withstand events like these, for it is made of endless strength. Count on that as I count on you. Love, Ellen Treadway

"Bless that woman a thousand times," Mrs. Stafford whispered, holding the card tightly and reading the message over and over again. Delmont left the room, using the excuse that he had to blow his nose. Moments later he returned and announced he was leaving for work. "Turn around," his mother ordered with a smile. He grinned at her and obediently shoved his behind in her direction. Poking out of his back pocket was a copy of Orwell's *1984*. A ragged bookmark revealed him to be more than three-quarters finished. Then he left for work.

"Boy's going to make it," Regina Stafford said proudly, standing in her small kitchen. Reflexively she straightened a pile of newspaper accounts of the school closings, tapping the edges to get them even. When this was done, she carefully tucked them into the pages of a hardcover copy of *Huckleberry Finn*. She never stopped smiling.

MY BROTHER'S KEEPER

BILLY BIGNELL'S mother is the first to say her seventeen-year-old son is lazy. She has practically put herself in the grave, she sighs, trying to get him to study. Every method known to man has been attempted, and still the main event of the day is getting him out of bed in the morning. Perhaps if school started at 3:30 in the afternoon, Billy Boy, as he is called by his four sisters and one brother, could make it on time. At least he'd have a fighting chance.

In middle school, Billy Boy got away with absences and missing home-work, but now in high school the repercussions have become serious. Billy Boy has been in trouble in every class, even gym, for which he just doesn't show up. Well, he shows up, but, coincidentally, it is usually just as the phys ed teacher is blowing the dismissal whistle. "The kid doesn't even get to the cafeteria with the rest of the students," one of his teachers observes. "As things stand now, there's no way the kid's going to make it through high school much less amass any record that'll allow him to move on to anything productive. Threats haven't worked, goading, urging, prompting, scaring, encouraging, the creation of rewards, nothing!"

Billy's after-school rituals are just as irritating to his family as the ordeal of getting him to school in the morning. With his arrival home, they hear the thud of his heavy book bag being dropped in the middle of the entrance hall. The crash sounds the daily announcement of his distaste for learning. The bag itself, seemingly, contains all his earthly possessions. The next stop is the kitchen for something sweet to eat. Cookies land in his mouth two or three at a time, milk is gulped, more cookies are shoved into pockets, maybe some peanut butter is tongued off a knife blade, a swig of cola washes it down, and then it's back to the entrance hall, where the royal blue schoolbag looms as a dangerous obstacle.

The book bag is carried up the stairs and into his bedroom, which is so messy one cannot even identify what appears to be growing in the closets and dresser drawers. No matter. It is dropped, heavily of course, a second announcement of his love for school. Miraculously, it lies on the floor too far away to be reached by someone lying on the bed or sitting at the desk, and that's where it remains, a modern sculpture, until the next morning, when the identical cycle of motions is replayed in reverse. Occasionally the bag is opened and a textbook placed on the desk or pillow. Occasionally that same book is opened, but Billy Boy admits it is rarely read. Math homework does not get completed, because it does not get started. English assignments are not read, because the books remain in the bag. The pages of his note-books remain as pristine as when they were purchased.

So Billy Boy Bignell is failing all his courses. He also is failing to keep up the act that he is even making a serious attempt to stay in school. He also is failing with girls, he says, and with his brother and sisters, who have lost all respect for him. His father is furious; his mother angrily concerned, though not particularly vocal about it; and his school perplexed. They know he is smart, but they're losing patience. Since his parents forbid him to watch television until his homework is completed, and everyone in the house knows that the term "completed homework" is for Billy Boy an oxymoron, he kills time listening to music, reading comic books and magazines, and tinkering with models he assembled years ago. That's the background on Billy Bignell, a boy of average height and weight, with shaggy blond hair, who every day dresses in ragged jeans, sweatshirt, high-top basketball shoes, never tied, and a baseball cap, worn backward. He's a boy who couldn't care less, apparently, about sports, academics, world events, his teachers, his family, or his future.

When you meet Billy, all the descriptions seem accurate. His look does seem empty and vague, just as his sophomore English teacher suggested. And the guidance counselor was right: Billy does have a habit of looking away as if there were something significant he didn't want to reveal. Billy Boy, it seems, has a secret. He's paying the price, it seems, of having done something real bad. Billy Boy, it is suggested, is living as if he had placed himself under house arrest. He's a kid perpetually on self-proclaimed proba-tion, or do his habits constitute some version of a furlough program? His routine is almost prisoner-like, with his self-imposed repetitive schedule making it impossible for him to break out of his own morbid thoughts. If you asked ten people what thought comes to mind when they peer into his deep-set, green-gray eyes, they would offer all variety of responses, surely, but the word "death" would emerge in most of them. "He is either grieving for someone or wanting to kill someone," the guidance counselor reports. "Mourning most likely. Maybe for the opportunities he's wasting. Or perhaps he's depressed, or feeling sorry for himself. Well, sure he's depressed. Worse still, maybe he's thinking of killing himself."

So I ask him that the next time we meet, on the day, actually, I learned that his I.Q. score is over 130, and he looks back at me as if I had just mistaken a rap artist for Whitney Huston.

"That's all you worry about," he remarked. "No, I don't think about committing suicide. Jesus."

"Well, then, Billy Boy," comes my presumptuous, even smart-aleck retort, "if you aren't planning to take your own life, is there anyone in particular you'd like to kill?"

"I don't believe this. Are these really the top-of-the-line questions you have for me? My mother and my father. Isn't that what you're supposed to answer? Innocent kids in a playground. Asian kids, right? That what you think? The President. How 'bout McCartney and lower the number to two? You happy now? Yeah, I'm a real killer. Wanna see my gun collection, or you just wanna come over my house and smoke dope? I can't believe this. What, do you all talk to one another? Is that the way this works? You, my father, the guidance counselor, the faculty, the principal. Guilty 'til proven real guilty."

"It's no conspiracy and you're not up for trial and my questions don't sound like any prosecutor's questions. Good try, anyway. So who did you kill?" My questions pour out like hot steel. For reasons I don't understand, there isn't a shred of compassion in them.

Billy Boy stares straight ahead, expressionless. We stand near a play field where groups of small children are running through elementary soccer drills. Little legs weave in and out between bright orange traffic cones. High-pitched shouts and giggles reach us, noises of play, not serious athletics.

"You damn well know who I killed."

"I know nothing. Why are you putting yourself in jail?"

"'Cause I killed my brother."

"Huh? What brother? I know your brother."

"Not the one I killed, you don't know. Nobody knows him. Obviously. God. I can't believe this. This is really stupid. There it is. You got your big payoff. Okay? One of those kids out there yours?"

"No. One of them yours?"

"What the hell's that supposed to mean?"

"It means, don't change the subject."

"What do you want? You got the big payoff. You got your reward. You gonna take me in? You gonna book me, Danno? We go right from here to prison or do we pass go and collect a couple of bucks?"

"My goodness, a clever twist on a board game reference, no less," I shoot back.

"Feel nervous talking with a killer?" he asks.

"Terrified. Haven't trembled like this since Glenn Close flew up out of that bathtub."

"Hey, I saw that."

"Like it?"

"Not really. You?"

"Not really. Scared me, though. Don't change the subject."

"You think they should let me stand so close to all those kids? Hey, if I killed my brother, maybe I'll kill those kids there. Why the hell not. What have I got to lose. How come you're not afraid?"

"'Cause you don't scare me half as much as you scare yourself."

"You get that line from a movie?" He's smiling.

"Not even guys in Hollywood write that bad. Go on, killer."

His smile vanishes. I made a mistake using the word "killer."

"You didn't frisk me or anything. I could have a couple guns on me, right? So, you taking me in? Who's shooting who first? Got that in your script?"

It is strange in these moments how Billy Boy reveals more energy, more forcefulness, than anyone imagines he possesses. If one iota of his anger could be siphoned off and used to run the machinery of nightly homework, the kid would fly into the Ivy League college of his choice. He doesn't even show this much excitement champing cookies. Finally, my response. Mature, sophisticated, therapeutic, from a movie, from a gutter, heaven only knows, but it is genuinely felt.

"Why the hell don't you shut up and tell me what the hell you're talking about."

He looks surprised, happily surprised, like a kid learning he just got an A on an exam he was certain he had flunked. He had to flunk it because he had sabotaged himself by never cracking a book. Billy Boy is actually laughing. No one has ever reported him laughing. It's not a completely ingenuous laugh, filled as it is with some haughtiness, but he's laughing, and shouting.

"I love it! I love it when people say shut up and tell me something. I love it! And a sentence with two hell's in it. What the hell this, what the hell that. Who's supposed to be the kid here, me or you?"

"Definitely you. You're the one who bragged he killed his brother, not me. Let's hear."

"Screw you!" he barks.

"Clever retort."

"Kiss my ass."

"Oooo. I love it when you talk dirty. The story. Remember? Stop ducking out. Your brother. He's dead. You're alive. I'm waiting."

"Him dead," Billy Boy whispers, "me Tonto. No. I'm not Tonto. Tonto was good. I'm Hitler."

"At least. 'Cause you killed six million—"

He cuts me off, despising the sarcasm. "I killed, all right? One. Not six million, asshole."

"I'm waiting. One dead brother story coming up. Hold the dressing. I'm waiting."

"What the hell do you want, anyway?"

"The truth."

"You want the truth?"

"What is this, Echo Park?"

"Don't be cute."

"Don't be coy."

"What's that mean?" he asks, a suddenly interested student.

"You don't know what 'coy' means?" I ask.

"Like shy?"

"Close enough. Listen, kiddo, you tell me you killed your brother. I don't know anything about a dead brother. I've known your family ten years. Who, what, where's a missing brother? And you stand there laughing at me turning this into a preparation course for college boards. Don't be coy. Coy. Coy. It's the first syllable of coyote."

"Kiss off, asshole."

"How original. You don't know 'coy'? How 'bout 'epithet'? Your brother."

"You're not going to stop," he states flatly.

"I'm going to have five birthdays standing here. No. I'm not going to stop. You tell me the story, I'll give you the definition of 'coy'."

Billy Boy glances toward the soccer players. In that moment I cannot understand what is impelling us through this bitterly masculine yet peculiarly intimate dialogue. I tap him on the shoulder to remind him of the obligation I've imposed. "May I cut in?"

"S.I.D." That's all he says.

"You had a brother Sid?"

"You really are an asshole. S.I.D." This time he spells it for me. "Sudden infant death. His name was Theodore, like my father. He died before he even lived a single year. I guess my mother always wanted . . ."

It takes almost an hour for him to tell the story, what with all the side-tracks and tangents. The whole time, I remain silent. No questions, no prodding, no support. One group of soccer children leaves and another group of older children arrives while Billy Boy tells his secret story of a teenage boy filled with guilt, so convinced is he that he is responsible for his brother's death. It is primordial guilt that has spawned the sarcastic anger of our dialogue.

Emerging from his account, as a subtext, is the family silence that continues to surround the death. Mother and children refuse to mention the boy, or have they been forbidden to? Not a single reminder of the child remains in the house. Weeks later I hunt unsuccessfully for even one. Mother and father have never spoken about it, and it happened more than a decade ago. Eventually, mother will claim that father set the tone, by never mourning himself and never allowing anyone else to release his or her feelings. The minister who presided at the funeral will recall the family's admonition to him: the ceremony is to be brief, private, perfunctory.

I learn that while the father indeed discouraged any expression of emotion, he never stopped blaming Billy Boy for the death. No death, he says after years of silence, is inexplicable; no death is without cause or reason. Six-year-old Billy blew it when, for the only time in his life, he was called upon to show he could be responsible.

"Yes, in a sense he is a murderer, and he'll have to bear the burden forever," says his father. "Certain things you don't forget, just like certain things you can't forgive. That's what makes man different from animals. It's not murder as we usually think of it, but there's responsibility there, and someone has to pay. He's a nice kid, but someone has to pay for what wasn't done. It probably all sounds unreasonable or unfair, but aren't these the same words you would use to describe the death of a tiny baby? Aren't they? A couple of feet long, if that much, and it just dies, and no one hears it, or goes to help it? There's nothing more unfair or unreasonable than that. Someone had to lift that dead child out of its crib, you know. Someone had to do that. So someone could have helped it before. He knows who he is. He knows what he's done. The boy carried my name, you know. I didn't request it. It was my wife's idea. He carried my name."

Every word is perfectly enunciated; the tone is unwavering. The eyes are clear. The demeanor permits no argument.

Even more furious after my talk with him, the father forbids me to see or telephone Billy Boy. I have opened the one family vault that was meant to be sealed forever, no matter what the toll on a teenage boy of average height and weight and shaggy blond hair. Months pass. A family therapist barely is accepted by the Bignells. The sisters, and particularly the youngest daughter, Lily, beg for openness and regular family meetings. The mother attends therapy sessions sporadically; the father appears at the opening session and none after that. Billy Boy's appearances are a touch more regular than his school attendance would predict. The therapist offers to go to the family's home. Some of the members join her there; others continually report previous commitments. When Billy Boy attends, he makes his points and sheds some of his emotional weight, as he says. Still, not too much has been resolved. Nor, for that matter, has anyone been absolved, and it turns out all the children live with guilt.

The family is on hold, Billy Boy reports to me by letter. The meetings aren't working all that well. There is talk of sending him to boarding school, an idea that offends and terrifies him, but he'll abide by his parents' decisions. His mother now agrees with his father that I have stirred up trouble. Baby Theodore's death had been silent history until I came along and won the mind games with Billy Boy. What is dead and buried, they say, should have remained dead and buried. Both parents also come to resent the therapist and fire her. The act causes Billy Boy to telephone me more frequently. He follows my suggestion to keep a diary, some of which he photocopies and mails to me, and some of which he expands and turns into Ms. Dunham, his English teacher, for academic credit. Learning of Billy's family situation from me, with his permission, she has agreed to let him use this writing for his assignments, if he promises to do the course reading. She never tells anyone of the arrangement. The plan is paying off. By the middle of his junior year, Billy Boy Bignell is riding the success of his English literature course to modest and then handsome success in his other classes. The photocopies keep arriving. He jokingly suggests that everything would be easier if Ms. Dunham and I bought fax machines. He has taken to reading diaries of writers and autobiographical novels.

Eighteen months after our fateful, sarcastic, guilt-filled talk on the soccer field, a confrontation Billy now proposes has earned me the title, Doctor Compassion, I receive a note from him. It reads in part:

A− in English, B+ in History . . . I think I have a girlfriend. I can just hear you saying, what do you mean think? You either have one or you don't . . . C− in math, a GREAT accomplishment. Don't know Spanish grade yet. Don't know Spanish language yet either. Could be bueno . . . Coy, from the French, coi. Shy, bashful, demure, retiring. I was right. How come you didn't tell me? Maybe you didn't know either . . . I don't bang the book bag like I used to. I put it down gently, you'll be happy to know. I do open it. Every night. You won't be happy to know that once in a while I think about suicide, but I'd never do it . . . There is one funny thing I remember. You actually thought my brother's name was Sid . . . If I apply to college could you write me a letter of recommendation? Do you do those? But what could you say . . . I want to do this on my own.

The story seems to be moving toward a happy ending. Ms. Dunham and other teachers are enormously pleased, and so are his parents, who rescind the gag order and allow me to visit Billy. In fact, we rarely get together, which is all right, he says. Nor do I ever meet with Ms. Dunham, who has become very close with the family, until one damp, cool night, when all of us convene at the suburban hospital near the Bignell home. The family is in shock, although Billy appears strong and solid. Lily, who has been struggling with anorexia for several years, has made a suicide attempt and now, in that ironic phrase, fights for her life. She has told her sister Miranda that since Billy Boy is doing well and has "come out of it," she's going to face her own guilt. But she has no strength.

Mr. Bignell avoids looking at me. Sitting across the visitors room, his wife is sobbing. No one consoles or even touches her. The children appear frightened and helpless. Billy pats me on the shoulder when I enter. He wants to embrace me, but something stops him. We talk some about Lily, but mostly about insignificant things. Later he hands me an envelope containing a photocopy of an acceptance letter from a college. It has arrived earlier than expected. He manages a weak smile. "The doctor says she'll make it. She better. She didn't warn us."

For an instant my tone from our infamous talk at the soccer field surfaces. "Did you?"

"Don't be coy, now, Doctor Compassion. Don't be coy."

I confront him, colleague to colleague. "Bill, this one's not your case, either. You understand?"

"I know. I know."

"College. You just got into college, not medical school."

"I know. I know."

I catch Ms. Dunham's eyes. She appears uncomfortable and confused. "We're here if you need us."

"I know. Yeah."

For a long while, none of us says anything. The hospital noises seem to recede. Then Billy, his hair still wet from the rain, takes a step toward me. He looks hopeful, and whispers, "Hey, Tom. Think Lily would like our soccer field?"

TEACHERS AND STUDENTS

THE LIFE studies in this essay derive from some work I have done wherein I sought to discover in various schools who the teachers are who seem to matter to students, whatever the word "matter" means. After conversations with these teachers—and, surprisingly, there is usually some agreement in schools as to who these teachers are—I then came to learn what students matter to them. The following are examples from two teachers and two students, all of them dealing with academic issues and some deeply personal ones as well.

I

Mind Tricks

This young woman is a seventeen-year-old high school junior. Her school is located in an affluent suburban community on the East Coast.

"IT HAS BEEN a terrible time for me and my brother. My grandmother's death, and then the news, practically at the funeral, that my parents are going to get a divorce, although anyone could see it was coming. I saw it coming and then I told myself, like, I don't want to believe it, so it's not really happening. If you tell yourself something often enough, it, like, sort of doesn't have to happen. I can do this with my mind almost whenever I want. Something seems to be coming out that is true, and then, like, I can sort of push it back in and not make it go away, exactly, but make it feel like it isn't there anymore. Or at least it won't hurt me wherever it goes. It's like what you can do on the computer, putting a document away and if you don't label it, it's very hard to find, but it's there. The nerds have to come and find it for you.

"But it doesn't completely work, because all you feel is sad. I was sad for the whole year. I'd cry anywhere where it was safe, especially at school. I wouldn't let anyone see me. If people see you, just their looking at you tells you that your little mind tricks aren't working. If they worked, you wouldn't be sad and you wouldn't have to cry in front of anyone.

"But then I did cry in front of my history teacher. She came up to me after class, sort of making me feel she knew there was something terribly wrong, which there was, and telling me if she wanted to talk she would be there. Did I just say if *she* wanted to talk? I mean if *I* wanted to talk. So now, like, I was frightened. My mind tricks were breaking down. Then I would think, how come if she wanted to talk to me, all my parents wanted to do was send me to the shrink, which I absolutely refused to do? At first I thought that's what she'd say, too, so I told her nothing was wrong. That went on for a couple of weeks. Then I did the anger number. I told her I was getting tired of her trying to dig stuff out of me. What the hell business was it of hers, anyway! That lasted, like I say, for about two more weeks. Then I spent two weeks doing the promising number. 'Yeah, I'm going to talk to you. I swear to God.' She absolutely didn't fall for this one at all! I remember the way she'd tilt her head like she was saying to me, Play it your way; I'm not buying a thing.

"Then came that one Saturday night where I really worked myself up into a mind state. I was drinking, like I did most every weekend, a lot more after my father left our house. And this was the first night my mother went out on a date. And she was with a man our family has always known. She told me it wasn't a date; he was only accompanying her. But I saw them walk to his car. I swear to God, I've seen people get sexually transmitted diseases doing less than what they were doing to each other. Accompanying each other? Yeah, right.

"So, I don't like talking about it, but that's the night I cut my wrists, and like a fool, one of my ankles as well. Pretty smart, huh? Like brilliant? My ankle, like I had to be different. My brother found me in the bathroom and called my father, who told him to call 911. I don't want to talk about the hospital. Let's just say, after that was the week I talked to Miss Lippincott. We talked a lot then. We never left the school; she never embarrassed me. She never let on that anything was going on. And then one day she said, 'Don't you just once want to cry? I have seen people cry before, you know.' Then she said, 'If you cry, I might cry, too, and we might both feel better.'

"I loved her for that. She knew I couldn't do a stitch of work. She knew things were so wrong it was like I had showed up in class one day weighing two hundred pounds more than the day before and told her, 'Why do you think something's wrong? Nothing in the world has changed.' She knew. She always knew. But she waited for me to come to her. She must have known things would have to be horrible horrible before I'd go to her. But she waited. I wish boys knew how to wait like Miss Lippincott. I wish my mother were taking her course, too. She needs to know how to love people and how when you hurt them they just don't come running back to you. I sometimes think my mother thinks I'm a little puppy. You whack him, he cries and then he jumps right back in your lap. I know Miss Lippincott thinks of me as just a kid in school, someone very sad who's trying hard not to make problems for people, except of course that one time in the bathroom when I thought I couldn't make it another night.

"She's one smart lady. She said to me once, 'I'll bet your brother's hurting, too, and I'll bet he has no one. And I'll bet you haven't tried to reach out to him.' Which is true. I haven't. I have to keep up the big sister tough act with him, which is pitiful. Miss Lippincott, who in my mind I call Beverly, said she was a big sister and did horrible things to her brother. So she knows all about it. She doesn't see through me, though. That's not what it is. She takes the time to look at me and find a name for everything she sees. She's the only person who's ever done this. And she doesn't have to. No one ever has to. When parents don't, it sort of, like, proves no one has to."

II

Cave Woman

In her midthirties, and the teacher of the young woman we met at the outset of this chapter, this teacher was once headed for a career in biology, but later switched her studies to art history and then again to American and European history. She teaches in a suburban high school.

"I SUPPOSE one mistake I continued to make early in my career was to believe either that I had to love all my students, or that they had to love me. Perhaps I believed—no, I'm sure I'm believed—that I would gain their love by openly loving them. And I worked a great deal on trust building. I never shortchanged them academically, but there was something palpable I needed to play out. Perhaps I recalled incidents in my own schooling where I imagined the classroom would have worked so much smoother had the teacher genuinely cared for us. Maybe we would have looked more at her, less at the clock or the reproductions of the Van Goghs. For me, perhaps, the origin of all this is in my childhood, buried in there somewhere, although I have always believed mine was a happy childhood. I know I was loved. I can still feel it. It too is palpable.

"I lingered with this feeling, remains of the school day, just as I lingered with that infamous phrase, 'Bev isn't working up to her potential.' It was the curse of the private school I attended. They wanted so much for us: the teachers, our parents, the janitorial staff, our dogs and cats. They wanted us to touch the sun, burnt wings and all, and there I walked, poor me, never reaching my potential. I bought into this one as well. Palpable. Always I could have done better. There was always another rung, here and in heaven, I'm certain. Every report card, irrespective, seemingly, of the grades, 'Bev is wonderful to have in class, but alas, she isn't working to her potential.' I always remember my mother, poor dear, I'm not sure what she made of that description of her beloved daughter. She always would ask so plaintively, 'You think it's true?' I always wondered, Do either one of us know what this comments even means? My father, who was a doll, he used to look at the report card and say, 'If you ask me, I think you've got the cutest potential in America.' I have no idea what he was talking about, but I knew the comment didn't bother him anywhere near as much as it bothered me.

"In reaction to this, I now believe, I pushed for love. Potential be damned, I must have decided. Let them feel my love. Enough of the carrot-and-the-stick routine and that deadly, dry feeling of being ever so close but never quite there. Alas, by definition, by the way the entire system was set up, never quite there. If we loved each other, I must have reasoned, then potential is erased. In time I proudly took the low road, only to discover that it was the path to a personal freedom and, I strongly believe, a path to a liberation in the classroom and the establishment of an enormous challenge. The question now would become, Were the students living up to their *actual*? Were they truly themselves in the classroom, and was this a significant ideal? Potential be damned; let 'actual' take center stage.

"So it was no longer, Were they doing their best? but, Were they being their truest to themselves and to one another in my presence? Was I helping them get to the heart of the matter and what mattered to them? Instead of attempting to win their hearts and to give them my heart, instead of being broken-hearted if I sensed they had turned away from me, instead of having heart-to-heart talks, instead of never wanting to appear heartless, I wanted to use materials and my being, somehow—this all sounds so lofty, I know, but I feel it—to put them in touch with their own hearts.

"It comes down for me to helping students, through the use of books or movies, whatever—the medium is not necessarily significant—discover their voices, their hearts, their being. They don't always understand this when I try to explain it to them, which, as you see, I don't do all that well. So in the last couple of years, I think I don't really explain it; I just live it out with them, although I warn them that at times, human explorations of the voice and the heart are painful. Of course, I will read materials from *Facing History*. It is important history, not-to-be-forgotten history, but its value lies also in that it is heartbreaking history. Toni Morrison, and Hardy, at times it must be heartbreaking to be heart opening. One must cry and shout and whisper and laugh and cough and probably choke and merely mouth messages in order to find one's voice. And one's heart must race and pump and throb and almost stop completely in order to be in touch with it. The cardiologists have no monopoly on the heart.

"So the love days have ended; the heart and voice days have taken over. It is not always there, it does not always happen, but nothing is more exquisite for me and perfectly joyous than classes where people reveal or discover their voices, their hearts, their souls, and, of course, their minds. It cannot be done without purpose; it cannot be done without experiencing pain, or humiliation, or shame, or guilt, or anger. Often students enter these very moist and seemingly dreary caves very much on their own. A television show has evoked something. Sometimes we enter it through literature or a piece of history. Lady Day singing the blues, *The Civil War* series, a soldier's recollections, the movie *Glory*, *Facing History*, Anne Frank, 'whatever turns you on,' I always tell my students. Wear old clothes; the caves are rich with dirt and strange fluids. We read together, we read out loud, we write, we vocalize, we share some of it, we converse, we befriend, we explore sometimes very, very dark caves. And no one knows for sure in what cave the person sitting right next to him might be groping about in. I grope toward my actual because it is a far greater challenge than mucking about, hoping to reach some fantasized potential that someone somewhere has calculated out for me on a magic slide rule. Potential yields little more for me than frustration and inherent failure: I can never be what I can be. Hunting for the actual frees me, because I can get there, and nothing thrills me more. The facades disappear, the dances disappear, appearances disappear, and occasionally in class, we stand there before ourselves, before one another, having discovered what it is about ourselves that makes us genuinely human. What it is that makes us us. Someone in that room has heard her voice, her true God-given voice. Not her mother's or her father's or her teacher's voice, not the voice that was supposed to occur after the curriculum was mastered or the test scores came back, but *her* voice. And someone else has made a mystical connection with her heart. For all I know, her heart beats along with her own soul. She's breathing, she's speaking, she's learning, she's alive. For moments, something utterly true has taken over her and she emerges from the cave, just like Greek mythology would describe, covered with sweat, exhausted perhaps, but clinging to her books and music and movies, smiling, comforted, joyous maybe. Joyous hopefully. She emerges with goodness she can share and give to herself as well.

"The trip has been successful, for the actual has been discovered, the potential merely another actual awaiting its turn. It will come, ideally, in another class, next week, next month, next year—who knows, next life. I know it never comes automatically with the next curriculum or the next educational policy statement, unless I am guaranteed these statements and curricula have been designed, executed, and tested on real live teenagers in human caves.

"So, Mom, to answer your plaintive question, no, it's not true. I do have moments when I have reached my potential, and the feeling is nothing like anything I ever experienced in school and one I wish more than anything else you, of all people, Mom, would someday know."

III

Brain Dead in School

SPECIAL EDUCATION has made enormous strides in both diagnosing children's learning problems and treating these so-called disabilities. For many children and their parents, the mere act of diagnosis, the mere presence of a label for a problem like dyslexia or attention deficit disorder brings instant relief; at last someone knows what the child struggles with and how to help him or her. Best of all, in many circumstances, parents learn that their child's problem was not caused by them or something problematic in the family.

Whereas the moment of diagnosis may bring instant relief to family members, to a child the diagnosis can evoke a host of other feelings as well. No one, after all, knows what having a learning disability is like better than the child who struggles with it. No one knows better what it is like to feel that one is stupid. "Face it," an eighth grader told me once. "Some people are just born dumb! You wouldn't understand this because *you* went to college!" In response, the parents of the child with the learning disability find themselves starting every sentence with, "He is very intelligent, but . . . " or "I know she is extremely smart; it's just that . . . "

So while relief may come to anguished parents, the child, now newly tested, interviewed, and diagnosed, may feel something different. The child may feel that this new label confirms once and for all that he or she is either permanently brain damaged or, even worse, stupid and uneducable! How else might the child understand comments such as "The boy learns differently," "It just takes her longer," "It doesn't work with him as it does with others," "You have to understand there is a wide range of what might be called normal," "She will have to be taken out of some classes and tutored," and "We have wonderful facilities for children needing special education."

The diagnosis of learning disability or some associated disorder may represent the first painful step toward productive schoolwork and, most likely, a concomitant rise in self-esteem. Yet there is a moment, a significant one at that, when these children learn of the nature of their own mind and their capacity to think, reason, and learn.

We know a little bit about the moment when children are told that they have a particular physical illness, such as diabetes or cancer. We know because we frequently ask children what their feelings and reactions are. In the world of psychology, however, we don't always ask, and so we don't always know what the child may be thinking. How ironic is that we ask children to tell us what they are thinking only *after* they have learned, or *believe* they have learned, that there is something woefully wrong about the way they think.

Speaking below is a fourteen-year-old boy from an urban school who has just been told that his results on a series of psychological tests yielded the diagnosis of a severe learning disability.

"I TELL YOU something. I am all alone in that school. They can have every single damn one of those meetings and class discussions they want and I am still sitting there in the middle of them, talking on like they think is fine, and I am all alone. There ain't no one else in that school for me. I can be there, go to the classes, buy the books, obey all their rules, show them I respect them which I don't always, but I am alone. There isn't one teacher understands what I'm about. There isn't one teacher in that whole place has the slightest feeling for what I go through everyday of my life now. Not one. I go through the faculty list, too, man, I read their names out loud to myself. One after the other. What a laugh. There's people in that school think they got the inside track on me. They don't know how damn foolish they sound. They put their arm around me, they tell me all this shit about how I'm making progress; they don't know anything. If they did, they'd keep their mouths shut. I don't need no friends out of that place. I don't need more parents out of that place. Man, if they could just take one look at themselves for a minute in a mirror they'd get the surprise of their life. They'd see what I see every day, every day, and they'd damn well shut up for a couple of weeks at least.

"Who the hell those people think they are, trying to tell me about the way I operate! Now you just stop for one goddamn minute and you think about what I say. You think about how you got to lead your life to come to the point where you can sit in judgment of someone and tell him, now you, *you're* smart. But you, young man, you're *not* smart. Fact is, you are one of *the* dumbest people on the face of this earth. You heard your mother tell you, son, you are the smartest little boy in the whole wide world. Fact is, you heard that a whole lot growing up, you know what I'm saying? All the time, she gives you that big wide grin of hers and she tells you, you are the smartest young person on the face of this whole wide earth. But not those folks in the school. No sir. No, they can't do that. They got a whole different set of rules they going to be playing by. They got rules you never heard of. Don't worry about changing the out-of-bounds? They go changing every goddamn rule you lived by throughout your entire life. Got rules from your mother; no, they go and change them. Got rules from your grandmother; no, they going to change them, too. Everything's gone and been changed.

"You watched them, you sat there, big people telling me how I was dumb, how I don't think right, the way I'm supposed to, tell me I need to go to school on top of school just to fix my brain, but don't worry, you remember them telling me this? You remember that shit? Don't worry about nothing, it ain't your fault. It ain't nothin' you've gone and done. You can't blame yourself for this. It ain't your fault. Ain't got nothing to do with fault. You remember all that? You picture this group of murderers telling me this. That's all they are, you know? Murderers! No it ain't my fault. It's the *government's* fault. They go and decide, we're going to wreck a few kids' brains today, so let's see, why don't we just start in Hartford, Connecticut. No, make that Providence, Rhode Island. No, make that Warwick. And let's see now, how about that kid there with the black hat? He looks like a good choice. What'd they do, put something in the cereal? Stick some poison in my hat? What'd they mean, it ain't my fault? Sure it's my fault. And that's what they ought to tell me, too. It's *your* fault, man. You got bad genes. I mean, we're talking *bad* genes. You might be able to sing, man, you might be able to run, man, you might be able do this or that, but where it really counts, you got bad genes. We're talking defective city here, man. Ain't your fault. My ass, ain't my fault. No, it's Santa Claus's fault.

"I got no one now, man. They're all going to be looking at me now, feeling bad, feeling low, feeling sad, looking at the pathetic little kid with the word 'dumb' stapled to his forehead. Sorry for you, man. We'll do what we can. We'll read a lot slower for you, and talk a lot slower for you, and answer all the questions a lot slower for you, you slow-down man. Ain't your fault; it's the genes.

"I'm not going to cry about this, man. I am not going to fall apart over this. They can tell me all they want about kids like me getting help, kids like me doing well, kids like me doing just as good as anybody else. Well, they can kiss my ass, 'cause it's all a bunch of bullshit, man. My life is over and they know it. That's what that meeting in there was all about. It's going to be all over this school; everybody's going to know about me. I can't come back here. I can't show my face in this place no more. You can't just walk around in a school knowing what I know and what they know about me. Ain't they got no sense of shame! My mother, she can't even tell my grandmother what happened. She knows it's all over. She knows. Every dream she ever had, it's all gone. I can't make it no more. And she counted on this, too. I know that for a fact. She can't tell my grandmother. It's going to be the first secret those two ladies ever had together. What's she going to say to my grandmother, 'Ain't his fault'? 'It's just a case of bad genes.' Well, let's put it on the table, like they did upstairs. It's *my* fault.

"I got no dreams no more. They went right through that table, right through the floor underneath. They're floating away in the sewer now. They're in the sewer with all the crap from that school, and I have no one to talk to. Five fouls, baby, and you're gone. You're *gone*. You can cry all you want to the ref, but you are gone. You are one gone man! Five fouls, kid, sit the fuck down! And I don't even have no coach standing up there fighting for me. I'll be sitting down there at the end of the bench for the rest of my life.

"You think that's wrong? You think I'm exaggerating this thing? My brain don't work, man. There is nothing you can say can make that right. I am dead in school. I am *dead* in school. You hear what I'm saying to you? I am dead in school, and I can't make it right and neither can anyone else. And I *wanted* it. I wanted it, man. I don't care what happened before. I don't care what I said to you before, or anyone else. I wanted it. I *wanted* it all the time, I wanted it.

"I prayed I could make it in school. I ain't never told nobody this. I would get down on my knees next to my bed and I would pray that God could help me make it, 'cause I knew I couldn't do it on my own. That's how much I wanted it, man. And now it's all been taken away, 'cause there is something wrong with my brain. Bad genes. Why didn't somebody tell me that when your genes come out the bad way that you can't dream no more. That you ain't entitled to dream no more. Why didn't somebody spare me all these problems and tell me when I was a little boy, face up to it, little man, you can act all you want and you can show 'em that smile of yours you got from your mamma, and you can show 'em all that respect you learned from her, too, but you're dead in school, little man, and don't you forget it. You are one brain-dead boy in every school you walk into. You hear me? On the streets, you better go live it up, 'cause in the school you are dead! Brain-dead, body-dead, dead."

IV

Never Read Kafka

In his early thirties, this teacher works in an urban high school where, because of his extensive education, he is able to teach in both the social studies and literature departments. He is the teacher of the young man whose words we have just heard.

"I VOWED I would never love them, never turn them into my friends. This was a willful effort. I knew from my own experiences in school that the best classes, the classes where I really learned, were those where the teachers were stern and tough, disciplined, and didn't make so much effort to get close to students and touch students and lament their problems as if they were psychically your own.

"I remember in graduate school a teacher who seemed to be pushing for a closeness, intimacy, pushing for all the psychological goo and stuff of help-ing kids work out their identity issues and their psychosexual diseases with their parents. Then I read Piaget and it was a breath of fresh air—not that he is easy to read. One longs for Kant. Here was someone interested in the way children learn, how their mind works. Piaget had the noble approach. He had it with ducks as well as children. Don't think of children as stupid, but don't spend your life trying to get to the root of their problems, their psyche, their armor, their unconscious. You can work hard with people and show them the utmost respect merely by helping them to learn to get excited with various fields of inquiry. What possibly can be wrong with that? In the end, if children cannot read and think and write, they will be lost souls. Yes, you reward them for their daily efforts, but you don't have to celebrate errors of fact and absence of knowledge, or looseness in thinking, or plain old-fashioned unenlightened outlooks.

"And why cannot the teacher advance moral precepts? I asked my colleagues over and over again. When you tell your class, 'Please don't speak while someone else has the floor,' you are then and there teaching moral precepts, whether you like it or not. And you outright lie when you advocate tolerance, because you will eventually reach the point of backing off from it. Tolerate gays? Yes. Tolerate interfaith marriages? Yes. Tolerate Nazism? Huh? Do I hear a swell of yesses now? So why not make it explicit! All they could say, my precious colleagues, was, 'We don't teach morality; we hold up various behaviors and help students clarify their positions, moral and otherwise, on these subjects.' The kids aren't the only ones exhibiting loose thinking.

"It never made sense. I never desired sternness, coldness, aloofness. I wanted students to understand and appreciate that what they were learning had great value for later in their lives: better jobs, better feelings about themselves, better human status in the world community. There is a degree to which learning and academic advancement require postponement of gratification. There ought to be a joy in the learning process, but it cannot always be consummated. I'm sorry; it's the nature of the beast, and it remains a very valuable beast. I believed I had a very substantial and defensible position, despite the students and some faculty who called me cool, or aloof, or, dare I even utter the word, unloving.

"And then one night I had this dream. I had been reading a book on dreams when I fell asleep and now, suddenly, I am immersed in a huge cave with spider webs hanging down from darkened walls and claylike ceilings. It is ominous in there; escape seems impossible. I am frightened and helpless. Then suddenly, this football player appears. He seems totally comfortable with the same circumstances that confront and frighten me. As we begin to talk, I realize I know all about him for some reason, which impresses him and endears me to him. Now we are walking with his arm around me and I have this thought, Is one of us or both of us gay? No, I assure myself, he is simply being protective and gregarious, although I am startled by his lengthy references to Dante, Schiller, Goethe, Milton, Socrates. I ask him, 'With all your prodigious reading, I must assume you have read Kafka as well.' This statement causes him to turn angry, almost furious. He brusquely takes his arm off my shoulder, as if I have deeply insulted him. 'Never, never, *never* read Kafka. It is obscene literature and must not be shown to children.'

Terrified by his response and fearing that he won't help me out of the cave, I reply, 'Oh, no, you are absolutely correct. I hope you understood my sarcasm, my irony, my sardonic wit. I knew of course that you would not like Kafka. Of course, of course I knew that.' He looks at me, for a long time I remember, and then smiles and puts his arm back around my shoulder, and we are once again walking along some avenue within the cave. I imagine that we are on our way out, because I feel relieved.

"I wake up terrified, but the terror quickly subsides when I realize it is just a dream. But for a day or two afterward I walk around feeling sad, melancholy—I use that word since I actually had found myself reading *Mourning and Melancholia* over the preceding week. You know it? Sadness, a terrific sadness haunted me for a couple of days. My mind wandered; my work actually suffered. For the first time ever, after teaching school for more than nine years, I think I began to seriously contemplate not teaching anymore. At any level.

"The sadness continued. I stopped reading the Freud, and then one morning, probably after another dream, I believe, I felt as if I had awakened to the meaning of the first dream. It began with the figure of the football player, a man I imagined who must have resembled some guy my dad went to college with who became a professional player. This always mattered to my father, somehow, that a friend of his actually played with the pros. But the clue for me was the reference to Kafka, and my demurring, cowardly retreat. Kafka is the one writer who conjures up in me the awful, unbearable pain of the relationship between father and son. I can barely read Kafka. I try not to assign him, but it's inescapable. So when the football player tells me, 'Never read Kafka,' I knew somehow the dream was about not facing something with my father.

"The choice of *Mourning and Melancholia* provided another piece of this mysterious puzzle, a puzzle I obviously have been repressing for years. The entire nature of my relationship with my father has been one of delayed gratification. Everything for him was a moral lesson. Every act, intellectual or otherwise, was one of utter seriousness, as if a time bomb were ticking and the entire civilization had but moments left to survive. My whole life has been lived, or was lived until that time, by something I think Brecht once said: "He who is laughing obviously hasn't heard the horrible news." And the horrible news was that he could not love me. Everything was in the effort, everything was in the activity, everything was in the final product, the accomplishment, the success, or at least the enormous effort that one was willing to make for the success. But there was no love. There could be no love, for love softens people, makes them into anything but tough, hard-nosed football heroes.

"I saw it all. My classroom philosophy, and demeanor I must add, though not entirely without foundation, were built essentially on my reaction to my father's inability to genuinely love me. The age-old expression holds true for him: he did the best he could. He thought he loved me; he imagined he loved me. Had I ever questioned him on the matter, he would surely have argued vociferously for his love—how could he not! But the fact is, I could never have asked that question, for fear of the response I think I must have gotten when the football player admonishes me to never read Kafka. Never ask your father whether he loves you, unless you are prepared to experience a pain that will cause you to feel melancholia and mourn for the rest of your days.

"It took me several weeks, months perhaps, to put the final connection on this matter, namely, that I had unconsciously decided to withhold love from my students, just as my father had withheld his love. I withheld it, too, for fear that had I offered it, it would not be requited. I withheld it because I felt it was a man's duty and obligation to provide strength and seriousness and armored morality in school. The rest belonged to the realm of women. But don't mistake this. This has nothing to do, I feel, with being feminine or gay or bi. It has to do with awakening a pain, an ache, a heartache I must have lived with all my life that the worshipping of my father, as people worship football players, meant that any reward that might come from work could not be the frivolous, joyous, comforting, and life-affirming reward that only love can bring. Only months before, I had read something I had never ever known: that Freud himself had written that love is the grand educator.

"It is so wondrously strange, there are dreams in sleep and dreams in wakefulness, there simply are so many fewer pieces of armor during sleep, and so many pieces of wonderful irony, enough to fuel my literature classes for centuries, along with a love of books and the children who hopefully will read them with me. And you know, of course, that my father, too, was a high school teacher."

A RAINY NIGHT OF POETRY

HEAVEN ONLY knows what American children feel about school assignments in which they are asked to write poetry. Some probably relish the idea of a short assignment; you can, after all, get away with a half-dozen lines, and nothing has to rhyme. Others probably view poetry as a bit mushy, or girlish, or frivolous, especially in today's era of power, money, and technology. Still others may imagine that the act of writing poetry puts them in touch with their nominees for the great poets of the generation: Dylan, Lennon, Wonder, Chapman, Sting, O'Connor.

Who, then, knows how a group of seventh graders in a Boston-area school reacted when their teacher announced that they would be creating poems, poems, and more poems. Presumably, the children believed they would write the poems, turn them in, get their grades, and go on to the next course unit. But this teacher had more extravagant plans in mind.

First, the poems were to be typed on computers and reproduced. A book would be fabricated, published, as it were, by the students themselves. Now what can make a young poet feel better than to have his or her poems published? The teacher wasn't finished. She then arranged for a poetry reading to be part of an evening program celebrating the arts. Titling the reading "Great Lines," she required every child to stand up in front of beaming and for once uncritical parents and read one poem. And each child did just that, concluding the reading by introducing the next poet in line.

The result was remarkable. Extraordinary words began to jingle in the little auditorium as Jessy, Timily, Kyra, David, Crystal, Mark, Tiesha, Sonya, Jason, Mike, Shariff, Danya, and the others read their poetry. In a matter of seconds, adults, who earlier must have smiled to themselves with the thought that Dryden, Wordsworth, Eliot, Milton, Blake, Heany, and Lowell hardly would be challenged this night, began to be moved, touched, and stirred by these children.

The poems spoke of death and loneliness, worrying and cruelty, suicide, the changing of the seasons, the paths taken by a mountain brook, a boy wondering what it would be like to be a woman, the counsel of grandparents, the pain of children who have been forgotten and neglected, and war.

From the start, I sensed the adults being drawn to the poetry and to the wondrous line of poets who read with a rare combination of emotion, innocence, and modesty. They heard lines like the following:

> The gravestone slabs stand among the shadows,
> Choosing to engrave the stone's writing with camouflage.
>
> The flaming wall around your heart,
> Blocking out all rationality.
> No matter when or how
> The pain and neglect is removed.
>
> The trees are attached by a web of silver thread,
> And the sledding hill is warmed with a blanket of diamonds.
> What if the sky was attached to sea?
> What if there was no one to look after me?
>
> No lives will pause,
> once I am gone,
> no tears shall be shed,
> as I lay upon my battlefield bed.
>
> Grandma always told me
> "Women have one button, men have two."
> Because men have less to hide
> And women have more.
> So I always went by her word.
>
> So alone am I now,
> For I lost her,
> I don't know how.
> How sweet her voice was
> On the wind,
> It's carried to me time and again.
>
> Don't rely on some handmade
> pieces of colored cloth.

No one can take your worry away.
It's your sin, your worry and no
Guatemalen legend can make it
disappear.

The night, seemingly disconnected from time, went on. Each child was videotaped as he or she read, as if to remind us of the century in which we live. Parents emerged with stapled pink booklets containing every poem. I quickly recognized the fonts and graphics of computers; a lovely blend, actually, poetry and that other variety of word processing. And then it was home to bed and preparations for another day, the children proud, surely, but making certain to get in their ritual grumbling about tomorrow's French or math homework.

Days later, I read more of the poems and once again was allowed entrance to some of the children's visions and frights:

No matter when in time
No matter the place
You shouldn't want to be alone
No matter what the cause.

Alone
lost
forgotten
parents fighting in court
to see what they can get
he has nowhere to go . . .

The cries of their sorrow, taking my sanity
The smell of death, taking my soul
The touch of the blade, taking my dreams
The sight of bodies dead in the field of death, taking my life
The blast of the bomb, Is the taking of me.

It had been a magical, almost ethereal evening. Having heard the poems, I required no tangible record of the event; the poetry and other memories would suffice. Poetry, after all, possesses its own endurance. True, there was the lingering shimmer of children's fears and hurts, but on this one night, the beauty of the words would win out.

Pens mightier than swords? Probably, but nothing political seemed at stake this one rainy spring evening, at least nothing that one wished to address at the moment. Children's art and children's truths were all that needed to be at stake; they would suffice this one evening for parents who also had put in a long day and could not quite glimpse the weekend. The debate over teachers' salaries, budgets, and cultural values would wait for the morning.

But something happened that night in the heart of one member of the audience. A single mother had heard all too well the plaintive poetry of her daughter, who had written of missing her father. His absence in her life had surfaced in her poem as death. The mother now embraced the metaphor as she would her child. Telephone calls were made, and within days a young poet met with a father she hadn't seen in years. A child's poetry had spawned communion.

Learning of this, the other poets, I imagine, thought again of just why it is that the human heart has always turned to poetry and why a solitary middle school English teacher might value this one discipline as well as children's capacity to dream and tell. If the people in the small auditorium didn't recognize it that one rainy night, they now stood absolutely assured that poetry, no matter what the contents of the metaphor, remains a life force and a mysterious path to the eternal.

In the end, it was again one of the youthful poets who described the transformation felt by the older audience and the tiny morsel of hope, not there that morning, they now would carry with them:

> The tear of happiness rolls down the smiling cheek
> The tear of happiness is only a joyful leak
> The tear of happiness is a way of being intimate
> The tear of happiness happens when your feelings are bent.

A FAMILY PREPARES
FOR COLLEGE

ONE OF THE infamous cliches of American culture has to do with the progress of its immigrant families. What these people want, it is said, is to make life better for their children. Each generation rests easy, it is also said, knowing that their children and grandchildren have opportunities they never knew. At the center of this generational assessment of progress is education, and particularly college. In many families, admission to college remains the ultimate measure of the family's success and status. There are families who report the college admission letter to be the indelible stamp of acceptance into America.

In some respects, it stands as a peculiar notion, inasmuch as contemporary America reveals an omnipresent anti-intellectualism. Moreover, populist ideologies often advance the sentiment that so-called prestigious schools are no better than state universities and community colleges, in the same way that designer jeans are no better than the standard fare. For this reason, certain schools have come to be called "designer schools." Still, having a child admitted to one of the so-called elite institutions may alter the destiny a family perceives for itself or at least for some family members. Thus tangible and intangible rewards earmarked for parents arrive in those infamous thick envelopes addressed to graduating high school seniors.

Years ago I began studying the lives of families living in poverty or working-class conditions. Among the questions I had for them were what they wanted from America and what kept them from getting it. Because the work essentially has followed an ethnographic approach over long periods of time, I have come to know a host of families rather well. Naturally, therefore, I have shared with them the momentous months of a child's senior year of high school. In many of these families, it's the very first time that the typical college application procedure is experienced. Even more poignant, the application process is the first time these families openly take stock of their status in society, in terms of their own sense of tangible success.

Not surprisingly, each family member experiences the application process in distinctive fashion. Often I find that it is the father who seemingly rests his entire sense of worth on the acceptance or rejection or, even more acutely, assesses his position on the basis of the schools to which his children apply. His wife, correspondingly, places less stock in the nature and reputation of the school and often attempts to reduce the pressure placed on her child by her husband. For many mothers, apparently, less rides on the acceptance or rejection; the mere idea that the child is applying to college is reward enough.

Now come the children themselves, feeling pressure, seemingly, from every corner of their life. At school, the talk focuses on college, and hence feelings of competition bubble to the surface. At home, the children recognize the significance of the act for their father and possibly feel slight confusion as they consider their mother's reaction. Is she attempting to make life easier for them, or does she genuinely not care all that much? When there is a younger sibling in the family, even more strain arises. The students, although proud to be the first one in the family heading for college, often wish at the same time to honor the accomplishments, present and future, of their brother or sister.

Probably, few families in our society approach the college application process with equanimity; everyone has something riding on the decision. But in the families with whom I have visited, a special strain is sensed, if not directly observed, as the senior year begins and young men and women start to narrow their options and envision the outlines of their future, and their family's future as well.

That I, too, in my own family and with a somewhat different agenda, have experienced this phenomenon, only sharpens my perception of the strain felt by these families. Occasionally, as best as the families attempt to hide it from me, it nonetheless comes forth with a power that angers, dismays, and ultimately confuses the various family members. It is no exaggeration to state that the psychological complexities attending the application process, embedded as they are in the life histories of family members, often immobilize the student. If in fact a child's admission to college is felt, even unconsciously, to be his or her family's ultimate admission to society, it is little wonder that some children find the process utterly debilitating.

What follows is an account of no more than ten minutes in the home of one of the families that I have been visiting for many years. Knowing that

I may write about my visits with them, the Lelands have been extraordinarily generous in letting me into their lives. But this account is not derived from the familiar interview schedule or question-and-answer routine. Rather it is based on catching a family almost off guard, when the profound significance of college admission is powerfully revealed.

To maintain anonymity I have changed all names. Equally important, each of the three family members presented here has read the manuscript and given permission to have it published. Finally, for those who wonder about such matters, as I inevitably do, this story has a happy ending, the precise details of which my promise of confidentiality prevents me from reporting. Suffice to say, the child in question, I have learned just this week, has been admitted to college.

IN A MIDDLE-CLASS neighborhood of Boston, Emma and Harry Leland are spending what seems to them an inordinate amount of time talking with their daughter, Tara, about colleges. Tara's senior year of high school has finally arrived. The last semester of important grades looms ahead of them—that is, of her—and they all have their sights set on the college board examinations. Every day the mail brings more information about colleges, most of it unsolicited. Colleges of all varieties seem to be rolling out their red carpets, making it appear that admission is an insignificant hurdle.

The family is passing through what salesman Harry Leland, who earned a college degree by taking evening courses, calls the enticing stage, the weeks when colleges attempt to lure prospective students. The Lelands, however, aren't falling for it. They know all too well the admissions statistics and the difficulties that can arise at any time. The Cs on the sophomore report card—will they come back to haunt Tara? Which teachers will write the best things in the all-important letters of recommendation? Should Tara have pursued more academic programs during summer vacations? Will there be sufficient extracurricular activities on her application, or will the list appear suspiciously long, as if she were trying to make an impression on admissions officers? Maybe she should simply document her talents and passions and let it go at that!

And what happens if her college board performance turns out to be mediocre, or even horrendous, even after two or three tries? Hadn't someone told the story of a student traveling to different states so that he might take the boards more than the allowed number of times? Tara was not the best of test takers, even though she'd performed more than adequately on the practice examinations the previous spring. Since her grades are borderline, her parents figure she needs an outstanding performance.

Harry Leland has begun to chastise himself for not sending his first-born child to private school. He gave in too readily, he claims, to his wife's belief in supporting public education. Besides, Emma never went to college. His dentist's children, to whom he alludes more frequently these days, are private school products. More to the point, they're Ivy League products.

"The whole system is one big crap shoot," he remarks bitterly, standing up from his chair near the television set. "My kids are as deserving as anyone's kid, but it's not a race with an equal start. It's a race with a staggered start, except the track's a straightaway, not an oval. Tara's in the middle, not at the end. She's certainly not at the front. Maybe it's my fault she's not there. I should have put her there. I shouldn't have listened to anyone on this. If you're going to sacrifice, you do it from the start. The private school kid starts out in front. I played it wrong. It's a crap shoot, like I say, but there are ways to play craps that give you better odds. You don't just let it ride. Not when it's your own kid's life at stake."

Emma, sitting at the far end of the beige couch, nods in agreement, but her expression communicates a sense of being tired with the college entrance process, and it has only just begun. She disapproves of the pressure high schools impose on their college-bound seniors and is troubled by her husband's competitive investment in the application procedure. "I don't even know why it all has to mean so much," she begins, speaking so quietly one can barely hear her. "It means too much to him. I only want her to be happy, but when I say that, he jumps down my throat."

"Indeed I do!" Harry Leland interrupts his wife, his hand pressed against his forehead. "Because this is a foolish discussion. These schools are not the same. Why kid yourself. And to say that all you want is for a kid to be happy is beside the point. Nobody wants their child to be unhappy. That's not the issue. You want her happy in an important school that can affect her life, or in a nothing place that leaves no impression on her? You tell people you went to one school, and they'll listen to you. Tell 'em another school, and it doesn't even matter you went to college. Believe me, I know. I've lived through it. Don't argue with me on this. I didn't design it this way. I didn't invent status, prestige, opportunity. But they are real, and they're out there, and a good parent sees to it that his children get the best shot at them. That's all it is. If the schools were identical, they'd be classified by numbers and you would get in by lottery. Don't keep saying all you want is Tara's happiness. It offends me, because it makes it sound like I want her to be unhappy. I want my child in an outstanding school so she'll be unhappy for the rest of her life!"

Emma's protests are stronger than her voice would suggest. "But there's a fit," she replies, sitting up erectly. "The school should be right for her. I don't want her spending four years of her life at a place only because it pleases us."

Harry looks incredulous, as if he's undertaking to convince a skeptic that the world is round. "First of all, you never said any of this when we picked a place to live and sent the kids to public school. Who asked her then, 'Do you think you can be happy here, Tara?' Nobody. We just sent her, for twelve years! Furthermore, do you honestly believe that every kid at Harvard and Dartmouth and Yale and Columbia is hating it, but staying there with great courage because they know it's making their parents happy? You really think all these parents are torturing their kids with demands that they go to Harvard or leave their house forever? Get serious. You don't just buy a BMW for status. It also happens to be a helluva car. I wish I drove one."

"You want the status for yourself, Harry. Where Tara goes to school is something you think you can use somehow. *You* need it!"

"And you don't?"

"No. I don't. Tara's Tara. That's all there is to it. She'll be Tara at Harvard, Tara at a state university, Tara at no college at all!"

Harry Leland is on fire. "That's a lie. You would die if she didn't go to college. You could never admit that to yourself. You were the one who got hot and bothered when her grades fell last year. You, not me!"

"I was concerned, but not for college." Emma Leland's voice remains surprisingly soft for a woman feeling such anger. "I thought she was having a problem she wouldn't tell us about."

"And you never thought about what that might mean for college?"

"No."

"Never?"

"Never."

"You're one great woman."

"What do you want me to say?" Along with the anger, Emma is embarrassed.

"You don't have to say anything. I paid you a compliment."

"That I'm a great woman because my daughter's college will not affect my feeling about her in the slightest." Her sarcasm is painfully evident.

"Damn it." Harry Leland has begun pulling off his tie. "Now you turn this into my liking Tara more if she goes to an Ivy League school. That maybe if she goes to some second-rate place I'll love her less. Or maybe I'll stop loving her altogether. Or maybe I don't love her at all. Ever think about that? I only love her accomplishments and this is the big one. Believe that. It will make you happier. You'll be able to sleep nights again. I don't love her or any of the children. I may love her, repeat, *may* love her if she gets into the big places. But a lousy school takes her, hey, I may end up hating her. Let's leave it at that, which will prove you were right. Tara goes to Dartmouth, I happily cough up the twenty-plus grand a year. Tara doesn't go to Dartmouth, I show my true colors and disown her. That's the proof you're looking for, isn't it?"

"She doesn't need proof." Emma's words are barely audible. Even Harry is straining to hear them. She has begun straightening the yellow throw pillows. "You just have to relax and let her lead her own life."

"Huh?"

"Let her lead her own life."

"You want me out of it, I'm out of it." His tie off, Harry is pacing in circles around the small living room, tapping the television each time he passes it. "I'm an ogre, after all. I mean, how could I be so cruel as to want my daughter in a first-rate college? I mean, that has to qualify as abuse, doesn't it? It'd be better if I beat her, wouldn't it? Why don't we get a good psychiatrist to treat us. Father who wanted good school for daughter sentenced to life on death row."

"Oh, stop it already! This whole thing is pitiful." Emma barks out the words at the same time an upstairs door slams shut. For several moments, no one speaks. The door slams a second time.

Tara has been listening to her parents. It is not the first time that a seemingly innocent discussion of college applications has erupted into this sort of argument. She cannot bear the scenes or the idea that this year seems to hold the confirmation of her parents' work for the last eighteen years. Everything they have tried to achieve seems to rest on the college admissions decision, and it does little good to mutter words like, 'Why can't they just accept me for who I am, rather than where I get in?' The notion that she might not be admitted anywhere causes such dread in her she can barely let herself contemplate it. She could probably survive total rejection from college, but her parents could not. Her father, she believes, would never be able to show his face. Even her mother, who talks such a serene game, would quake.

Tara herself has told friends she wouldn't mind not going to college right away. Maybe she could take a job somewhere, or travel. But she is lying to them. On the outside she tries everyday to give the same impassive, carefree impression that her mother gives, but inside her competitive drive is exactly the one articulated by her father. To her friends she acts nonchalant; inside, she feels an almost uncontrollable drive to get to where she believes she belongs, no matter how foolish or crude this sounds. She tries on occasion to rid herself of the feeling that impels her toward the competitive and high-status avenues of the world, but she knows she is fooling herself. Her parents' arguments hurt her, but at the same time they reveal the truths of her own conflicts. Neither of them is saying anything that she hasn't already battled internally. But their conflict, her conflict, is keeping her from acting, and this troubles her. She agonizes over her utter inability to do anything.

Unbeknownst to her parents, she has not yet begun to apply even for college application forms. Her list of potential colleges, categorized as dream places, possibles, and fallbacks, has yet to be filled out. It is increasingly evident to her that she will spend the year confronting her own fears and feelings and working out ways to relate to her friends, all of whom, she imagines, will be experiencing much the same thing. All of them will have to negotiate the slippery shoals of competitiveness. They will keep up with one another, root for one another, compare themselves with one another, pretend that they aren't doing any of this, and hope. Tara Leland's inner drive will only intensify as the semester progresses.

On this particular afternoon, after twice slamming the door in anger and disgust as a signal to her parents to stop yelling, she realizes that the fear of getting into college is mislabeled. It isn't that she fears she won't be admitted. More precisely, she fears the power of her undying need to achieve and what she might do if she fails, not in their eyes, but in her own.

As the door slams she is left utterly terrified, grabbed by some momentous force in herself that the prospect of applying to college has awakened. To quiet this force, she turns again to the device that seems to silence it: total inactivity. She hasn't chosen colleges or sent for applications, and she won't just yet. Everyone will call it procrastination, but for her, for now, anyway, it is a life-sustaining action. Maybe it will quiet all of them.

Tara Leland stands motionless in the middle of her bedroom, listening for whatever words might filter up from the livingroom. Hearing nothing, she moves to her bed and sits down. She throws a fashion magazine on the floor, picks up an oversized paperback book, and resumes reading, an action that almost at once calms her. The book is *Peterson's Competitive Colleges—314 Colleges That Attract the Nation's Top Students.* She reads,

> Franklin and Marshall College, Lancaster, Pennsylvania . . . Applying—Required: essay, high school transcript, 2 recommendations, SAT or ACT, 1 Achievement, English Composition Test. Recommended: 3 years of high school math and science, 3 years of high school foreign language, interview . . .

IV

SOCIETAL PERIL

A COMMON CRITICISM of Freud's theory of the personality is that it overlooked the power of society and culture. While there are many things to criticize in Freudian theory, the absence of society in the development of the personality is not one of them. In the constructs of the ego and superego, Freud early on postulated the contributions to the emerging self made by society in the form of values, rituals, conventions, and morality. Interestingly, at almost the same time that Freud was writing, the French sociologist Émile Durkheim was suggesting that society exists exclusively in the minds of individuals, a point Erich Fromm later formulated when he wrote that parents and teachers are "agents of culture."[1]

The point of all this is only to remind us of the palpable realities constituting society in the lives of citizens, realities that frequently come across as unjust, as in the case of unemployment or a government's neglecting not only the people it is charged to serve, but also the very people it employs. We know well the problems revolving around crises in the public trust, just as we know the dynamic of a society shaped by matters of social class.

Consider for a moment the notion that cities, beyond being human settlements, are symbolic representations of a society. More than buildings, streets, and centers of commerce, cities, and what we call city life, contribute to the conceptions people hold of themselves and the world. Strange to think that the reality of a neighborhood or community may actually be related to health and illness. We think of urban pollution as a lethal element, which of course it is. But pollution, filth, noise, sheer ugliness, or barrenness also affects moods and ultimately people's images of themselves and others. Not unlike the societies that form and inform them, cities intrude in people's lives, often in salubrious ways and often, too, in the most destructive of ways. Granted, there are many people left out of society, "ground down by poverty," as Matthew Dumont has written, and obliged to go without certain objects and physical necessities.[2] But society can grind people's spirits down, just as it can uplift them, usually in the forms of injustice and justice, and in this conception, objects and possessions may play only a minimal role.

If culture teaches us how the world works and, for that matter, how people work, as Mary Douglas and Steven Ney suggest, society might be said to be the stage on which individuals, as actors, play out their understanding and misunderstanding of these various meanings.[3] The actuality of justice or injustice is part of the stage direction, part of the ecology—who knows, justice and injustice may also be part of the props and sets of the culture. We must keep in mind that many of our mental representations are constructed from societal elements, philosophies, rituals, and conventions of which we may be barely aware. Sadly, for me, too many in the culture continue to believe that only the highly educated, formally trained, or especially skilled comprehend this power of society and are able to articulate it, much less discern societal elements living in their own minds, exactly as Durkheim postulated.

By the time we reach adolescence, we are familiar with the idea that people engage in interactions wherein each participant understands or is supposed to understand the fundamental mutuality of the connection. All you have to do is ask teenagers about dating rituals, and they will have much to say about mutuality and the rules governing it. Yet adolescents recognize something else constituting the enactment of mutuality. They recognize that laws, rituals, and morality transcend individual mutuality and ultimately govern the ways in which this mutuality comes to be enacted. Adolescents understand, moreover, the necessity, even goodness, of these laws and hence recognize for the first time the purpose of society. Now, because their ubiquitous assessments of unfairness come to have a greater potency, it no longer suffices to attribute their gripes to mere rebellion or excessive hormonal production. Because of their capacity to abstract ideas and hold competing abstractions in their minds, they are able to contemplate the realities of society and appraise the degree to which they are products of it, and it products of them. They may speak of "the system" with derision, but they are properly referring to societal elements and the legitimacy or illegitimacy of particular features and conventions.

Individuals' capacity not only to comprehend the conventions, rules, norms, and values of society but to embed them in their personal narratives is what this book is about. Every personal account, no matter how idiosyncratic it seems, inevitably contains sociological insights and reasoning. A child who says, "I don't think it should be this way," and an adult who comments on the unequal distribution of goods and services testify to the individual's sociological eye. The moment a child looks not only at his or her own test results, but at the results of others in his or her class and school, other schools, and other communities, the child engages in sociological inquiry.

Like children scanning test results posted outside their classrooms, we all need to know where we stand, and for this we look to society and culture. We also seem to need evidence of whether we are good, worthy, and significant, and for this, too, we look to society and culture. Granted, we have a tendency to credit ourselves during moments of success and blame society during moments of failure or hurt, but this is understandable. We've all felt guilt over having done something unacceptable or unjust or even contemplated doing it. Similarly, many of us have known shame, yet another residue of injustice. We know what it's like to have society, through its agents, proclaim not only that we have done bad, but that we *are* bad. We have known, too, the utter humiliation of shame, the reluctance to show our face in light of supreme failure or hurt.

A parent finds her child hiding under his bed: "Go 'way," he shouts. "Don't look at me." The long-term unemployed man hides out in his home, venturing outside only in the evening, when he may not be spotted or recognized. A woman feels that the neglect shown her and her community can only mean she is remiss, lacking, defective, and unworthy. She has been shamed, actually, by her environment, her surroundings literally underwriting the most intimate appraisals she renders of herself. Injustice shames; just as we wear it on our faces, we house it in our bodies, and, most interesting, once there, it seems never to fully disappear.

Most of us recognize the role fortune plays in our lives. The people whose stories are presented in this book fully recognize when misfortune collided with injustice to put them in harm's way. And this is only a part of their comprehension, experience, and ongoing felt sense of injustice; it is only part of their shame. It is part of the shamefulness, too, of a society that promises so much and comes through for so many, but not for all.

ONE JOB AND THEY WOULD'VE HAD SMOOTH SAILING

Ed Zegler was in on everything. What he didn't actually witness, he heard through the floor, or his wife heard, or his children heard. All the residents of 1826 South Peletus knew about Peter and Stacy Bennett. They knew when he was hitting her, when she was hitting him, and when one of them was beating up their children, and particularly when it was the baby, Margaret Ann, who was only a year and a half. Ed Zegler composed a nursery rhyme:

> Peter, Peter, pumpkin eater,
> Lost his job and couldn't feed her.
> So he beat her.

In the beginning, it gave his wife and some of the neighbors a bit of a laugh. Later, when it was obvious to everyone that Peter Bennett's employment situation was uncertain, to say the least, Ed Zegler's nursery rhyme brought not even a smile. His wife, Frances, told him, "The Bennetts aren't going to make it. If you have to write something clever, it probably should be something for their gravestone. That family is going down."

"Hey, let's face it," Ed Zegler always said, "we're bad off in this neighborhood. We're barely working around here. What's going on downstairs with the Bennetts is going on in every apartment in this neighborhood. Nobody understands what it's like over here."

Tommy was the oldest of the three Zegler children. At sixteen, he was a tall, strong boy who, despite the styles of the day, wore his hair short and combed forward, so that he resembled an ancient Roman soldier. His friends razzed him about his appearance, but he remained a respected young man. Everyone believed he someday would become a lawyer or a politician. Perhaps he could do something for his neighborhood, with its high crime and unemployment rates, its population shifts, its bad garbage collection system, and the lack of play space for children.

Tommy only grinned when told of destiny's plan for him. "Kids around here," he would say, "have a better chance of ending up in prison than law school. And besides, not too many politicians from around here do anything for the people they grew up with. You'd think they'd see how the people here need jobs. But they don't do anything but ask people to vote for them. There hasn't been new industry 'round here for years, and the job corps centers are the biggest waste anybody's ever seen. My father thinks I'd be a good politician, but I wonder whether I'd even come back here. The place eats you up. You live here despite what it does to you, and you got to be strong to make out. Believe me. When you're poor and you end up without a job, the only thing left is to drink or do something corrupt if it'll make you a couple bucks. People here, they don't know what to do. They tell you one thing one day, another thing the next. Look at the Bennetts.

"There's a family lives in the same building where we live for maybe four years. The first day they came, the first thing they said to my mother was, 'We aren't going to be here long. We'll just get settled a little, you know, then find a better place.' They didn't understand they were insulting her. They didn't even live here and they're already telling her what a cheap place their apartment is, and the neighborhood, too. All right, you figure the guy is between jobs, or something bad happened. Maybe he used to live in the suburbs. That happens, you know. We got a few families come 'round here who had money once. The Friends family used to live over on St. James Place. He once owned an enormous farm in Belvedere. He took a bunch of kids out there once and showed it to them. But something happened, I think maybe he was caught with his hand in the till of some big corporation. They put him in prison and he lost everything, so when he got out he came here. He couldn't get a job. Just like Bennett.

"Anyway, my mother didn't know about the Bennetts. Maybe they had money once. But nobody around here needs to be told we ain't Belvedere. The rich don't come here. Nobody comes here. I got a friend, Timmy Mc-Carthy, a nut, but real smart. Lives on Baloil, two blocks from here. He says this neighborhood is so lousy we don't even have college students living here. You know these kids who want to pretend they don't have money? Not even those kids come here. I remember my mother telling my father about the Bennetts that first night. My father laughed. I was insulted. I really was. 'Whoever he is,' my father said, 'the guy's a loser pretending he's someone important. Only losers are here. Nobody else. You got your old-line families who stay on, but new people, they're losers. If they don't have family here, they're in real trouble.'

"I sort of liked Bennett. I didn't like his wife so much. She was stuck up. She didn't have too many friends, neither. Nobody liked her, probably 'cause she acted like she didn't want to be liked. Like, my sister Terry used to baby-sit for them and she said Mrs. Bennett treated her like she was a servant instead of just a baby-sitter. Lots of times they didn't even pay her. They said they would and then they'd forget all about it. So my mother would have to ask them for, like, eighty cents or a buck. Peanuts, nothing. They had the money; they just didn't want to cough it up. My mom knew they had it. She said Bennett always had his hands in his pockets jingling his money, so she knew he had it.

"Oh, here's an amazing thing Terry said. They used to come home when she was baby-sitting, you know, and tell her all these things they'd done, like go to a show, and then some nice place to eat. So she figured after a while they were doing pretty well, 'cause they'd go out two, three times a week. People 'round here go to the show, but not three times a week, and restaurants. She knew they were drinking, but they weren't drunk. I mean, they didn't come home sloshed or nothing. So they could have been going to these swanky places like they said. But it didn't seem right. With this little apartment, and no car, and everybody knew Bennett had no job. So where'd they get it? We thought maybe the guy was a crook.

"So one night Terry starts talking to them about the movie they'd been to which she saw, too, only they didn't know it. And she's asking them all these questions about it and it turns out they didn't see it. They were lying to her. So this other night, and this was pretty cruel, this guy Ronny and me, we followed them, and all they did was go to a bar about two miles from here, probably so they wouldn't be recognized, 'cause if all you want to do is drink there're a million places to go 'round here. I always say, the more the job rates go down, the more the number of bars goes up. But all Mr. and Mrs. Bennett were doing was drinking. Nothing else. I really felt sorry for them. Part of me was glad to find out they were phonies like my father said, but then I felt sorry for them. Why they have to pretend they're something they aren't? It's kind of sad. So they didn't have money. Why they have to make people believe they're rich? I wanted to go up to them and say, 'Hey, we're good people 'round here. You don't have to lie to us. Don't waste your time trying to prove something, walking two miles to a crummy bar where you can't talk to nobody 'cause they'll find out what we know.' They'd have been a lot better off being honest. If people are honest with you, like the

Bennetts should have been with my mother, then my mother's going to help. I'm going to help. Hell, Terry would have baby-sat for free if they'd just told her what was going on. Nobody's going to let anything happen to their kids.

"You got three kinds of sickness around here. First, you got the people who drink. Every family, practically, has someone who drinks too much. Maybe they aren't what you'd call alcoholics, but they drink, 'til they fall out. Then you got drugs. Not as much as the newspapers make out, but you got a lot of people with that problem. Kids in school with me, maybe since they're ten years old, hooked on something. You can't believe it. They always need help or money. Pretty soon their families can't make it with them, so they throw 'em out of the house and the next thing you hear, they're in jail. The lucky ones go to the rehabilitation places, but there's not too many of those places.

"Now we have the real sickness. If they cured this one, they'd cure the others: guys without jobs. That really kills these families. That's the Bennetts. You can see it. Guy's working and everybody thinking he's doing fine. They don't talk much about it. Then you hear he's been hanging around in the day. Maybe he'll tell people he's on vacation, which can happen. Most of these people take vacations in the summer, but they get a week here and there in the year, too. Then he's hanging around a long time, and maybe he'll tell people he's on sick leave, taking a little insurance. Most people 'round here, they'll tell you straight out they lost their job. Why lie about it? If you tell the truth, people don't laugh at you. But a man like Bennett, you could tell by looking at him he's going to be the type to feel ashamed. Or maybe his wife made him feel ashamed. Anyway, after a time everybody knows this guy hasn't worked in months. That's when a lot of them move, you know. Or they'll change their name or switch places with some other family they know. Lot of them leave 'cause they can't pay their rents. Or like, all of a sudden the man disappears. You figure, he's got a new woman or he's lost his job. You can't blame the guy. He's got to work. He's got to go where the job is; nobody's calling him up and asking him to come to work. You go out and hustle no matter where it is.

"But that's where Bennett made his mistake. He and his wife seemed to be into this thing of not admitting they were sick. They were always pretending things were better than they were. Only once do I remember him admitting it to my father. We were outside, standing 'round, and he told my father, 'It'd sure be different if I could come up with something. Anything.' My father said, 'You sound like a guy saying, if only I had one drink, just one drink.' Bennett looked real surprised, like he knew my father understood what was wrong. He should have talked to my father. My father's been out of work in his life. Couple of times. He came out of the service and got a job right away, then lost it two months later. But he kept going. He didn't quit like Bennett. And he didn't lie to nobody. 'Course, maybe he felt like the country owed him something. But when Bennett talked to my father, my father understood him. He was silly not to keep going with my father. He could have been his friend."

Nobody believes that Ed Zegler is forty-five years old. Most people guess his age as middle thirties. He's a man who prides himself in taking care of his body. The secret, he says, is to watch the waistline: "You can't eat too much or work too much. One rots your body; the other rots your mind."

Ed Zegler has worked steadily with a sewage pipe firm. When he first began with the company, they had him in the trenches. Knee-deep in mud, he fit the four- and twelve-inch pipes into place. It was tiring work, but Ed took it as easy as he could. "No sense rushing," he'd tell his co-workers. "Keel over in this crap and that's where we'd leave you." His friends admitted that no matter what the job, Ed set the pace, and it was always the right pace. The work got done, yet the men weren't exhausted at the end of the day. If the job took a day or two longer than it had been contracted for, Ed would speak up for the men. The job dictates the speed, he would say, not the workers. He soon became the crew's choice for foreman, but he never achieved it. He dreamed of it often enough, but he never got beyond the street crews. When he inquired about the foreman position, he always heard the same words: "We don't feel you'd push the men hard enough."

Perhaps it was true. Ed Zegler was not a pusher. He valued work, and saw how unemployment destroyed people, but he never felt right about pushing a man. He knew all about a person's breaking point or getting the most out of him, but he always believed powerful people pushed workers until they dropped. "The bosses," he said, "they want people to drop dead from exhaustion before retirement so they can save ten dollars."

Although he disliked Peter Bennett, Ed Zegler never wrote him off completely. He felt for the man, and although he never sat down and analyzed Bennett's life, he knew from the little he witnessed every day exactly what was happening to the Bennetts.

"I saw the man hit his wife on two occasions. I heard them fighting first. She's yelling, 'You couldn't hold a job if they tied it to your neck, for Chrissakes. You're the biggest phony I've ever met. Grown man not working. There are jobs. You just don't want to work.' She'd give it to the guy real good. But he'd come right back at her. 'If you're such a big deal,' he'd be yelling, 'why the hell don't *you* get a job? You think they're so easy to get, *you* get one.' 'I'll work over your dead body,' she'd tell him. 'You run around like a guy with no arms. You're a goddamn baby.' I mean she'd pull out the guns on him. She could be a devil. But he'd sulk around. I was in their kitchen one night and in front of me they put on one of their shows. I was a little alarmed at first. It started slowly, so I couldn't tell for sure if they were even serious, although we'd heard them fight before. But in the beginning they'd push at each other or shove, like little kids who want to fight but don't know how. And then, this one time, while I'm standing there not sure whether to stay or go, she begins yelling at him:

"'You're a bust, a failure, I want you out of here. I can always get a man who'll work, not scum like you.' And they're pushing and poking with their hands, like they were dancing. She pushes him, he pushes her, only she's doing all the talking. Bennett isn't saying a word. Then all of a sudden, she must have triggered off the right nerve, because he lets fly with a right cross that I mean stuns; I mean she goes down like a rock! Right on the kitchen table. And he's swearing at her, calling her every name in the book. I didn't know what the hell to do. What I wanted to do was call the police, but I figured, How can I call the police and add to this guy's misery, because she was pushing him. I'd have testified in court on that one. She was really pushing him about not working. I might have done something to her myself. I mean, that's the way you got to gauge these things. What she was doing, see, was trying to convince him he was no better than a baby. She said it right to his face: 'A fucking baby girl can do more than you. Probably bring in more money than you, too.' That's what she said. Then she worked on his manhood. 'You lost your balls a million years ago.' Hey now, you don't talk that way to nobody. I know men don't talk that way to each other. He could never convince her how hard it was to find work. I tried the best I could to say something, to defend him, because it's a miserable time. But I figured, If I talk, how can that hold much weight when I'm working? She's just going to say, 'Zegler works so why can't you?' But he flattened her that time. I couldn't believe it 'cause they were just pushing and poking each other up to that time.

"Then another time, he really got it from her. I heard him yelling, 'You friggin' slut, you pig whore.' He must have caught her or heard about something, 'cause he was on fire. And I happen to know that was a night he'd just been told a part-time job he had was going under, so again the guy was down-and-out, and probably afraid to go home and tell his wife. And on top of that, he's got to find her with somebody. I mean, this is what I imagine must have happened. But they were throwing chairs at each other, pushing over tables; it was unbelievable. And the amazing thing was that their children were sleeping through the whole business. You can't imagine these things happening. A man's out of work, his wife tells him he's no longer a man, she goes and finds another guy, and they're fighting to beat the band, and this time Bennett had an enormous gash on his arm 'cause she was breaking bottles and throwing 'em at him, and you have these two little children, and they sleep through the whole thing.

"You know, when I see a thing like that, I'm always telling myself, Here I am, sitting in front of the TV, tired, maybe bored with my life. The same events, same routines, I can see now exactly where I'm going, and I sit there wondering, what am I feeling so special for, feeling this way, because everybody in the country feels this way more often than they'd like to admit. I figure, money separates me from the guy below me and the guy above me. But the rich know loneliness and boredom and all the things I know. They got their problems, their share of divorces, their parents dying. So I tell myself, maybe everybody's watching the same television program and feeling the same kind of things. But then you go into the Bennetts' apartment, and you know, they were calling for us like they were children or something, and we're supposed to be their parents. They're practically ready to kill each other, and crying and screaming and calling for my wife and I. Once, they were screaming at each other during the day. I was at work, my wife was shopping, but Tommy happened to be home sick. They're going at it and he hears it, because the walls in these buildings aren't all that thick. And this time they're calling for him. They must have known nobody else was at home. So this kid goes in there—and there's no telling how seeing scenes like he saw can mess up a young person's mind—and there they are. Bennett is naked, and his wife is in her slip, and they're going at each other, are you ready, with knives and forks. Stuff is flying through the air and they're swearing, and here's my boy, coughing and sneezing, and he walks in on these two very sad people and he sees what he sees. But he stopped them. Because they were like children. A fourteen-year-old kid comes in and tells them to stop and behave themselves, and they stop. Like children.

"But again that time, the topic was his not having a job. It drove her crazy, not to say what it did to him. It was more than money and security with them. He was drawing a little welfare. You don't get much, but he had a legitimate claim. He could have worked with us. I've known guys with less skill and a helluva lot less interest in working. He wanted to work. But Mrs. Bennett, she was an unusual sort of person, considered herself to be special.

It was like she once had money, or position. It was his not working that ruined her, not even the small apartment with not much furniture. I have to laugh. When I say they threw furniture at each other, I'm not exaggerating. I mean, they threw all the furniture they had, it all went. But it wasn't not having possessions that bugged her, it was the fact she couldn't walk down the street and tell people, 'I can't talk long 'cause I got to go home and prepare dinner 'cause my husband's coming home from work.' That's what got her. There was no respect. That's what I want to say. There was no respect they were going to get from nobody.

"Look. You meet a person you don't know and you start a little friendship with 'em. What's the first question you're going to ask? Tell me, pal, what do you do? Now, a person, say, like Bennett, he's going to look away. So you figure, the guy's lame and can't work or he's not lame and can't find work. He sure isn't rich and doesn't have to work, because men like that don't look away from you like that. They're proud as hell to tell you they don't have to work. Look at the state of the economy. How many people out of work? Eight percent? Five percent? You know it's higher because things are at least twice as bad as the government admits, right? So if you look at it that way, there's no reason to be ashamed if you're not working. You're not stealing when you cash that insurance check. You're willing to work, but the country has no place for you. Nothing to be ashamed of. But you take every man I've ever met who's out of work, he'll do two things. First, he'll tell you the country's sick, there should be jobs for people, he's just a statistic, one of the injured. It's like war. Nobody's surprised to learn that someone died in a war. You're sorry, but you aren't surprised. That's the way they talk about unemployment. They're the statistics; it's the government that's at fault, and the whole economic system. I don't blame them, either, for talking like that. What are they supposed to say?

"But they don't stop there. Then they say it's them. The country's bad, but it's their fault they're out of work. It's them. They turn their own arguments right around. One minute it's not their fault; the next minute it's all their fault. So you ask, How can it be both ways? Because people out of work are beaten people. Like the Bennetts. They do to themselves the same thing not having a job does to them. They beat themselves, and they beat each other, physically, 'til they really get hurt. The Bennetts acted like children because they are children. What's the difference between a man and a boy? The man has responsibilities; he works for a living. Even if the boy has a few responsibilities, he still doesn't work for a living. His father or his mother works for a living and he rides that living. The Bennetts were riding other people's living, and it made them into babies. We had four children, not two children, living below us. That's the God's honest truth. Mrs. Bennett, she told my wife once, 'You think of me as a child, don't you?' My wife said, 'No, of course not,' but she did a little, because they *were* like children.

"Tell you the truth. In the beginning, I thought they were both nuts. Honest to God. I felt ashamed that what they were doing to one another was going on under the same roof. You're out of work, that's your business. You want to talk to me about it, I'll talk to you anytime you want. But go 'round belting your wife, or husband, or carrying on like a couple of maniacs, I don't want any part of that. I'd tell the same thing to my own children. There have to be rules and you have to behave like an adult, even when you're going through tough times. But I never realized how this unemployment business was affecting people, changing 'em. The Bennetts were dying on the floor below me. They were dying and I'd joke about them. I've talked to a million guys about being out of work. I was out of work in my day, too. But you don't remember what it does to you, and in my case, I never saw what goes on in a guy's home. Talking in a bar is one thing, but it's just words. But here you have a chance to see what happens day by day, minute by minute, and they were being killed by it. I think about them now and I feel ashamed how I joked about it. They never knew, of course, but I know. That's all that's important to me now."

Frances Covell Zegler has four sisters. She grew up in a building two hundred yards from where she, her husband, and children presently live. Her father, Frank, worked for a pipe company until he suffered a stroke. He was in his middle forties at the time. A strong man with energy neither his daughters nor fellow workers could match. He never made much money, not that anyone faulted him for it. No one in his family ever mentioned the subject of his finding a job that paid more or taking on extra employment. He worked steady jobs, brought in money, and rarely complained, except about heat. He despised hot weather and always promised that when he got rich he would vacation on the North Pole. He even bought toy penguins for his daughters to remind them of his imaginary North Pole expedition. Frances Zegler remembers the stories her father used to tell about the North Pole. He was so accurate in his details that Frances believed he had been there. Her father always said Francie was the most gullible of the daughters, but gullibility was the sign of trust.

On a viciously hot July afternoon, Frank Covell awoke with a headache. By late afternoon he was feeling pain throughout his body. In the hospital, the next afternoon, it was determined that he had suffered a stroke, although the doctors believed there might not be excessive damage. A week later, he suffered a second stroke and a heart attack and was left a man with severe disabilities. Because Francie's mother was not a strong woman, the responsibility of nursing Frank fell on the daughters, who worked indefatigably, hoping that their assiduous care would restore their father's health. But Frank Covell never recovered. It was a relief to everyone when he died, at age forty-nine. The strain had been too great. Francie had always imagined that one morning he would jump out of bed and go to work. For it was his not working that perplexed her. The idea of her father staying home all day seemed peculiar, even though she knew he was desperately ill. If it had been her mother, it would have been easier to comprehend.

No one needed to tell Francie that her reactions were curious. She loved her father and was herself stricken by his illness. Yet, deep down, she was angry with him for not being the strong man he was supposed to be and not being able to work. She never revealed these feelings, for she knew they made her sound disloyal, but when her father died, she felt no small amount of relief. When her mother died five years later, she mourned again for her father and feared she would never regain her strength and confidence. There was a bit of relief in her mother's death, too, for still another of her burdens had been lifted. She was tired of playing mother to people who weren't her children. She was tired of the incessant talk about insufficient money, jobs that paid too little, and unemployment.

Early in their courtship when it became evident that Ed had marriage in mind, Frances said to him, "Promise me we live alone. No parents." Ed never pursued the point with her. He knew what she had gone through, and how important it was for him to work and to provide for her so that she would feel she could be her own woman. She was entitled to a life in which people gave to her instead of her having to nurse them. Ed entered marriage certain that when a man can no longer work, like his father-in-law, the burden it places on his family is too great. He resolved that if he couldn't work properly, he'd take his life. If, God forbid, that day ever came, Francie would understand.

Frances Zegler said she smelled the smell of death when she first met the Bennetts. They could not have been more charming, more pleasant or neighborly, but there was something they were hiding. When Mr. Bennett was seen hanging around the apartment house during the day, she knew precisely what these two sad people were facing:

"At first I thought he might have been a mental case. Or maybe she was. Or maybe they both were. I didn't really feel they were crazy, but something was off. Then it came out that Mr. Bennett hadn't been able to find work and Mrs. Bennett felt it wasn't her place to work. She thought it would only hurt him if she worked when he couldn't. She told me she was willing to take the welfare 'til he found something. She always seemed reasonable when she talked with me. Nothing like how he was going to end up being a bank executive. He'd get steady work, she said, and they'd be able to straighten their lives out. I never liked the way she talked about the neighborhood as if it were a railroad stop; like they were going to be moving down the line when things got better. That's what she'd say: 'When it's better.' I let it go. You never like to hear that someone can't wait to get out of a situation which is the best you'll ever be able to afford. I never told her that. By the time I decided to, I saw how bad off they were. All the talk about moving where it's better was part of the lie they kept with one another, and everybody else. So I accepted it.

"As for the hitting and screaming, I guess I never knew people did it like that. In many ways, I had a very sheltered life. My parents never fought; the buildings we lived in always had quiet people. I had girlfriends who told me how their parents fought, but I thought fighting meant some shouting and then it's quiet again. But the Bennetts were at war. I never went down there when they were like that, although I wanted to more than once. I had this idea I'd go in there when they'd call for one of us and take them both over my knee and spank them 'til they were silly. But they were sick. You don't live without a job and get by for too long, emotionally I mean. It'll take the best out of any person.

"Mrs. Bennett came up to our place every once in a while. Never stayed if anybody else was home. I'll never forget that woman's face as long as I live. You knew she was young. She couldn't have been more than midthirties, but she looked like she was in her midforties. She had these terrible lines on her face and this terrible purple color around her eyes, like she was an actress with makeup, only this wasn't makeup. Her teeth were bad, too, and her hair always seemed so dirty. But the thing I remember the most was the way her eyes looked like they had been cried out. Like she had no more tears to cry. Ed saw it in their eyes, too. He called them the couple with the workless eyes.

"There was only a few conversations, nothing too much, but enough to know what their situation was all about. He'd lost maybe a half-dozen jobs, and it was eating the two of them alive. He'd try to get work; she'd say he wasn't trying hard enough. He got angry at her pushing; she thought if she didn't push he wouldn't try at all. She told me, like she was confessing to her priest, that she fought with him and refused to sleep with him in the same bed. She said she knew it wasn't a good idea but she had her principles. I told her once it was none of my business but since the job market was so terrible, it didn't make much sense for her to be tough on her husband. She said she knew that but she had her pride. She couldn't go home to see her mother because her mother wouldn't talk with her until Mr. Bennett got a job. She got terribly angry about this, which isn't hard to imagine, and told her husband he was the reason she couldn't have a relationship with her own mother.

"Then she told me how she had two sisters, both of them married to men with steady jobs. Then, damned if one of her sisters' husbands goes out and loses his job. So this man is out of work, according to Mrs. Bennett, the same time Mr. Bennett is out of work. But they never got together. Each one was afraid to tell the other the trouble they had. Then she went on to say how her sister left her husband because he couldn't find work. She put up with it for a while; then after a couple of months when she saw how terrible it was going to be, she told him, 'Bad times or not, I'm giving you exactly six months to find a job. And not just any job, but one that looks like it's going to last.' Six months, and she's going to leave him. I couldn't believe her sister saying this, but that's what happened. Six months later, this poor man had still not found anything, and she did it. She left him. And listen to this part. She walks out on him and leaves him with the kid. So here's this guy without a dime, without a job, and full responsibility for a six-year-old child. She told him, Mrs. Bennett said, 'If a man can't provide, a woman can't raise a child.' Then their mother, she takes back this sister, into her house. Received her with open arms. But she won't talk to Mrs. Bennett, who's trying to hold on even with all the problems, and she was a good mother, too, given the circumstances. You can only do the best with what you've got.

"That's how it went. I'd be ready to slap her or bawl her out, and she'd come to me, a perfect stranger, and tell me her side of the story. I couldn't do anything. I never helped her, poor thing. I never did a thing, because she was trying to tell me she had pride and a sense of shame; she knew exactly what was going on. But her position was not, Feel sorry for me, but Look what I'm doing, what I'm putting up with, when my sister walked out on her situation and got the blessing of her mother after she did it. That's the part that was so strange. Mrs. Bennett believed she was doing a great thing staying with her husband and children. There's a lot of people would tell you that everyone would have been better off if she walked out on him a long time ago. Nobody likes to see a separation or divorce, but many times it's better than a family being together when it's at war. But she stayed. That was her act of courage; I think you could call it that. She was a courageous woman, even with all the terrible things she did, and he did.

"I'd call them both courageous in their way. They both knew what the future held for them. They got drunk and fought and acted like they were blind to what was going on, but they knew. Nobody needs to tell anybody how their lives are. Nobody knows better than the person themselves. They knew exactly what the future would bring, and when it would bring it. When you have a situation like theirs, deep-rooted unemployment which gets worse everyday, you begin to see the future very clearly. People who go into the hospital sick enough that they're going to die, they know it. I go in with pain in my stomach or legs, I know I'm sick, but a little voice inside me says, 'You're scared, and you're in a lot of pain, but you know you're not going to die. Maybe the next time, but this time, no.' I'm sure your body tells you: Be sick, but don't worry.

"But the Bennetts, they knew when they moved into this building they were dying. When she said to me that first day, 'We're only going to be here a little while,' that time I got so insulted, I knew what she was saying. She was telling the world, I'll be here 'til I die. This is the last spot on earth I'm ever going to live in. So you think, now, if a job, not even the greatest job in the world, had come up, those people might have been spared all they had fall on them. No one needed to tell them about other families going through the same thing. Didn't she have her own sister who made a life for herself? They needed some company to come to them and say, 'Here, Mr. Bennett, here's a job. You need a job, here's a job.' He wouldn't have cared if it was a gift or what Ed calls a fool's job, which is just making a place for someone who needs work. One job, and they would have had a little smooth sailing, a little more time. That's all you can do for people like that, give them time. But there was no way I could give her time. She never asked me for a thing, especially for something she knew I couldn't give. All the days she was living here, I wished I was the president of some corporation so I could go down-stairs and knock on their door and tell them their unemployment days were over. What a feeling that would be. You wonder sometimes, Aren't there corporation presidents who, if they heard about cases like the Bennetts, could come up with a few jobs? I realize what you need is hundreds of thou-sands of jobs, but people like the Bennetts, they're the extreme case. I'll bet there are more people like the Bennetts suffering from their unemployment disease than anybody could imagine. Not everybody ends up like them, but they come close, mighty, mighty close."

Frances Zegler was awakened by the commotion that cold February night. Ed Zegler woke first, certain that their apartment was being robbed. Listening more closely, he realized the noise was coming, as usual, from the Bennetts. But it wasn't fighting or furniture being thrown. There had been an explosion. He roused Frances and told her what he had heard. Frances told him he was dreaming. No, he protested, it wasn't a dream. He had heard something that sounded like a gunshot. "Did either of the Bennetts have a gun?" he asked. "How would I know?" she answered with irritation. Then, as she was about to reprimand him, they heard a second explosion, a gun firing, and they saw lights going on in the apartments across the courtyard. It was two-thirty in the morning.

Ed and Frances Zegler pounded on the Bennetts' door for more than a minute before Ed tried opening it. The door was unlocked. The lights in the Bennetts' livingroom were on, and a strange smell hung in the air, as if someone had burned food. Ed told Frances to go back upstairs to their own apartment and telephone the police. Then he tiptoed into the kitchen. He found Stacy Bennett dead, seated in a chair, her head lying face down on the table, which was covered with blood. She was wearing a blue bathrobe and was barefoot. He ran from the room, left the Bennetts' front door open, raced upstairs to his own apartment, locked himself inside, and leaned against the door as if he were preventing anyone from entering.

Within minutes, the police arrived to find the body of Peter Bennett lying on his bed. He had shot himself in the head. Unbelievably, the children had slept through the noise. They weren't even awake when the police began their examination of the apartment.

Ed Zegler has never been able to determine whether he remembers a great deal or nothing at all of that night. At times he can replay the events in his mind without missing a detail, but at other times he can recall nothing, not even seeing Stacy Bennett dead in the kitchen. One fact, however, he always remembers. A tall policeman who struck him as being unusually old asked him whether he knew Mr. Peter Bennett. Ed Zegler nodded. Then, with his pen poised to record Ed's answer, the policeman asked, "Any idea what he did for a living?"

DYING FROM THE LINES

Sixty-two-year-old Amos Payton, an African American man born in Tennessee, has lived in Boston for the last thirty-nine years. He spoke with me in his home several days after the death of his older brother, Clinton. Both men had known periods of unemployment and the physical and psychic toll that being out of work can have on a person. Both men had experienced discrimination, sometimes in subtle ways and often in grotesque and ugly ways, and had been exhausted by it. And finally, Clinton, if Amos Payton's words accurately describe the situation, knew what it was to quit, to give up, to "turn his body quietly over to the angels."

To listen to the Payton family—Amos and his wife, Ruby, Clinton's widow, Cleo, and the uncles, aunts, and cousins who live close by—Clinton Payton died because he chose to. Amos explains it this way: "My brother could have gone on, a long time too, if he'd wanted to. Folks in my family live a long, long time. They always did, anyway, 'til the smart ass ones like me thought they'd do better in the city. Stay out there in the country, western Tennessee where we were brought up, the eight of us, and you lived a good long time. But, I suppose, when you're young you don't think about none of that. Get it in your head you're going to live forever. Old Clinton and Amos did. We just picked ourselves up, and here we are. Here I am, I mean. Lost my next older brother now, and like I say, he could have gone on a whole lot longer.

"Know why my brother died? 'Cause he chose to. 'Cause he told himself, How long you want to fight it, boy? How long you want to put yourself through the pain of it, the living up here with all the hustle and bustle, and the people huffin' and puffin'? Tell you why he died. Did I say he chose to? 'Cause he chose to. You know how people talk about poor folks like us living off welfare or government pensions or whatever we all got? Folks say how we need a home and food, health care, all the stuff. Sure we need that stuff. For God's sake, everybody needs that. But you don't just die when you don't have it no more. You don't just die when you lose a job, or go a long time without working. That don't just kill you. All those things, they all add up, but they're just pieces of the puzzle. You ever seen a puzzle? You know how you can look at the pieces? You can look at just the lines, too. What do you see connecting all the puzzles? Is it the pieces, or is it the lines? It's both, but most folks, they're so busy looking at the pieces they don't see the lines, and all the patterns those lines are making all over the puzzle.

"You know why Clinton died? From the lines. The lines are the connections, and the connections are what supports you. Clinton lost the connections, so he lost the supports. You see what I'm getting to? The man had some of the pieces to the puzzle. Had a little money, and a little home, had a good woman caring for him. Went to the hospital when he had to. Time to time he had a little job, nothing all that much, but good enough. But all that, see, is just pieces. No lines yet. Man couldn't find support. The stress killed him. The stress of just being around, being alive. Had the pieces all right, but they weren't connected. Doctor told me, man had a bad heart, bad liver, bad kidneys, nothing no good. But he didn't have no disease. Least so they didn't tell me no name of no disease. Man had all his insides going bad, but nobody found a disease. Died because there weren't no support.

"You want to know why he died? Why he quit going on? 'Cause of all the potholes in the streets. Believe that? That's one of the connections. Walking down the street was a pain to him. Man hated looking at the street, hated driving on the street. Hated the idea nobody came around to fix them holes. So he gave up on that. Know why he died? No light in the hall. Never no light in the hall. Never no light on the street, never no light going up the stairs to his front door. Stressed him. Thirty years, never no light. Summer, winter, late at night, early in the morning, couldn't never see a damn thing. Wasn't nothing to see, 'cept that's not what folks think about. Stressed him, not seeing. He brought home the bulbs. Never worked. Someone took 'em. Someone broke 'em. 'Lectricity would go out. He'd go buy some more. Same story. No light, no support.

"Know why he died? Non-human noises. That's what I call 'em. Noises no human being's going to make. Child gets whupped by his father, starts bawlin', that's a human sound. You don't mind that noise. But you go hear a child crying 'cause his old man beats him for no good reason, only 'cause he's just so miserable hisself, that's a non-human noise. Going to kill you, that noise. Who knows, maybe you gone and done that yourself. I'm not saying my brother did or didn't beat up on his children. I'm only saying maybe he did, and maybe the pain of doing it lay too heavy on the man. That can stress you, too.

"No good religion, always cold inside the church, people freezing in the winter, church in bad shape, potholes in the streets walking to the church, buildings coming down, or s'posed to be coming down—that's what folks gotta see walking to the church. Sidewalks cracking, got places where folks can't walk where they're s'posed to be fixing the sidewalks, got those places blocked off for years, it seems, but no one comes to do nothing about them. That sort of thing ate the man up. Used to look at all that and tell me, 'I can't eat when I see it. And nobody in the world can explain it?' All that stuff stressed him.

"Dirt. If you knew my brother you knew he didn't keep hisself all that clean. I mean, he'd wash, but I'd see him at the table with his hands dirty. Cleo would have to tell him, 'Clinton, you wash your hands or prepare your-self to watch us eat!' He'd obey when she talked, but he was never no clean gentleman. But even that way like he was, I'd watch him rub his finger along some windowsill and shake his head. Or he'd stare at the garbage piling up out back of his house. You could see him standing there, not saying a word, and not looking all that clean hisself, but you'd see him shaking his head. Just having to live with it, it stressed him. Man died from garbage. Man died from seeing it, living alongside it everyday over the last forty years. Smell got in his nose, sight of it got in his eyes. What stressed him was how ugly it was. Made him think there wasn't no hope, no reason to hope about noth-ing else in the world. Garbage killed my brother. Man watched for too long folks dumping their garbage out back, thinking it'd be gone by the end of the week. Animals running wild over it. Looked out his window and watched the dogs running all over the garbage. Seeing it that way just hurt him.

"You know how those folks read your hands and tell 'bout your lifeline? I'll tell you about the death lines. Two of 'em. Angry. Being angry about all these things, and not being able to do nothing in the world about it. Can't fix the problem, and you can't yell nothing to nobody. Even when you do, you know you got the wrong guy, 'cause the guy you're yellin' at, he's just trying to make out in the same community with the same horrible problems as you got. You can live like that, maybe, when you're twenty, but you don't cotton to it no more when you're old. World stressed Clinton. Only fought back with his own stress, which turned him right around back on hisself. I told him, 'Relax. What's it going to get you being so angry all the time?' Man didn't answer me. But he was thinking, You got to be dead not to be angry about all this.

"Anger and fear. That's the other one. Afraid you might get beat up. Afraid you might lose your job. Afraid someone's getting sick. Afraid you won't get everything you need. Afraid you can't be the man you want to be. Afraid for your life; afraid for your death, too. Clinton used to tell me, 'You know something, I don't know what I got to do to turn off the fear. 'Fraid of getting angry, and getting angry 'cause I get afraid. Hell, man, afraid of not being angry no more.' He knew the only way you stay alive 'round here is stay a little angry, and a little afraid. Just cutting it out for yourself everyday, no matter what's going on, you got to stay up on your toes. Anger and fear, they're gonna keep you alert, like an animal. Got to keep on the prowl. May be fun when you're young, but it's got to stress you when you're old. Comes a time when folks need to rest; folks got to recover from all that being afraid and being angry. Men like my brother, 'cause all they see and hear bothers 'em so much, they don't never know no relief from being alive. So they tell themselves, fight's coming to an end.

"I believe all sorts of strange things can happen to a man when he decides he's going to die. He can make hisself do it. For all I know, Clinton picked out the date from off the calendar. Man waited 'til after the New Year started. Like to say, well, I didn't want to make nobody unhappy at Christmas. Like to see one more year start, just to see maybe they're going to make it different 'round here now. Maybe now they're gonna fix some potholes, put some lightbulbs in the hall. Maybe they'll take away the garbage. Man waited. Then he probably told himself, Ain't no supports in this city and I'm tired. Tired of the same old pieces, tired of not being able to find connections. So, like I say, the stress got him. That's my theory, anyway.

"When the doctors look at a man like my brother, they look maybe at his insides, and all they can say is everyone of 'em is in bad working order, but still he don't have no disease. Man had his sick days, but nothing ever serious. But now they say his organs have all gone. Man never felt like nothing about his life was supported; that killed his heart. Bet you his brain was working, never stopped thinking. Might have been better if he did. Only way to beat the stress is to pay it no mind. Pretend it ain't there eating you up alive and you just standing there not being able to do nothing to protect yourself, 'cause all you got is the pieces to deal with but none of the connections.

"Point is, you might have the supports, but you need more. You can have all your big muscles, but some folks can't get over the pain of a rotten pothole. Potholes, rows of 'em, most likely, might have killed my brother. Maybe that's why the doctors couldn't find no name for the disease that killed him. Wasn't no disease to be found."

DR. PAULIE'S SNOWSTORM

RAYMOND PAULIE CRIGHTON is a tall, frighteningly thin boy of thirteen. I met Paulie years ago, when he was only five, when I came to know his family and many other families as part of research I was doing on how families without fathers were faring. Although one of his brothers was in jail, there was no way to tell, of course, how little Paulie would turn out. I remember thinking at the time that this boy had one of those sweet, innocent faces that prompted people to call him "Sugar."

I am told by his mother that Paulie flunks most of his courses, shows up for classes only 50 percent of the time, and never stays for more than 50 percent of the day. His friends call him "the fifty-fifty man." Strangely, I often use the word "brilliant" to describe him, but it may not be accurate. Truthfully, I have never observed him doing anything long enough to know just how smart he is.

One might say that Raymond Crighton is a successful businessman, if that term applies to a boy barely in his teens. On good days he takes in $600; on bad days, around $100. He might work three days a week, or he may go seven. He keeps only a percentage of what he earns, but it is more than sufficient. Paulie Crighton sells drugs. He sells them, seemingly, everywhere and to everyone. He sells on the street, and he sells in shopping malls, restaurants, office buildings, hospitals, furniture and liquor stores, and supermarkets. He'll sell wherever you want him to sell. You tell him, and he'll be there. He's rarely late to an appointment, returns phone calls, is always reachable; he wears a beeper on his belt for just that reason. You can contact him and have him bring any amount of cocaine you desire. He handles complicated payment programs—installment strategies with interest—and rarely makes an error.

He may be "Sugar" to his relatives, "the fifty-fifty man" to his school chums, but the boy who calls himself Dr. (a reference to his "medicinal" business) Paulie (Paul being his father's name), is handling thousands of dollars a month. And partly because of this, and partly, too, I imagine, because of the supreme danger of his work, he has mastered the big man image and the art of bravura. His pockets bulging with money, he will say to me,

"Hey, doc, tell me what you need? Name it, you got it. I got TVs, doc. You want 27 inches, you got it. You want the floor models with the colored lights, consider it arranged. I got friends in high and low places. Real low places. Refrigerators? Tell me the color. Got all kinds of gadgets on 'em; throw ice in your face if you hit the right button, doc. Microwaves. They're safe, doc. Checked 'em out myself. Nah, I didn't really. How'm I gonna check a microwave? I can't even figure how those suckers work. You get the steak warm, how come the dish don't get warm? They teach that in my school; I might just sit there awhile. Radios? Boxes, doc, stick 'em in your room, plug 'em in your ear. Pick a color, pick a song."

Now, years after our initial meeting, we stand together on a street near the projects where he lives. It is an area where the crime rate is high. Nightly, police answer calls of knifings, shootings, and drug overdoses, and the large majority of them involve children. He stands in front of me in the sunlight, shifting his weight from one foot to the other, a sprinter awaiting the order to enter the starting blocks. He is revved, always revved. The tone of his voice rarely changes; it is always enthusiastic. There are never problems he can't handle and never a reason to be pessimistic.

"What do you ask these questions for doc?" he responds when I start once again on the subject of his staying in school. "I do what I do. I make money off people like you, doc. They want drugs, I get 'em drugs. I'm no different, doc, than half the people you know. Everybody's doing the illegal thing or the stupid thing or the killer thing. They go to court, they do their song and dance, and they walk. The bankers do it. The doctors do it. Politicians, too. Don't make out like everybody's clean. This guy makes money with money. This guy makes money with cars. This guy sells TV sets that cost him a few bucks. He makes a killing while you go off thinking you made a killing.

"I stand there, doc, next to guys in the stock market business. They're on the phone getting some sucker to buy a stock. They're there guaranteeing him, and while they're doing this, they're writing notes to each other 'bout this and that. I don't know if they're lying. I don't understand what the hell's going down. Everybody's screaming and yelling, about what I couldn't tell you. Hey, I know when to keep my mouth shut, and my beeper on!

"You know why I'm there, doc? 'Cause these yellers and screamers want my drugs. Want 'em for their recreation. Their recreation makes me get my recreation, see what I'm saying? They act so smooth all the time, but if I don't come up with what they want, they go out of their minds. I saw a guy a few weeks back, he made someone buy something or sell something, 'cause the sucker owed me money. I'm standing there while he's making some fool spend his money or lose his money to pay a thirteen-year-old kid who gets him drugs. You understand that? All I care about is the man pays me good old American cash.

"Doc, I make more money in two hospitals than I make out here in the streets for two weeks. Doctors with keys to cabinets with painkillers that could put me out of business, buying from me. You believe what I'm tellin' you? I'm saying old guys. Young guys can't afford my show. We're talking honest to god docs wearing white coats so pressed you can 'bout see your face in 'em. I been in their offices with the pictures of the wife and kids on the desk. Frames could send me on a trip somewhere. Some dumpy little picture in a hundred-dollar silver frame. Man don't ask me a question 'bout nothing,' 'cept maybe how my mother's doing. But he don't like this now 'cause I bring my mother to him when she got sick and he can barely look at me. He knows the game. He treats her, I treat him. He knows, I know, my mother knows. Whole damn hospital knows, for all I care. He does his work for her. He's a helluva doc. I know that. I don't let him down, but he's ashamed. I see it in his face. She comes in for treatment, he does his job, but he won't call me for weeks. I sit tight. He'll call. He ain't goin' to kick nothin' anymore. He ain't goin' to change his life. Not for himself, not for all the people in the picture on his desk, and not for me, you can bet! Man's stuck on my show.

"Nurses too, doc. Good-looking nurses standing 'round waiting for me to visit. I come in there, I find out from my contact people they been asking for me, doc. They got people bleeding and dying and falling all over the place, and all these nurses can think about is, when's Dr. Paulie coming? And doc, I ain't payin' no visit without someone callin' me first. Too great a chance you lose out on another score. You call, you talk money, I'll be there. There are people, you know, who can't go to the wards and I get to go, 'cause folks up there say I'm this one's son or this one's brother. They do business right there, since no one will suspect 'em of nothin.' Right out in the open.

"I got a dentist near where you live, doc; man's got more money than god. Gambles. I got a cousin helps him lay bets. I get him drugs. We meet in a goddamn MacDonalds. You believe this? That's the way he wants it. They ain't never ashamed. You thinking we're hiding around doing this? Hell no. People could be watching us like we were on TV. These people are giving me money in the open, doc. Sometimes no envelopes. Give me IOU's, man.

"The place is wide open drug crazy. I'll bet I been places you never been. I sold drugs, man, to a judge in a court. You think I'm lying, doc? I went to this court with a friend of mine. He was up for something he never did. Anyway, we're talking, and this man comes up and tells me this judge is a head. Man does cocaine. Gets stuff through a guy who's been in prison. So he says, 'You want business, Dr. Paulie?' I say, 'In here man? In a goddamn court? You got to be kiddin' me.' He says he'll fix me up. Judge pays me cash. Calls me on the beeper. Man's got to be sixty years old, and he's calling Dr. Paulie to get stuff. Man told me if I told someone 'bout him he'd have me in his court. So who you think is crazy, doc?"

There is obvious danger at almost every turn of Dr. Paulie's life. That he returns home every night is a miracle. That he avoids fights and shootings is extraordinary. His innocent smooth face saves him. His youth saves him, too. Astonishingly, he has never been robbed, though his pockets veritably bulge with the bills he receives from his clients. There is danger as well for those who associate with him, and especially those who supply him drugs. Then there is the matter of his moral dilemmas.

He is openly angered, for example, to learn that a friend does drugs, but he articulates his rage ten minutes after he has sold cocaine to someone. He brags to me of living without conflict, but just when I conclude that his sanguine outlook is nothing more than psychopathy, he turns around and ruminates on his destiny, as he does on this one hot afternoon near his home.

"My mother will tell you she takes my stuff and doesn't care how I got it. We both know she's lyin.' Ain't many people in the world breath easy knowing how things have found their way in their home. Money ain't stole or nothin,' but it's dirty. Hey, I'm the one saw where the money comes from. I know better than anyone how people are beggin' for the show. I might have already put someone in the grave. I've taken money from some of the sickest folks anyone could meet. They're wearin' clean clothes and all, but they are sick! But I'm the one took their money.

"You wanna know if I'm a criminal? I'm a criminal. Bad one, too, which makes everybody who knows what I do a criminal. That means my mother, my sisters, my brother. 'Course I got cop friends who gotta know what's going down. They ain't never been in our house, but if they don't do nothin' it's because they pretend they can't see nothin.'"

He's probably right about this. Police admit to their frustrations in dealing with child drug dealers. Most kids like Dr. Paulie will walk free from the courts, and besides, it's the older dealers and organizers the police seek.

"Think about this, doc. You got a thirteen-year-old kid making more money than most everybody in the country. And how many hours a day I work? Four? How many people you know dealing with big shots like I do? Lots of time I walk around here feeling like some kind of big shot myself. Feels good being somebody people can see. I don't need school now. I don't do drugs. Don't drink. Too young for sex, right, doc? Take care of my body. So what's wrong 'bout this arrangement? You wanna know? Plenty times I thought about it and it always comes out with the same answer."

Now his tone and mood begin to vacillate. One minute I hear the big man bravura, and the next he reveals contrition, even remorse. Similarly, his argument at times loses its logic and impact, and his accounts seem contradictory. Whatever his verbal shifts and inconsistencies, he never stops talking.

"I'm a damn criminal who maybe ought to be killed for what he does. I'm the one who goes between the people killing people and the people getting killed. I ain't the gun, I ain't the guy killing the guy; I'm the bullet. Boom, off into the air I hit this guy right between the eyes. Do it so clean the guy don't even know he's hit. That means someday, when they find one of these people who dies from the show, they're going to do one of their examinations and find the bullet. They're going to hold it in their hand and say, 'Well, I'll be, here's the first time we laid our hands on the bullet that killed all these folks, or made 'em poor as hell, and wouldn't you know, it's old Dr. Paulie.' Probably knew it all the time. But it don't matter 'cause I'm still the bullet. I can tell myself what I'm doin' don't hurt nobody but it's lyin.'

"Don't want nobody to tell me I'm dumb. I know what's happening. Whole thing's too big now. It's like a snowstorm. It's going to blow down on folks as long as it likes. People think they can stop it. No way. You put me away today, they got ten million kids, most of 'em younger than me, waitin' to get hold of my client list. Hundreds of guys comin' out of school saying, take a look at me, boss, I'm the new Dr. Paulie. Most of 'em already got their names, like the Croacker, Roach, Spider Man, The Slider. Got their names, but they're all criminals.

"I'm doin' lots of things bad, doc. Gonna get caught, but I can't stop the show now. Too late for that. Guys like me, we don't go to court, 'cept to sell drugs, I s'pose. We die. In the streets, back of someone's car somewhere. We don't go to court. Too many people sittin' ready to get even with us if we make a mistake. I figure I can make it a few more years. All's I want is to live longer than my mother. Hope she's got a lot of time, but the doctor don't think it looks good. That's why I keep gettin' her everything she ever wants. No one else did. When she dies, I ain't going to turn myself in or nothin,' but then everything can go away.

"I ain't in it 'cause of her. I ain't sayin' that. I'm only sayin' I stay as long as she stays. That crazy? She ain't gonna be healthy just 'cause I go home some night and tell her I'm out of work and goin' back to school. She ain't gonna suddenly say good-by to cancer. She dies, I quit. Maybe. I'll tell you then. But I got to pay a price somewhere, don't I? I ain't foolin' myself. This is a bad act, doc. Can't get out of it. Don't know if I want to, either."

Nothing I say ever seems to affect Dr. Paulie. His grandiose offers of products continue, and our discussions go on in cars, hamburger joints, ice cream parlors, and shopping malls. No one takes note of us; no one sees anything out of the ordinary. In subsequent conversations, however, I begin to hear increasingly more references to penance, punishment, and guilt. There are also more references to death as a logical and preordained solution. And for the first time since I have known him, I see his fright. I see a thirteen-year-old boy fearing things with which he should never be bothered.

Whereas once I dreaded telephone calls from this young braggadocio, now suddenly I worry when I don't hear from him. Many in his family are worried as well. The murders of children continue in our city, and what Raymond Crighton calls "the snowstorm" has barely abated. So I welcome his calls these days and listen to his grandiose promises of free TVs and refrigerators. After all, no show runs forever, and no actor, no matter how superb his performance, is immortal.

MEN WITH NO ANSWERS

DESPITE SOME recent accounts, the story of the Atomic Veterans, a group of some 250,000 former American military personnel, remains relatively unknown. In some cases, their anonymity barely troubles readers of history; after all, most men and women who served their country and then left the military to resume their civilian lives have stories that probably would not interest most of us, unless, of course, they contain graphic tales of war. So, we honor these people who, as they say, serve our country, or even protect and defend it, but seemingly remain relatively disinterested in the lives and jobs they had in the military.

In the case of Atomic Veterans, however, the accounts that have been slowly accumulating over the last thirty years ought to have special relevance to all of us, because these are the men who survived what most of us dread more than anything: nuclear explosion. These are the men who can answer the question, What would happen to us if we survived a nuclear holocaust?

Even after the horrendous deaths of thousands of Japanese and the unbelievable destruction wrought by the bombings of Hiroshima and Nagasaki in 1945, the U.S. government oversaw almost two hundred atmospheric and underground nuclear test explosions. Known by such names as Bikini, Smokey, and Operation Dominic, these tests required the presence of military personnel, mostly men, who often witnessed extraordinary explosions from positions dangerously close to the detonation sites.

Devices of all kinds were examined, as were the physical and psychological reactions of the men assigned to participate in these tests, men who often worked at close range to detonation sites. The data stemming from tests on the devices are well known; the results involving the men have been shrouded in military secrecy and, in some cases, misrepresented. Indeed, for more than a decade, two organizations, the National Association of Atomic Veterans (NAAV) and the Center for Atomic Radiation Studies (CARS), have devoted themselves to learning essentially two things. First, what did happen to the men who participated in these tests? Second, and more generally, what is the effect on a human being of having been directly exposed to certain forms of radiation?

The answers to these questions are fraught with legal, medical, sociological, and historical complexities. But while the men and their families await a final verdict from the U.S. government on whether the military in fact knew the dangers facing Atomic Veterans and will properly compensate them for damages due directly to radiation poisoning, thousands of men live their lives and reflect on their peacetime military obligations. Some have not yet made a connection between their illness and their proximity to detonation sites decades ago. Others died of cancers in their thirties, forties, and fifties, having revealed to their spouses nothing of what they did, saw, and felt during their years of military service.

In many respects, the government has not been forthcoming. Legal suits have been lodged to procure medical information, and journalists have made intensive investigations, but the medical and psychological histories of the Atomic Veterans remain incomplete. The answers, therefore, lie not in military records, some of which have mysteriously disappeared or been burned, but in the personal accounts of the veterans themselves. Here's the problem: many of these men have died or presently are dying from various forms of cancer, some of which medical science was utterly unprepared to treat. Even more, and the issue that has the CARS scientists convinced that there is a connection between these men's exposure to radiation and their cancer, the children of these men also have been diagnosed with cancer at rates far exceeding what normal cancer statistics would predict.

Now, primarily because of the work of NAAV and CARS, more Atomic Veterans are coming forward to offer their accounts, motivated mainly by their existing medical problems or their children's illnesses. It should be noted, however, that the men themselves, most of whom possess unswerving patriotic attitudes, are not always certain of a connection between their roles at test sites and their present medical conditions. Many simply were never told the details and potential dangers of their nuclear assignments. Others, to this day, have no idea of the existence of these issues or, for that matter, the work of CARS and NAAV. Still others, out of denial or a refusal to believe that the military would knowingly use them as guinea pigs and place them in jeopardy, seek to obtain incontrovertible proof of the effect of radiation exposure on the development of cancer cells. CARS scientists also seek this proof, but unlike the veterans, they now are convinced of the connection.

Some Atomic Veterans read a great deal these days about nuclear radiation, underground and above-ground tests, and hazardous wastes. They write letters to government agencies and journalists, consult psychologists and psychiatrists, attend Atomic Veterans organization meetings, and wonder why the majority of Americans either have forgotten them or never knew about them in the first place. And a few tell their stories and draw their own conclusions. Over the years I have interviewed a host of Atomic Veterans, believing that each of their stories represents one more piece in a perplexing and often terrifying mosaic whose ultimate shape will reveal the effect of low-level ionization on the human body. The following are the accounts of three of these men.

I

Ten years ago at an NAAV meeting in Boston, I met veteran Bob Grober, who was then forty-five. Of Dutch and German descent, Bob is a tall, strong-looking man with thinning blond hair and pink skin. Most people would describe his face as kindly and gentle, despite the skin around his eyes, nose, and mouth, which is mostly scar tissue.

Married and the father of three children, who at the time he and I talked were ages fifteen, fourteen, and twelve, Bob Grober has his own military story to tell. It begins in 1962, when he was eighteen and a fresh recruit in the U.S. Navy. His first command placed him on a ship that had been used primarily for testing surface-to-air missiles off the California coast. He remembers the ship as an old sea plane tender whose cranes had been replaced with technology used for guided missile launchings. Eventually, the ship drew an assignment known as Operation Dominic, which called for it to sail to some distant Pacific island area for nuclear testing. As far as Bob can recall, the orders were just that vague.

The flagship of Task Force 8, the vessel made its way toward the Johnson Islands accompanied by a Polaris submarine. Upon reaching the test site, the sub launched a missile into space. When the missile reentered the atmosphere, it was detonated. According to Bob, the purpose of the test was to determine the effects, if any, of the reentry process on the atomic warhead.

"We were down there—it was hot, the sun, what have you—we were down there a couple of weeks and, well, I was ill a number of times," recalled

Bob. "As I recollect, we hung around doing [radiation level] readings, measurements, and so forth. We all had film badges on, and we came home. So I never thought much of it. We were told we had no radiation, all the dissemblers were negative."

Three months later, Bob developed what was diagnosed as a sty in the margin of his left eye. The ship doctor prescribed an ointment for it and told him that regular application would cause it to disappear. Six months later, with the ship now on the East Coast about to be decommissioned and fitted with a new superstructure, the sty was still there. Bob consulted a second military physician on board the ship and then a third physician on the base. The diagnosis: basal cell carcinoma syndrome. A form of skin cancer, basal cells, he was advised, can grow into the tissue of the brain and cause serious damage. Bob also was told that the condition was hereditary, although his parents, his grandparents, and his seven brothers and sisters had never contracted it.

"Nothing to really get excited about, you know," said Bob. "One or two, you have them removed and that's the end of it. I spent six months in the hospital having one or two removed." Bob grinned at me, and chuckled, something he often does when anger moves about inside him. "I think that at that time I had one hundred and fifty removed while I was in the hospital. And now the disease I have is claimed to be hereditary. I just keep going and have them cut off when they get to the size that I feel they should be removed. I think a conservative guess right now is that I've had two thousand of them removed since I've been out of the service. I seem to grow them quite readily. I'm looking for somebody that wants to buy basal cells.

"But now my kids have come down with it. Two have been diagnosed. One is—wait a while and she'll get it. In other words, she has the right characteristics and so forth. I really never related this until last year. I got thinking about it, wait a minute, I was in nuclear tests. So I started pursuing this angle. I do get a fifty percent disability from the government for scar tissue. Not basal cells, scar tissue. They admit I had basal cells. I was discharged from the service with basal cells, but they've used every excuse in the book to say that something else causes it. 'It just happened while you were in the service.' If I had it prior to going into the service, it was not detected. I had a physical going into the service, and I came out of the service with a mass of them. Is it a coincidence?

"The Navy responded with a letter explaining the operation I was on. There were three hundred and twenty-seven people on board the ship, and all dissemblers were negative. The bomb blew up a thousand miles down range. We stayed down there a couple of weeks, but to interpret the letter, we steamed right home, it said. But also the paper said that there was thirty-six tests done in this area over a year and three weeks. So I feel that we could have gotten the fallout from another test. Or maybe we did steam down to where they detonated it to take the readings. I have no idea. I only have one piece of paper from the Department of the Navy that says that we steamed home after the tests. We were one thousand yards off the side of the submarine that launched the missile. Everything seemed to start happening after that.

"The prognosis of this illness? Just keep having them cut off. It's going to continue. I spent fifteen years, more or less, in research. I have a doctor that tried everything in the book to control it, but they haven't. I've got a lot of respect for these people, because they've really tried. I hope someday they do get it, so the kids don't have to go through the same thing, amount of pain and agony, whatever you want to call it. I'm needle shy. Basically that's it. Nothing fancy. I mean there are plenty of other ideas of how I got it and so forth; some of them I disbelieve. It's something that happened and I have to tolerate it. I don't feel that the Navy gave it to me. I have it and I have to tolerate it, so I'll live with it. There was a complete amount of ignorance with these tests. I am more appalled, I mean, by the predecessors to these tests. What right did they have to make them march into a hot spot! I mean, today, to go into a reactor, you have to put on a suit, and still, still they only allow them twelve minutes in there and they have taken their total rhems. They have to lay off work for three months. And I don't call myself an anti-nuke. I would like to see atomic power better controlled and the waste bio-degraded. But I won't sit here and tell you I want all the nuclear stopped. The bomb? Yes, I'm against the bomb. I'm against nuclear weapons. But I think the atomic energy can be used peacefully and correctly if the energies are properly put there.

"You know, I can sit back and say that I got the same symptoms as every-body else. I got headaches, disorientation. There's times I can't remember how old I am. Like the [NAAV] meeting we were at the other day. 'How old are you?' 'Thirty-eight.' I'm not; I'm thirty-seven. It's close, but I have to stop and think, Now wait a minute, what year was I born? I get fifty per-cent disability now; somewhere around three hundred and eighty dollars. I don't know [exactly] how much I get. It all goes into a bank and I don't worry about it. It pays the mortgage and that's the end of it. I assume that one hundred percent would be around twelve hundred dollars with the kids and wife. But I lose a tremendous amount of work out of my own pocket. I work for the post office; they give you two weeks a year. I work on the platform, throw those sacks around in the weird hours of the night. They give me what they call 'leave without pay,' which also is deducted from my retirement date, also deducted from the annual leave next year. This year, I've lost five hundred and sixty hours in pay, which amounts to, in round figures, fifty-six hundred dollars. Last year, it was four hundred and twenty-six hours, which would be forty-two hundred dollars. So that every year you are losing money straight out-of-pocket because of the leave without pay, as well as the difference between the possible fifty percent compensation and the one hundred percent compensation."

At present, the Grobers are struggling. Mrs. Grober is totally disabled, her husband reports, with phlebitis. Able to function fairly well at home, she nonetheless feels intense discomfort all the time. Personnel from Social Security attempted to find employment that she could manage before concluding there was absolutely no job she could handle, since she is unable to sit, stand, or lie down for any significant period of time without pain. The Grober children are responsible for cleaning the house, going to the grocery store, and doing other chores, something their parents feel is unfair to them. Still, as Bob says, what choice do they have? With his salary and his wife's disability payments, the family gets by.

"I get angry at times. I'm not one to sit here and point my finger and say, 'Look what you've done to me.' I don't believe that anyone did anything to me intentionally. Ignorance played the biggest part of it, and maybe there is a possibility that the tests had nothing to do with it, too. I don't know. But I think there is the possibility. My doctors have told me there is. But I'm not one hundred percent ready to sit down and say you people did it, you know. I can't do that. I can probably sit down and say you people aggravated it, but I can't really say they *caused* it. I think you need black-and-white evidence to say something like that. I haven't gone on looking for other people on the boat, because I can't remember their names. I could get the captain's name because I have a nice document of 'Congratulations, you served with the atomic . . .' They're very proud, they're very proud. But I haven't made a big effort. I've tried to sit back and think of names. I can remember one guy's first name, another's last name. I don't remember where they come from. So you know, I go around looking for Bobkins. Any Bobkins in the world?

"I think things are going to work out. I am an optimist, let's put it that way. The disease that I have—there's no telling. I can start growing cells on the brain tissue. But to sit back and say, 'Hey, one of these days I'm going to become a vegetable,' you can't do that. You've got to live; you've got to keep going. You can't just sit down and say, 'I quit, and that's it.' Where are you going to get off? The world is not going to stop. Sure, I would like to see somebody do something. I would like to see someday you take a pill or something and your system charges up and attacks everything and you clear it. I don't know if I'll ever see this day; I have hopes for it. I'm worried about the kids. It's not fun to go through. The boy has had two removed, and my daughter has had one: the nose on my son and the back of the neck on my daughter, which kind of supports the U.V. (ultraviolet) theory that I got basal cells in places that never see the light."

Bob chuckled. "I have a U.V. theory of basal cells. I mean, they told me everything. 'Have you had arsenic?' 'Yes, I take it daily.' 'Have you had hydrocarbons, U.V. radiation?' I don't even understand why up until a year or two ago I never even gave a thought about radiation. And maybe I didn't get it, but we went into an area where all of these tests were going off. I don't know. I don't have any answers. I still haven't lost faith in the government."

II

It sounds like the introduction to a television program, but Gerald Murphy's story begins decades ago and thousands of miles away.

Operation Castle. Joint Task Force 7. March 1, 1954. In the morning, a fifty-megaton atomic bomb is dropped. At the time, it is the largest blast ever detonated. Gerald Murphy is among hundreds of military personnel on the ground 180 miles from the explosion site, an atoll at Bikini in the South Pacific. He and his comrades are safely protected, they are told by authorities, in aluminum huts. They are also advised that in three days a radioactive cloud will float above them. As it happens, the wind shifts, the atmospheric pressure changes, and it rains. No one seems to know if these meteorological shifts will reduce or heighten the danger of radioactive fallout. Thirty-four years later, Gerald Murphy, an overweight man who appears far older than his sixty-one years, remarks, "Atomic is a very nebulous, intangible area." With clear eyes, this proud man, obviously ailing, recounts a brief moment of his own and America's history:

"All right, when I came out of the service I experienced headaches, like I couldn't sleep for two weeks. No temperature, and blood started coming down, nosebleeds. I would say this was a year and a half later. I was going to college and it knocked me right out because I had these wicked headaches. I had headaches for ten to twelve years after that. They didn't know what it was. The doctors said they couldn't give me antibiotics because I had no temperature. I said, 'I've got to have something.' One fellow eventually diagnosed it as a nervous breakdown. He was an eye, ear, nose, and throat man, and he said it sounded to him like a nervous breakdown.

"I had lost most of my taste, ninety percent of my smell, and blood kept coming down, ears, headaches, sore throats—for twelve or fifteen years. And I'm impotent. That came after March 1, 1954, as well, and I've been having a rash and undergoing treatment with a doctor from 1955 on. I am still his patient. I'm still having problems. Growths, eyelid growth four years ago. I don't feel too well. I'm on welfare, living in one room. I've got all these problems. I'm under psychiatric care. I've had these rash problems. Before, I was in good shape. I had all my hair. I lost all my hair. I guess I may develop cancer, right? I've had all these growths. Eyes. They were diagnosed as selasians [cysts], whatever that is. I suppose when I get something like that there's a possibility of malignancy. So I don't know, you know. Naturally there's, I suppose, some apprehension.

"I have no family. I never got married. My parents are dead. I have one sister. I like people very much. I have a number of friends, but I'm pretty much of a loner. I don't have my own family, you know. I probably would have if I didn't have all these physical problems.

"I'm convinced heavy radiation caused a great deal of damage. I would imagine it would be common knowledge; there should be just certain levels of acceptable radiation. Those people, I think they said it was a thousand to two thousand times an acceptable level from that blast. Now that I think about it, when I draw a picture of it, I think it's unbelievable, you know, because many of those people, all their hair fell right out on the spot.

"I feel about ninety. I feel like a vegetable. My appetite is completely gone. Gone in 1963 for some reason. Nothing works. Nothing works. I never get hungry. I could go without food. I would look at it perhaps, but I would never have any muscular contractions associated. I don't feel hungry, full up; that's gone. I could go out and eat a good meal or something and I would feel nothing. I could eat ten more after that. I could drink unlimited. I'm just existing, is all it is. If I could just try to find out what the matter was, what's happened here.

"I would like to work. I don't think I'm unable to do anything. I'm told that I'm unemployable. I can't really do anything. I can't. I don't seem to do anything. I don't seem to have any concentration. I couldn't sit in one place at one thing for an hour. I've been drinking a lot of coffee. I'm on welfare. I've been lost in the general scheme of things. That's the way it goes. I could probably get Social Security disability, I don't know.

"I would say I have no future unless I can help somebody to do something; be of some assistance to someone. I don't even know what I'm doing, you know? I'm just what they call 'free falling.' There's no plans or anything. I used to try to make plans; there's no concentration. I feel like I'm in a fog. I have been called a vegetable. I don't read the newspaper. I try. It's just that I can't really concentrate. I used to.

"I wanted to be good, productive. I was brought up in that type of atmosphere. There was everything I ever wanted. Then I was in the Air Force and I went to college. Then I got the headache—it blew my head right off. It blew it right off. I don't know what that was. I don't know why the hell I would have gone through a nervous breakdown. That thing just blew my head right off. Blood came out of my sinuses.

"I only wish I could do something that would be helpful to others. That's what I would like to do, that's the way I am. If I can help anybody, that's the way I am. If I can do anything that will help anybody, you know, that's what we're here for. That's what we're supposed to be doing. You know what I mean? We're all brothers. Instead of killing each other, screwing each other forever, try to help each other and give some meaning to life. That's what it is."

III

New Englander George Wiltshire, a marine, was part of a special force sent to Nagasaki to unload ships and clean up after the blast. Soon after the bombs were dropped his military company, oddly, was disbanded and a new one formed. He remembered it being called Fleet Marine Forces Pacific— Special Services. Their assignment seemed innocent enough: unload ships that had been left by the Second Marine Division and then load them up again with materials previously unloaded in the atomic area. The Second Marine Division earlier had been dispatched as part of the Japanese invasion force. Wiltshire and his comrades had heard a rumor that D day had been set for sometime in the following November, not June as it turned out to be.

When the bombs exploded and Japan, as Wiltshire would say decades later, "just quit," a new occupational force had to be sent in. Battle-ready, loaded with supplies, this new force braced itself for the possibility of a last-ditch battle from the Japanese army, which still numbered millions of men. But the army obeyed the emperor's order to lay down its arms, and the war ended. Now, while millions of people around the world celebrated the Japanese surrender and the conclusion of World War II, a group of American marines began clearing an area in the middle of the atomic zone. Reconstructing a railroad track to be used for hauling materials from the docks, they soon were able to establish a large supply depot.

Then, as George Wiltshire recalled, something peculiar occurred. A group of scientists appeared on the scene and began studying the environment. No one informed the troops that it was radiation levels these scientists were examining. Wiltshire remembers signs in Japanese and English reading NO UNAUTHORIZED PERSONNEL ALLOWED BEYOND THIS AREA, but he never connected this warning with radiation. He merely assumed the American military was concerned with protecting the millions of dollars of supplies and machinery being unloaded daily.

Years later, when he reflected back on the scene, he realized that the men unloading supplies were working at ground zero, "give or take a few thousand yards," without a hint of the potential dangers of radiation. The scientific group, meanwhile, had ordered the Second Marine Division out of the area, advising them to leave their supplies behind and be gone. Wiltshire reasoned that they no longer wanted these men exposed, but he and his comrades were left with cleanup duty. They were joined by a small force of military police but no other military outfit.

The cleanup and unloading took almost three months. In January 1946, George Wiltshire was on an LST (Landing Ship Tank), the first leg of his journey back to the United States. Now, something else peculiar happened. With no reasons given, Wiltshire's outfit was disbanded and became part of a new supply company, a company, he claims, of which there has never been any record. Sixty or so men constituted this undocumented outfit. A medical doctor and a corpsman were assigned to them, and they were provided their own poorly stocked PX. Again, there was never official record of this company existing. Said Wiltshire, "I think now they're sorry for even moving the material out instead of making a dump for it somewhere. But they salvaged millions of dollars of material. It was salvage. Millions of dollars of materials and supplies, and we were expendable, sixty of us."

By the end of 1946, George Wiltshire had returned to New England and begun working as a salesman. In the spring of 1947, he came down with an illness that never left him. It began one night on a business trip, in a small hotel, where he collapsed in his room with dizziness and nausea. Unable to sleep or eat, he felt the room floating about him. He remembers taking off his tie and feeling the need to learn whether he could drive. Amazingly, he drove home that same night, 150 miles. When he reached his house, his wife called a doctor. Wiltshire was diagnosed as anemic and given liver shots. The injections seemed to help. He soon was back on his feet, but from that point on he experienced chronic fatigue. And that is how it went for forty years.

"I had times I didn't take a lot of vitamins. I got poor—which I'm poor most of the time, anyway—and didn't buy them. I'd go right downhill. I could always feel myself dropping right off. I'd borrow some money or whatever to get some vitamins, and in a week I'd start coming back up. There were times I'd work on a job, and then I'd lose it, 'cause I was tired. One fellow called me lackadaisical. It seemed as though I would just get to the point where things would be going good, and then I'd go right back downhill again.

"It was after I read about some atomic test that I began to think that maybe there was a connection between my laziness, or whatever they wanted to call it, and radiation. I remember I went to the doctor once, and he wanted to know, of course, 'Well, what's your trouble?' 'Well, I'm awful tired. I'm so tired it was all I could do to get in here. I'm too tired even to go home.' And he said, 'What do you think is doing it?' And I said, 'Well, I was wondering whether it might be radiation?' And he sat back in his chair, and he laughed. 'Hah, hah, hah!' That was the first time in my life that I ever really got laughed at. And I got up and walked out."

There were other symptoms, such as severe headaches, which started a week after he returned home in 1946 and lasted for twenty years. Doctors also discovered nasal polyps, which frequently caused bleeding. At the same time, lesions began appearing on his legs. They would flare up and then disappear. In 1975, George Wiltshire was diagnosed as having diabetes. Frightened by the illness, he began reading as much as he could about it. Because his mother was a diabetic, he initially assumed his own illness was genetically caused. However, he discovered research indicating that exposure to radiation may damage the thyroid and pituitary glands, which in turn affect the pancreas, ultimately leading to diabetes. One study offered a statistic he never forgot: "If you have been involved with radiation you have a better chance of getting diabetes than if you've got ten people in your family with the disease."

With every doctor who examined him, George Wiltshire raised the possibility of a connection between his symptoms and radiation. None of them took him seriously. Several of them scoffed at his suggestion. Unable to afford a private physician, George received all his medical services at the local veterans hospital. There, only one doctor who treated him listened to his theory that exposure to radiation at ground zero, Nagasaki, could be the source of his physical ailments. The doctor, head of the nuclear medicine division, never offered a comment.

If the work of the NAAV and CARS redounds to one matter, it is this connection between exposure to radiation and the emergence of severe physical illness. Indeed, what these two organizations have attempted to demonstrate is that exposure not only to the blasts in Nagasaki and Hiroshima but also to hundreds of subsequent nuclear tests has caused all varieties of illness in the men exposed as well as in their children conceived after their exposure. In fact, there now is evidence that the grandchildren of Atomic Veterans present a disproportionately high frequency of cancer-related illnesses.

Every day, the U.S. government receives material generated by NAAV, CARS, and individual Atomic Veterans arguing for the relationship between servicemen's radiation exposure and illness. But there's a big difference between considering the data and accepting them as scientific fact. Accepting these reports as scientifically valid would mean that the government finally would have to take responsibility for its role in nuclear cleanup operations of the sort that George Wiltshire and his fifty-nine comrades carried out.

One wonders whether the group of scientists that departed Nagasaki after two weeks realized the perilous conditions faced by Wiltshire's force. Did they cover up their findings to defend themselves from exactly the sort of medical problems reported for years by Atomic Veterans? And if they covered up, is it because they knew that someday they would be obliged to compensate the Atomic Veterans, as they were obliged to compensate the Japanese and the Marshall Islanders where nuclear tests were undertaken? Is it possible, moreover, that some men of power continue to believe that radiation exposure at a nuclear test site or at ground zero, Nagasaki, poses only minimal health risk? George Wiltshire offered his own perspective:

"If what they're telling the American people, that there is a problem with radiation, that you have to be careful, that you have to wear protective clothing in these buildings, that you have to go to all this expense to protect things from radiation, is true, then there's a connection. But if not, if they're lying about these things, then you can run around and pick up plutonium and put it in your hip pocket and go all over with it, instead of setting up roadblocks and spending millions of dollars for protection. Then there's nothing to it.

"I was in Nagasaki. It was a plutonium bomb that was dropped. This plutonium saturated the earth, and we worked it. There is no way that anybody could come out of there. The fellows that went in there first and cleared out this area where we put this material, they worked with bulldozers, they worked with tractors, they worked with front-end loaders and construction equipment to clear this area off. If you ever saw a man when he was done working on a bulldozer, you'd imagine how he was covered with radioactive dust. And he had to go wash in radioactive water. Those fellows came out of there and they were sick. They had nausea, they had diarrhea, they had dizziness, they had headaches, and when this survey team got done, they shipped them right back to the States and discharged them. Why? No medical treatment at all! They didn't take them into a hospital and treat them. They didn't do anything for them.

"The Defense Department itself and the Nuclear Agency had put out in the Nagasaki area that anything from zero to a hundred rhems: no sickness. That's zero to a hundred rhems. Let's think back to this less-than-one rhem business that they put out just recently. It was in the newspapers and broadcast all over. One hundred to two hundred rhems: a little sickness, slight nausea, no ill effects. Two hundred to a thousand rhems: survival on the low end of the scale, death on the high end of the scale. And the symptoms of the two hundred bracket and higher are dizziness, headaches, nausea, diarrhea, exactly the same things the fellows had who were sent home.

"Two hundred rhems, and they tell you from the defense group that there was less than one rhem—the damnedest lie they ever put out! And done to hurt the best—done to hurt American citizens. And they compensate the Japanese, who were our enemy at the time. They compensate *them*! They take care of them! They sent people over there, they sent medicine over there, they took care of the sick people they hit with the bomb. And don't think there weren't medical teams that went into Japan after the bombs were dropped. They went in there and they kept records, and they know exactly what happens to people over a period of twenty years. They've got documents, medical documents, volumes of them. But they don't apply to me, and I was there."

For more than a decade, George Wiltshire, growing increasingly ill, made attempts to gain compensation or reparation from the government that had sent him to war more than thirty years before. More significantly, he sought to have the government clarify its position on the Atomic Veterans and to announce once and for all that it knew of the dangers of radiation exposure. Aided by NAAV, he brought to his various hearings hundreds of pages of letters and documents that he hoped would prove conclusively the connection between radiation exposure and severe, if not fatal, illness. Each attempt failed, and many were met by officials with bemusement or even open hostility. No one acknowledged his altruism; all the officials he approached re-acted only to what they saw as his misguided self-interest.

Toward the end, his strength waning, George could offer little more than corrections to the inaccuracies he read in the responses to his hearings. In one such letter he wrote,

"It was not my intention at any time to be judged disabled by reason of insanity, incompetency, or mental instability as their [a doctor's and a judge's] reports seem to indicate. I was told that I would be examined by a medical doctor to determine my disabilities. They were diagnosed in 1975 as diabetes mellitus, atherosclorotic cardiovascular disease, and episodic pe-riods of premature contractions, hiatal hernia, unstable sacroiliac joint and osteoarthritic changes in the left knee and both hips, and chronic ob-structure [sic] pulmonary disease.

"This was the evaluation of three medical doctors with many years of medical practice from Boynton V.A. Hospital. Two of the staff doctors are now, and may have been then, the Chief and Assistant Chief of Medicine. Six doctors made their rounds together each morning on Ward 4 North, checking each patient. The report that Dr. Romer and Judge Markson re-ferred to is a report from a medical student, Dr. William Sanders, who did not have the benefit of an experienced doctor to consult with while making his rounds. And not once did any other doctor examine me except when I was taking the stress test. Dr. Sanders' report was signed by a Dr. Bolston and a Dr. Landrum, who only passed by my bed once in my thirty-five days as a patient, let alone examine me."

George Wiltshire died in February 1988. His son, William, had died nearly ten years earlier of lymphoma, a form of cancer. William's son, now seven, has been in regular treatment for leukemia.

I collected this account from George in conversations with him over a period of years. He felt passionately about the plight of the Atomic Veterans. Long ago, this former marine had lost faith in his government, and more recently he had feared that his investigations and inquiries would bring re-prisals. Still, he disliked our conversations, believing that he sounded fool-ish and unintelligent. Most of our talks began with his showing me recent scientific reports or materials gathered in CARS newsletters. They typi-cally ended with this sort of fatalistic and self-deprecating comment from George: "Oh, I imagine I'll be like the other fellows someday. I'll get one of the types of cancer, I expect. Okay? Was I good enough? Can I go now? Did I ramble and shoot my mouth off enough so that they can put a contract out on me? Have I proven myself a nut already?"

HOCKING A LIFE

There can be no more immaculate housekeeper in the world than Ina Merman. At fifty-three, she has mothered three children, been married to the same man for thirty-two years, worked in part-time and full-time jobs, and never once failed to keep her three-bedroom apartment as neat as a pin.

The Mermans have never had it easy; they have worked hard for everything they have. They know full well that they will go to their graves owing a whole lot of money to a lot of people. But they have never been bitter or complaining. With everyone else in the country, they watched the purchasing power of the dollar fall and, when advised to do so pulled in their belts. They heard the clichés, the economic predictions, and the voices of the optimists as well as the doomsayers, and they pulled their belts in even tighter. Over the decades, Al worked either a job-and-a-half or two jobs. Ina worked full-time, part-time, and then full-time again. "You work or you bitch," Al Merman has said over and over. "Let the rest of 'em bitch; we'll work!"

So they worked, Al and Ina Merman, from the time they were fifteen. Al never completed high school; Ina did, but by then she was already working twenty-five hours a week. In time, they created a lovely home for themselves. "Let's say we kept our foreheads above water," Al often remarked. "Chins, no; from the hairline up. But no more, baby. No siree. Them days are gone, and we are sinking in the mud. I've had it, she'll have to tell you."

Ina Merman stands in the corner of her small kitchen. Not a pot or piece of flatware is out of place. Even the drawers and cabinets are immaculately maintained. As her own mother would say, "You could eat off the floor and not collect a virus." Still, Ina stands there with a look that says, What do I begin to clean? What do I fix up first? Where do I start to straighten?

"What's there to tell?" she begins. "It's America, right? It's the 1990s right? So what's there to tell? Have we worked? Have we paid our taxes every year? Have we broke our backs? Did we do a good job with our children? Did we send them to good schools? Did they honor us? Did we ask for too much? Did we say something out of line, insult, maybe, a congressman? Did we vote wrong? Did we vote right? Why all this punishment? Nobody, nobody can explain to me what inflation's all about, where it ends, where it begins, more importantly. Wage freeze? A laugh! I never made enough, no matter what. Al, he's a man, he should have earned more. They would have asked for a leg, he would have cut off his leg for them. Price freeze? Are we serious here? This is some kind of a joke, I hope.

"You want a joke? Ice freezes, and ice costs more than it did, what, ten months ago. Liquor, we drink liquor? Do we smoke? Two years ago Al Merman, the man in the next room, and I went to a movie. Two years ago! A rerun of Gene Kelly and Judy Garland. I'm on a mailing list to get cable for my TV. I can't really afford it. Do we eat like kings and queens? You want the truth? I'm embarrassed by what I put on the table sometimes. I'm old-fashioned; I'm in charge of the food department; it belongs to me, and I'm embarrassed. I swear to you. It's nutritious, but it's sparse. Sparse, what kind of sparse? I'm hungry all the time. He's hungry. We don't watch our diet? We don't take all this medical advice seriously? Oh, you take it seriously, but you can't live by it. What goes on in a supermarket now, I laugh. Do you know it? I laugh. Sure I'm a pro in the supermarket. I watch these items, I watch those items. I study the sales, I clip from the newspapers. Big deal! No matter how I play it, it doesn't work out. Al's right. He's not exaggerating: we're drowning!

"We cannot live on what we earn. Now, he's not well. He's got to pull back now or he'll drop dead on them one of these days. He'll never tell you, but believe me, it's not good. The stairs coming up to this apartment? He's stopping, I've noticed, on the second floor. Always he's looking for something. You know what he's looking for? His breath. They're taking it all away from us. They're crippling us. In my mind, I've got a connection right to Washington. Those guys take a vote on something, the oil big shots come up with another wise decision, in my mind something happens. They're changing me. You hear that? They're changing who I am, who I was, who I'll never be now. That's some power you've got in a vote, wouldn't you say? You make it like this, you make it so people can't eat what and when they want, they can't relax, you'll tear up their insides. Every time I turn around, the government's on television telling me to pull in my belt. And we're what they call one of the working families, am I right? Pull in my belt? I'd like to tell them just once how they're pulling in my mind! Their politics is making me retarded. I can't think right. They're ruining my life. What do they think, that people like us don't read the papers or listen to the radio? They think we aren't affected by the corruption? How can people like us, working people, feel about millionaires who don't pay a penny in taxes? What do you think crosses my mind when I read a man has donated a billion dollars, a billion dollars to something? You think we salute their intelligence? You think we're proud of them, our fellow Americans? People are being laid off left and right, or they're working all the time and still they don't have enough, and somehow, somewhere a man wants to be president and over-night, overnight, he's got his hands on millions of dollars. Where's all that money come from, as if we didn't know.

"I won't even mention what's fair and what's not fair. My point is this: it's so hard now that our bodies and our minds are being affected by it. All right? I can't sleep through a night. I'm worrying. I'm always worrying. We don't have and it's getting worse. I work at one job, I say to myself, you should have a better job. I blame myself every day for being uneducated. We saved money; we put it away. Every week we did this. It's all gone. Long ago, gone! We had children, but we had parents, too, and it all costs, it all costs. So what do I do now when I'm having diarrhea or constipation and I find myself like an idiot comparing prices of laxatives? I'm hocking our belongings. You're surprised to hear this? It's true. Why would I lie about this? A year ago when we couldn't manage the heating bill and the electric bill and the phone bill, we hocked some stuff. Who missed it! Six months ago, some more things. A few dollars here, a few there. Now I've reached the point where I'm beginning to sort through the stuff that means something to me. All right?

"Three weeks ago, to this very day, I took the valuables, the keepsakes, the objects you've sat with, the objects you've lived with that nobody can give you enough money for because some things in life you don't have a price for, all right? And I hocked them all. I don't go around here, 'cause at our age we don't need people to see what we're doing. I looked like a refugee that morning, but I got my money. I got good money, too. And was I alone in that hock shop? Not on your life! I waited in line forty-five minutes and heard every single other person in there say exactly what I was feeling. Every one of them. They can't make it, and I'm pretending to everyone I'm hock-ing this stuff because I got so many possessions I don't have closets anymore for all of them.

"How can America be this way? A wife is dead, a husband can't work. This bill isn't paid, so they're turning off the heat. What's going on in all these capitals? On Wall Street? In the Arab countries? In Iraq? What's going on in the world that all these people are hocking their belongings just to get through the winter, or get through the summer? They're breaking our minds, I'm telling you that. They've destroyed everything we've worked for, which isn't all that much in case you haven't noticed. They're making me give away everything I ever had. They're turning me into a I don't know what 'cause I'm not a person anymore. I'm certainly not the person I want to be. And what, Al is? I'm humiliated; I'm defeated! I'm made to feel I'm little, and look at me, I already am little, so how much more can they shrink me! Dignity? Haven't seen his face in a decade. Intelligence? Once, maybe, I thought I had some. Now? Nothing. Pride? Wouldn't know him if I saw him and he went out of his way to introduce himself to me. Shame? It's my skin.

"I stand in those lines with my suitcase full of things to practically give away, I stand in that freezing cold hock shop, except in the summer when you could die in there from the heat—open a window, how much can it cost!—and I tell myself that I feel my entire life is being sold. Years, effort, risk, sweat, work, lots of work, that's what I'm hocking. I'm hocking my dreams in that shop. Believe me when I tell you. I'm hocking the little iddy biddiest dreams. A little peace in old age? A little forgiveness for my parents? It's all hocked! A little joy in the coming years that maybe I could share a little something good with my husband? Hocked!

"If today I met the man running for president, I'd tell him exactly what I'm telling you. You want my vote? You want what they call my support? Then don't make me hock my life away. I beg you. Let me hold onto all those things which the man in the hock shop looks at with that cocked eye and bald head of his. This is one bored man like you've never seen, but he doesn't know what I'm doing? He wouldn't like, just once, say, 'Here, lady, you, shrinking lady, here's some money, hold onto this stuff, I can't take it; it's your life you're asking me to price.'"

WITNESS TO JOY

I

ON A BLUSTERY February morning, I arrive at the unconscionably rundown Boston housing project that a policeman friend of mine believes should be evacuated and bombed. The scene of this sorrowful edifice is at the same time so dangerous and depressing, I fully understand his exasperation. Together, we have wondered how people can live in such untenantable conditions, tolerate the constant smell of human waste in the hallways, and endure the noises that never cease.

I have been visiting families here for twenty years, and every time I approach the neighborhood, the same thoughts come to mind, almost ritualistically. Magical mechanisms, they serve, somehow, to keep me from feeling frightened. I wonder how it is possible to live in these buildings and not feel one was about to go crazy. I wonder what kind of world allows this sort of harsh existence. I wonder where the children, especially the little ones, who live here get the strength to just keep going when their home environment seems to be as far from a sanctuary as one can get.

After all these years, I have many friends at this project, some who still appear bemused by my inquiries and periodic incredulity. Most of the families accept me, giving me credit for at least being a regular visitor. But where we find common ground is in our observations of the children. Some of the children scare us with the intensity of their anger, and some sadden us with their quiet, brittle manner that almost suggests they have quit on life. Many children, however, dazzle us with their infinite capacity to discover and nurture joy in activities and settings one would think could breed only frustration and tears.

It's 10:30 when I enter 808 Langley Court. Residents here call it "C Entry." It has an infamous history. In the past year, a woman was stabbed on the very spot on which I now stand. Leaning against the wall to the right of the front door, where once mail boxes were located—they long ago were ripped out, leaving space open to studs and lathes—a nineteen-year-old woman waited to be picked up by her boyfriend. Suddenly, the door flew open and a fourteen-year-old boy rushed in wearing black leather pants, high boots, and a t-shirt. Breathless, manic, pushed to the edge by drugs and alcohol, he spied her and impulsively went to tear at her clothes. When she resisted, he drew a knife and slashed her ten times, one of the cuts ripping open her cheek.

The attack occurred at 11:00 on a Monday night, a school night. Only later, days after her hospitalization and the news that she would not lose the sight of her left eye, we learned that her nine-year-old brother and seven-year-old sister had been waiting with her in the hallway and had witnessed the entire episode.

There is more to the history of 808 Langley Court. Here in the past two years, a twenty-four-year old man died of AIDS, and a young woman of twenty-two died giving birth to a premature baby. Finding no one to assist her but her nine-year-old sister, she succumbed to a hemorrhage. Two other deaths involved elderly residents. A man and a woman in their seventies, passed, as the people here say, in the company of their families. In both instances, children witnessed the deaths. They heard the shouts for help, the wailing, and watched with terror and excitement as police and firefighters rushed into the building through this very entrance.

Ascending the stairs, reflecting still on these juvenile witnesses to death, I ask myself, Doesn't witnessing these sorts of events make these children, to use the jargon of the day, victims of posttraumatic stress disorder? What sort of life can it be to watch a sister die in childbirth? How does this even happen, when a few miles from here stands one of Boston's preeminent hospitals? I doubt many women die in childbirth there. And surely, on those rare occasions when they do, no child would ever witness it.

The elevators in the entrance hall haven't operated in all the years I've been coming here, so I walk along the first-floor cement corridor toward the stairs. Up the stairs to the first landing, where I am met with the usual building noise: motors droning, people yelling, dogs yapping, and always the children. Some of them are crying, others scream or shout to one another, and some of them laugh. In this setting, in this darkness and raw coldness, their laughter is an incongruous sound.

On the second-floor landing, a group of eight-, nine-, and ten-year-olds, who should have been in school, has devised a game that one can only describe as joyous. These children are feeling joy in a lugubrious hallway lit only by slivers of light coming in through a narrow window that has been partially boarded up. On the floor, the children have placed two rotting mattresses. Still emitting the smells of urine and vomit, the mattresses nonetheless provide the padding the game requires. On the wall opposite the stairs leans a third mattress, also decaying but with its padding, too, more or less intact.

Suddenly, from the third floor, Derond Sommerset, nine years old and wearing nothing but brand-new, black, high-top sneakers and pink shorts, this despite the cold, takes a running start and slides down the ten stairs on a metal cafeteria tray. Barely long enough to span the distance between stairs, the tray actually provides him a surprisingly smooth ride to the bottom, where he flies off and plops down on the mattress. Four children watch his descent, which proceeds perfectly. Clatter, clatter, clatter, splat, and the small audience explodes with laughter and cheering.

Derrick Whittier's turn comes next. Although he is laughing, his face reveals apprehension. Seeing this, I tell him he doesn't have to follow Derond. "It's alright, Derrick," I counsel him, "to say you just don't want to do it." The other children, all of whom I know, look at me as if to say, You crazy, man? What do you mean Derrick doesn't have to go? "He's riding. You're riding, ain't you, Derrick?" Derrick looks first at me and then at them. The children's joy has turned to sternness. With no other adults in the hall, the dilemma must be settled exclusively by the children. If Derrick Whittier could suddenly announce, "I think I'd rather not, I'm scared," I would nominate him for a Nobel prize. But there's about as much chance of this happening as there is that the building's elevators will be fixed by the end of the week.

Derrick pauses, his body rigid, and looks about at the other children, who barely breathe. The silence is broken with the announcement: "He's gonna ride!" The children scream with excitement. Joy has returned. They're having fun as few people know it; at least that's how it appears to the outsider.

No one in the hall utters a word about Feliciano Daniels, the eight-year-old who split his head open three weeks ago playing this same game. The cut required more than thirty stitches. The police were called, and finding no adults at home, they asked Feliciano's older sister to accompany him to the hospital. Lucky for Feliciano that Betina had also skipped school, for there was no one else looking out for him that morning. When Feliciano's mother returned from work that evening and learned of her son's accident, she spanked the boy and warned him there would be hell to pay if she ever caught him playing roller coaster again. Feliciano is not one of the children in the hall this morning.

I step over the mattress and head up the stairs, two more flights, to Lynn and Jared Swilling's apartment. Naturally, I pause long enough to watch Derrick. Still frightened, he takes a diffident, walking start and lights upon the tray at the top of the landing. Within seconds he hits the mattress. He's made it. My own pulse rate has increased, I notice. I fear that someday a child is going to die from playing this game. I look down at Derrick, prone on the mattress, wishing he would return my look. But no, he is absolutely joyous, along with the other children, who, recognizing that he has beaten his fear, happily jump all over him on the putrid-smelling mattress.

II

Rural New Hampshire has a magnificent feeling about it. Even in the poorer regions there is a glow in the low hills that compels one to pause and take in the scene. The colors on the hills arrange themselves on this one morning like shifting fabrics, and the lines of pine trees disappear in the gullies where the rock formations make it difficult for much to grow.

Willie Dillmeister's family lives in a small white house with forest green shutters on a farm that has sat at the base of the low hills for more than 125 years. I am two hours by car from Boston, but it feels as if I'm a million miles from anywhere. Out here I better understand what it means when people refer to a place as God's country. The air is clear, the maples are just commencing to bloom, and the smells of the pines bring to mind the aromas of sumptuous foods.

Nine-year-old Willie Dillmeister is one of four children, all of whom, even four-year-old Charlie, help with the farmwork. Willie says he hates his older sister because she's always bossing him around and making him do her chores. He says school is okay, he doesn't like to be around when his parents argue, and he worries that the family will not have enough money to get through the winters. It is a matter Ted and Martie Dillmeister wish their children knew nothing about. They try to keep their discussions about money problems out of earshot of the children, but there is no way Willie could be ignorant of the daily facts of small-time New Hampshire farming. He understands about thunderstorms, low water levels, long cold spells, and dangerously low bank accounts. He knows what happens if the land absorbs too much rain, especially if it is acidic, and what takes place in the rolling fields if the mountains beyond the foothills did not receive sufficient snow-falls during the previous winter.

There is always an air of trouble in this friendly but modest home. Ted has enlarged the house over the years, but it remains too small for the family. Martie works alongside her husband of thirteen years almost twenty-four hours a day. Both wonder how long they should go on in this manner, or whether the present New England economic crisis will finally drive them away from their beloved home in the foothills.

I have known the Dillmeisters for several years. We met when I was inter-viewing families about unemployment. Somehow I ended up having meals with this family, whose terror of going under is never far from the surface. These days, all the Dillmeisters seem more agitated than ever. Money, as Ted has always remarked, remains the root of his own personal evil.

Rivulets of water line Interstate 87 leading to the outskirts of the little town in which the Dillmeister farm is located. Minutes from their home, I am still constructing questions about joy, but everything I see intimates the ravages of a New England recession. The family claims to be excited by my arrival, but I nonetheless find it difficult to tell them I want to know how Willie and his sister Christina—known by the family as Teenie—find joy, or what they even take this word to mean. "Dr. Tom," they reassure me, "you're always investigating something personal." At lunch, Martie insists to me that my latest investigation makes a great deal of sense. She herself often calls Willie a joyful child and knows precisely from what sources he draws his joyous pleasures, although she challenges me to discover them on my own.

It isn't difficult. Willie responds openly and quickly to my questions. His pets, nature, the farm animals, and, in some strange way he cannot make sense of, the land are what make him joyous. And then there is the matter of his mother's reading to the children at night, a ritual that no amount of fi-nancial or marital tension has ever curtailed.

"Do you know, Willie, what I mean when I ask you about joy?"

"Of course. Like, when I run down Post Road with my dogs I feel like, that could be joy. I'm happy then, right? That's what joy means, right? I like being outside, playing with animals, or going fishing with someone, or by myself. I can fish for a long time by myself. I think I'm joy, with joy, however you say it."

"Joyous."

"Yeah. Right. But the best is when my mother reads to us. I feel real happy then. Joyous, right? And safe. Everything seems okay, you know?

Sometimes I just listen to her voice. If she asked me, like a teacher, you know, what we've been listening to, I wouldn't really know, 'cause I'm just lying on the bed listening to her voice. But I'm, like, happy, you know, listening to her read. It's the best. It's like I say, I feel happy and safe, not that anything's going to happen to us while we're in the bed."

Later that afternoon, as Willie and I walk around the outbuildings and watch the steam from our breaths magically disappear in the cool air, I imagine he is right at the edge of telling me that joy for him comes from being, somehow, transported. Whether it is by nature, the scents rising from the fields, the wild runs with Pepper and Geronimo, the Dillmeisters' golden retrievers, or just lying on Christine's bed listening to his mother read, Willie seems to grope for the words to capture transcendence and moving beyond the everyday realities of rural New Hampshire living. His joy is palpable. A joyous look comes over him as, squinting slightly, he scans the foothills, letting his eyes roam the boundaries of his family's property. The expression was not there earlier when I asked him about school, hoping, I suppose, that he might find something joyous about education. The look returned when I asked him how he would spend his summer, and he spoke dreamily of going swimming in a pond nearby and in the rushing current of the Calhoun River and taking overnight hiking trips with his father.

When I ask him whether he thinks about what he might like to do when he gets older—a question I normally find painfully uncreative—I detect a different look, one of concern, perhaps, or guarded anticipation. If I had to bet, I'd say that Willie will not end up on this farm. I'd say that ten years from now he'll have to find new sources of joy and that his sensing this fact causes him sadness. Willie seems so young when we speak about his joyous pursuits and so much older when the conversation shifts to what he might become.

His experiences of joy don't last long, Willie concedes. I suspect his joy lasts only as long as he lives these experiences, and particularly when he is allowed to be alone with his thoughts. Then again, I keep telling myself, he is only nine. It is tempting to say that the land, somehow, ages him, but this is not so. The fright of financial ruin and the fear that economic conditions may cause his parents to separate truncate the joy I am convinced I see in him.

His parents recognize this as well and lament it. Martie says she wishes only for her children to be happy, but she is not certain that her love and concern are enough to give rise to some permanent joyfulness of character in her children. In her eyes, and mine as well, Willie is a touching admixture of joyfulness and apprehension. It seems a strange recipe for a child, but, come to think of it, the children sliding down the stairs on trays in 808 Langley Court revealed the same antinomious qualities.

Willie laughs at my description of the Boston children. It prompts him to tell me about leaping into a mountain pond after pushing Geronimo in before him. "That was my favorite day so far," he says. In fact, he cannot tell the story of how Geronimo, once out of the water, slipped on the rocks and fell back in, without erupting into gales of laughter. "That's the biggest joy," he continues, trying to give a good answer to my questions, just as his mother has admonished him. "The really biggest joy so far."

Driving home well before the sun disappears behind the hills, I wonder whether a child like Willie Dillmeister makes up answers to appease people like me, as well as his parents? Does he hunt for joy because I ask him about it? Does he contrive the feeling because at some level he feels his life to be joyless and oppressive? Is joy, in other words, a compensation, akin somehow to the response one hears from adults who grew up in poverty but claim that when they were young they thought all people lived as they did? It is a sentiment difficult to accept in this generation, as television introduces people to the face of wealth at every turn of the dial. There's not a quiz show, talk show, sitcom, newscast, or other program on the tube that doesn't bespeak affluence, if not extraordinary wealth. Today's poor children know full well that not everyone lives as they do.

So does Willie Dillmeister honestly know extended moments of feeling the sensations of pure joy? I suspect he does. His mother prays that he does. His father believes joy isn't something one need bother oneself about, particularly when crops are meager and money scarce. Without his uttering a word, I know that Ted considers my investigation to be an act of extravagance and leisure. Perhaps it is, but I will insist to him, should the opportunity ever arise, that children must know periods of joy. They must know how to play and to mine an activity so that it yields joy. They must know how to derive joy from something they do with their brain or muscles. They must learn that just as feeling competent in something may yield joy, so, too, might intellectual discovery or the ability to be touched by the strength and beauty of one's physical environment.

III

Nine-year-old Hillary Franklin knew joy the day she came home from school having rehearsed the role of Mary for the Christmas play. Marian Franklin claimed her daughter was literally off the wall with happiness. Her child was so excited about the play she actually forgot to sit down in front of the television, as she did most every afternoon. Even *3-2-1 Contact*, her favorite show, went by the boards. Knowing of my interest in the sources of joy, Marian tried to write down verbatim Hillary's words.

"I have to sing this song," Hillary began, "and it's long, real long, about Jesus. And Mr. Treblehorn said I did it great. He said 'great!' He said it a lot. Great, great, great. And you know how you know when some teachers say things they really don't mean but they have to say it because, like, it's their job? Well, he meant it. He told me he did."

"What makes you feel the happiest about it?" Marian asked her daughter, later admitting she thought she sounded more like a psychologist than a mother.

"I like being the star of the play," Hillary replied. "I really do, mom. This is what I'm going to do, you know."

Again Marian responded in what she thought was an artificial manner. "It is? Well, this is the first I learn of this." Her description of her own affectlessness reminded me of the manner I affected years ago, when I did my training at Boston's Children's Hospital. I saw the children more as patients, obsessive-compulsives, trauma victims, nocturnal bed wetters, and aggressive acting-outers than as simply children, sometimes triumphing, sometimes even joyous, but mostly struggling and confused.

"Oh, Mom," Hillary proclaimed, not without some impatience, "I've always wanted to be a star. You knew that. I told you that a hundred times."

"You never did, darling," Marian protested.

"You're lying, mom. You're lying, which is the worst thing you can do. I always know when you're lying 'cause your nose sort of wrinkles up."

"Like how?"

"Like that! And you want me to be a star, too, don't you, mom? I mean, I'm not always going to get good parts, like Mr. Treblehorn said. But he said if that's what I want to do that's what I should do."

"And you should," Marian responded. Later she said her role in the conversation felt a bit like confronting a runaway freight train.

"I will, I will, I will," Hillary shouted.

By all accounts, Hillary Franklin sounds joyous. It seems her feelings were born in some fabulous connections she made, Mr. Treblehorn being a significant part of them. She discovered an activity that "joyed" her (to use the expression of six-year-old Benjamin Parsons, another child of exceptional talent and passion whom I know). What joyed her was the feeling of something that thrilled both her and someone else, someone apparently,

whose assessment meant the world to her. Listening to Marian read her account of her conversation with her daughter, I was struck with the almost
defiant inner strength that Hillary had brought to the conversation. She had
found the outlines of a dream, and a teacher had made it seem possible. It
mattered little what her mother thought; Mr. Treblehorn had sanctified the
dream and, with it, a whole new sense of competence and definition of self.

Identity, Erik Erikson wrote decades ago, is a complex combination of
change and continuing sameness. The child knows both ingredients. Indeed, a child probably knows all too well the static and dynamic truths of
his or her life, as Robert Pirsig has written, despite our belief that such concepts are too recondite to be grasped by the likes of Willie Dillmeister, Hillary Franklin, or even little Benny Parsons.[1]

It is the sense of continuing sameness from which a New Hampshire
farmer's child draws some joy. Even at nine, one suspects Willie already is
apprehensive about departing the rural landscape, with its predictable chores
and constant beauty.

In a suburb of Providence, Rhode Island, Hillary Franklin has found joy
in change. Having discovered yet another layer of this magical thing called
the self, she is not today what she was yesterday. A new layer, a new cavern,
a new landscape has opened for her. She may be nine years old, she may
adore television, but on this one afternoon she has discovered one of the
mysteries constructed by heaven knows what. Genetics, biology, physiology,
chemistry, temperament, talent, environment, parental behavior—whatever
it is, something has been awakened in her. So today, she and "it" together
are verbally cavorting about, in a sense celebrating a special sort of birthday.

Hillary's joy represents the discovery of a form of intelligence: she can
perform. She can act and sing. For her the world is no longer what it was
this morning. Something has emerged in her, something that she herself
fetched from some inner space, without even thinking about it. But there it
was for people to witness. And come the week before Christmas, still more
people will witness it. Contrary to her mother's nervous concern, the fact
that others watch her only makes her more joyous.

Do children understand the differences between the static and dynamic
or between the sense of sameness and the sense of continuing change? In
my mind, they do. Surely they know the difference between the boredom of
certain static properties and the serenity of other ones. In the same way, they
know the thrill of certain dynamic qualities and the terror of other ones. To
conjecture further, I suspect children are able to distinguish between a personal discovery, one, say, that transports them to a new station in life, and a

distraction that is meant to carry them away from some present, ongoing station but in the end rarely yields them anything resembling genuine joy.

The culture thrives on entertaining young children, getting their minds "off of it," whatever "it" may be. Granted, children may feel outright enjoyment in front of movie and television screens, but I am convinced it is not joy that is being instilled and felt, since joy is not a substance to be instilled. For many children, joy comes as the result of mining something unique and wondrous about themselves from some inner shaft. Distractions may please the child, even as he or she turns from one form to another. But even with children's ability to remember rap lyrics or complicated choreographies, it is not until something from the inner world has been triggered that genuine joy can rise to the surface.

All these thoughts were inchoate the night I telephoned Marian Franklin and heard the details of her conversation with Hillary. Self-discovery and finding that one has worth remain awfully close to the realm of joy, assuming the discovery has gone well, I told Marian. Sometimes self-discovery yields pain. But who knows, perhaps the pain of certain self-discoveries lies closer to joy than does the dullness and flatness emerging from the unexamined life. Even for children.

"And children can do all this?" she asked.

"But of course," I replied confidently, knowing in my heart that romanticism and exuberance rather than hard-earned data braced my theory. "Hey, what the hell, Marian, if you don't feel joy when you learn you're doing great being the mother of Jesus, then when are you going to?"

IV

The magic of Hillary Franklin's joy was made possible in part by the unknown Mr. Treblehorn. I shall never know what he did or said, but he conveyed something more than his love for her and capacity to guide her. There was a sense of approval, genuine esteem-promoting approval, that this child felt coming from Mr. Treblehorn. With his aid, she was able to lower herself down into those magical caves of her essential being.

Approval, I've often argued, is the lubricant of the child's search for his or her inner selves. When you hate yourself, you don't go looking for yourself. You don't play this sacred hide-and-seek game, because you're convinced all you'll find is confirmation of the "data" that convinced you to hate yourself in the first place. Self-hating children experience little joy. Children like those sliding down the stairs at Langley Court remain unaccepted, I think, by a greater unseen culture that never would admit to it, but nonetheless must take responsibility and offer explanation for the children's treacherous living conditions. But these children are not necessarily self-hating. Certain factors and people have intervened to buffer them against some of the assaults of the dominant culture.

I speak here of nothing mystical or evanescent. Consider, for example, ten-year-old Maya Pinkerton, who was often beaten by her father before he finally abandoned the family. It seems possible that someone may have sexually molested this child as well. Her mother, having given birth to Maya when she herself was only fourteen years old, is rarely at home. Maya's cousin, Janet, who is a few months older, was also abandoned by a father and raised by a drug-addicted mother, who coerced the child to smoke cigarettes when she was six. Neighbors report that the woman also attempted to turn Maya and her two brothers onto drugs before their tenth year. Nevertheless, Maya and Janet know joy; I have witnessed it. Sometimes it appears when I watch them playing together on the back porch of Maya's tiny two-room apartment in a poor neighborhood of Boston, but mostly I detect it when they cook with their grandmother.

Anna Turnbull, a woman in her late forties, has committed herself to making these two children happy and successful. She knows well the handicaps she faces: the mothers—her daughter and daughter-in-law—who have transgressed and the fathers who, uneducated, and unable to find steady work, eventually abandoned their families. She is perfectly willing to admit that she has selected these two grandchildren at the cost of losing her other ones, but she seems not to question this decision. The very definition of her being is to make these girls, in her words, "come alive" and "know the greatness that's sleeping there somewhere." When these three people cook together, which they do whenever Maya and Janet request it, there is consummate joy in the tiny alcove that serves as "Mamo's" kitchen.

It is not only joy that one notices, but intense concentration, hard work, and responsibility. Mamo barks out the orders with good nature and the two girls jump to the bait. Eating seems almost anticlimactic. Again, I see the communication of approval and, in turn, the children's sense of confidence emerging.

A peculiar combination of experiences appears to unfold in these cooking sessions. The children are simultaneously playing and working; that goes without saying. It also goes without saying that if schools could capture this spirit, that is, if more teachers could capture this spirit, children would long to be in class. They may even petition for the schools to remain open during the summer months. But to listen to Mamo tell it, these children are being rescued as well. Redemption is being served up in that kitchen. Maya and Janet are being pulled back from social and human dangers, no matter what the sources.

Certain theorists suggest that children face an almost insurmountable task in attempting to overcome absent or unloving parents. Little, these theorists suggest, can ever compensate for the loss of parental love and approval; they remain palpable hurts never to be fully healed. In contrast, other writers suggest that children require and will take support and love from any quarter; it almost doesn't matter who provides the love, although often they look to the mother's mother to become that special wellspring, even if she failed to provide in this manner for her own children.

Mamo Turnbull is actually no different from many grandmothers (most of them considerably older than she) whom I have visited over the years. She is quick to point out that the joy she never provided her own children, given where she was in her life when they were small, she can now provide for her grandchildren, or at least these two girls. Like many other grandmothers, Mamo believes that joy must come from within, but at least one significant person, someone who regularly befriends and openly loves the children, must help them find joy within themselves and bring it forth.

Mamo's notions seem simplistic, probably, to sophisticated students of psychology. What allows a child to feel joyful often seems bitterly complex. One imagines joy as a flame. Like all flames, it needs oxygen; some life force, a combustible material, say; a significant activity; and the white heat of profound effort or activity leading ultimately to inner satisfaction, if not ebullience. The flame one finds in Mamo's kitchen is the result of powerful love forces and exquisite hands-on teaching techniques battling against the forces of despair, poverty, abandonment, pain, and humiliation. Perhaps joy only emerges as some antithetical dynamic: pleasure winning out over pain; competence winning out over incompetence; and a belief that one is good, sound, and smart winning out over a conviction that one is bad, worthless, sorely incomplete, and ignorant. Children who in one manner or another describe themselves as damaged goods rarely reveal joy.

This explanation of what in the nature of rudimentary kitchen practices could produce joy in a child also must sound childishly simplistic. Still, two thoughts come to mind. First, I think that at some level, joy eternally remains a childlike sensation. Joy is child-size rapture and ecstasy. Once felt, it is probably never forgotten, although it may not be easily reexperienced. Adults who recall going on joyous fishing trips, being absorbed in a game of checkers, or playing catch with a parent feel that childlike sense of joy, although tears may accompany the recollection. "Tears of joy" we call them.

Adults who master something and for an instant feel youthful, immortal, and blessed with unlimited capacities also feel that joy. The body figuratively tingles with it. The little flame still burns, we tell ourselves, but how can we keep it alive when we're encumbered, if not oppressed, by repetitive actions that open no new life corridors or secret attics? Many creative artists report that the joy they feel is unquestionably part of their childhood keepsakes, keepsakes into which they intentionally tap. What some of us call mere objects, more creative persons view as toys, and what some of us call satisfying accomplishment, these persons call sheer joy, unwilling, apparently, to part with childlike characteristics.

My second point regards the matter of one person's making childhood joy possible for another. Once again, it seems simplistic even to suggest it, just as it seems simplistic to state that little boys and girls do best when raised by men and women who love them and each other. Still, I am struck by something about the funerals I have attended for members of the many families whom I've been visiting over the years. Among the wealthier families, the loss of a parent seems almost unbearable to the mourning child. Among poorer families, these same feelings are revealed upon the deaths of grandparents as well, and particularly those special grandmothers, the Mamo Turnbulls of the world.

How many times have I, while standing next to a grave, in a church, or days later in a home, heard a reference to the end of joy. "Now with her passing, I can't ever be happy again," said ten-year old Miko Dwyer, her cheeks bathed in tears, upon the death of her grandmother. She added, "She was the only person in the world who ever made me totally happy. I'll never feel that way again. She stole all my joy when she died."

Those of us who have known Miko Dwyer all her life know the importance to her of that noble grandmother. All of us know as well that a light that once shown in Miko's eyes has gone off. It has been ten years since Mother Accosta passed away.

A few months ago, now thinking a good deal about children and joy, I asked Miko whether she still thought her grandmother's death was truly the completion of any joy in her life. "So far," she replied laconically.

"It's almost as though," I suggested, "if we could pump it up from the cemetery ground, maybe we could get it back for you."

Miko smiled. "I wish we could. But I'll have to find it somewhere else so my own children get their share. It's not enough to make them laugh," she concluded. "You have to do what my grandmother did, and I think the secret's buried with her. Well, you know what sort of person she was. She just had joy in her heart, like the minister said. And she gave it all to me."

V

Miko Dwyer's words hardly confirm social scientific hypotheses, but they do reinforce my suspicion that adults need to give joy implants to those special children who clearly need something far more complicated than amusement. To smile and laugh is not necessarily to know joy. Indeed, one often suspects the presence of joy among children as they toil hard at some task. The heavy breathing, the intense concentration, the extraordinary physical or intellectual effort, and then the joy of the "Eureka!" Ask teachers about this probably too simplistic matter, and many of them, at least those who themselves know joy, will say they believe the search for it in a classroom is the supreme academic requirement.

One such teacher is Melanie Dickerson, whose Boston fifth-grade classroom regularly resounds with antic discussion and highly theatrical exchanges. I can't state with certainty that joy abounds in this classroom every day of the academic year, but something goes on here that causes the children to report unanimously that Mrs. Dickerson is the greatest teacher in the whole wide world.

Among her charges is eleven-year-old Tanya Dade, a tall, slow-moving child with sunken eyes that are always looking down at the ground. Tanya is more than shy; it's evident that somewhere along the line she has been hurt. Her story is all too familiar to Mrs. Dickerson, a woman in her late fifties who came back to teaching ten years ago, after a layoff of fifteen years while she raised her own three children. Now she has committed herself to raising the twenty-six children in her precious fifth grade.

"Tanya is the American story," she tells me. "I rarely saw it before I took my time off. Now it's an everyday occurrence." Apparently Tanya's parents went through an angry separation that essentially has never been resolved. Although legally divorced, the parents continue to battle and disparage one another, whether in earshot of their children or not. Mrs. Dickerson also suspects that Tanya was molested. The child has spoken of nightmares and some peculiar flashbacks and reveals a rather angry self-dislike. She cannot stand receiving praise and refuses presents from anyone. Moreover, she periodically exhibits the characteristic startle pattern of victims of trauma. A door closing in the classroom goes unnoticed by most of the children, but

Tanya's body lurches and she throws her head around as if ready to confront a dangerous perpetrator, or so it seems to this perspicacious middle school teacher.

After six months of working with the children, Mrs. Dickerson begins to see progress in Tanya. By "progress" she means more than an improvement in grades, which she always has claimed are an impediment to teaching. She, too, is looking for a spark in the eyes, that flame again, or merely an increase in the number of minutes per day that Tanya will look up at her and her classmates rather than peer down at the floor. She looks for signs of enthusiasm, an interest in something beyond normal classroom assignments. She looks for a momentary lifting of Tanya's mood that like a heavy cloak engulfs this child and palpably drags her down. She looks for "signs of life from the inside," as she calls it, and enjoys any allusion to the child's inner caves and the human expedition to personal truths. In this case, however, she knows that Tanya is only too familiar with the caves. If in fact there has been trauma, this child, presumably, remembers enough of it. The question is how to get at it and not let the memories remain as permanent sources of torment and grief.

Noting Tanya's sadness, along with a host of other problems in several of her students, Mrs. Dickerson proposes that the children keep diaries that no one will be allowed to see. Tanya and the others are free to write and draw in their books whenever they wish and are not obliged to show their musings and representations to anyone. Interestingly, before she has written a single word or sketched the barest scene, Tanya expresses a fear that her diary may be discovered at home. Accordingly, Mrs. Dickerson not only offers to keep the diary for the child, but promises to take it home with her every evening if Tanya so desires. Tanya smiles her acknowledgment. It is exactly what she had hoped for. Amazing, I note to myself, how good teachers not only train young minds to read, but read the minds of those they train.

Starting early in the fall, Mrs. Dickerson brings the diaries to class with her. They sit in a locked cabinet to which only she carries the key. I notice that at almost no time does any child threaten to read the diary of another or even tease a child by pretending to read over his or her shoulder. The respect for the diaries and the recorded privacy they contain is exemplary. (How ironic that these same children cannot contain their reactions in the presence of a child who is obese.) Nothing, moreover, is said about Mrs. Dickerson's reading the diaries. Whether or not the children assume she will read them remains yet another classroom mystery.

My own guess is that the children want her to read every word and inspect every drawing. Knowing the impeccable integrity of this one teacher, I bet she would not dare to open a book without first telling the author. But I am wrong. In fact, she regularly inspects these documents and, in one subtle manner or another, brings certain issues to the attention of people who might help a child.

In truth, a game is being played here. The children are using the diaries to work out issues they may or may not understand and communicate their findings to a trusted friend. Tanya clearly is doing this. She is unloading details of her childhood—as if at eleven she had completed childhood—in the hopes of accomplishing something that Mrs. Dickerson and I are not quite sure of. But evidently there is an urge to seek out those inner caves where pain and joy live and then share her daily journey with her teacher.

At one point, I mention to Mrs. Dickerson that Tanya seems to be doing therapy on herself, and the teacher responds by saying she believes the work of this one saddened eleven-year-old is free association and hence psycho-analysis. Her accompanying look tells me there is no room here for me to disagree.

After six months of diary work—psychoanalysis, if you will—Tanya Dade is changing. The eyes are lifting, the morose mood is in retreat, and I see occasional smiles on the face of this ostensibly lonely child. Nothing goes better at her home, or homes, I should say, since Tanya splits her week in the houses of her mother and father. Their own battles continue apace, but some inner peace seems to have taken hold in Tanya, barely but perceptibly. Months before, she felt anxiety even thinking about the Tuesday/Wednesday stay with her father. Months before, she dreaded bedtime and postponed its arrival by using every child's trick in the book, which meant of course that she came to school exhausted every morning. But this, too, changes somewhat. Just before Thanksgiving vacation, Mrs. Dickerson, recognizing Tanya's bedtime terror, suggests a simple assignment. "Do you think you could draw a nightmare?" Tanya nods yes.

Now, months later, Mrs. Dickerson tells me that Tanya looks directly into her eyes and smiles and eagerly responds to questions put to her in class. In December and January, Tanya's diary becomes saturated with what she calls her "nightmare series," dozens of drawings capturing her fright and the re-current theme of being overwhelmed and ripped open by a huge, overpow-ering monster. Never once does Tanya raise the question of whether Mrs. Dickerson is reading her diary; the game continues to be played. The child knows the teacher is peeking; the teacher knows she is meant to peek. I find the entire process perfectly legitimate and beautifully symbolic. How else will we ever learn anything about our true selves or the selves we claim to love if we never peek?

In this same light, the children who feel joy at the exact moment they swim underwater for the first time with eyes open cannot wait to surface and scream for their mother's attention. Peek at a diary? Why, most children only draw so that their parents will exclaim over the new creation and stick it on the refrigerator door.

Mrs. Dickerson is peeking; she even writes notes to Tanya. There is growing evidence to support the hunch that there has been some form of assault or molestation. Tanya seems increasingly eager to make this point known. Seven months since the inception of the diary exercise, Tanya Dade, her teacher reports, is approaching that feeling of relief that both of them describe in one form or another as joy. Tanya is admitting to herself that trauma has occurred and is beginning to control the nightly arrival of the nightmare terror born years ago, allegedly, by a nighttime attack. She is beginning to realize, furthermore, that she can make herself safer, if only by believing that the past will not return with full force and in full reality. In part she wards off the demons by essentially facing them dead on, if not recalling them and thereby reliving some of her earlier experiences.

There is, furthermore, a witness to her internal odyssey. Mrs. Dickerson lovingly accepts every description and representation. Tanya Dade is drawing nightmares. She is drawing molestation. She is drawing people fighting, people frightened, people yelling, people being hurt. "And what is happening here?" Mrs. Dickerson asks, pointing to one corner of a drawing. "And what do you think the child is feeling here?"

Is it therapy, this march toward freedom and joy? To be sure, although Tanya would never consider visiting a psychiatrist or psychologist. Don't think her parents haven't tried to get her "to see someone," as the expression goes. Anyway, she knows she is doing the required work with Mrs. Dickerson, whom she tells me is the only woman in the world she can trust.

"Are there men in the world you can trust?" I ask.

Tanya looks at me, and for the first time ever I see her smile so broadly her teeth actually are visible. She utters not a word. The message is plain: men are not yet to be trusted. She continues to grin.

Mrs. Dickerson claims Tanya now appreciates something resembling joy. It is not the eureka phenomenon or the experience of competence, although this surely is part of it. Nor is it the joy of cooking cheeseburgers with peppers under the tutelage of one's grandmother or sliding down the stairs in a dim hallway on a serving tray.

In Tanya's case, Melanie explains, the child for the first time in her conscious life is able to recognize that she can pull herself back from a dangerous precipice. She can control her life, or at least some of her primary feelings. She has indeed regained control. No longer a terrified victim (as it turned out, of a male baby-sitter's assaults), she is discovering strength, external and most assuredly internal strength. She has spent seven months operating on herself, the diaries confirming that almost daily she has dared herself to go one more step, and then still one more step in the direction of those inner caves.

The diaries confirm, Mrs. Dickerson alleges, that not only does Tanya fear less on the outside and inside, she is growing less fearful of feeling fear. This is Tanya's new joy: that life can be led without trepidation and doubt, without an almost instinctual diffidence. She is now daring to live, Mrs. Dickerson observes. The description is apt.

VI

On a beach ringed with high, rocky cliffs that jut into the sea, forming lacy coves, I observe two examples of children daring. The first is a lovely girl with blond hair the color of straw and a husky voice. She appears to be somewhere between four and five years old, but her speech is that of a child younger than three. The child's face reveals her genetic condition: Down's syndrome.

Protected by a tan umbrella, she sits in the sand between two women I presume to be her mother and grandmother; a man sits nearby. Suddenly she manufactures a game. She grabs the sun hat off her grandmother, who just as quickly grabs it back and replaces it on her head. The child watches carefully and then, predictably, grabs the hat a second time. Again, the grandmother fetches it back and puts it on her head. By this point the child clearly is evincing joy, and I know that a third, fourth, and fifth recurrence of the vaudeville-like ritual is in the offing. Her face veritably dances with delight. She has created a game of simple rules but spectacular results.

Grandmother plays her role to the hilt, and the child roars with laughter. What has started as a daring escapade has evolved into a ritual of pure joy. Suddenly, mother barks, "Stop!" and father barks, "Bad!" The child's face falls; it is no longer the same face. Joy is gone. Grandmother does not protest. The dare has not ended well, or lasted long enough.

Down the beach in one of the rocky coves, some small children climb to a small promontory, from where they will leap into the sea. I am barely in earshot of their jibes at one another, but their bodies tell the story of their constant daring, the acceptance of the dares, and the utter dejection caused by the refusal to accept. When the children leap from the rocky shelf and discover upon emerging from the black water that they have survived, their whoops of joy sound over the surf, echoing the joyous cries of the children on the stairs at Langley Court.

From the safety of my beach chair I think, If children allegedly believe they will live forever, an assertion professionals put forth as a reason for wild driving, drinking sprees, and drug experimentation, why do these little children, who have never steered a car or poured a drink, know the joy that comes from escaping serious injury or death? Do children believe in their own immortality except on those occasions when they fear they may die? Is there some confusion in psychologists' thinking, or is it possible that the two sensations coexist within the developing mind? Challenging death surely brings forth the propensity for joy; believing in one's immortality, apparently, doesn't even ward off depression in some children.

The children who smack into the mattresses or disappear beneath the swirling water evidently have won something. They show the same ebullience young athletes show when they win or accomplish something even more outstanding. Winning at something, therefore, also carries the propensity for joy in the child, although, as I have noted, it is hardly the only requirement.

I watch a child, probably nine or ten, begin to have a tantrum in the middle of the field when the referee calls him offside. He stomps and yells and starts to cry. Moreover, to the chagrin of his parents, standing on the sidelines, he is swearing. His coach, a young man with an athletic body, runs onto the field and embraces him so that he cannot move. At first, the boy squirms violently and pounds on the coach's arms. Finally, the boy's efforts subside and he walks off the field, head dramatically downward. He will have to sit out five minutes, the coach announces. "Players must be in a good frame of mind in order to perform at their best." He is also told he should construe the action not as punishment but merely as a rest.

An hour later, the child's team has won. Now we all witness joy. High-fives, low-fives, bumping chests and arms, a happy scene of affluent suburban children in blue-and-white uniforms showing how well they have learned the choreography of joy from athletes on TV. They are rehashing the game, reminding each other of this particular play or that game-changing moment, all the while laughing about how they faked out this guy or outran that one. Once again we witness the consummate joy of winning and, if we dare look to the opposite side of the wide, green lawn, the sloped shoulders and shuffling gait of the children in red-and-gold uniforms that bespeak only defeat. No joy there, although it is interesting to note that several of the boys appear to be laughing.

A few points strike me on the soccer field, most of them inappropriate to the time and place, but, alas, my observations of children rarely are free of social realities and political bias.

First, I remark to myself how many of these children fail to show the athletic work ethic that would land them in the highest circles of sports fame. Said simply, their social class has taught them this is a game, no more, no less. No one plans to do this for a living, so let's not take it all that seriously. In contrast, children in other parts of the city know full well that their ability on a blacktop basketball court may hold the proverbial ticket to success. The odds are long, to be sure, but, unlike suburban soccer, hoops may be a life or death matter, even for small children, and hence a work ethic can be discerned. The city basketball players know joy, all right, but it's joy with the slight weight of contingency attached to it.

Next, it occurs to me that this soccer game, one of several that will be played this one autumn morning, is the product of a host of people whose ingenuity, efforts, and, yes, property taxes have conspired to yield healthy physical effort, along with tantrums and joyous celebrations. There is barely a town center in this one community, and PTO meetings attract minimal attendance, but enough is being done to underwrite what seems an endless conveyor belt of soccer players. And lest anyone believe that the feminist movement hasn't hit this and adjoining towns, there are just as many girl leagues as boy leagues. In fact, at the younger ages, the girls and boys play together, and each child demands that the others hold up their end of the bargain, regardless of race, creed, or gender.

It makes for a lovely piece of America, I think. It reminds me of an almost epiphanal scene I witnessed early one April evening as the light slowly disappeared on a Boston suburban baseball field: A team practicing for an upcoming game. Girls wearing batting helmets. Girls taking hefty cuts from both sides of the plate. Girls razzing each other about a huge swing that yielded a piddling ball hit toward short. And everywhere girls squealing with joy when one of their teammates did something sensational. "Way to hit it, Lizzie." "Whee, let's hear it for the Lizard!" And of course the consummate confirmation of joy: "Awesome!"

Did that one girl over there with the freckles and long pony tail and wearing the bright yellow sweatshirt feel the same joy when Lizzie rifled one past the left fielder as when she herself did it? For that matter, could she do it? She did seem diminutive, even for this group of nine- and ten-year-olds. Did she even have to blast one into left field to experience joy? It seems to me that a boy has to be the agent of the action to derive the joy, but these girls, playing the sport I played a thousand years ago at the same time of day, dusk, when only athletes can see, are finding joy in other people's accomplishments. Imagine that! They are so in tune with their baseball community and hence with the communing portion of the practice that they actually delight in anyone's success. There is only one word to describe the joy I feel in witnessing their joy: Awesome!

Leaving this scene, I once again reflect on a community's commitment to children. Some of the parents are active in it, but other people, unrelated to the children, also play roles, perhaps even more important ones than anyone in the culture ever acknowledges. I love scenes of this type, and yet invariably they evoke a bitterness in me. Why is it that America lets so many children get injured, die, fall out of school, or live with illnesses their families cannot afford to have treated? Why does our culture refuse to find the resources to uplift each child and allow each child to discover the intelligences, no matter what their form, that he or she possesses?

"Bleeding-heart liberal" I'd be called if I ever made these sentiments known in precisely these terms. But how many children will bleed tonight from a gunshot wound, a stabbing, a battering, or one of the freak home accidents that occur more frequently in poor, urban homes than in affluent suburban ones? Bleeding-heart liberalism or no, class-dominated culture or not, no one can deny that anyone who works with children earns significantly less money than does a person performing the identical or an analogous task with adults. One need only compare the salaries of the kindergarten teacher and the lawyer dedicated to juvenile work with those of the university professor and the attorney practicing adult criminal law.

Sometimes joy comes from community organization, which means that town budgets and a culture's value structure become invisible integers in the algebra of joy. Children don't wrack their minds over such deliberations, but many of them have learned not to wait for the community of adults to bring them joy or joyous possibilities. If necessary, they will find it in a putrid mattress and rusting tray or on the narrow, grassy path leading to the low foothills.

VII

Baseball scenes remind me of one of my own joyous moments. It was some-time in the 1950s, and a grade school classmate's parents had arranged to bring Jackie Robinson to speak to our entire student body. It cannot be true, I thought. Jackie Robinson under the same roof as the rest of us? Jackie Robinson in our rather lugubrious auditorium, looking out at us from his place on the stage under the banner printed with the motto, "A school should be a model home, a complete community, an embryonic democ-racy"? Jackie Robinson standing beneath that word "embryonic," whose meaning I never bothered to look up in the dictionary?

We waited, as quiet a group of students as ever assembled in those uncomfortable wooden seats. The time passed; he didn't show. I knew he wouldn't come. It would remain an empty fantasy to all of us save Mickey, whose parents had actually dined with Jackie Robinson in their own home.

And then, just as we had reached that restless, irritable grumpiness that regularly characterized our lack of enchantment with school, the rear door of the auditorium opened, and there stood Jackie Robinson. First a hush, then a collective breath being inhaled, and finally an explosion of noise. Screaming, stomping, clapping, whistling, we showed our adoration for this, well, God. I didn't know the word then, but the scene surely would have earned the accolade "awesome!"

Tall, handsome, and clad in an elegant dark blue suit, white shirt, and four-in hand tie, Jackie Robinson strode slowly down the rubber-matted aisle, barely a few feet from us, toward the stage. I can still see his black shoes and pigeon-toed walk. Our joy reached its crescendo when he was introduced—as if he really needed to be—and we watched him step to the center of the stage.

What happened next is the reason I bring forth this cherished recollec-tion in an essay on children and joy. With the noise absolutely deafening and teachers abandoning any thought of containing us, Jackie Robinson looked at us, which meant, of course, he looked at me; then smiled broadly at us, which meant, of course, he smiled at me; and finally spoke to us, which meant, of course . . .

In this utterly magical moment I now see a final aspect of joy. It is recog-nition, and let me assure anyone who doubts it, the feeling quite literally is awesome!

Seeing Jackie Robinson brought me intense, almost painful joy, the sort of wailing, crying joy many female rock fans exhibit, and the phenomenon of recognition lay at the heart of it. In recognition, we literally re-cognize something or someone. Somehow, we know again this something or someone, not only readjusting our sights on the object, but now reestablishing it in a familiar, if not intimate, context. Jackie Robinson dining with Mickey's parents in their very own home was pure anomaly. Jackie Robinson belonged in a uniform on a field. It was sheer incongruity to place him in street clothes in a friend's dining room. But now he was walking down the aisle inches from me, and I recognized him. And when he said "Hello" to all of us, that is, to each of us, he was recognizing us. I see you, which means, I know you. In response, we re-know him, for the joy obviously wouldn't exist if we didn't already know him from that other context.

Joan Erikson wrote of the birth of recognition when she described the mother looking at her newborn. Psychologist Jerome Kagan and his colleagues later reminded us that this primitive "I know you" phenomenon requires the mother to be looking full face at the child. Seeing this full face, most babies smile, and their arms and legs lift up off the mattress as they reveal a pattern of primitive recognition.[2] In that instant, they are as excited to see and be seen as were the children who overcame their fear and leapt into the sea. Come to think of it, those children, too, were gaining recognition, as was Lizzie when she smacked that ball to the left-field wall. We saw that! the girls were implicitly yelling out to her. And we saw you, too, doing that.

Recognition has a more familiar meaning. It suggests superior status. When a person gains recognition, we place the person on some higher level. Recognition in this context is granted and received and thereby connotes a social status. Thus, personal and social recognitions that also carry the propensity for joy constantly take place for the child. Children are seen and then reseen in new contexts—like Hillary Franklin—and in this way, they end up being something different from what they were moments before. The so-called moment of recognition for the child, therefore, not only marks a notable moment on an old clock, but also starts up a new clock, confirming the child's old being while simultaneously launching a new being. Recognition is central to Erikson's definition of identity as containing both static and dynamic components.

At eight, nine, and ten years old, children reveal another aspect of the joy of recognition. It appears in their complicated ambivalence about being seen or noticed. Children often claim they enjoy looking at people, but we all know that being seen is the rich reward of people's watching. Tanya Dade's habitually downward gaze literally had to be lifted by Mrs. Dickerson in order for the child to receive recognition. The action highlights what we mean when we say, "I need to talk with her eyeball to eyeball."

Children walk through school unaware of what in this instant is making them self-conscious. Is it that they are looking at someone and fearing that they may be caught in the act? Are they perhaps fearing (or wishing) that a certain someone will look at them and then—awesome!—know their names? In fact, many children will tell you complicated stories of why they don't like their names, and although some of these convoluted or nonsensical accounts bespeak their battles with parents and family origins, identity formation, esteem, and heaven knows what else, they also reveal a foundation of recognition. When someone, after all, knows my name, I am recognized. I could not have written this essay if Jackie Robinson had stopped in front of me and said, "Hi, Tommy," for I would have dropped dead on the spot!

What's in a child's name? Merely the commencement of his or her capacity to be recognized. "How'd you know my name?" one child asks another on a playground, partly bemused, partly curious, but mainly enthralled. Why collect an autograph if a name is not a slice of human recognition? The child is now in touch with the author of the autograph. The autograph symbolizes a personal connection between two people, or at least a child feels it this way. And recognition and joy spill all over it.

Great teachers recognize their students, not merely their students' work. They touch them, hug them, honor and love them, and make them feel special. In their early teenage years, children barely are able to articulate what they may be feeling about this recognition. But at eight or nine and then again in high school, there is no holding the child back. Children are quick to tell you of the joy they feel from having a teacher adore them. Part of the privilege of being thirteen is to grumble, "It doesn't matter." Part of the makeup of the nine-year-old is being able to tell your parents how much you really love Mrs. Dickerson.

A final word about recognition.

When Tanya Dade looks deep within herself and lets go of some of her secrets—when, in Melanie Dickerson's terms, she performs her psychoanalytic work—a form of recognition is taking place. Tanya is reknowing herself, which provides her yet another opportunity to develop new feelings about herself, or at least this new and transitory self. Tomorrow, when she explores more of the inner caves, she begins the process of reknowing, recognizing, and, ideally, reliking herself all over again.

In this regard, amusement and entertainment do not carry the day. Partly they fail because too little is explored or learned, and little resembling recognition takes place. The child is only being diverted or having something evoked that is quickly dismissed in favor of yet another diversion. Such activity may be pleasurable when it is not alienating, but it rarely provides the path to genuine recognition and joy.

Missing here is not only the opportunity to rediscover yourself, recontextualize yourself (as Hillary Franklin was doing), or re-create yourself (as Mamo Turnbull was attempting to do with her granddaughters), but the possibility of falling in love with yourself all over again. I have consistently argued that good families, good schools and communities, and good teachers and coaches, among other things, allow children the opportunity to fall in love with themselves. I have never been concerned about children's getting fat heads; it's the thin heads, like Tanya Dade's, that disturb me. Besides, the notorious children with fat heads are merely compensating for the fact that they cannot locate lovable qualities in themselves.

Psychoanalysts call the process healthy narcissism. If I examine my own image in that mythic pool and decide that it's lovable but don't fall in and drown, I am on my way to knowing joy. In contrast, when I learn that nothing about me is lovable, nothing I do allows me to love me, then ultimately I suspect my life to be a joyless pursuit of inevitably empty tasks or accomplishments. I weep for children who remain friendless and answer as best I can their parents' questions regarding the origins of this aloneness and its possible ramifications. But more than anything, I lament the fact that these children will not know the joy of being loved by someone their own size. A pet may bring joy, and surely adults do, but the love of people my size remains enormously important. In fact, as a parent, I imagine I still crave the love of people smaller than me. Then again, who's to say that the child seemingly without friends isn't deriving joy from some of the same tasks and endeavors we have been exploring in these pages?

VIII

In more than a quarter century of observing, speaking, and playing with children, I have learned that one child may be, not so simply, born with a capacity to find joy, whereas his or her very own brother or sister may be a complete stranger to it. Little seems to please this child, and not that much provokes a laugh. It is as though the joy wiring has not been hooked up. I am continually struck by this temperamental variation when I observe poor children who have been diagnosed as malnourished and yet who at times squeal with joy. I think of it, too, when I see depressed children who live in homes of grandeur and wealth. What could have gone so wrong that these children don't know feelings like glee and perpetual giddiness and joy?

Of course, we know the answers to these questions. With every social advantage leaning their way, affluent children, albeit carrying with them a sense of entitlement, as Robert Coles described it, by temperament or experience may be a million miles from joy.[3] Classical psychotherapies, furthermore, may not always be able to draw them closer to the sources of it.

Not so strangely, in all of the homes I visit, grand and poor alike, televisions blare and children sit before them. All of America's children see all of the shows they are "meant" to see. They know all the American actors and all the American music and lyrics. Joy or the lack of it somehow is bound up with this electronic phenomenon, but I'm not certain that anyone yet knows precisely what the correlations or even the variables may be. One thought, however, on the connection between joy and television comes to mind.

It goes without saying that television is fundamentally a visual medium that cannot truly develop vocabularies. In fact, it stunts and abbreviates vocabularies, so that, for example, children feel perfectly comfortable with the slang verb "dis," which is television-like shorthand for showing disrespect. Television of course, does develop visual imagery and in its way produces an elaborate cognitive apparatus, inasmuch as the child's consciousness is being bombarded by visual stimuli that rarely last more than a few seconds. I liken the process to fireworks—brilliant and consciousness consuming, to be sure, but with no possibility of enduring.

The concomitants of recognition, seeing and being seen, necessarily are accentuated by television; the medium does at least offer constant practice in viewing, if not in imagining. But something appears to be missing: the ingredients that would help children connect visual representations to their inner world, where they construct significant calculations, interpretations, and analyses, and let us acknowledge that they are constructed at complicated levels even by small children. Presently, the connections appear to be made only between visual images and evocative expressions. The redundancy here is intended: television too often evokes little more in the child than evocation.

At the very least, children, in what Jerome Bruner calls narrative thinking, must learn, first, to represent and describe experience to themselves and then to make sense of that experience.[4] One wonders whether television, in its essentially entertainment mode, helps children to make sense of any reality. If they do make sense of reality, must this sense ineluctably be couched in primarily visual terms? Although there is no question that visual stimuli and the responses to them can produce joy—there is, after all, the phenomenon the Greeks called *amor*—I don't know that joy as we have examined it here is enhanced by this constantly changing rush of visual treats.

A more benign view of television has it that postliterate children, those belonging to what some authors call the new age of electronic tribalism, are encountering new definitions of joy. In addition, because of television, the narrative form of reasoning probably is undergoing profound transformations. After all, in the electronic age, what is reality to the child but anything that can be seen? "I saw it on television," the child states with confidence, echoing Neil Postman's observations, so it must be real and true. (In this same line of reasoning, that which is read presumably cannot be real and true, for nothing has been seen.)

The child, not ironically, makes the same claims about his or her dreams. "I saw it in my mind's eye and so it must be true." Or, similarly, "After seeing something I felt something and that's it." What need is there for old-fashioned reason, if seeing and feeling are all that are required for genuine action? Tanya Dade's exquisite life work in fifth grade demonstrates a different sort of seeing and believing, ultimately leading to a new self-recognition and joy. I hope television possesses the same capacity as a simple diary. In the main, children appear to recognize its evocative power, and stuff becomes stirred up inside them, but the question is, What happens to it? Do children have the intellectual equipment to make any sense of it, as narrative reasoning demands? Joy, after all, requires more than stuff being stirred up. A certain intellectual and reasoned capstone must sit atop the evocation, so that, as the artist might say, "it all works."

I linger over the matter of television and joy, because clearly television is the most powerful cultural force the child experiences. It is hardly the most powerful human experience the child will know, but with television we have a medium with which adults maintain some intellectual and emotional control of the child. It is evident that the very nature of consciousness is shifting by dint of people's ongoing television viewing. If nothing else, the capacity to make sense of utterly unending messages and themes builds an inherently ahistoric intellectual foundation in the child. In turn, the child's sense of causation is affected, since interconnections of television themes and story lines are often tenuous. Thus, new premises of joy most likely will be born of these new cognitive demands and styles. Surely the proclivity for joy in discourse already has been eroded.

In truth, we don't yet know what the effect of the medium on something as precious as the child's sense of joy will be, although we already are witnessing the effects of a culture that seems to have abandoned the art of reading and writing. Willie Dillmeister not withstanding, I suspect that fewer and fewer children are gaining joy from what we ancient ones used to call without shame "the life of the mind." Even college students tend often to view the life of the mind more in terms of academic requirement than in terms of mind play. To mimic something in the way children do when they sing the commercial jingle or lip-sync the hottest rap lyric seems to be eroding the source of joy in creating. At least, I fear this to be the case. Then again, as Pirsig and others warn, we must not only perpetuate the old but also establish the new, so perhaps children do find joy in being able to do what their hero does: sing, dance, slam-dunk a basketball, walk that special walk, wear those special shoes.

A final point. There can be no question that one of the implicit messages of television is that personality is all and all. We even have a new vocation known as the "television personality." For children, the major dynamic at work here is classical identification with, ironically, the smaller-than-life figures they see on the tube. Heroes or not, real or not, television has created a whole new meaning of the concept of celebrity. To see a rock or television star in person—an interesting phrase—surely brings joy to the child, as I mentioned earlier in discussing recognition. But think now of small children's unconsciously believing that celebrities truly are the way they appear on television, modeling their lives after them, and experiencing joy as taught by these people through scripts and character development.

Ever since popular music emerged as big business, teenagers have screamed with almost sexual delight at the sight of their icons. Now, because of television, this psychological phenomenon has spread down to children six, seven, and eight years old. Often their joy is derived from "contact" with the stars, as the culture urges them closer to show business and further from the professions that my parents put forth as acceptable options. Every popular performer is called "artist." Where now is the fool who once remarked that the more things change the more they stay the same!

The emphasis, therefore, on the new joy may lie in this identification with the major players of popular culture, the new class of artists. For children, the implication is simply that the sort of quiet reminders required in traditional schools—such as psychology, religion, and personal discovery—must give way to new dramaturgies of popular culture performance. Parents and teachers will have to perform, for children are learning that the mainstream action of the culture lies in performance of one sort or another.

This means that the grand reward for children is applause. Without an audience there can be no grand reward. One can preach as often as one likes about work's being its own reward, the supreme values being the intrinsic ones, and how people must plumb the depths of their souls and worry not what critics write, but many children raised on television are learning that genuine joy is defined as a crowd going mad over your last public display. So what if you are required to do it all over again tomorrow, it's worth it if the audience rises in a standing ovation, the Nielson ratings look promising, and the dollars roll in.

I hope that the reader detects here not just my cynicism but also my lamentation for children whose entire being and hunt for joy are captured in what four decades ago David Riesman called the "other directed" soul.[5] I eagerly await a discourse on why it is that television watching and drug use have hit children at the same time. Can there be some cognitive connections between these two foods, neither of which is nourishing and both of which are exciting, evocative, distracting, and arousing?

The new joy, therefore, is often little more than heightened sensation. The new sensation, moreover, leads one to believe in the literalness of an altered state, albeit an externally generated one. Having their state altered allows some people to feel joy, or at least puts them on the road frequently traveled to finding joy. The opposite of joy? Easy: "Bummer." As Benny Parsons reminds us, something either "joys us up" or brings us down, be it an experience or pill. The brain, obviously, is involved, but it's not the cerebral cortex that has been called into action, but rather compartments far more primitive.

Many critics of our culture are correct when they say our society increasingly acts in animalistic fashion, as if instincts by definition always are meant to be honored. If constraint was an art for Goethe, it now has become a hangup. Children are advised to "go with the flow," "let it all hang out," and "go with their gut," and many are taking these admonitions to heart, as their communities seem to offer little or no constraint. The right to express oneself has become the byword of the day, even for small children demanding their rights.

In the end, the new joy, somewhat tribal in origin, clearly electronically generated, and aided and abetted by a cult of personality, the search for a new consciousness and altered states, the sheer glory of public approval of popular performance, and the apotheosis of celebrity, will only grow in the present environment. For the climate these days is hardly one of child protection, adoration, worship, or even fundamental appreciation. The new age relies on exploiting child and teaching forms of joy commensurate with this exploitation. That television host Mr. Rogers would hit a nerve when he announced to children that he liked them exactly as they were and there was no one else in the world exactly like them bespeaks the danger in the new joy. But it also offers hope that certain segments of the culture may regain those community and family values required to nurture children, values that recently have come under assault by commercial forces and a capitalism often out of reasonable control.

Applause is wonderful for children, but only the children themselves know the degree to which it represents transitory compensation for things far more significant and healthy. "Joy must be like electricity," a grandmother living in Boston's Roxbury neighborhood told me years ago. "The child must always be able to turn it on, or know they can get at it. All those rich folks who buy their little precious ones everything they want before they even know what they want, they aren't making electricity. That will never make for a joyous child. You watch those children and see just how long their smiles last. Believe me when I tell you, and I don't lie, those smiles of theirs aren't lasting anywhere near long enough."

IX

Having had lunch and conversation at 808 Langley Court with Lynn Swilling and her husband Jared, who hasn't worked for thirty straight months and hasn't known joy in a long while, I'm about to take my leave. The children on the stairs have disbanded, and the halls outside have become peculiarly quiet for this time of day, although through the walls I can still distinguish the sounds of at least four different television sets. The Swillings themselves habitually have two playing for almost the entire time they are awake.

From the single bedroom of this small but neatly kept apartment, seven-year-old Luanda Swilling appears, her face creased from being buried in pillows as she slept. Seeing me, she appears startled, for she is somewhat uncomfortable with visitors. Then she spies her mother, a woman not much older, actually, than my own eldest child. Luanda has stayed home from school this morning with a head cold, and it's clear from her sniffling and puffy eyes that she is in discomfort. "I can't breathe, Mommy," she says, walking toward Lynn. "I can't breathe, Mommy."

Lynn moves toward the child as simultaneously Jared rises from his chair in front of the window. Within moments, Luanda is being carried to a chair at the small table where our lunch dishes still sit and is buried in her mother's body. Jared walks up behind his wife and gently strokes his daughter's hair. No one speaks as we listen to Luanda's sniffling and coughing, the results of her cold and her having started to cry.

Suddenly, this lovely child lifts her head and stares up at her mother and then beyond her mother's face at her father. Still sniffling, she looks at me and grins widely, revealing precious white teeth as neat and straight as ever they could be. Then, obviously contented and reassured, and, I think to myself, joyous in the best of senses, she once again buries her head in her mother's arms and breasts.

Lynn looks at me and giggles. What more is there to say to an aging psychologist speaking to families about children and joy! Jared, who has seemed especially low this one cold day, glances at me and asks softly, "That the sort of thing you looking for, Doc?"

AFTERWORD
Life Studies and the Value of Stories

There ought to be a place in the world for the sociologist who is also an artist . . . That is why the really great men of sociology had no "method." They had a method; it was the search for insight. They went "by guess and by God," but they found out things.

WILLARD W. WALLER, *On the Family, Education, and War*

My studies in Judaism have taught me that each person is an entire world and to lose one person is to lose that irreplaceable, individual sphere of experiences, memories, and wisdom.

DONALD PALLADINO JR., *"Seeking the Spheres"*

When our analysands tell us about their inner life, they describe to us a country to which we have never been, a country to where we can never gain direct access.

HEINZ KOHUT, qtd. in A. Goldberg, *Advances in Self-Psychology*

YEARS AGO I listened to one of America's outstanding social scientists speak about his work. He told his audience that he had collected some unusually complex and fascinating data and, unfortunately, he had not been able to include it in his final report. Because the material was too difficult to code, he explained, he had omitted it. How strange, I thought, that the very data he himself found to be most significant, the data we typically assign to the "other" category because we don't know what to make of it, was being left behind, and most probably would never be published. Then again, I mused, in an admittedly cynical manner, most of the rest of us are also being left behind, since the world doesn't seem to know how to code us, either.

At that time in my life, I was hard at work turning young people's responses on a questionnaire about perceptions of time into mathematical

271

scores punched on IBM cards. Truthfully, I was mesmerized not only by the numbers but by the technological processes that gave birth to seemingly scientific findings: The stack of IBM cards increased in height, the printouts came chugging out of the machine, and there I was, making social science! There was a problem, however, not only with the nature of the research: I never dared to admit that the methods of data analysis rather than any ideas had come to dominate my entire social scientific enterprise. More significantly, I had the feeling I had lost my voice. This work I was doing was not my style. I didn't feel comfortable with the esthetics of the inquiry.

That ideas were abandoned in the hunt for proper operational methods was one thing. More important, it was not me doing the work; I was merely part of the machinery of the inquiry, and the machinery offered had no room for human temperament or sensibilities. The data, I felt, should tell a story, preferably a moving one. At the very least, they had to meet V. S. Naipul's criteria of a successful novel: human data had to enlighten and evoke.[1] At the time, I had no idea that the value of storytelling would spawn an expansive literature, as typified by these observations from Jack Maguire: "We all are made of stories. They are as fundamental to our soul, intellect, imagination, and way of life as flesh, bone, and blood are to our bodies . . . Story-knowing represents our naturally evolving memories—our instinctive recording, in our own language, of the most impressive life experiences we've lived through or heard about . . . As human beings, we have a fundamental affinity for storytelling, and it represents a divine energy burning within us."[2]

Years before, a professor had remarked that a good piece of research leads the reader like a good drama to that one special table of tables where an informational denouement may be experienced. He was right, except that I preferred to conceive of the denouement in human terms. A good story for me was one that a person told in his or her own words. (The seed for this interest of mine, I believe, was the joy I experienced as a child when my mother read stories to me and, even more, when I listened to her tell stories. I rarely saw her as happy as when, surrounded by friends, she told long, wondrous stories filled with humor, pathos, drama, and, I truly believe, essential human truths.)

Perhaps it comes as no surprise, then, that a few years after my entrance into the social science profession, I realized that what lay behind my research concerns was an interest in collecting other people's stories. The essence of the work is to capture the way people lead their lives as evinced in the stories they tell and to faithfully reproduce the stories in the language, rhythm, and meter of these storytellers. In the words of John Dewey, I was interested in nothing more and nothing less than the uncommon stories of common people.[3]

The type of work I do is called clinical history taking, psychohistory, journalism, and even nonfiction short story writing. I use the term "life study," to distinguish this form of inquiry from the classical clinical case study. In recent years, however, I find the terms "story sociology" and "narrative" to be congenial, because both suggest a jargon-free approach to this form of inquiry. Perhaps the term that best describes this sort of work is the one put forth by Sara Lawrence-Lightfoot and Jessica Hoffman Davis, who call it "portraiture."[4] Still, the word "story" tends to put this form of inquiry into a teller-audience context. For there to be a story, there must be a teller and a listener, someone who has lived the life and someone to witness the narrative of it.[5] The term "story" need not suggest an oral account; in fact, it often suggests a written account, although in this form of research the writer and the storyteller are not the same persons. But this obvious point raises a more complex one.

Using the word "story" may suggest the notion of a contrived account, something a trifle fictionalized. We speak, for example, of a "tall story," or we admonish people, "No stories, please, just the truth!" I rather like this somewhat shadowy aspect to the word "story," because we must never lose sight of the fact that no one can render a wholly objective, value-free accounting of human experience. There is always bias, prejudgment, subjective interference, contrivance, and other forms of "research noise." The storyteller makes the story a little better or worse, just as the listener—or witness—does while listening and then again when repeating or reproducing the story. Ever the poet-scientists, Lawrence-Lightfoot and Hoffman Davis speak in this context of "refining the lens." Not so incidentally, Ellen Langer uses this same word, "lens," to remind us of another value of stories: "In the perspective of every person lies a lens through which we may better understand ourselves."[6]

No matter what our intentions, conscious or unconscious, or, for that matter, our social scientific safeguards, stories develop twists and turns and inimitable stylistic and substantive variations. Moreover, these variations should remind us of the origin of the experience being rendered or recounted, not to mention the human being who sits (or, in the case of a child, runs, plays, jumps, or squirms) before us as storyteller. Every conversation—and they *are* conversations, rather than question-and-answer sessions—runs the danger of factual slippage; classical memory experiments confirm this. A story passed from one person to another arrives at the final witness significantly altered from the original version, though usually with certain fundamental elements intact. Indeed, the essence of mythology rests on the variation of the story, as it passes on (and hence breathes life) from teller to teller, witness to witness.[7] In the adumbration and embellishments one finds the subjective contribution of each person—teller and witness—as well as remnants of his or her culture.

Just as ecological theory suggests culture becomes a highly significant feature in storytelling research. Consider, for example, John Van Maanan's explanation of culture: "A culture is expressed (or constituted) only by the actions and words of its members and must be interpreted by, not given to, a fieldworker. To portray culture requires the fieldworker to hear, to see, and most important . . . to write of what was presumably witnessed and understood during a stay in the field. Culture is not itself visible, but is made visible only through its representation." And if we worry that versions of a story may vary, as John Kotre assures us they will, then we may take heart in Langer's thoughtful reminder: "Would I be inclined to listen to you if you said something at all similar to something else you once told me and I remembered every word you said? Would I taste the food I'm eating if I simultaneously remembered exactly how it tasted the last time?"[8]

This last point deserves attention. To say that a piece of research results merely from listening and recording and then recounting someone's story sounds cavalier. Surely there is more to a story than that. The researcher asks questions and requests clarification, and pieces of the story come to be confirmed in one manner or another. On the other hand, some might ask, How could anyone consider a story, and especially a highly personalized account, social science? If for no other reason, one person's story or account is by definition idiosyncratic. It may even change as a function of the audience. What possible generalizations, therefore, may be drawn from it?[9]

In fact, little generalization is possible. As in many cases involving human inquiry, one's goal is better described as conceptualizing rather than generalizing, and hence the single narrative or portrait, albeit an idiosyncratic version (the storyteller, after all, may tell that story differently three weeks hence) remains of the utmost value.[10]

But even this is not the central point. More important is that the version proffered by the storyteller bespeaks a true account in all senses of the word. For not only do we find people telling their story, but, when allowed to continue their story, they offer as well their *accounting* of their experiences. That is, one finds in the "good" story not only dramatic details and inner feelings associated with them, but also the teller's interpretive variations.

Thus, in the telling we hear the experiences along with their meanings and implications, at least as proffered by the teller.[11]

I raise these points because one of the criticisms of life study research is that authors fail to interpret their "data." In truth, when one presents a sufficient amount of material, the teller's own interpretations tend to be found within the story. That is why we remain alert to the notion that storytellers build their accounting into their accounts. Granted, as researchers, we reserve the right to reinterpret the account, but we must hold in mind that, inevitably, our work is a reinterpretation. Not only do we (re)tell the story we have heard firsthand, but our interpretations, by definition, become a secondhand retelling.

Notice here the problem of interpreting data as the story unfolds. Psychotherapists may offer interpretations to their clients, as might interviewers to their "subjects." The person following closely all the questions put forth in an interview schedule presumably tries to remain indifferent to the material—and perhaps to the respondent. Somewhere between these extremes lies the life study researcher. Although in the life study one tends to steer clear of explicit interpretations, on occasion one finds it necessary to offer interpretive remarks, almost in the form of concert program notes. Still, the point of these remarks is to communicate one's responses to the story. The goal is not necessarily to help the teller understand the deeper ramifications of his or her story; this is not part of the life study contract. In fact, there are no clear-cut deeper ramifications to this form of story sociology. The story, like the immediate moment for Henri Bergson, is all! When the story is told, and witnessed, it is by definition interpreted; hence the double meaning of the word "account."[12]

To those who wonder whether a witness is required for a life study to be born, the answer is assuredly no. Every minute in what Jerome Bruner and Donald Polkinghorne call narrative thought, people tell stories to themselves and attempt to make sense of them. In fact, one finds these "narrative accounts" or moments of "self speak" coming forth from children playing by themselves. When made aware of the witness, children most likely cease their public (self) storytelling.[13]

While the thrust of life study research appears to proceed at a conscious level, the studies actually arise, if Freud is to be believed, from preconscious materials, since the researcher asks people to speak about things, presumably, that they were not thinking about at that particular moment. Indeed, people regularly ask researchers; "What exactly am I supposed to be talking about?" Unconscious materials, too, make their way into the accounts. In psychoanalytic terms, telling the story is akin to recounting a dream or, more precisely and again in Freud's terminology, to *interpreting* a dream.[14]

We recall that Freud considered a dream interpreted when the dreamer, the storyteller, has exhausted all conscious associations to the forms, substance, and symbols of the dream—he or she literally has run out of associations. Freud explicitly indicated that although from time to time he offered interpretations of his own, it was the analysand's associations and not the analyst's codification of the material that constituted the genuine interpretation of the dream. In this same way, the themes and variations of the story, its twists and turns, and, of course, the free associations all contribute to the analysis (really the account) of the story.

In addition, it is impossible for the sort of stories to which life study researchers listen to be completely interpreted. Just as, by definition, a final version of a story cannot be constructed, so a story cannot be completely interpreted. Whereas a dream has a finite number of interpretations or associations to be teased from it, there is no limit to the number of associations to a story involving the ways one leads one's life. This, in part, is what makes the story uncommon. Because the very purpose of the life study is to accumulate through a person's narratives as much as one can about his or her life (as is true for the goal of all worthwhile biographical and psychohistorical enterprises), the very living of a day furnishes the person with a range of potential versions for old and new stories alike. If, as Heraclitus warned, one cannot enter the same water twice, then surely the same story cannot be recounted the second time as it was the first; inevitably, the first recounting shapes the second.[15]

As a child, I heard my mother tell one story exactly twelve million times. With each telling I felt I couldn't survive hearing this story one more time. In retrospect, I see that each version was different, and, like a great stage actor, she told each version with the allusion that this was the first time the story had ever been told. Keep in mind that, by pure chance, her audience had heard that story four million times! Keep in mind as well these words from Alan Parray and Robert Doan: "But each person is freed from the assumption that a grand narrative tends to foster—namely, that each person is entitled to only one self."[16]

In response to the simple question, How are you? we may respond, Am I glad you didn't ask me that last week! This common response suggests that we change. Our experiences grow in number, the meanings we make of events shift and mature, and because our stories accumulate, they are altered as a function of both changes in mood and the inevitable accumulation and interpretation of experiences. As the structure of our mind changes, we speak to ourselves and others in a slightly different way than we did perhaps a few hours ago. The river isn't the only thing that has changed.

If one looks closely at the life study form of research, one recognizes that it relies on people's constantly bringing their stories forward. In a sense, the teller catches the researcher up, filling in the blanks as well as adding to the store of information. Only death ends the story, and then, as in the construction and evolution of myth, others carry it on, which is to say others carry on the teller as well. One hears a man's story of his life and then the versions of it told by his heirs. In this regard, some of the more fascinating accounts are those undertaken of people whom the researcher never meets, as was the case with the unemployed family whose story I present in the Societal Peril section of this book. Ineluctably, autobiography and biography remain intermeshed. For obvious reasons, all accounts marry the contemporaneous with the historical. All stories are made in and shaped by time, and no one is more aware of this than the storytellers themselves. And all of this is background for the emergence not merely of a story but of a person's fundamental identity. As Erik Erikson observed, we live simultaneously with the sense of permanence and a sense of change; at all moments we are what we were and also something different.[17]

Two points about the nature of the story: First, by definition, the most personal life stories, or life studies, involve cultural and institutional factors as well as purely personal ones.[18] If the single story is seen to be idiosyncratic, its scaffold is at the same time systematically underwritten, in that broad cultural and institutional features shape and refine the story. In part, this is what is described by ecological theory.

Second, often the story one hears relates more to an interior narrative, "self speak," as it is called, than to neatly etched external experiences. I use the word "experience" here rather than "event" to suggest, following the lines of Robert Kegan's writings, that an experience may be viewed as an event to which a person has rendered meaning. An event, in other words, does not shape us until we have assigned meaning to it. Kegan suggests, actually, that humans' fundamental activity is to make meaning of events.[19] Perhaps this meaning making is what distinguishes humans from other animals. Surely it is at the heart of story telling and witnessing.

In other words, there are always affectual, cognitive, and experiential aspects of the story to which researchers must attend. I tell something, I feel something about what I am telling, and what I feel becomes part of what I tell. In addition, I reason something out that clearly shapes my original definition of the event and now exists as part of that experience. Even more, my reasoning shapes the story I now recount; most likely, it constitutes the structure of the account. In this regard, the process of collecting the story becomes a quasi-clinical as well as journalistic endeavor, a social-psychological as well as biographical enterprise. This is precisely what the sociologist Jan Dizard means when he describes research of this sort as "treading a fine line between anecdote and systematic data" and "between journalism and sociology."[20]

Furthermore, the researcher as listener, or witness, becomes aware that feelings and experiences are evoked in him or her by dint of hearing the story (V. S. Naipul's evocation criterion) and moreover, that the approach to the material that is evoked must also be along clinical, journalistic, social psychological, and biographical avenues. In all, four discrete stories are going on simultaneously as the teller and witness come together. The teller has an interior story as well as the one he or she publicly recounts. Similarly, the witness has two stories to consider, the one being told and the interior one that is evoked or stimulated.[21]

Put all these stories together, and one is left with a combination of the interior and exterior worlds. Daniel Frank spoke of the matter in this way: "The most value laden areas to study are mental states and social institutions; to study them together forces the researcher into the abyss of the subjective world."[22]

Over the years, I have repeatedly heard the observation that life study research is highly personal, subjective, and idiosyncratic. Clearly, the observation is intended to reflect the teller's experience. The listener's personal responses and evocations, however, also assume important roles in this personal enterprise. Keep in mind that the phrase "bearing witness" hardly connotes a passive act. The word "bearing" carries definitions such as carrying, transporting, giving, giving birth, holding up, sustaining, offering, and supplying. In the act of communication, nothing could be more active.

ANY AUTOBIOGRAPHICAL narrative must contain its cultural and institutional trappings. One of the ironies of life study research is that it remains essentially anthropological. Our "informants," naturally, are instructed to speak only for themselves, but this is no reason to think they will ignore the social and cultural features that may occupy our ruminations. Therefore, we learn from "informants" not only individual or idiosyncratic stories but also about cultures and social structures. Beyond a person's experience of unemployment, for example, we learn about the concept of work as it is defined by a society or culture.

In this regard, biography involves attending to features of history and society that underwrite the story one is telling. If there is one finding that derives from life study research, it is just that: by definition, storytellers are historians, anthropologists, and sociologists. Their awareness of historical and cultural features, both tangible and ephemeral, are heard in almost every account.

As an explicit matter, storytellers reveal their awareness or lack of awareness of social and historical facts. Often, that which the research asks of them they have already asked of themselves. In this light, I imagine that the subjects of life study research tell us stories which they feel fulfill the mission of the work as they define it. The storytellers' asking "Is this the sort of stuff you want?" becomes particularly poignant when we consider that they may be seeking some sort of recognition or assurance from us for the work they have done in preparing and performing their accounts and stories.

It would be inaccurate to suggest that the structure of any person's story represents the sociological or anthropological structure underwriting the story as it actually evolved in the person's living of it. Yet, if one listens to stories—and everyone, recall, is an expert storyteller when the stories are genuinely his or her own—one invariably hears people struggling to locate and define cultural forms and social structures that they might use to frame and stabilize their ostensibly subjective and highly idiosyncratic accounts. (As an amateur carpenter, I call these stabilizing references the "stud walls" of the story.)

Having recounted some of the basic tenets of the life study research, I'll now underscore the dangers and difficulties one experiences in defining what the task of data analysis might be. Does one dig deeply into the fabric of an account and tease out the threads and themes that lie there? Or does one "lift" the material into some higher analytical or theoretical plane?[23]

I find these questions to be as vexing as any the research confronts. Over the years I have taken the position that the more explicitly one interprets the data, no matter how faithful to the data one attempts to be, one inevitably injects one's prejudgments (and probably ideologies as well) and moves away one very significant step from the delicate originality that is the person's own autobiographical testimony or narrative.[24] There is, then, an intellectual or methodological dilemma to be considered. There is also a political one, as Howard Zinn reminds us.[25]

When the words of the storyteller are presented only to be followed by detailed analysis of some sort, either qualitative or quantitative, I always fear that I have implicitly been made party to a precarious political arrangement. Presumably, what the storyteller has revealed is not suitable, sufficient, or comprehensible, or perhaps the interpretation represents refining mere raw data. To make the data acceptable—which in a sense means to make the teller more acceptable—or to make it comprehensible, we analyze it. And analysis here means lifting the data (the story, actually,) to some "higher" level.

In effect, there are two currencies at play: the teller's and the listener's, with the latter emerging as legitimate, sophisticated, and professional and the former being, shall we say, raw, primitive, and unsophisticated, the currency seemingly lacking sufficient credit. So we transliterate the illegitimate or counterfeit currency, thereby rendering it legitimate. In the process, we go beyond analyzing the data to laundering it.

Philosophers of science provide us one way out of the dilemma. Drawing on the work of Willard Waller, we may argue that the purpose of the life study is to gain insight. But insight is not simply learning something about someone; rather it is the ability to perceive various parts of the perceptual world and how they appear to cohere. Even more, we can perceive a causal interconnection between these various parts. This is what we mean when we suggest that the life study helps us understand how people lead their lives and what sense they make of them. The sense, in other words, is represented in the interpretations they offer or the coherence of their various insights.

The story itself has an internal coherence—it may appear as an aesthetic—that the teller provides. As witnesses, we need not impose this coherence or interpretation on the story; the words speak for themselves, because the internal logic and order of the story offer the coherence of insights. That is why the storyteller recounts this event before that one or concludes that one experience has resulted from another. This is the essence of what Dewey meant by reflective thinking. And this is really the point. One need not impose an *external analysis*, because analysis has already been done *internally* by the teller in the arrangement of the parts that unfold as palpable coherence. As Parray and Doan observe; "A story told by a person in his/her own words of his/her own experience does not have to plead its legitimacy in any higher court of narrative appeal, because no narrative has any greater legitimacy than the person's own."[26]

In this same context, Waller writes, "All science depends upon perceptions *reconstructed* and *fitted together* in imagination, upon an artistic *recreation* of event." But it is not the listener (the scientist, perhaps) who Waller says undertakes these mental activities; it is the storyteller. Of course, the listener brings to the listening process conceptions (and preconceptions) that can be both fruitful and harmful. Again from Waller: "Without concepts as an aid to observation we could see almost nothing, and yet concepts hinder us from seeing things afresh."[27] These conceptions naturally influence what the listener hears and how he or she privately (internally) makes sense of the story. In the end, however, the listener must provide that material that allows the reader to perceive and appreciate not only the particular threads of the story, but their coherence as well. Again, it is in the coherence that one discovers the causal connections, the interpretation of the story's themes, and ultimately the insights to be unearthed.

As I say, this form of interpretation or transliteration potentially contains strong political overtones. Either we use occasional citations or anecdotes to illustrate or flavor our more "serious" and "thoughtful" theoretical points, or we run the risk of leaving the impression that the story requires our interpretations in order to be understood or appreciated.[28] Lurking in all of this is a provocative message: in and of themselves, these stories, and therefore these storytellers, do not carry sufficient weight. Perhaps legal testimony is something like the process activated by the life study, inasmuch as people hear testimony all the time and must react to it in terms of what is emotionally and intellectually evoked by it. One danger of this analogy, however, is that the "ideal" story hardly develops with the listener shaping and forming it through questions, points of clarification, and rules of evidence and inquiry.

The main political point here is that all stories must be heard. All testimonies must be accepted for what they are and not primarily for what they tell us about issues that concern only the listeners. To honor the story is to honor the teller. In a sense, this would be enough, even though by now we know there is a whole lot more to this form of research. The point is made rather blatantly in Sandy Coleman's review of the book *Teach Me* by Murray Levin: "In this context, Levin's insistence on interpreting what a student has just said comes across as insulting. He wants to allow the students to speak for themselves, but he assumes they cannot be understood."[29]

It is this same thought that Peter Woods seeks to convey when he writes that ethnography essentially works "from *within* the group, and from within the perspectives of the group's members. It is *their* meanings and *their* interpretations that count." Ethnography, furthermore, as Helen Roy argues, "allows the researcher to live with the characters of the story, then re-create the scenes and bring them to life by telling the story."[30] In this regard, every storyteller is an ethnographer, or at least a narrator.

Along with the political aspect of the story's interpretation, there is a personal one. Although the moral and ethical considerations inherent in undertaking life study research are rarely noted, this seems the appropriate forum to remind ourselves of them.

At the outset of our work, we not only ask the person for permission to report his or her words, but also describe as fully as possible what we will do with the accounts, how we will work with them, and what the person can expect from us as an interviewer/listener as well as from our final written product. Yet no matter how precise our descriptions, much of what we say as the months of our association with the tellers pass and they become our friends, our work becomes, if not invisible, then surely an unobtrusive feature of the friendship.

Consciously trying to keep all physical and mechanical evidence of a conversation like a tape recording out of this friendship, the data-gathering procedure ideally becomes an unobtrusive by-product of our many conversations. Typically, I have found it best to refrain from a great deal of note taking until I have left the person, so that everything about my way of dealing with the person appears somewhat normal and routine. No one needs to remind a storyteller or his or her family of our abiding interest. Yet this rather cumbersome and questionable quality tends to diminish with time. After months of conversation, the storytellers simply cannot keep calling this visitor to their home the census taker. (Witnesses, too, require a little recognition from time to time!)

The research goes on, existing in the bond that ties the witness to his or her special friends. It is a bond, not so incidentally, that implicates the researcher in the lives of those he or she "studies" or, better, befriends. I suspect that all biographers sense this bond. Yet, just as the friendship is born in the context of research, so does it evolve with that element of human inquiry that attends the rituals and conventions constituting human exchange. It is not difficult to see, therefore, why the interpretations of the stories one chooses to recount in a written document would have profound ramifications for the tellers. Analysts and critics may wish to know more or less about the quality of these interview-conversations, but the tellers of the stories read the researcher's final documents with a wholly different agenda. They wish to know how they have been seen and heard by the researcher, for there is a certain immutable truth to the written portrait, as Lawrence-Lightfoot and Hoffman Davis point out, just as there is in the painted one.[31]

Let us remember that millions, perhaps tens of millions, of words are uttered over these years of friendship, but only a few thousand are selected for public presentation. No trial sketches to examine in this exposition, just the final display. So the process of reduction already has its political and human implications for the tellers. "That's it? That's all you have to say?" they might ask, when actually they wish to know, "Is that all I mean to you?" Similarly, the tellers are more likely to interpret our interpretations as an indication of what we actually think of them or a sign that taken by itself, their story does not meet the standards of genuine scholarship or human inquiry. Reproducing their stories gives them voice—as if they didn't have one before our encounters with them! Adding our interpretation ostensibly gives their story credence and ultimately "acceptability." Complex and sensitive, this matter, too, lies at the root of Dewey's phrase regarding the uncommon story of the common man or woman.

The problem before us may be the taproot of the life study inquiry. The researcher's intention is to produce reliable data, systematically collected and appropriately analyzed, with the final product representing an objective account of, well, the teller's account. As if this weren't difficult enough, at the same time the researcher has insinuated him- or herself into the storyteller's life, such that it seems impossible for the final product to be anything but subjective. Indeed, the life study seems to be the natural form of the subjective inquiry.

How many times have people counseled, You can't make science and friendship with the same folks; either you study them, or you look out for them, but you can't have it both ways. That is precisely why we invent words like "subject" and "informant"—to differentiate a particular population of people from one's friends and associates. Rightly or wrongly, it is true that I choose not to associate with my clinical clients outside the professional context. I have made a conscious decision not to mix the work in the office with the informal contexts of friendship outside the office. Why, then, would I attempt to meld the objective with the subjective, and how, theoretically, can I combine these two avenues to make a justification for the enterprise?[32]

My response goes this way: After I realized that my own voice and temperament had become lost in the earlier work I had undertaken, a different form of research presented itself that appeared more consonant with my sensibilities and ways of viewing the world. Well aware of the fact that social scientists distinguish between so-called masculine, objective, hard data and so-called feminine, subjective, soft data, I nonetheless sought a conflation of the two approaches. I found it in some of the writings on moral development, and in particular, the work of Carol Gilligan and several scholars associated with the Stone Center of Wellesley College in Massachusetts.[33]

From the Stone Center authors we learn of the importance of human relationships in terms of the development of the ego. Years ago, one of these authors, Jean Baker Miller, wrote that, unlike boys, girls tend to develop their egos through constant interaction with others.[34] The self, in other words, is primarily a product of contact, attachment, and mutuality. Boys, in contrast, appear to have their ego development dictated more by abstract reasoning and analytic constructs. This development, moreover, appears to evolve free of personal associations. Thus the so-called feminine personality and the concept of morality derive in some measure from mutuality, the constant interplay of people, and not necessarily from purely analytic notions or abstract constructs.[35]

From Gilligan we learn that morality can be viewed and experienced fundamentally as acts of care. If morality is seen in part as the ways human beings conduct themselves with one another, then respect and care may be placed as the centerpiece of this concept of moral development, in contrast to the more masculine underpinning of morality, namely, justice, as advanced by developmental psychologists such as Lawrence Kohlberg. Putting aside for the moment precisely how methodologically these researchers derived their notions, think only of the distinction between (masculine) justice and (feminine) care. For Kohlberg, individual human acts are judged either just or unjust, irrespective of context or external consideration.[36] For Gilligan, individual action is assessed in the context of caring or beneficence.

The connection of this literature to life study research becomes clearer as we take both notions, justice and care, as guides for assessing our research. The data that we present must be a just representation of the work. That is, we seek to do justice to the accounts and lives of the people who were good enough to reveal their stories. At the same time, however, by insinuating ourselves into the lives of the tellers, we also must reveal a level of sensitivity and faithfulness to the people as well as to the data and, ultimately, care about them.

In the end, our accounts are judged as just and caring, or unjust and uncaring, and hence, one is tempted to add, they may be evaluated as moral or immoral enterprises. For whether or not we choose to look just at the so-called hard (masculine) data, accounts of storytellers ineluctably become the products of telling and witnessing, interaction and mutuality. The soul, Walt Whitman suggested, is a bit like a spider. It sends forth filaments that it hopes will connect with other filaments of other souls.[37] And in attempting to discover the soul, we at least imagine that we have gone to unusual depths.

IT MAY BE HELPFUL at this point to review a few research procedures I have found to be useful. Whenever possible, I have asked that storytellers read my accounts before they are made public. At the outset I promise them the opportunity to do so and explain that they may offer corrections in substance and tone. Interestingly, only rarely does anyone have even the slightest suggestion for alterations. What people do ask, however, is to delete a particular passage on the grounds that although it seems to them an accurate rendering of the truth, they would feel uncomfortable having members of their family read it. Normally I honor these requests. The first allegiance must be to the storyteller, not to the story. The process of data gathering is sufficiently delicate and intrusive that the researcher must not cause additional burdens for the teller.

Parenthetically, I find a dangerous laxity in the procedures supposedly arranged to safeguard research subjects, and medical patients, for that matter.[38] My own procedure is to guarantee anonymity to storytellers; indeed, I insist on it even when they find the procedure superfluous, which is common. I discourage people from letting their identities be made known to friends and relatives to whom they wish to show the accounts or with whom they may share the research experience. I discourage photographs being taken of them to accompany published stories, just as I discourage their being interviewed on radio and television. Rarely have I found that the publicity that accrued to those who chose to make their identities known was productive or valuable. In particular, when children who have been mistreated are found to be the subject of controversial reports, even those that advocate the rights of children, I have too often seen the child become the object of envy or disdain. Institutions generally are uncomfortable with special status among those in their charge.

People learn at once that in the notes I take during early conversations and the publications that result I use fictitious names and false identification of places and various matters just as long as this intentional falsification does not significantly alter essential issues of the account. Placing a person in Providence, Rhode Island, instead of New Bedford, Massachusetts, presumably has no bearing on the matters considered in an account.

All the safeguards notwithstanding, a researcher's relationship with a storyteller becomes the central concern.[39] Indeed, it was the lack of relation-ships with anyone that initially turned me away from the sort of inquiries I undertook when I first entered the profession. Whereas one social scientist may call on his or her data to illustrate or explain some phenomenon, I turn to my research friends as a way of bringing to life that very same phenome-non. As we have seen, the life study reveals how unemployment, racism, poverty, welfare, jail time, school suspension, special education, divorce, and suicide are lived. The storytellers are the true witnesses of peril.[40] We listen to their testimonies because we seek to humanize the sociological and psy-chological factors we are researching. And we emphasize again that life sto-ries constitute genuine social scientific data, as well as interpretation of those data.

Hopefully, life studies generate a type of data that augments information generated by other forms of inquiry. Granted, the story approach is bound to be more dramatic, evocative, or even personally unsettling for the wit-nesses. Yet what troubles many of us is the idea that dramatic, evocative, or personally unsettling data should be found invalid precisely because they have these effects on us. Psychotherapy also has these effects on both thera-pist and client, and it remains a powerful tool for the collection of "life data" as well as clinical data.[41]

The word "data" should remind us that this type of inquiry possesses its own special forms of systematic data collection, interpretation, and analysis. The very selection of the material, the process by which one engages in classically subjective forms of human inquiry, represents a form of interpre-tation. To some degree, the selection process becomes part of the interpreta-tion. Necessarily, a host of principles, theories, and variables, many of them purely experiential, govern the selection of materials to be presented in doc-ument form; the interconnections within the material; and, importantly, the techniques and styles—some of them esthetic—in which the data ultimately may be presented. Thus traditional as well as more contemporary methods and theories give structure and direction to life study research. Simply put, the ostensibly straightforward task of gathering stories is hardly free of re-search biases and prejudgments.

A word now about the accuracy of the accounts in this book.

Obviously, accuracy is the goal. Anything short of it is not only a failure in the scientific enterprise, but a violation of one's friendship with the story-teller. That said, complete accuracy without mechanical devices is impos-sible. Yet I hardly think this distracts from the ultimate validity of the work.

Inasmuch as comprehensive reliability is itself nearly impossible in the social sciences, some of the traditional checks on validity and reliability become more difficult features in life study research.

The important point is that no story is told free of the influence of a real or imagined audience. One could argue that the audience may be among the more important ingredients of the stories. We are in great measure a compilation of both our experiences and our stories of them, which, again, represent the meanings we have attributed to events. Kegan appears to be correct: human beings at core are meaning makers; our stories represent our reports of the present state of this ongoing meaning making.[42]

In the story we draw our accounts for others and ourselves and at the same time are forever taking stock of our ongoing life inventories. The researcher surely influences the substance and tone of the story—these are, recall, the two features that we ask tellers to examine when they read manuscripts. Yet without the audience, there is no public version of the story. Our relationship with the teller appears in the story if for no other reason than that the present is partly constituted by the past. (Perhaps this feature is also part of Gilligan's care component.)

Thus it is foolish to believe that the method of psychological treatment has only minimal effect on the substance of a client's or patient's utterances. The very social structure of the real and imagined therapeutic process in great measure shapes and drives the transaction and hence the narrative; it lies at the heart of the established mutuality. As Parry and Doan point out, "It is a world in which every perception of reality, of one another, and of oneself—including those of the therapist, including this assertion itself—is but an act of interpretation. No person, no theory, no point of view has privilege at the expense of anyone else's."[43]

When a critic of life study research justifiably asks the researcher to provide more details of his or her participation in the storytelling process (although some critics insist that the witness's presence be kept out of the story altogether), we must be reminded that the interviewer/witness is as much a part of the story as his or her friendship with the storyteller is part of the dynamic that gave birth to the research in the first place. Rollo May wrote of such friendship, "It is the experience of the instantaneous encounter with another person who comes alive to us on a very different level from what we know *about* him. 'Instantaneous' refers not to the actual time involved but to the quality of the experience . . . *The essence of relationship is that in the encounter both persons are changed.*"[44]

Once again we are reminded of the level of care that insinuates itself into the storytelling process, a process that in some people's minds feels irreal, not unlike psychoanalysis, although hardly unreal; we simply don't have conversations of this sort everyday. As educator Vivian Brown has observed, we don't speak the deep truths of our lives to one another very often, if ever. Is it, she wonders, because the truths of our lives are constituted of exquisite pain?[45]

For these and other reasons, I propose that the life study researcher must be part clinician, part social scientist, part journalist, part diarist, and surely part storyteller. I do not mean to suggest that the desire to witness stories masks a secret desire to become the subject of the story. Although this may be true inasmuch as being human seems to be defined as being a storyteller, in the final analysis the life study researcher appreciates the idea of a life story because of the substantive and aesthetic ingredients constituting the leading of a life. In both explicit and implicit fashion, life study research subscribes to the notion that all of life, all of existence, seemingly, is constituted by our stories. Stories therefore are not all that we have to impart; they are all that essentially we are. They are life and legacy. Literally, they "call up," "call out," or "lead out of the self."[46] For the story necessarily is already known to the teller, and hence he or she is essentially recalling while creating for the listener. As the saying goes, we all have a novel in us. (Or is it that we are ourselves novels?)

The acts of storytelling and bearing witness to stories are not only acts of self-reflection, self-consciousness, intimacy, sharing, mutuality, and care. They may constitute as well the most tangible and lasting form of human exchange. Jean Baker Miller and Irene Pierce Stiver argued strongly for this position when they wrote:

> In our view, the goal of development [is in forming] relationships that foster the well being of everyone involved. Our fundamental notions of who we are formed . . . within the mutual interplay of relationships with others. In short, the goal is not for the individual to grow *out* of relationships, but to grow *into* them. As the relationships grow, so grows the individual. Participating in growth-fostering relationships is both the source and the goal of development.

> We believe that our focus on connection and disconnection speaks to the core of the human condition, the foundation that has remained obscure and out of focus. While all theories have spoken about relationships, this core has remained obscure because these theories emerged from an underlying preoccu-

pation—though one not usually made explicit—with individual gratification and power . . . Once we examine more accurately the lives of all people—women *and* men—we find ourselves moving away from this preoccupation and toward a recognition of the necessity of human connection and the sources and consequences of disconnections.[47]

The act of storytelling represents a pact with another person, what may properly be called a *covenant*, in that a series of promises occupies a central place in the relationship between teller and listener. At the very least, one invokes the promise to truthfully represent another person's life. Hence the covenant becomes a sacred trust. The terms we use, such as "mutuality," "relationship," and "pact," barely serve our purpose. For the connection is a *binding* of two people of an almost sacred nature. Anthony Giddens spoke of this matter in these words: "The pure relationship depends on mutual trust between partners, which in turn is closely related to the achievement of intimacy. In the pure relationship, trust is not and cannot be taken as 'given': like other aspects of the relationship, it has to be worked at—the trust of the other has to be won . . . What matters is that one can rely on what the other says and does."[48]

If, as the Bible instructs, the act of living is a gift, then the living representation of this gift would be that which we give to and receive from others. As Maguire put it, "Our stories are sacred to us. They become even more spiritually potent when we take special care of them and craft them into more conscious and complete—or, if you will, holistic—form." Stories are what we tell; confess; admit; proffer; part with; and most assuredly leave behind as legacy, lore, myth, tale, or history. The story represents not only individual experience but also the human substratum of culture. Stories, after all, are the products of cultural transmission. Let us bear in mind Clifford Geertz's definition of culture as a "historically transmitted pattern of meanings embodied in symbols, a system of inherited conceptions expressed in symbolic form by means of which men communicate, perpetuate and develop their knowledge about and attitudes toward life." Maguire, too, may have had a conception of culture in mind when he wrote, "When we reconstruct an incident from our past, we inevitably rebreathe the atmosphere that we shared with other people, retrace the ties that linked us one with the other, and remind ourselves of our 'fit' in the human community."[49]

To bear witness to someone is also to bear witness to that person's historical and cultural determinants and influences. And as the storytelling and witnessing play their essential role in human exchange at personal, interpersonal, and more broadly conceived collective levels, so, too, do they play a role in the shaping and creating of wholly new conceptions of social science, as well as procedures for collecting human information.

Always there is a story. Everyone has a book—or at least several chapters—inside him or her. As I hear the stories come forth, I typically justify my presence in a person's home and my role as witness or chronicler by reminding myself that we all want to tell our story, we all want to get into the act (of storytelling)! It's only that we're not certain we have an audience, or even one person who will hear us. We wonder, even with one person, how he or she might react to our sadness or fright, our anger and hurt, our forms of intelligence, our knowledge or lack of it, and our experiences and stories of peril.

Perhaps, as Dewey suggested, many of these tellers are so accustomed to being a country's silent, invisible, or even exploited population that they cannot believe or trust anyone claiming to take interest in them. America, after all, is a high-speed culture dominated by recognition, fame, and celebrity. You have to own a famous face, engage in infamy, or have one whale of a story for the culture to pause to listen to you. Nowadays, the ultimate judges of stories are the members of the media, and surely they have complex agendas and criteria to which they attend.

The significance of freedom of the press to a democracy has been discussed again and again. Our very civilization depends on the right to investigate, seek, and report truth—however that slippery term is defined—or just report the uncommon stories of common people. As part of this freedom, we assume an authority of voice in storytelling, a substantial authorship of our words, and of course an appeal to validation, whenever possible, of fact. Although, philosophically speaking, it is impossible to know precisely the truths that any of us seek in witnessing stories, we know surely when we are presented with hunch, mere possibility, or outright gossip.

The culture lurches backward or may even commence to unravel when we push words upon one another, either as storytellers or witnesses, that do not do justice to human experiences and the public narratives of them. In newspapers, magazines, and movies and on radio and television, too, even with all the visuals, in storytelling and witnessing it is all in the words. Hence it is in the words that the ultimate responsibility of life study research lies: to honor the power of the word, the majesty of literacy or the oral tradition, and the complexity of thoughtful investigation, discourse, and imagination and, finally, to recognize that the stories we tell are the palpable substance enhancing the integrity of our inner selves and our visions of the world, as well as the living tissue connecting us to one another. I am reminded of this comment by the novelist Toni Morrison: "As subtle as a movie can be, as careful and as artful as it can be, in the final analysis it's blatant because you can see it. You can translate certain things, make certain interpretations, create wonder, certainly there can be mystery, but the encounter with language is a private exploration. *The imagination works differently*."[50]

All we are as civilized people, seeking to battle our own forms of peril, shame, or an existential loneliness, are the stories that we tell, to others and ourselves, and the stories that are told to us. May wrote, "Our seeing each other allays the physical loneliness to which all human beings are heir. Another level is that of *friends*: we trust—for we have seen a lot of each other—that the other has some genuine concern for listening and understanding. Another level is that of esteem, or *agape*, the capacity . . . for self-transcending concern for another's welfare. Another level will be frankly *erotic*."[51]

Life study research is more than mere reporting; it is human connection, attachment, and definition. Inevitably it contains the care feature discussed earlier: care for the truth, care for the teller, care for the facts, care for the feelings. In part, the sensibilities of life study researchers determine what they believe to be sensible, responsible, and just language. Given the nature of the medium, television allows for neither this sort of sensibility nor the fundamental attachment that remains available to us through the written and spoken word.

It is not metaphor, therefore, to say that the civilization unravels when our accounts cannot support the weight of human stories and the truths and untruths they contain. It is not mere metaphor to assert that those who decide what is essential for the rest of us to know take into account that these deliberations affect our very essence. So it is not surprising that when hearing stories of peril we should ask ourselves, What do we tell our children about all of this? What do we tell each other? What do we tell ourselves? Important questions all, and they, too, begin with words. It is these written words that become not only our encounter with literacy, but commence our thinking and reasoning and ultimately form our definitions of being alive.

BEFORE CONCLUDING, I'd like to offer some thoughts on the philosophical nature of the life study.[52] From May and from Richard Rorty's notion regarding teaching we know that the life study form of research is somewhat erotic in nature. There is something in the relationship between storyteller and listener that is more, even, than irreal. The connection, the attraction through the story, defines an almost erotic coupling. Perhaps the eroticism derives from the teller's vulnerability and, quite frankly, the vulnerability that is required in good listening as well as in intimacy. Anthony Storr might have been speaking about the relationship between teller and witness when he said of psychotherapy, "In no other situation in life can anyone count on a devoted listener who is prepared to give so much time and skilled attention to the problems of a single individual without asking for any reciprocal return, other than professional remuneration. The patient may never have encountered anyone in his life who has paid him such attention or even been prepared to listen to his problems."[53]

On closer inspection, we are not drawing life as much as we are drawing *out* life. This is the basis of our queries and the friendship that makes life study research possible. In this posture of "tell me more," we ask people to go deeper into themselves and draw out what they perceive to be the truths of their lives or at least the experiences (and their renderings of them) that ultimately define for them these truths. It is perhaps this point that Kegan makes when he describes human beings as meaning makers.

In drawing (out) lives of storytellers, we are alleging that the story represents the present state of a person's sense of self and, in addition, the present state of his or her self-representation, self-knowledge (knowledge of the self, really), personal and social recognition of the self, and hence reputation. For in reputation, as in the life study, we let out bits of ourselves. It is in the stories that we tell, as well as the stories that are told about and to us, that we derive our reputation. (Is not gossiping referred to as "telling tales?") But the notion of reputation should not be misleading. It is not status, per se, that we intend, but rather the ongoing acts of self-revelation that lead to self-discovery.

The danger is that some will perceive the work of life studies as an act of self-recognition, self-celebration, or outright narcissism, but this is not the case. Self-celebration and self-discovery are not to be confused. The former rarely leads to the latter. If anything, the genuine revelation of the self—I was tempted to write the soul—normally yields pain or discomfort. If storytelling reveals how life is led, it draws people to the place where they feel themselves to have been thwarted or they outright failed. If an argument can be constructed, therefore, that a problem inherent in storytelling (and collecting) is that all we are left with, in a postmodern sense, is a collection of particular events rather than universal truths, we might also argue that people appraise their own stories according to ideals they may or may not reveal in their accounts.[54] Again and again, we hear people not living up to what they once imagined or hoped they might have become. So stories are also about human possibility and impossibility.

They are also about esteem, *agape*, for, as Heinz Kohut reminds us, the establishment of self-esteem is predicated not only on self-conception but on the establishment of the imagined perfect self.[55] All assessments are made against this perfect self. Not only that, we are encouraged in our life study enterprise by Kohut's insistence that the self wishes to reveal itself to the world. It wishes to say, "Look, whatever I am I am." It says this not with grandiosity and self-aggrandizement, but with what psychoanalysts call healthy narcissism, the belief that I am whole, intact, lovable, loving, and probably, too, in no way imperiled. The life study ought to be a life-sized study. When it is larger than life, as ineluctably it is in public relations, it becomes grandiosity.[56] Storytelling, moreover, is hardly a celebration of the self, although it may be a celebration, however bittersweet, of the *exploration* of the self, the journey of the self toward personal recognition and (personally determined) reputation.[57]

In the end, storytelling is one of the ways we learn about life, ourselves, and most assuredly others. It is an exploration of the self and an exploration of another's self. As listeners, we are the witnesses of stories, the witnesses of a life imperiled or not. Life literally is being recounted in front of and directly to us. Ideally, the journey is one of enlightenment and self-discovery (literally the discovery of the self), and hence every story may reveal ignorance as well, the ignorance that each of has regarding our self, history, and circumstances.

In this journey, the self is being *drawn out* and *called up*, which means that self-knowledge is being drawn out and called up. This makes sense, given that the storyteller is necessarily calling up materials with which he or she is already familiar. Even if the story is complete fiction, it is not being spun out of whole cloth—the threads must be known to the fabricator. (Moreover, the fabricator knows the true threads from the counterfeit ones.) No, this is movement toward a truth of self, perhaps the very basis of the *authentic self*, and in this regard a movement away from unadulterated narcissism or self-love. For in the story we discover our sense of strangeness along with our sense of being identical to others. We also discover the love of another, the love, really, of another's self, which in part accounts for that notion, generated from Rorty, that the basis of the research construction may well be erotic.

It is often argued that to base knowledge on mere personal stories is to avoid a significant force in human reasoning: the power of criticism. If all we do is collect stories, how do we ever step back and make judgments about them? To this I respond, judgments about what, precisely? If in constantly telling stories I reach closer to that elusive truth of my self or the truth of another's being, am I not making judgments about my own account, as well as the account of this other person? Do I not know whether I am heading toward or swerving from the truth of the self?

For Kohut, there is a legitimate enterprise known as "the acquisition of objective knowledge about the inner life of another person." Ironically, to gain this objective knowledge, one resorts to *empathy*. For Kohut, empathy is the "feeling in" or "feeling toward" someone else, a force prominent in conducting life studies. More appropriately, as Timothy Kunzier points out, in empathy—perhaps the primary action of the listener—one accepts and confirms, just as one feels the echoes and evocations produced by the teller. Along with empathy, Kohut admonishes us to create the proper atmosphere and assume the proper attitude. Together, these features become the foundation or posture of the listening stance.[58]

Related to empathy is what Waller calls "sympathetic penetration." This represents a form of insight that

> is based upon the fact that the behavior of others, either directly perceived or mediated to us ... starts certain mental processes in ourselves ... [Sympathetic penetration] is derived from contact with the minds of other men, through communication, which sets going a process of thought and sentiment similar to theirs and enables us to understand them by sharing their states of mind ... But it remains true that nearly all of the things that people most want to know about other people are accessible only through sympathetic imagination.[59]

It is in the telling and listening—each requiring the other—that I learn when I have moved off track, when literally I have moved against my self and thus against self-recognition, regard, and love. (To a certain extent, this is the process Freud called resistance.) Clues that I have slipped off the track of pursuing (self) truth are the aforementioned strangeness and recognition. I am off the track of self-discovery when I sense a story is strangely not me (hence the concept of personal estrangement from the self) or, similarly, when I cannot recognize my self in my own accounts. At some level, I always know that I am lying to myself (falsifying my self) and hence my account is fatuous. (Jung called this process the development of the false self.) It may well be that I must make myself the center of my story before I can gain access to the path of self-truth. Although resistance and false selves play important roles in the evolution of the self and the path of self-truth, they also tend to block the self from ultimately discovering and defining itself. Frank perhaps provides an antidote to this when he writes, "Passion describes an experience of connection. In one form, passion allows a person to come forth beyond the walls of inhibition and privacy, to reach out and create through deliberate acts of engaging with the world. The person is freed from a sense of limitation in order to foster a sense of possibility."[60]

We come now to the last justification for undertaking the life study. I have argued that storytelling is not only the grammar, syntax, and words that constitute a human account of the self. Equally important, the building of the story is the building of the self we seek to preserve. As Giddens notes, "Autobiography—particularly in the broad sense of an interpretive self-history produced by the individual concerned, whether written down or not—is actually at the core of self-identity in modern social life. Like any other formalized narrative, it is something that has to be worked at, and calls for creative input as a matter of course."[61]

The story is the product—my self—I present to friends and strangers alike, as well as to myself. The stories we tell and listen to, moreover, may represent the best "teaching material" any culture possesses for helping us to understand who we are. As Clifford Geertz reminds us, a fundamental ingredient of culture is the transmission from person to person, generation to generation, of what life is about and what therefore we mean to ourselves.[62]

Surely we have literature for accomplishing this purpose, since, as Dennis Donoghue writes, literature reminds us of how we are different from one another. But is not literature, another fundamental ingredient of cultural transmission, merely another form of storytelling? Like literature, each of our stories provides a basis for comprehending the authenticity of culture or at least human experience, all forms of it, similar and diverse, strange and familiar. If stories tell us anything, it is that people embody the judgments and claims about them made by others as well as by the culture. In this way, as Erich Fromm suggests, we are all cultural agents, just as we are all magnificent autobiographers and narrators. And as autobiographers, we are capable of drawing out genuine accounts of our selves, just as we are capable of editing these accounts, correcting the language and grammar as we proceed. Storytellers, as we see from the accounts presented in this book, edit as they go, sometimes rather scrupulously.[63]

Finally, to hear a story is to hear a judgment of the self, often of personal, cultural, societal, or moral failure, for judgment requires the presence of ideals that the storyteller makes relative to his or her ultimate accounts. Sadly, the storyteller also often is unable to recognize that the very failure underlying the account—the failure, in other words, to reach some inherent self-proclaimed ideal—is precisely what gives the account an authenticity. For everyday interactions, the real conversations as compared to the sort of irreal ones observed in the life study process, rarely dip to this depth of (self) understanding. They are meant more likely to perpetuate the self as human product or serve as rituals of comfort, conviviality, and communion. The genuine life study is predicated on these variables but seeks as well a higher and more virtuous purpose. Clearly, it seeks this higher purpose because the storyteller does.

NOTES

Introduction: The Ecology of Peril

1. Ellen J. Langer, *The Power of Mindful Learning* (Reading, Mass.: Perseus Books, 1997).

2. Christopher Lasch, *The Culture of Narcissism: American Life in an Age of Diminishing Expectations* (New York: Norton, 1978).

3. Gerald Fain, "Special Education: Justice, Toleration, and Beneficence as Duty," *Boston University Journal of Education* 180, no. 2 (1998): 41–56.

4. See William K. Frankena, *Ethics* (Englewood Cliffs, N.J.: Prentice-Hall, 1963).

5. "Homeless Families with Children," Fact Sheet No. 7, (Washington, D.C.: National Coalition for the Homeless, 1998), http://www.nch.ari.net/families.html.

6. "Young Children in Poverty: A Statistical Update" (New York: National Center for Children in Poverty, 1999), http://www.cpmcnet.columbia.edu/dept/nccp.

7. See Thomas J. Cottle, *Hardest Times: The Trauma of Long Term Unemployment* (Westport, Conn.: Praeger, 2001); Jeremy Rifkin, *The End of Work* (New York: G. P. Putnam's Sons, 1995); William Julius Wilson, *When Work Disappears: The World of the Urban Poor* (New York: Knopf, 1996).

8. Cynthia Crosson-Tower, *Exploring Child Welfare* (Boston: Allyn & Bacon, 1998), 118, cited in Lisa Mitrano, "Children at Risk," unpublished manuscript, Boston University, 1999, 4.

9. See Lisbeth Schorr, *Within Our Reach: Breaking the Cycle of Disadvantage* (New York: Anchor Press, 1988).

10. See Adam Rogers, Pat Wingert, and Sharon Begley, "Why the Young Kill," *Newsweek*, May 3, 1999, 32–35.

11. Stephen Nathanson, "Are Special Education Programs Unjust to Nondisabled Children? Justice, Equality, and the Distribution of Education," *Boston University Journal of Education* 180, no. 2 (1988): 17–40. See also Stephen Nathanson, *Economic Justice* (Upper Saddle River, N.J.: Prentice-Hall, 1998).

12. Interestingly, the law speaks in terms of *meaningful* access.

13. Rollo May, *The Discovery of Being* (New York: Norton, 1983).

14. Theodore Roszak, *Person/Planet: The Creative Disintegration of Industrial Society* (Garden City, N.Y.: Anchor Press/Doubleday, 1978), and *The Making of a Counter*

Culture: Reflections on the Technocratic Society and Its Youthful Opposition (Garden City, N.Y.: Doubleday, 1969).

15. Alexis de Tocqueville, *Democracy in America*, trans. Henry Reeve (1835; reprint, New York: Knopf, 1994).

16. Edwin J. Delattre, *Character and Cops–Ethics in Policing* (Washington, D.C.: American Enterprise Institute for Public Policy Research, 1994), 154–55, cited in Thomas W. Nolan, "Character Education for Police Officers: Station House as Moral Milieu," unpublished manuscript, Boston University, 1999.

17. U.S. Bureau of the Census, *Health Insurance Coverage*, 1998, Current Population Reports, P60–208. 1999. These data are reported in the March, 1999 Supplement to the Current Population Survey.

18. CHIP enrollment increased almost 55 percent from December 1998 to June 1999. The enrollment of children in federal and state programs (including Medicaid and CHIP) in some states declined by nearly one million between 1996 and 1999, this being the result of welfare reform's not functioning well. In twelve states, fewer children were covered by insurance in 1999 than in 1996. The states are Arizona, California, Florida, Georgia, Illinois, Louisiana, New Jersey, New York, North Carolina, Ohio, Pennsylvania, and Texas. On this point, see *One Step Forward, One Step Back. Children's Health Coverage after CHIP and Welfare Reform* (Washington, D.C.: Families USA, 1999).

19. The data on infant mortality come from the National Center on Health Statistics, which is affiliated with the U.S. Department of Health and Human Services, and were reported in *Boston Globe*, October 6, 1999, A12. The statistic on men with lung cancer is from Richard A. Knox, "Racial Gap Found in Cancer Care," *Boston Globe*, October 14, 1999, A6.

20. "State-Specific Maternal Mortality among Black and White Women—United States, 1987–1996," *Morbidity and Mortality Weekly Report* 48, no. 23 (1999): 492–96. See also http://www.cdc.gov/epo/mmwr/preview/mmwrhtml/mm4823a3.htm.

21. Gretchen LeFever et al., "The Extent of Drug Therapy for Attention Deficit-Hyperactivity Disorder among Children in Public Schools," *American Journal of Public Health* 89 (1999): 1359–65.

22. It is estimated that 12 percent of America's children reveal some difficulty in performing at school because of a learning disability or a communication problem of some type. See Federal Interagency Forum on Child and Family Statistics, "America's Children: Key National Indicators of Well-Being, 1999" (Washington, D.C., 1999), http://www.childstats.gov.

23. Stephen Kemmis, "Action Research and the Politics of Reflection," in *Reflection: Turning Experience into Learning*, ed. Rosemary Keogh, David Walker, and David Bond (London: Kogan Page, 1985), 139–64 (I am grateful to Arthur Beane of Boston University for calling my attention to this volume); John Kotre, *White Gloves: How We Create Ourselves through Memory* (New York: Free Press, 1995).

24. See, for example, Erwin A. Gutkind, *Community and Environment: A Discourse on Social Ecology* (New York: Philosophical Library, 1954).

25. Urie Bronfenbrenner, *The Ecology of Human Development* (Cambridge: Harvard University Press, 1979), and Urie Bronfenbrenner, ed., *Influences on Human De-*

velopment (Hinsdale, Ill.: Dryden Press, 1972); see also David Kaplan and Robert A. Manners, *Culture Theory* (Englewood Cliffs, N.J.: Prentice-Hall, 1972).

26. Clifford Geertz, *The Interpretation of Cultures: Selected Essays* (New York: Basic Books, 1973).

27. Elizabeth Goodman, "The Roles of Socioeconomic Status Gradients in Explaining Differences in US Adolescents' Health," *American Journal of Public Health* 89 (1999): 1522–28.

28. On this point, see Salvador Minuchin, *Families and Family Therapy* (Cambridge: Harvard University Press, 1974).

29. John Santrock, *Adolescence*, 7th ed. (New York: McGraw-Hill, 1998).

30. Anne Hunsaker Hawkins, *Reconstructing Illness: Studies in Pathography* (West Lafayette, Ind.: Purdue University Press, 1993). I am grateful to Donald Palladino Jr. for this reference.

31. On this point, see Richard H. Price, "Psychosocial Impact of Job Loss on Individuals and Families," *Current Directions in Psychological Science* 1, no. 1 (1992): 9–11.

32. Seymour S. Bellin and S. M. Miller, "The Split Society," in *The Nature of Work: Sociological Perspectives*, ed. Kai Erikson and Stevan Peter Vallas (New Haven, Conn.: Yale University Press, 1990); André Gorz, *Farewell to the Working Class: An Essay on Post-Industrial Socialism* (Boston: South End Press, 1982); Abraham Maslow, *Toward a Psychology of Being* (Princeton, N.J.: Van Nostrand, 1968), cited in Arthur Beane, "Student Teacher Supervision: An Emphasis on Self Reflection" (Ph.D. diss., Boston University, 1999), 190, emphasis added.

33. John Dewey, *The Child and the Curriculum, and The School and Society* (Chicago: University of Chicago Press, 1956).

34. Bronfenbrenner, *Ecology of Human Development*. See also John Dewey, *Democracy and Education: An Introduction to the Philosophy of Education* (New York: Free Press, 1966).

35. Jeffrey G. Johnson et al., "Childhood Maltreatment Increases Risk for Personality Disorders during Early Adulthood," *Archives of General Psychiatry* 56 (1999): 600–606; Cathy Spatz Widom, "Commentary: Childhood Victimization and the Development of Personality Disorders," *Archives of General Psychiatry* 56 (1999): 607–8.

36. Herbert Anderson and Kenneth R. Mitchell, *Leaving Home: Family Living in Pastoral Perspective* (Westminster: John Knox Press, 1993), 144, cited in Timothy Kunzier, "Preserving the True Course," unpublished manuscript, Boston University, 1999, 10.

37. John Dewey, *How We Think* (Amherst, N.Y.: Prometheus Books, 1991), 25.

38. William Ayers, *To Teach: The Journey of a Teacher* (New York: Teachers College Press, 1993), 8.

39. It is interesting, in this regard, that one of the tenets of the American School Counselor Association is: "Each person has the right to self direction and self development." Not so incidentally, another tenet reads, "Each person has the right to respect and dignity as a human being."

40. Society, Durkheim wrote, lives exclusively in the minds of its members, while

Fromm referred to parents as "society's agents." Emile Durkheim, *On Morality and Society: Selected Writings*, ed. Robert N. Bellah (Chicago: University of Chicago Press, 1973).

41. May, *The Discovery*, 128, cited in Beane, "Student Teacher Supervision."

42. Paulo Friere, *Pedagogy of the Oppressed* (New York: Continuum, 1993); see also Paulo Friere, "Cultural Action for Freedom: Author's Introduction," *Harvard Educational Review* 68 (1998): 480–98, cited in Beane, "Student Teacher Supervision," 221.

43. On these points, see Carl Germain and Alex Gitterman, *The Life Model of Social Work Practice* (New York: Columbia University Press, 1980), and R. Greene and Paul Ephross, *Human Behavior Theory and Social Work Practice* (New York: Walter de Gruyter, 1991).

44. Nathanson, "Are Special Education Programs Unjust."

45. Editorial, *Journal of Education*, March 1950, 2, cited in Evgenia Tsankova, "Justice and Education," unpublished manuscript, Boston University, 1999, 4; Gerald Grant, *The World We Created at Hamilton High* (Cambridge: Harvard University Press, 1988), 4, cited in Tsankova, "Justice and Education," 4.

46. John Rawls, *A Theory of Justice* (Cambridge: Harvard University Press, 1971).

47. See Fain, "Special Education."

48. John W. Gardner, "Excellence and Equality," in *The Nation's Children: Development and Education*, ed. Eli Ginzberg (New York: Columbia University Press, 1960), 227, cited in Shira Weinstock, "The Power of Justice and the Future of Children," unpublished manuscript, Boston University, 1998, 9.

49. Francis W. Parker, *Talks on Pedagogics: An Outline of the Theory of Concentration* (New York: John Day, 1937), 340.

50. On this point, see Julius Stone, *Human Law and Human Justice* (Stanford, Calif.: Stanford University Press, 1968).

51. Fain, "Special Education," 41.

52. *Ibid.*, 55.

53. Mia L. Pringle, *The Needs of Children* (New York: Schocken Books, 1974).

54. Robert Kegan, *The Evolving Self* (Cambridge: Harvard University Press, 1982).

55. Laura E. Berk, *Child Development*, 3d ed. (Needham Heights; Mass.: Allyn & Bacon, 1994).

56. The inventory is also similar to Richard Eberst's six categories of health: physical, emotional, mental, social, vocational, and spiritual. See Richard Eberst, "Defining Health: A Multidimensional Model," *Journal of School Health* 54, no. 3 (1984): 99–104, cited in Elisabeth Bridges, "Healthy Children in Today's Society: An Environmental View," unpublished manuscript, Boston University, 1999.

57. Erich Fromm, *Escape from Freedom* (New York: Farrar & Rinehart, 1941).

58. Since he wrote from the perspective of someone having survived the Holocaust, it is interesting that Fromm likened nationalism to incest.

59. For example, Erik Erikson, *Identity: Youth and Crisis* (New York: Norton, 1968), and Erik Erikson, *Childhood and Society* (New York: Norton, 1950); Minuchin, *Families*.

60. Abraham H. Maslow, *Religions, Values and Peak-Experiences* (New York: Pen-

guin Books, 1976); Mihaly Csikszentmihalyi, *Creativity: Flow and the Psychology of Discovery* (New York: HarperPerennial, 1996); Mihaly Csikszentmihalyi, *Flow: The Psychology of Optimal Experience* (New York: HarperCollins, 1990).

61. Erikson, *Childhood and Society*.

62. On a related point, it is interesting that research indicates that deprivation of maternal and environmental conditions can produce developmental, physical, intellectual sensory processing, and social delays. See Sharon Cermak and Lisa A. Daunhaurer, "Sensory Processing in the Postinstitutionalized Child," *American Journal of Occupational Therapy* 51 (1997): 500–507, cited in Renee Devereux, "Child Care in America: Whose Responsibility Is It?" unpublished manuscript, Boston University, 1999.

63. Roberta Wollons, ed., *Children at Risk in America* (Albany: State University of New York Press, 1993), ix.

64. According to Susann R. Hill and Toni R. Tollerud, dignity is also an inherent aspect of human life. To enhance this sense of dignity, they suggest the importance of safety, autonomy, belonging, self-esteem, and self-significance. See Susann R. Hill and Toni R. Tollerud, "Restoring Dignity in At-Risk Students," *The School Counselor* 44 (November 1996): 122–32.

65. Not so incidentally, the American School Counselor Association lists four basic tenets of counseling. The first three are that each person has the right to respect and dignity, each person has the right to self-direction and self-development, and each person has the right of choice and the responsibility of goals reached.

66. Unfortunately, at the time I was not aware of the now well known Tennessee study that showed that when class sizes were reduced from the normal size of twenty-two to twenty-five students to thirteen to seventeen students, children in the first three grades scored better on both standardized and class tests. In addition, the study showed increases in minority students' scores, leading to a 54 percent reduction in the black-white testing gap. These data are reported in *Boston Globe*, October 22, 1999, A22.

67. On this point, see Gitta Sereny, *Why Children Kill: The Story of Mary Bell* (New York: Henry Holt, 1999).

68. I am grateful to Emily Weber for providing me with these statistics on out-of-wedlock births. The statistics on the rise in child abuse and neglect are also reported in David Anspaugh, Gene Ezell, and Karen Nash Goodmerry, *Teaching Today's Health*, 3d ed. (Columbus, Ohio: Merrill, 1990), cited in Bridges, "Healthy Children." According to the *1999 Kids Count Data Book*, the years 1985 to 1996 showed a slight increase in the proportion of low-birth-weight infants, a slight rise in the teen birth rate, and an increase in the percentage of families headed by a single parent. On the positive side, the same source indicated that the child poverty rate dropped from 21 percent to 20 percent, and the number of teen deaths due to accident, homicide, and suicide fell from 63 per 100,000 to 62 per 100,000.

69. The reader perhaps recognizes the reference to Howard Gardner, *Frames of Mind: The Theory of Multiple Intelligences* (New York: Basic Books, 1983), and Howard Gardner, *Multiple Intelligence: The Theory in Action* (New York: Basic Books, 1993).

70. Delattre, *Character*, 154.

Health Peril: Introduction

1. Michael Lasalandra, "Increase Is First Time in More Than a Decade," *Boston Herald*, March 29, 1999, 3.

2. David Nyhan, "It's Mostly Bad News for the Poorest People on the Planet," *Boston Globe*, October 1, 1999.

3. On this point see Paul Wise, et al., "Assessing the Effects of Welfare Reform Policies on Reproductive and Infant Health," *American Journal of Public Health* 89 (1999): 1514–21.

Children at Risk: The Case for Youthful Offenders

1. Robin Karr-Morse and Meredith S. Wiley, *Ghosts from the Nursery* (Boston: Atlantic Monthly Press, 1998).

2. Jonathan Alter, "Crime Is a Serious Problem at Schools, Survey Finds," *Boston Globe*, March 20, 1998, A3; "U.S. Youth Are Called Likeliest to be Shot," *Boston Globe*, February 7, 1997, A3.

3. For a general discussion of this point, see Roberta Wollons, ed., *Children at Risk in America* (Albany: State University of New York Press, 1993).

4. This material comes from U.S. census data.

5. "Monitoring the Social Well-Being of the Nation. Special Focus: The Social Health of Children and Youth" (Terrytown, N.Y.: Fordham Institute for Innovation in Social Policy, 1989).

6. Children's Defense Fund, *Reports*, February/March 1990, 14.

7. See Peter Freiberg, "Killing by Kids 'Epidemic Forecast,'" *The Monitor*, American Psychological Association, 22, no. 4 (1991): 1ff.

8. W. Yule and R. Canterbury, "The Treatment of Posttraumatic Stress Disorder in Children and Adolescents," *International Review of Psychiatry* 6 (1994): 141–51.

9. *Children's Defense Fund Reports*, "News and Issues," February/March 1990.

10. I am grateful to Kimberly Kline for compiling many of these statistics in a class report, Boston University, School of Education, 1998. See Carolyn Piver Du-Karm, Robert S. Byrd, Peggy Auinger, and Michael Weitzman, "Adolescent Substance Abuse: Gender and the Risk of Violent Behavior," *Prevention Researcher* 6 (Spring 1999): 3–4.

11. For more general discussion of these points, see Alan Gartner and Dorothy Kerzner Lipsky, "Children at Risk: Students in Special Education," in Wollons, ed., *Children at Risk*, 157–82.

12. See David Finkelhor, "The Victimization of Children: A Developmental Perspective," *American Journal of Orthopsychiatry* 65 (1995): 177–93; see also David Finkelhor, "Dissociative Disorders in Children: Behavioral Profiles and Problems," *Child Abuse and Neglect* 17, no. 1: 39–45.

13. Naomi Breslau et al., "Traumatic Events and Posttraumatic Stress Disorder in an Urban Population of Young Adults," *Archives of General Psychiatry* 48 (1991): 216–22.

14. Bessel A. van der Kolk, *Psychological Trauma* (Washington, D.C.: American Psychiatric Press, 1987).

15. See J. S. Wodarski et al., "Maltreatment and the School-age Child: Major

Academic, Socioemotional and Adaptive Outcomes," *Social Work* 35, no. 6: 506–13, cited in Beverly Chase, "Applications of Vygotskian Theory to a Remedial Curriculum for Sexually Abused School-age Children," unpublished manuscript, Boston University, 1998.

16. The *Diagnostic and Statistical Manual of Mental Disorders*, quoted in James Morrison, *DSM-IV Made Easy: The Clinician's Guide to Diagnosis* (New York: Guilford Press, 1995), 269. See John S. March, Lisa Amaya-Jackson, and Robert S. Pynoos, "Pediatric Posttraumatic Stress Disorder," in *Textbook of Child and Adolescent Psychiatry*, ed. Jerry M. Wiener (Washington, D.C.: American Psychiatric Press, 1997), 507–24.

17. Judith Herman, *Trauma and Recovery* (New York: Basic Books, 1992).

18. Thomas J. Cottle, *Children in Jail* (Boston: Beacon Press, 1977).

19. On this point, see Jennifer Egan, "The Thin Red Line," *New York Times Magazine*, July 27, 1997, 20ff.

20. J. S. March, Lisa Amaya-Jackson, and Robert S. Pynoos, "Pediatric Posttraumatic Stress Disorder," in *Textbook of Child and Adolescent Psychiatry*, 2d ed., ed. Jerry M. Wiener (Washington, D.C.: American Psychiatric Press, 1997); see also Spencer Eth and Robert S. Pynoos, eds., *Posttraumatic Stress Disorder in Children* (Washington, D.C.: American Psychiatric Press, 1985), and Spencer Eth, *Post-Traumatic Stress Disorder in Children* (New York: Pergamon, 1990).

21. William Pollack quoted in Patti Doten, "Without Guidance Boys Will Be Troubled Boys," *Boston Globe*, July 20, 1998, C7, C11.

22. Sigmund Freud, *New Introductory Lectures on Psychoanalysis*, trans. and ed. James Strachey (New York: Norton, 1965).

23. Janae B. Weinhold and Barry K. Weinhold, "Shift Happens: Becoming Masters of Our Fate," unpublished book proposal, 1998, 3.

24. Allan Young, "Suffering and the Origins of Traumatic Memory," *Daedalus* 125 (winter 1996): 245–60; see also Allan Young, *The Harmony of Illusions: Inventing Posttraumatic Stress Disorder* (Princeton, N.J.: Princeton University Press, 1995).

25. Elisabeth Kübler-Ross, *Coping with Death and Dying* (New York: Ziff-Davis, 1973), and Elisabeth Kübler-Ross, *Death: The Final Stage of Growth* (Englewood Cliffs, N.J.: Prentice-Hall, 1975).

26. Bernhard Schlink, *The Reader*, trans. Carol Brown Janeway (New York: Pantheon, 1997), 217.

27. See March et al., "Pediatric Posttraumatic Stress."

28. Frank J. Sulloway, *Born to Rebel: Birth Order, Family Dynamics and Creative Lives* (New York: Pantheon Books, 1996); Salvador Minuchin, *Families and Family Therapy* (Cambridge: Harvard University Press, 1974).

29. John Bowlby, *Attachment and Loss* (New York: Basic Books, 1980); see also Mary Ainsworth, *Patterns of Attachment: A Psychological Study of the Strange Situation* (Hillsdale, N.J.: Lawrence Erlbaum Associates, 1978).

30. Felton Earls and Mary Carlson, "Towards Sustainable Development of American Families," *Daedalus* 122 (winter 1993): 93–122.

31. See Thomas Ashby Wills and Marnie Filer, "Stress-Coping Model of Adolescent Substance Abuse," in *Advances in Clinical Child Psychology*, volume 18, ed. Thomas H. Ollendick and Ronald J. Prinz (New York: Plenum Press, 1996).

32. See Martin Heidegger, *Being and Time*, trans. Joan Stambaugh (Albany: State University of New York Press, 1966).

33. Herman, *Trauma and Recovery;* Anthony J. Marsella, ed., *Ethnocultural Aspects of PTSD: Issues, Research and Clinical Applications* (Washington, D.C.: American Psychological Association, 1996).

34. For an intriguing discussion of the experience of emptiness and the need to fill it, see Mark Epstein, *Going to Pieces without Falling Apart* (New York: Broadway Books, 1998).

35. See David B. Herzog and Eugene V. Beresin, "Anorexia Nervosa," in Wiener, ed., *Textbook of Child and Adolescent Psychiatry.*

36. On this point, see D. Roberts, "Child Protection in the 21st Century," *Child Abuse and Neglect* 15, no. 1 (1991): 25–30; see also Arloc Sherman, *Wasting America's Future* (Boston: Beacon Press, 1994), and Sylvia Ann Hewlett, *When the Bough Breaks: The Cost of Neglecting Our Children* (New York: Basic Books, 1991).

Feeling Ill with the City Disease

1. P. B. Warr, "Job Loss, Unemployment, and Psychological Well Being," in *Role Transitions,* ed. V. Allen and E. van de Vliert (New York: Plenum Press, 1984), 263–85; and S. P. McKenna and D. M. Fryer, "Perceived Health during Lay-off and Early Unemployment," *Occupational Health* 36, 1984, 201–6.

2. E. Palmore, "Physical, Mental, and Social Factors in Predicting Longevity," *Gerontology* 9 (1989).

Family Peril: Introduction

1. D. W. Winnicott, *Home Is Where We Start From: Essays by a Psychoanalyst,* ed. Clare Winnicott, Ray Shepherd, and Madeleine Davis (New York: Norton, 1986).

2. Rollo May, *The Discovery of Being* (New York: Norton, 1983).

3. Salvador Minuchin, *Families and Family Therapy* (Cambridge: Harvard University Press, 1974).

4. Erich Fromm, *The Art of Loving* (New York: Continuum, 1992).

5. Felton Earls and Mary Carlson, "Towards Sustainable Development of American Families," *Daedalus* 122 (Winter 1993): 93–122.

6. Erik H. Erikson, *Childhood and Society* (New York: Norton, 1950).

Mind Shadows: A Suicide in the Family

1. Kathleen Stassen Berger and R. A. Thompson, *The Developing Person: Through Childhood and Adolescence* (New York: Worth, 1995).

2. Ann F. Garland and Edward Zigler, "Adolescent Suicide Prevention," *American Psychologist* 48 (1993): 169–82; Cynthia Crosson-Tower, *Exploring Child Welfare: A Practical Perspective* (Boston: Allyn & Bacon, 1998).

3. Garland and Zigler, *Adolescent Suicide.*

4. Melanie Bellah, *Tammy: A Biography of a Young Girl* (Berkeley, Calif.: Aten, 1999); Edwin S. Shneidman, "Suicide," in *Psychology,* 2d ed., ed. G. Lindzey, C. S. Hall, and R. F. Thompson (New York: Worth, 1978). See also Alex D. Pokorny, "Prediction of Suicide in Psychiatric Patients: Report of a Prospective Study," *Archives of General Psychiatry* 40 (1983): 249–57.

5. Garland and Zigler, *Adolescent Suicide.*

6. Susan J. Blumenthal and David C. Kupfer, "Overview of Early Detection and Treatment Strategies for Suicidal Behavior in Young People," *Journal of Youth and Adolescence* 17 (1988): 1–23; Judith L. Rubenstein et al., "Suicidal Behavior in 'Normal' Adolescents: Risk and Protective Factors," *American Journal of Orthopsychiatry* 59 (1989): 59–71.

7. G. R. Patterson, Barbara D. DeBaryshe, and Elizabeth Ramsey, "A Developmental Perspective on Antisocial Behavior," *American Psychologist* 44 (1989): 329–35; David K. Curran, *Adolescent Suicidal Behavior* (Washington, D.C.: Hemisphere, 1987); Jerome B. Dusek, *Adolescent Development and Behavior* (Upper Saddle River, N.J.: Prentice-Hall, 1996); Roy F. Baumeister, "Suicide as Escape from Self," *Psychological Review* 97 (1990): 90–113; Susan Harter, "Causes, Correlates, and the Functional Role of Global Self-Worth: A Life Span Perspective," in *Competence Considered,* ed. Robert J. Sternberg and John Kolligian Jr. (New Haven, Conn.: Yale University Press, 1990).

8. Stuart T. Hauser and M. K. Bowlds, "Stress, Coping and Adaptation," in *At the Threshold: The Developing Adolescent,* ed. S. Shirley Feldman and Glen R. Elliot (Cambridge: Harvard University Press, 1990).

9. Salvador Minuchin, *Families and Family Therapy* (Cambridge: Harvard University Press, 1974); J. Haley, *Leaving Home* (New York: McGraw-Hill, 1980); Virginia Satir, *Conjoint Family Therapy,* 3d ed. (Palo Alto, Calif.: Science and Behavior Books, 1983); Murray Bowen, *Family Therapy in Clinical Practice,* 3d ed. (Northvale, N.J.: Jason Aronson, 1985); Augustus Y. Napier and Carl Whitaker, *The Family Crucible: The Intense Experience of Family Therapy* (New York: Harper Perennial, 1978); Philip J. Guerin Jr., *Family Therapy: Theory and Practice* (New York: Gardner Press, 1976).

10. Haley, *Leaving Home.*

11. Minuchin, *Families.*

12. Salvador Minuchin and H. Charles Fishman, *Family Therapy Techniques* (Cambridge: Harvard University Press, 1981).

13. Minuchin, *Families;* D. Daniels-Mohring, *Family Systems within Educational Contexts: Understanding Students with Special Needs* (Denver, Colo.: Love, 1993).

14. Minuchin, *Families.*

15. Susan B. Silberberg and Laurence Steinberg, "Adolescent Autonomy, Parent-Adolescent Conflict, and Parental Well Being," *Journal of Youth and Adolescence* 16 (1987): 293–312.

16. Bowen, *Family Therapy.*

17. Don Jackson, "The Question of Family Homeostasis," *Psychiatric Quarterly Supplement* 31, part 1 (1957): 79–90; Paul Watzlawick, John H. Weakland, and R. Fisch, *Change: Principles of Problem Formation and Problem Resolution* (New York: W. W. Norton, 1974).

18. Minuchin, *Families.*

19. John Kotre, *White Gloves: How We Create Ourselves through Memory* (New York: Free Press, 1995).

20. Robert Kegan, *The Evolving Self* (Cambridge: Harvard University Press, 1982).

21. William Earle, *The Autobiographical Consciousness* (Chicago: Quadrangle Books, 1972).

22. Donald P. Polkinghorne, *Narrative Knowing and the Human Sciences* (Albany: State University of New York Press, 1988), 15.

23. Daniel B. Frank, "The Live Creature: Understanding the School and Its Passions," *Child and Adolescent Social Work Journal* 15 (1998): 419.

24. John T. Maltsberger and Mark J. Goldblatt, *Essential Papers on Suicide* (New York: New York University Press, 1996); Alec Roy, "Family History of Suicide," *Archives of General Psychiatry* 40 (1983): 971–74.

25. Minuchin, *Families*.

26. Rollo May, *The Discovery of Being* (New York: Norton, 1983).

27. J. Novick, "Attempted Suicide in Adolescence: The Suicide Sequence," in *Suicide in the Young*, ed. Howard Sudak, Amsa Ford, and Norman Rushford (Boston: John Wright/PSG 1984), 115–37; Joseph Sabbath, "The Suicidal Adolescent—The Expendable Child," *Journal of the American Academy of Child Psychiatry* 8 (1969): 272–89.

28. Heinz Kohut, *The Kohut Seminars: On Self Psychology and Psychotherapy with Adolescents and Young Adults* (New York: Norton, 1987).

29. David Luterman, *Counseling Parents of Hearing Impaired Children* (Boston: Little, Brown, 1979).

Women Who Kill

1. Richard J. Gelles, *Family Violence* (Newbury Park: Sage Publications, 1987); and David Finkelhor, *The Dark Side of Families: Current Family Violence Research* (Beverly Hills: Sage Publications, 1983).

2. Angela Browne, *When Battered Women Kill* (New York: Free Press, 1987).

School Peril: Introduction

1. Craig T. Ramsey and Sharon Landesman Ramsey, "Early Intervention and Early Experience," *American Psychologist* 53 (1998): 109–20.

2. Howard Gardner, *Frames of Mind: The Theory of Multiple Intelligences* (New York: Basic Books, 1983).

3. Edward Hallowell and John Ratey, *Driven to Distraction* (New York: Pantheon, 1994); John Ratey, *Shadow Syndromes* (New York: Pantheon, 1997).

4. On this point, see Kevin Ryan and Karen E. Bohlin, *Building Character in Schools: Practical Ways to Bring Moral Instruction to Life* (San Francisco: Jossey-Bass, 1999).

5. Amy Gutmann, "Education for Citizenship into the Twenty-first Century: Deliberation and Democratic Education," unpublished manuscript, Aspen Institute, 1996, 3, cited in David Steiner, "Searching for Educational Coherence in a Democratic State," in *Citizen Competence and Democratic Institutions*, ed. Stephen L. Elkin and Karol Edward Soltan (University Park: Pennsylvania State University Press, 1999), 253.

6. David Steiner, "Searching," 225–57.

7. Katherine Newman, *No Shame in My Game* (New York: Knopf, 1999).

8. William Ayers, "Democracy and Urban Schooling for Justice and Care," *Journal for a Just and Caring Education* 2, no. 1 (1996): 85–92.

NOTES

Societal Peril: Introduction

1. Erich Fromm, *Escape from Freedom* (New York: Rinehart, 1941).
2. Matthew Dumont, "Zen and the Art of Poverty," *Readings* 14 (September 1999): 16–19.
3. Mary Douglas and Steven Ney, *Missing Persons: A Critique of Personhood in the Social Sciences* (Berkeley: University of California Press, 1998).

Witness to Joy

1. Erik Erikson, *Identity: Youth and Crisis* (New York: Norton, 1968); and Robert M. Pirsig, *Zen and the Art of Motorcycle Maintenance: An Inquiry into Values* (New York: Morrow, 1999).
2. Jerome Kagan, Richard B. Kearsley, and Philip R. Zelzzo, *Infancy: Its Place in Human Development* (Cambridge: Harvard University Press, 1978).
3. Robert Coles, *Children of Crisis, Privileged Ones: The Well-off and Rich in America* (Boston: Little Brown, 1977).
4. Jerome Bruner, *Actual Minds, Possible Worlds* (Cambridge: Harvard University Press, 1986).
5. David Riesman, *The Lonely Crowd: A Study of the Change in American Character*, in collaboration with Reuel Denney and Nathan Glazer (New Haven: Yale University Press, 1950).

Afterword: Life Studies and the Value of Stories

1. On the more general point, see Louis Cohen and Lawrence Marion, "Introduction: The Nature of Inquiry," in *Research Methods in Education* (New York: Routledge, 1989) and Ken Metzler, *Creative Interviewing: The Writer's Guide to Gathering Information by Asking Questions* (Englewood Cliffs, N.J.: Prentice-Hall, 1974).
2. Jack Maguire, *The Power of Personal Story Telling: Spinning Tales to Connect with Others* (New York: Jeremy P. Tarcher/Putnam, 1998).
3. John Dewey, *Characters and Events: Popular Essays in Social and Political Philosophy* (New York: Holt, 1929).
4. Sara Lawrence-Lightfoot and Jessica Hoffman Davis, *The Art and Science of Portraiture* (San Francisco: Jossey-Bass, 1997).
5. See Joseph Aux Maxwell, *Qualitative Research Design: An Interactive Approach* (Thousand Oaks, Calif.: Sage, 1996).
6. Lawrence-Lightfoot and Hoffman Davis, *Art and Science*; Ellen J. Langer, *The Power of Mindful Learning* (Reading, Mass.: Perseus Books, 1997), 135.
7. See Joseph Campbell, *The Hero with a Thousand Faces* (Princeton, N.J.: Princeton University Press, 1972); Joseph Campbell and Marie Jeanne Abadie, *The Mythic Image* (Princeton, N.J.: Princeton University Press, 1984); and the classic study, Thomas Bullfinch, *The Art of Fable* (New York: Dutton, 1979).
8. John Van Maanen, *Tales of the Field: On Writing Ethnography* (Chicago: University of Chicago Press, 1988), 3, cited in Helen Roy, "Inclusion: Voices from Inside" (Ph.D. diss. proposal, Boston University, 1998), 44; John Kotre, *White Gloves: How*

We Create Ourselves through Memory (New York: Free Press, 1995); Langer, *The Power,* 83–84.

9. On this point, see Alan Parry and Robert E. Doan, *Story Re-Visions: Narrative Therapy in the Post-Modern World* (New York: Guilford, 1994).

10. Alan Parry, "A Universe of Stories," *Family Process* 30 (1991): 37–54; Shirley Brice Heath, "What No Bedtime Story Means: Narrative Skills at Home and School," *Language in Society* 11 (1982): 49–76.

11. Miller Mair, "Psychology as Story Telling," *International Journal of Construct Psychology* 1 (1988): 125–37.

12. Henri Bergson, *Time and Free Will: An Essay on the Immediate Data of Consciousness,* trans. R. L. Pogson (New York: Macmillan, 1913). As an aside, I hesitate to call any person in research of this sort a "subject," for although his or her account is in fact the subject of our work, the subject of the account may change with each new uttered paragraph. To call the teller "subject" runs the risk of imbuing him or her with a passive posture that we, as witness, are about to manipulate or control, as in a laboratory experiment.

13. Jerome Bruner, *Actual Minds, Possible Worlds* (Cambridge: Harvard University Press, 1986); see also Jerome Bruner, *Acts of Meaning* (Cambridge: Harvard University Press, 1990), and Donald E. Polkinghorne, *Narrative Knowing and the Human Sciences* (Albany: State University of New York Press, 1988).

14. Sigmund Freud, *The Interpretation of Dreams,* trans. and ed. James Strachey (New York: Basic Books, 1955); see also Bert O. States, *Dreaming and Story Telling* (Ithaca, N.Y.: Cornell University Press, 1993), and Massimo Ammaniti and Daniel N. Stern, eds., *Psychoanalysis and Development: Representations and Narratives* (New York: New York University Press, 1994); and Jack D. Douglas, *Creative Interviewing* (Beverly Hills, Calif.: Sage Publications, 1985).

15. Paul Ricoeur, *Time and Narrative* (Chicago: University of Chicago Press, 1984).

16. Parray and Doan, *Story Re-Visions,* 27.

17. Erik Erikson, *Identity: Youth and Crisis* (New York: Norton, 1968).

18. See Frederic Jameson, *The Political Unconscious: Narrative as a Social Symbolic Act* (Ithaca, N.Y.: Cornell University Press, 1981).

19. Robert Kegan, *The Evolving Self* (Cambridge: Harvard University Press, 1982).

20. Jan Dizard, letter to author, September 22, 1999.

21. See Tom Andersen, "The Reflecting Team: Dialogue and Meta-Dialogue in Clinical Work," *Family Process* 26 (1987): 415–28.

22. Daniel B. Frank, "The Live Creature: Understanding the School and Its Passions," *Child and Adolescent Social Work Journal* 15 (1998): 419.

23. For an expanded discussion of these points, see Elliot W. Eisner, *The Enlightened Eye: Qualitative Inquiry and the Enhancement of Educational Practice* (New York: Macmillan, 1991).

24. See Ruthellen Josselon and Amia Lieblich, eds., *Interpreting Experience* (Thousand Oaks, Calif.: Sage, 1995).

25. Howard Zinn, *A People's History of the United States* (New York: Harper & Row, 1980).

26. John Dewey, *How We Think* (Amherst, N.Y.: Prometheus Books, 1991); Parray and Doan, *Story Re-Visions*, 26–27.

27. Willard W. Waller, *On the Family, Education and War* (Chicago: University of Chicago Press, 1970), 129 (emphasis added), 128.

28. See Herbert Kelman, *A Time to Speak: On Human Values and Social Research* (San Francisco: Jossey-Bass, 1968).

29. Sandy Coleman, review of *Teach Me: Kids Will Learn When Oppression Is the Lesson*, by Murray Levin, *Boston Globe*, November 9, 1998, C6.

30. Peter Woods, *Inside Schools: Ethnography in Educational Research* (New York: Routledge & Kegan Paul, 1986), 4, cited in Roy, "Inclusion," 45.

31. Lawrence-Lightfoot and Hoffman Davis, *Art and Science*.

32. On this point see Eisner, "Objectivity and Subjectivity in Qualitative Research and Evaluation," in *The Enlightened Eye*.

33. Carol Gilligan, *In a Different Voice* (Cambridge: Harvard University Press, 1982); see also Jean Baker Miller and Irene Pierce Stiver, *The Healing Connection: How Women Form Relationships in Therapy and in Life* (Boston: Beacon Press, 1997).

34. Jean Baker Miller, *Toward a New Psychology of Women* (Boston: Beacon Press, 1976).

35. See Mark B. Tappan and Lyn-Mikel Brown, "Stories Told and Lessons Learned: Toward a Narrative Approach to Moral Development and Moral Education," *Harvard Educational Review* 59 (1989): 182–205.

36. Lawrence Kohlberg, *Essays on Moral Development* (San Francisco: Harper & Row, 1981). See also Lawrence Kohlberg and Carol Gilligan, "The Adolescent as Philosopher," in *12–16: Early Adolescence*, ed. Jerome Kagan and Robert Coles (New York: Norton, 1972), 144–79.

37. Walt Whitman, "A Noiseless Patient Spider," in *Walt Whitman: Complete Poetry and Selected Prose*, ed. J. E. Miller Jr. (Boston: Houghton Mifflin, 1950).

38. I have written elsewhere of this concern. See, for example, Thomas J. Cottle, *Private Lives and Public Accounts* (Amherst: University of Massachusetts Press, 1977).

39. See Sara Lawrence-Lightfoot, *I've Known Rivers* (Reading, Mass.: Addison Wesley, 1994).

40. See Shelley Roberts and Suzanne McGinty, "Awareness of Presence: Developing the Researcher Self," *Anthropology and Education Quarterly* 26 (1995): 112–22.

41. This seems a good place to refer the reader to Sigmund Koch's provocative essay "The Nature and Limits of Psychological Knowledge," in *Century of Psychology as Science*, ed. Sigmund Koch and D. E. Leary (Washington, D.C.: American Psychological Association, 1992).

42. Kegan, *The Evolving Self*.

43. Parry and Doan, *Story Re-Visions*, 22.

44. Rollo May, *The Discovery of Being* (New York: Norton, 1983), 92, 128.

45. Vivian Brown, personal conversation with author. It is this same pain, not so incidentally, that Reb Midrash speaks to when he calls on the Jews to "search out the depths of one's own suffering."

46. Donald Palladino Jr., "Seeking the Spheres," unpublished manuscript, Boston University, 1998, 18.

47. Baker Miller and Pierce Stiver, *The Healing Connection*, 22, 195, cited in

Scott L. Horton, "The Healing Connection: A Relational Perspective," unpublished manuscript, Boston University, 1998, 13, 1; I am grateful to Mr. Horton for sharing his work on this topic.

48. Anthony Giddens, *Modernity and Self-Identity* (Stanford, Calif.: Stanford University Press, 1991), 96.

49. Maguire, *The Power*, 39, 21; Clifford Geertz, *The Interpretation of Cultures* (New York: Basic Books, 1973), 89, cited in Timothy Kunzier, *"Revealing the Mystic Cipher,"* unpublished manuscript, Boston University, 1998, 5.

50. "A Conversation between Michael Silberblatt and Toni Morrison," *Los Angeles Times Book Review*, November 1, 1998, 3, emphasis added.

51. May, *The Discovery*, 21.

52. I am grateful to four colleagues in the School of Education at Boston University for aiding my thinking in this discussion. They are David Steiner, Victor Kestenbaum, Alan Gaynor, and Gerald Fain.

53. Richard Rorty, *Objectivity, Relativism and Truth: Philosophical Papers* (New York: Cambridge University Press, 1991); Anthony Storr, *Solitude: A Return to the Self* (New York: Ballantine Books, 1988), 7.

54. See David Elkind, "Children with Special Needs: A Post-Modern Perspective," *Boston University Journal of Education* 180, no. 2: 1–16.

55. Heinz Kohut, *The Kohut Seminars: On Self Psychology and Psychotherapy with Adolescents and Young Adults* (New York: Norton, 1987).

56. See Kunzier, "Revealing the Mystic Cipher."

57. A possibly apocryphal story from Freud's notes adds some color to this complex process. It is said that a patient of Freud's arose from the couch one day, very early in his analysis, and told his doctor just how marvelous he thought the process of psychoanalysis was and how much he had already derived from only a few sessions. It is said that in response Freud admonished the man, "When we begin to make progress, you will be crawling out of the office."

58. Heinz Kohut, cited in Arnold Goldberg, *Advances in Self-Psychology* (New York: International Universities Press, 1980), 485; Kunzier, "Revealing the Mystic Cipher," 25.

59. Waller, *On the Family*, 120.

60. C. G. Jung, *Aion: Researches into the Phenomenology of the Self*, trans. R. F. C. Hull (Princeton, N.J.: Princeton University Press, 1979); Frank, "The Live Creature," 432.

61. Giddens, *Modernity*, 76.

62. Clifford Geertz, *The Interpretation of Cultures: Selected Essays* (New York: Basic Books, 1973).

63. Dennis Donoghue, *The Practice of Reading* (New Haven, Conn.: Yale University Press, 1998); Erich Fromm, *Escape from Freedom* (New York: Farrar & Rinehart, 1941).